EMOTION-FOCUSED THERAPY FOR COMPLEX TRAUMA

EMOTION-FOCUSED THERAPY FOR COMPLEX TRAUMA

An Integrative Approach

Sandra C. Paivio
Antonio Pascual-Leone

AMERICAN PSYCHOLOGICAL ASSOCIATION
WASHINGTON, DC

Second Printing, December 2010
Published by
American Psychological Association
750 First Street, NE
Washington, DC 20002
www.apa.org

To order
APA Order Department
P.O. Box 92984
Washington, DC 20090-2984
Tel: (800) 374-2721; Direct: (202) 336-5510
Fax: (202) 336-5502; TDD/TTY: (202) 336-6123
Online: www.apa.org/books/
E-mail: order@apa.org

In the U.K., Europe, Africa, and the Middle East, copies may be ordered from
American Psychological Association
3 Henrietta Street
Covent Garden, London
WC2E 8LU England

Typeset in Goudy by Circle Graphics, Inc., Columbia, MD

Printer: Maple-Vail, York, PA
Cover Designer: Berg Design, Albany, NY

The opinions and statements published are the responsibility of the authors, and such opinions and statements do not necessarily represent the policies of the American Psychological Association.

Library of Congress Cataloging-in-Publication Data

Paivio, Sandra C.
  Emotion-focused therapy for complex trauma : an integrative approach / Sandra C. Paivio and Antonio Pascual-Leone. — 1st ed.
     p. ; cm.
  Includes bibliographical references and index.
  ISBN-13: 978-1-4338-0725-1
  ISBN-10: 1-4338-0725-4
  1. Emotion-focused therapy. 2. Post-traumatic stress disorder. 3. Psychic trauma—Treatment. I. Pascual-Leone, Antonio. II. American Psychological Association. III. Title. [DNLM: 1. Stress Disorders, Post-Traumatic—psychology. 2. Stress Disorders, Post-Traumatic—therapy. 3. Adult Survivors of Child Abuse—psychology. 4. Emotions. 5. Psychotherapy—methods.   WM 170 P149e 2010]
  RC489.F62P35 2010
  616.85'21—dc22
                                    2009031075

British Library Cataloguing-in-Publication Data

A CIP record is available from the British Library.

Printed in the United States of America
First Edition

We stood, literally, on the shoulders of giants—our fathers,
Allan Paivio and Juan Pascual-Leone.
Figuratively, we stood on the shoulders of
another giant—our mutual mentor,
Leslie Greenberg.
This book is dedicated to them.

CONTENTS

ACKNOWLEDGMENTS

We would like to acknowledge the dedication of many professionals and trainees to learning emotion-focused therapy for trauma, and their contributions, through research and practice, to development and refinement of the treatment model. Above all, we want to acknowledge the courage, openness, and willingness of dozens of clients to share their struggles in therapy and to participate in research so that other trauma survivors might be able to heal wounds and live meaningful and productive lives.

EMOTION-FOCUSED THERAPY FOR COMPLEX TRAUMA

INTRODUCTION

Trauma, in general, involves emotionally overwhelming experiences that can have devastating psychological, physical, and societal effects. Complex trauma, in particular, typically involves repeated exposure to violence and betrayals of trust in relationships with attachment figures. Abuse and neglect at the hands of caregivers and loved ones at any age can be devastating, but when these experiences occur in childhood, they can have deleterious effects on development and result in a constellation of long-term disturbances. Well-documented sequelae include chronic posttraumatic stress disorder (PTSD), other anxiety disorders, depression, substance dependence, self-harm behaviors, and personality pathology. Perhaps most devastating are the negative effects these experiences have on emotional development and competence, the person's sense of self, and his or her capacity for interpersonal relatedness. Although experiences of abuse and neglect involve exposure to trauma and feelings of helplessness and terror, PTSD is not necessarily a defining feature of the difficulties that can ensue. Many painful and threatening emotions, besides fear, are considerable sources of distress to individuals with histories of abuse. These include guilt, shame, and self-blame for victimization; anger at violation and maltreatment; and sadness

3

about the many losses associated with trauma, especially trauma perpetrated by loved ones.

Childhood maltreatment is disturbingly common, both in the general population and even more so in clinical samples. Most experts agree that exposure to trauma during childhood development is far more prevalent than trauma beginning in adulthood (e.g., van der Kolk, 2003). Among clients in psychotherapy, prevalence estimates for a history of child abuse trauma are as high as 90% (Pilkington & Kremer, 1995). Furthermore, because child abuse trauma is a significant risk factor for repeated victimization, most of these individuals have been exposed to multiple types of abuse and neglect, often at the hands of multiple perpetrators. Simply put, most clinicians will work with clients who have a history of complex trauma, and many are already routinely treating adult survivors in their practice.

Because noncompliance with exposure-based procedures and dropout rates are both notoriously high in this clinical group, it is particularly important for clinicians to be aware of effective treatment options. Emotion-focused therapy for trauma (EFTT) provides a strong and unique contribution to theory, research, and practice in this area.

WHAT IS EFTT?

EFTT is an effective individual treatment modality that targets the constellation of disturbances associated with complex trauma. In addition to symptoms of distress and problems in functioning, EFTT particularly focuses on resolving issues with past perpetrators of abuse and neglect, usually attachment figures. Clients not only are disturbed by their current problems but have been unable to heal these specific emotional injuries. Resolving issues with significant others, together with cultivating a strong therapeutic relationship, translates into reduced symptom distress, increased self-esteem, and improvements in global interpersonal functioning.

To date, EFTT is the only evidence-based (Paivio, Jarry, Chagigiorgis, Hall, & Ralston, in press; Paivio & Nieuwenhuis, 2001) individual therapy for both men and women who are dealing with different types of childhood maltreatment (emotional, physical, sexual abuse, emotional neglect). Other than research supporting EFTT, almost all other studies of individual therapy for complex trauma have included only female sexual abuse survivors diagnosed with PTSD (Chard, 2005; Resick, Nishith, & Griffin, 2003), whereas only one additional study included female sexual and physical abuse survivors (Cloitre, Koenen, Dohen, & Han, 2002). However, the negative effects of child abuse are not exclusive to this subgroup, and, as noted earlier, a diagnosis of PTSD is not necessarily a defining feature of complex PTSDs (van der Kolk, 2003). Clinicians frequently are confronted with complex cases of depression or anxiety that are clearly related to a client's personal history of childhood abuse, yet they may not meet diagnostic criteria for PTSD. In addition, because current evidence indicates few differential effects among different types of childhood maltreatment, EFTT targets those disturbances that are common across different types of abuse and neglect. At the beginning of this treatment, clients identify the experiences and the abusive/neglectful others they want to focus on in therapy. Following that, the protocol is sufficiently flexible to address individual client treatment needs.

Developments in the Emotion-Focused Approach

EFTT is among a growing group of psychological treatments identified as emotion-focused approaches for particular disturbances or disorders. As such, the current treatment for complex trauma has adapted the general emotion-focused therapy model (Greenberg & Paivio, 1997) by modifying its interventions and by tailoring its structure and emphases to the specific needs of trauma victims. These developments are based on a long program of research and have resulted in some key differences from the original model to better suit the targeted population.

In contrast to depressed clients being treated with emotion-focused therapy, for example, there can be inherent differences in clients who have suffered chronic interpersonal trauma, and this is especially the case with respect to issues of symptom management and emotional regulation skills. Moreover, individuals who suffer from PTSD or complex PTSDs frequently have disturbances in narrative memory and difficulties with labeling or describing their feelings (i.e., alexithymia). It is also common that they have comorbid social anxiety and are reticent in new relationships. All of these client difficulties can require a slightly more directive style from the therapist as well as changes in emphases from the original emotion-focused therapy model.

Furthermore, the classic empty-chair procedure used in emotion-focused therapy for addressing longstanding interpersonal issues or "unfinished business" with significant others is not always suitable or appropriate, in its original form, when addressing issues with perpetrators of abuse. Traumatized clients can experience considerable difficulty in imaginally confronting perpetrators, and interventions frequently require more attention to affect regulation or the use of alternative interventions for these individuals. Compared with the original model, this task in EFTT more explicitly involves principles of gradual trauma exposure. Thus, working with complex trauma has necessitated changes to interventions as well as the addition of memory work to address a new set of treatment needs.

Finally, although the general model of emotion-focused therapy can incorporate tasks to address self-criticism or self-interruptive processes and longstanding interpersonal injuries, these tasks may be used independently of each other and do not occur in any specific order. In contrast, observations of therapy with victims of complex trauma indicated that treatment required addressing both self-related and other-related disturbances. Moreover, we found that clients were unable to resolve past interpersonal issues until self-related disturbances (fear, avoidance, self-blame) were first reduced. The end result is that EFTT is a treatment innovatively structured in four sequentially ordered phases, each of which can be later revisited in a recursive fashion.

Treatment Indicators and Contraindicators

The characteristics of client suitability for EFTT are consistent with best practices for most trauma therapies (e.g., Courtois & Ford, 2009; Foa, Keane, Freidman, & Cohen, 2009). In general, EFTT is designed for clients who are suitable for short-term trauma-focused therapy who have the capacity to form a therapeutic relationship over a few sessions and to focus on a circumscribed issue from their past—in this case childhood trauma. The standard version of EFTT is not suitable for clients whose primary presenting problem is severe affect dysregulation with a risk of harm to themselves or others, whose current problems take precedence over a focus on past issues (e.g., domestic violence, substance dependence), or who wish to focus primarily on current rather than past relationships (e.g., a focus on parenting, marital distress). Even so, brief treatments aside, aspects of EFTT have been integrated into longer term treatments, ones that devote more time to training in emotion regulation skills and to addressing current life difficulties that may be among the sequelae of past trauma.

Strengths and Distinctive Features of EFTT

The two primary change processes in EFTT are the therapeutic relationship and emotional processing of trauma memories. These are similar to the change processes posited in other psychological treatments for trauma. Emotion-focused therapies, however, make distinct contributions to understanding and promoting these change processes. First, we emphasize advanced empathic responding as the primary intervention used throughout therapy. An empathically responsive therapeutic relationship enhances emotion regulation, promotes emotion awareness and competence, and helps to correct the effects of early empathic failures. Second, emotion-focused therapies such as EFTT are characterized by a highly differentiated approach to understanding and treating different emotion states and processes (e.g., Greenberg & Paivio, 1997; Greenberg, Rice, & Elliott, 1993; Pascual-Leone & Greenberg, 2007). For example, the pain of sadness and loss, and the "bad feelings" associated with depression (which can include sadness at loss), are both aversive and people can exert considerable effort to avoid both of these types of experiences. However, these involve different change processes and require different intervention strategies. Similarly, hostile and rejecting anger (or rage) at rejection, suppressed anger at violation, and anger at self for having been victimized are different experiences that each requires different intervention strategies.

Another distinguishing feature of emotion-focused approaches is their emphasis on changing emotion with emotion rather than with rational cognition or interpretations (Greenberg, 2002). Information associated with healthy adaptive emotions, such as anger at maltreatment and sadness at loss, is used to modify the maladaptive meaning associated with emotions such as fear and shame. This is particularly relevant to therapy for complex trauma, because many people who have been victimized learn to suppress their feelings of adaptive anger and sadness and so have been unable to assert interpersonal boundaries and grieve important losses. EFTT also draws on well-developed technology in the experiential therapy tradition for overcoming experiential avoidance, accessing inhibited emotion, promoting meaning construction processes, and resolving attachment injuries. In this book, then, we present guidelines for cultivating a strong therapeutic alliance and for implementing different interventions specifically tailored to these different types of emotion and emotional-processing difficulties.

PLACING EFTT IN CONTEXT: AN INTEGRATIVE APPROACH

Emotion-focused therapies, including EFTT, integrate recent developments in emotion theory and research and affective neuroscience that emphasize emotion as an adaptive orienting system (e.g., Damasio, 1999; Fridja, 1986; Izard, 2002; LeDoux, 1996). The EFTT emphasis on adaptive processes also is consistent with recent interests in the phenomena of trauma resilience and posttraumatic growth. EFTT, in particular, draws on the vast theoretical, research and practice literature in the areas of trauma and attachment (e.g., Courtois & Ford, 2009; Solomon & Siegel, 2003). Strengths from the cognitive and behavioral traditions, for example, include the construct of exposure to and emotional processing of trauma memories as a mechanism of change, as well as the use of memory work and emotion regulation techniques (e.g.,

Cloitre et al., 2002; Foa et al., 2000). EFTT also integrates work on narrative processes in trauma therapy (e.g., Neimeyer, 2001). Similarities with the psychodynamic tradition include an explicit focus on working through the effects of negative attachment relationships and the therapeutic relationship as a corrective emotional experience. Outside the emotion-focused therapy tradition, technically, EFTT is most similar to recent experiential/dynamic or relational approaches (e.g., Fosha, 2000; Mitchell, 1993) that emphasize therapist empathy and experience-near interpretations. Moreover, in outlining concepts and treatment interventions in this book, we present comparisons with other treatment approaches to highlight similarities and differences. Consequently, we expect that this manual will be useful to practitioners from divergent theoretical perspectives and professional backgrounds.

EFTT also is fully integrative at the level of theory, research, practice, and training—each aspect informs the other. First, as described, the model is based on a sound theoretical foundation. Second, the EFTT model is based on our combined years of training and clinical experience treating traumatized individuals, which have shaped and refined the theoretical underpinnings of the treatment. Third, EFTT is based on an empirically verified model that identifies steps in the process of resolving past interpersonal issues and attachment injuries (Greenberg & Foerster, 1996; Greenberg & Malcolm, 2002). The EFTT treatment model has been further developed and refined through more than 15 years of programmatic research that has involved randomized clinical trials (e.g., Paivio & Greenberg, 1995; Paivio et al., in press; Paivio & Nieuwenhuis, 2001), as well as observation and analysis of hundreds of videotaped therapy sessions with clients working through complex trauma (e.g., Paivio, Hall, Holowaty, Jellis, & Tran, 2001; Paivio & Patterson, 1999). This research supports the posited mechanisms of change in therapy and is highly relevant to clinical practice. Finally, the model has been further refined through clinical training and in dialogue with dozens of trainees from divergent backgrounds. This book reflects this larger integrative framework by richly illustrating concepts and treatment principles with clinical examples and by describing the supporting research.

ABOUT THE BOOK

This book presents a manualized treatment that, on one hand, is sufficiently specific and rigorous to be used in research and, on the other hand, is sufficiently flexible to be used by clinicians in their daily practice. The text also can be used in graduate training programs and is consistent with the American Psychological Association's recommendations to provide training in evidence-based approaches. Ultimately, the aim of this book is to present theoretical and practical aspects of EFTT (as well as supporting research) with enough specificity that clinicians from different theoretical perspectives can apply the complete package or integrate aspects of the model into their current practice. The model can be modified, while keeping with key intervention principles, to meet the needs of different clients in terms of trauma type and severity, symptom profile and severity, and length of treatment.

This book is presented in two parts. Part I, Theory, introduces general concepts that are important throughout the treatment. As such, it includes four chapters that describe relevant features of trauma (chap. 1), a model of how EFTT addresses these features (chap. 2), and the core constructs of emotion and experiencing (chaps. 3 and 4).

Part II, Intervention, describes processes and procedures in each of the phases of EFTT:

- Chapters 5 through 7 cover Phase 1 of therapy, which focuses on cultivating the alliance. This includes instruction on establishing a safe and collaborative therapeutic relationship, introducing the primary reexperiencing procedure used in therapy, and promoting client experiencing that is the basis for all tasks and procedures used in therapy.
- Chapters 8 and 9 cover Phase 2 of therapy, which focuses on resolving self-related difficulties, that is, reducing fear and avoidance and transforming guilt, shame, and self-blame. These processes interfere with emotional engagement with trauma memories and with appropriately holding offenders responsible for harm.
- Chapters 10 and 11 cover Phase 3 of therapy, which focuses on resolving past interpersonal issues by accessing adaptive anger at maltreatment and sadness at loss. Experience and uninhibited expression of these emotions and their associated meanings are the catalyst for resolving issues with offenders.
- Chapter 12 covers Phase 4, which focuses on the termination of therapy.

Intervention chapters in Part II include sections on the relevance of a particular emotion or process to trauma work and guidelines for distinguishing among different types of emotion and associated emotional-processing difficulties. These chapters also outline the central principles and goals while giving step-by-step guidelines for conducting interventions and completing therapeutic tasks. Finally, they provide guidelines for addressing client difficulties and therapist errors that typically occur in this type of therapy.

In describing the phase-by-phase treatment process, this book presents clinical material drawn from a wide range of clients, all of whom have given permission for their participation in research and in professional communications. Identifying information for these clients has been deleted. Actual client material frequently is presented verbatim, although some cases are composites, and, in other instances, dialogue has been modified to better illustrate intervention principles. When a particular case is referred to repeatedly in the book, we have used pseudonyms to provide continuity for readers examining various aspects of a client's process across treatment.

I

THEORY

1

TRAUMA AND ITS EFFECTS

The first author Sandra Paivio's interest in trauma began as a result of conducting therapy with one client early in her career as a psychologist. "Monica" sought therapy to deal with the suicide of her mother, by gunshot, more than 30 years prior to treatment. Following the suicide, the family basically fell apart. The father died of alcoholism a few years later, and the three children were placed in a variety of foster care settings. No one ever talked about the mother's death; the message was, "Forget it, let it go, she was a sick woman, get on with your life." The mother's suicide became the family's "ugly secret" and Monica could not forget about it. Although she functioned extremely well on the surface, she struggled with recurrent episodes of post-traumatic stress disorder (PTSD; e.g., avoidance of reminders, anniversary reactions), as well as feelings of shame, depression, and anger at her dead mother, the "atrocity" she committed, and her abandonment. Therapeutic work with Monica exemplified the richness, challenges, and rewards of trauma work, as well as the incredible resilience and courage of trauma survivors. The process of therapy with Monica has been analyzed from multiple theoretical perspectives, and this case became the inspiration and prototype for emotion-focused therapy for trauma (EFTT). We refer to aspects of therapy with this client throughout this text.

The overall purpose of the present chapter is to describe the nature of trauma and its effects. How these effects are addressed in EFTT will be presented in chapter 2, which outlines the treatment model. These chapters, therefore, should be read as a pair.

DEFINITION

The *Diagnostic and Statistical Manual of Mental Disorders* (4th ed., Text Revision [DSM–IV–R]; American Psychiatric Association, 2000) criteria for trauma include both the nature of the event and emotional reactions to the event. Accordingly, a traumatic event involves actual or perceived threat of death or physical harm to self or others; a threat to the integrity of self; and reactions of horror, terror, or helplessness. From this perspective, the focus of pathology is on the emotion of fear.

However, many experts understand trauma to mean not only "capital T" trauma as defined by the *DSM–IV–TR*, but "small t" trauma that involves incidents of humiliation, rejection, and experiences of neglect or attachment difficulties (Shapiro & Maxfield, 2002). From this perspective, trauma involves many emotions and emotional difficulties. Emotions and reactions associated with the original event are stored in memory, and, with repetition, those parts of the memory network become predominant and reactions become generalized.

VARIOUS CATEGORICAL SYSTEMS

There are several ways of categorizing different types of traumatic events, and these various categorical systems partly reflect distinct ways of understanding the nature of trauma. Briere and Scott (2006) identified 12 types of trauma, and their categories are strictly based on the content of an event. Neborsky (2003), in contrast, identified a spectrum of small "t" and capital "T" trauma based on distinctive features of the relationships and emotions involved, and these reflect potential themes for therapeutic exploration. However, even in a system based exclusively on content, the distinct features of different types (e.g., natural disaster vs. sexual assault, assault by stranger vs. assault at the hands of a loved one) are associated with different problems that have implications for therapy. For example, if the perpetrator of the crime remains unidentified or unapprehended, therapy may need to focus on managing a very real risk of revictimization. Crimes that do not result in severe physical injury can be met with minimization by others so that victims feel invalidated and isolated. Crimes and vehicular accidents can involve prosecution and severe losses to self, including physical injuries that require lifelong rehabilitation combined with psychological treatment.

Types I and II Trauma

The trauma literature most frequently distinguishes between two broad categories of traumatic exposure that differ in terms of type, severity, or breadth of effects (Pelcovitz, Kaplan, DeRosa, Mandel, & Salzinger, 2000; Scoboria, Ford, Hsio-ju, & Frisman, 2006; van der Kolk & McFarlane, 1996). Type I trauma refers to single episodes, such as a car or industrial accident, a natural disaster, or a single assault. These are thought to result in the disturbances that characterize PTSD, which is described in a later section. In these instances, it can be the severity or extremity of the event that causes disturbance. Some single events, such as suicide of a loved one or physical and sexual assault, can have severe long-term effects. The suicide of a loved one, as in the case of Monica, typically takes place in a complex environment and can result in a chain of events that can last a lifetime.

Type II or complex trauma, which is the predominant focus of EFTT, refers to repeated exposure to threat of violence, including social and political violence through war or torture, domestic violence (as victim or witness), and childhood abuse. EFTT particularly focuses on complex interpersonal developmental trauma (Type II) related to childhood maltreatment. Reactions to these experiences appear to be much more complicated and are often classified in terms of cumulative trauma disorder, in the case of refugee trauma survivors, or disorders of extreme stress not otherwise specified (DESNOS; van der Kolk et al., 1996), in the case of childhood abuse and neglect. Disturbances in affect regulation and problems with maladaptive meaning, which includes perceptions of self, others, and traumatic events, are at the heart of these reactions.

War and combat trauma are examples of complex trauma that are characterized by their severity, confluence of victim and perpetrator, and lack of societal support, as in the case of veterans of the Vietnam war. The torture and political violence experienced by refugee trauma survivors and asylum seekers often involve destruction of an entire community and may or may not involve a perpetrator known to the victim. Frequently, however, perpetrators of interpersonal trauma are known to the victim. Instances of domestic violence and sexual abuse, for example, most frequently involve friends or loved ones as perpetrators and are followed by shame and minimization or denial, as well as social isolation. These offenses also involve betrayal of trust and unresolved anger and sadness regarding significant others that eventually become the focus of therapy. Victims may also be trapped in ongoing abusive situations due to financial, physical, or emotional circumstances. Individuals can be further victimized by unhelpful others who minimize damage if the assault did not result in severe physical injury, by myths about rape that generate shame and self-blame, and by procedures of the judicial system. Documented effects of sexual assault include PTSD, sexual dysfunction, and cognitive–affective disruptions such as guilt, shame, and self-blame.

Finally, interpersonal trauma perpetrated by intimate others can occur at different developmental stages, most frequently at critical ages or transitions when vulnerability to psychological disorganization is high (Cichetti & Toth, 1995). The trauma involves, for example, betrayal by caregivers, violation of self, and violation of the fundamental moral values or beliefs that compromise normal development. The most well documented types of these traumatic experiences are childhood physical and sexual abuse and victimization through exposure to malevolent violence (sexual assault, domestic violence). Betrayal at the hands of primary attachment figures, such as the case of Monica, who was essentially abandoned by her mother's suicide, can have profound and devastating effects on development.

The distinctive features of complex trauma in childhood include the vulnerable developmental stage and repeated exposure over an extended period. The three main interrelated sources of disturbance are exposure to trauma, attachment injuries (e.g., abuse, neglect, lack of love and safety), and reliance on experiential avoidance as a coping strategy for dealing with the intense negative affect generated by these experiences.

It is now recognized that PTSD from exposure to a single traumatic event is relatively rare compared with cases of exposure to multiple traumas (van der Kolk, 2003). Most people who develop PTSD symptoms and seek treatment have experienced multiple traumas stemming back to childhood. For example, in a study of cognitive–behavioral therapy for PTSD stemming from adult sexual assault (Resick, Nishith, & Griffin, 2003), half of 121 therapy completers had an additional history of child sexual abuse. Thus, psychological treatments for many types of trauma can end up focusing, at least in part, on issues of childhood victimization through abuse and/or neglect.

PREVALENCE AND RISK FACTORS

It is important to distinguish between exposure to trauma and development of disturbance. Each of these is associated with different prevalence rates and risk factors. Many more individuals are exposed to trauma than develop disturbance. However, in general, risk of both exposure and disturbance increases with each exposure. It is sad to note that the more vulnerable an individual is to begin with, the more likely she or he is to be exposed to trauma and to suffer long-term negative effects. The following review of statistics concerning prevalence and risk factors is intended to highlight the need for effective treatment options and clinician training in this area.

Prevalence of Exposure

Exposure to traumatic events, in general, is no longer considered rare (Foa, Keane, Friedman, & Cohen, 2009). Most adults (69%) living in urban areas of the United States report experiencing one or more traumatic events in their lives (Norris, 1992). This includes being criminally victimized at least once (Resnick, Kilpatrick, Dansky, Saunders, & Best, 1993). Even among relatively young, well-educated, and insured populations, prevalence estimates are as high as 39% (Breslau, Davis, Andreski, & Peterson, 1991). Trauma exposure also is common among university students. Vrana and Lauterbach (1994) found that 84% of undergraduate students at a major Midwestern U.S. university reported exposure, with 33% stating that they had experienced four or more traumatic events. Our research (Paivio & Cramer, 2002; Wild & Paivio, 2003) found similar results in samples of Canadian undergraduate students.

These rates do not reflect the increasing numbers of refugee trauma survivors who now live in developed countries, including Canada and the United States. The United Nations reported that 11.5 million individuals seek asylum annually, and most of these individuals are escaping severe social and political violence, including direct and indirect torture.

In terms of Type II trauma, despite increased attention to issues of family violence and child maltreatment by public policy and mental health professionals, recent surveys indicate that child abuse in the general population remains disturbingly common. It currently is recognized that repeated exposure to trauma in the home is far more prevalent than single-incident trauma. Furthermore, multiple types of maltreatment usually co-occur in the same family so that victims are exposed to multiple types of trauma. A large-scale study in Canada of child abuse among Ontario residents (MacMillan et al., 1997) reported rates of sexual abuse perpetrated by adults at 13% for females and 4% for males, and rates of physical abuse were 21% for females and 31% for males. These rates are consistent with national and international estimates (Finkelhor, 1994; Yamamoto et al., 1999). Although there are few estimates of emotional abuse (defined here as verbal derogation, threats of violence, and witnessing family violence), a recent study of Ontario university students indicated rates of emotional abuse at 25% for females and 35% for males (Turner & Paivio, 2002).

Experts also agree that an overwhelming majority of victimization occurs before adulthood (Finkelhor, 1994; van der Kolk, 1993). This means there is a particular need for effective treatments for the effects of interpersonal developmental trauma. Furthermore, as we have seen, early victimization increases the risk of subsequent exposure through, for example, family violence or criminal victimization such as rape. This compounding of risk, in addition to the extremely high prevalence of childhood maltreatment in clinical samples (Pilkington & Kremer, 1995), argues convincingly for the long-term negative effects of these childhood experiences. Thus, most clinicians will need skills in treating the complex disturbances that commonly occur in this client group.

Prevalence of Disturbance

Breslau et al. (1991) found that approximately 25% of those exposed to a traumatic event ultimately developed PTSD. Still, even though most people exposed to traumatic events do not develop PTSD, estimated rates for the disorder in the general population are high, and its onset can be delayed for months or even years following the traumatic event. In the United States, the National Comorbidity Survey (Kessler, Sonnega, Bromet, Hughs, & Nelson, 1995) indicated a lifetime incidence of PTSD at 8% of the adult population. Moreover, the effects of this disorder can be quite long-lasting.

Of course, even higher rates of PTSD are reported in higher risk populations. For example, almost one third (30%) of Vietnam war veterans developed PTSD, and 15% of them still had the disorder 15 years after the war had concluded (Coleman, 2006). Similarly, the National Women's Study found that 13% of American women experienced a completed rape at some time in their life, and nearly one third eventually developed PTSD (Kilpatrick, Edwards, & Seymour, 1992). Breslau, Davis, Andreski, Federman, and Anthony (1998) found that assault violence, including rape, induced the highest rate of PTSD of all traumatic events measured. Prevalence of PTSD in the general population ranks behind only substance abuse disorders, major depression, and social phobia in its frequency rate. Despite the high reported rates of abuse, there are few existing estimates of PTSD in children.

Although well-controlled studies of prevalence in developing countries are scarce, many scholars believe that rates in these countries are higher than in more economically developed regions because of a lack of resources with which to avert disasters and mitigate their aftermath (De Girolamo & McFarlane, 1996). Currently, there are increasingly large numbers of refugee trauma survivors in North America from both developing countries as well as "failed states." In addition to enormous adjustment issues, many of these individuals have serious mental health problems as a result of cumulative trauma and the many losses they have endured. Prevalence of PTSD and related health problems in this refugee population is underestimated because these individuals frequently are reluctant to use mental health services on account of financial and language barriers as well as uncertain refugee status. Furthermore, these individuals are rarely questioned about trauma history when they arrive at emergency clinics. This large-scale migration is a relatively recent phenomenon, and there is ignorance on the part of many health care professionals about the mental health needs of this group.

EFFECTS OF TRAUMA

Outlining symptoms and the particular ways in which individuals are affected by trauma helps to delineate the specific presenting targets for treatment and the deeper biases, dispositions, and deficits that people suffering from trauma also experience. These can present complications to treatment over and above the initial presenting symptoms. In this section we outline the effects of trauma in terms of symptoms and associated cognitive and personality characteristics; self, interpersonal, and emotion regulation difficulties, as well as specific effects of different types of development trauma. We conclude with treatment implications.

Symptom Development

Traumatic experiences are thought to be encoded in memory as a multimodal network of information or fear structure (Foa, Huppert, & Cahill, 2006; Foa & Kozak, 1986). Information includes neurobiological, cognitive, affective, and stimulus–response aspects of the traumatic situation. Stimuli resembling the traumatic event activate the entire network or structure. We will see that this understanding of the development of trauma symptoms forms the basis of most trauma therapies, including EFTT. From a learning perspective, classical conditioning is thought to account for the development of chronic PTSD, whereas operant conditioning is thought to account for maintenance of disturbance (i.e., avoidance of trauma feelings and memories is a negative reinforcer). PTSD reactions occur, not only in response to reminders of the trauma but also in response to intense albeit neutral stimuli (e.g., loud noises), indicating a loss of stimulus discrimination.

Most studies suggest that trauma memories tend to be implicit, behavioral, and somatic. They also tend to be vague, overgeneralized, fragmented, and incomplete, and as such are associated with disorganized personal narratives (van der Kolk, 2003). One theory is that traumatic experiences are encoded primarily in right-brain experiential (nonverbal) memory, in the form of emotions, images, and bodily sensations, but are not processed on a symbolic or verbal level and are left unintegrated with other life experiences (van der Kolk et al., 1996). Results of neuroimaging studies of individuals recalling trauma memories (e.g., Lanius et al., 2004) suggest increased sensory processing, especially of visual information, accompanied by decreased verbal processing. These findings are consistent with conclusions drawn from clinical observations of low verbal processing and high sensory experiencing by trauma survivors. This supports the need for therapeutic procedures, such as those used in EFTT that access experiential memories and help clients to verbally symbolize their meaning.

Posttraumatic Stress Disorder

By definition, PTSD is an affective disorder, and psychological treatments, regardless of theoretical orientation and techniques, need to address these affective disruptions. PTSD is diagnosable following a traumatic event and after 1 month of symptoms from each of three clusters: intrusion, hyperarousal, and avoidance.

Intrusive symptoms include phenomena such as nightmares and flashbacks. In essence, traumatic experiences are unforgettable, outside of an individual's ordinary experience, and not easily integrated into one's current meaning systems. Intrusive memories, rumination, and perseveration are conceptualized as attempts to process and integrate the trauma (Briere & Scott, 2006). A diagnosis of PTSD requires endorsement of at least one of five symptoms listed in the intrusion cluster of the *DSM–IV–TR* (American Psychiatric Association, 2000). Severe intrusive symptoms need to be managed to permit processing of trauma memories.

Hyperarousal refers to chronic overstimulation of the nervous system, whereby the body constantly is on the alert for danger (van der Kolk & McFarlane, 1996). Symptoms include increases in heart rate, blood pressure, and skin conductance in response to sounds, images, and thoughts that resemble the trauma. These responses eventually can get paired with neutral stimuli as well. Chronic irritability and anger are manifestations that can be particularly problematic; anger control problems often are comorbid with PTSD and can be an intervention priority. A diagnosis of PTSD requires endorsement of two of the five symptoms listed in the hyperarousal cluster of the current *DSM*. Hyperarousal can result in psychosomatic complaints and physical problems such as headaches, hypertension, back pain, and gastrointestinal difficulties.

Avoidance essentially compensates for intrusion and hyperarousal. Avoidance strategies include "shutting down," dissociating, suppressing feelings and memories of the trauma, avoiding situations reminiscent of the trauma, and using maladaptive behaviors such as substance abuse and self-injury. Numbing is thought to be the hallmark of PTSD and linked to depressive shutting down. Avoidance is adaptive in the short term but in the long term is thought to prevent processing and integration of trauma and to perpetuate trauma symptoms (Foa et al., 2006). A *DSM–IV–TR* diagnosis requires endorsement of three of the seven avoidance symptoms listed in this cluster.

Cognitive Disruptions

Cognitive disruptions in the form of shattered assumptions about self, others, and reality (Janoff-Bulman, 1992) also frequently result from trauma. The current *DSM* lists these as associated features. People's previctim view of self and the world involves basic assumptions about invulnerability, personal safety, others as mostly trustworthy, and a just world. Trauma introduces new data that are incompatible with these assumptions. Following exposure to a trauma, people are hypervigilant and can experience self-blame, survivor guilt, distrust, and alienation.

Furthermore, the National Comorbidity Study found that PTSD is associated with increased rates of major depressive disorder, substance-related disorders, panic disorder, agoraphobia, obsessive–compulsive disorder, generalized anxiety disorder, social phobia, specific phobia, bipolar disorder, and borderline personality disorder. These can precede, follow, or co-occur with PTSD (American Psychiatric Association, 2000). Thus, psychological treatments for PTSD frequently need to address multiple disturbances. EFTT views depression as the activation of a "weak/bad sense of self" (Greenberg & Watson, 2006) developed in early attachment relationships and the collapse into feelings of powerlessness and worthlessness. Similarly, EFTT views anxiety disorders as the result of growing up in an environment of fear, uncertainty, and constant negative evaluation by attachment figures. This leads to development of a core sense of self as insecure, defective, and/or inferior and therefore vulnerable to harm, negative evaluation, and abandonment. These client problems have implications for therapy processes in terms of difficulties establishing safety and trust in the therapeutic relationship and participation in key interventions.

Disorders of Extreme Stress Not Otherwise Specified

The complex array of disturbances associated with exposure to interpersonal violence beginning in childhood is commonly referred to as DESNOS, which we described earlier while discussing types of trauma. Again, PTSD symptoms may be part of this array, but a diagnosis of PTSD is not the defining feature of complex PTSDs, and many emotions besides fear (i.e., rage, shame, resignation) are at the heart of disturbance. Overall, it seems clear that effective psychological treatment for prolonged exposure to complex interpersonal trauma must be multidimensional and integrative.

Trauma symptoms also may be especially severe and long-lasting when the trauma is complex and interpersonal in nature and particularly when these traumatic experiences occur in childhood. These types of experiences during childhood and a DESNOS diagnosis are associated with high (50%–75%) PTSD prevalence (Kessler et al., 1995) and also with chronic self-regulatory deficits (Cichetti & Toth, 1995; Roth, Newman, Pelcovitz, van der Kolk, & Mandel, 1997), substance abuse disorders (Chilcoat & Breslau, 1998), persistent anxiety and affective disorders (Polusney & Follette, 1995), externalizing disorders in childhood and adolescence (Ford et al., 2000; Pelcovitz et al., 2000), and medical morbidity (Walker et al., 2003). DESNOS also co-occurs with borderline personality disorder (McLean & Gallop, 2003). Results of a study of the factors associated with a DESNOS diagnosis (Scoboria et al., 2006) further suggested that anger dysregulation is a distinct factor separate from impulse control. Thus, effective therapy needs to focus on anger, per se, and distinguish this from managing behavior problems such as substance abuse or self-harm. According to work by Scoboria and colleagues (2006), appraisals of self, relationships, and broader systems of meaning or hope all clustered onto a single factor, which suggests that these symptom features are interrelated rather than distinct. This suggests that a treatment focused on changing maladaptive meaning should include and integrate these elements.

Self-Related and Interpersonal Problems

Both self-related and interpersonal problems associated with attachment injuries are well documented (e.g., Courtois & Ford, 2009; Solomon & Siegel, 2003). Perceptions of self and others formed in early attachment relationships are encoded in memory and act as enduring prototypes that influence current perceptions and behaviors. Attachment theorists and researchers (e.g., Sroufe, 1996) emphasize the importance of parental empathy as the basis for establishing healthy representations of self and others and a secure attachment bond. This bond, in turn, is the basis for developing emotion regulation capacities, self-confidence, and interpersonal trust. Through empathic mirroring of feelings and needs, the child learns to recognize, label, and describe emotional experience. This contributes to self-control, self-definition, and interpersonal connectedness through the development of communication skills.

Self-Related Problems

Impairments to the sense of self that result from childhood maltreatment include a limited awareness of internal experience (i.e., feelings, wants, needs, values) that allows individuals to build a sense of self as separate from others. More concretely, this results in identity confusion and fragmentation, guilt and self-blame for the abuse, and a pervasive sense of worthlessness, powerlessness, and victimization. These problems represent a core set of underlying dimensions that are responsible for regulating self-esteem through skills such as affect regulation, tolerance for being alone and of criticism, self-soothing, and a sense of personal agency (McCann & Pearlman, 1990). Underlying dimensions such as these are captured in the emotion-focused therapy construct of different emotion schemes (Greenberg & Paivio, 1997) that regulate one's sense of self in the world.

Autobiographical Memory. The area of autobiographical memory and disruption of narrative processes through trauma have recently received considerable attention. All too frequently, trauma survivors have not developed a clear understanding of their experience and how it fits into their life story or have not identified and processed feelings associated with the trauma (and associated information). These individuals are more likely to produce fragmented, disorganized narratives indicative of inner confusion and distress. The quality of trauma narratives has been used as an index of emotional processing or resolution of traumatic events (Pennebaker, 1997). Several studies have documented a link between the impoverished quality of trauma narratives and PTSD (see O'Kearney & Perrot, 2006, for a review). Qualitative dimensions that are indicative of trauma resolution include coherence (Fiese & Wamboldt, 2003), such that a story has continuity, directionality, and meaning, as well as causal and insightful thinking and references to self and feelings.

An integral component of this autobiographical memory is the concept of experiencing (see chap. 4, this volume, for further discussion). *Experiencing* refers to the capacity to attend to and explore the meaning of subjective internal experience. Thus, the experiencing construct captures many of the features identified in other studies of narrative quality. Our research group has shown that trauma narratives of individuals who were externally oriented and had difficulties identifying and labeling feelings were also low in experiencing (Le, 2006). This indicates there is an association between the phenomenon of alexithymia, which literally means "no words for feelings" (Taylor, Bagby, & Parker, 1997), and the capacity for experiencing. Results of a study by Kunzle and Paivio (2009) further indicated that lower levels of experiencing in the trauma narratives written by EFTT clients before treatment were associated with more pretreatment trauma symptoms. Again this supports narrative quality as an index of trauma resolution.

This connection between unresolved trauma and narrative quality can be attributed to a number of factors. There is some neurobiological evidence that trauma affects areas of the brain, such as the hippocampus, that are responsible for meaning creation and autobiographical memory (Siegel, 2003). In addition, PTSD is associated with memory gaps because overwhelming fear interferes with the capacity to process information. Memory gaps, in turn, interfere with the capacity to make sense of the experience, thereby affecting narrative coherence. So, one of the goals for reexperiencing procedures in trauma therapy is to access trauma memories to fully process or integrate relevant material. Moreover, trauma disrupts meaning ("shattered assumptions") and the capacity of individuals to make sense of their experiences, to put the trauma into perspective, and to fit it into their life. Avoidance of trauma feelings and memories, a symptom of PTSD, compromises the capacity of people suffering from trauma even further as they try to integrate or make sense of these events.

Ultimately, impoverished autobiographical memory and personal narratives reflect an individual's self-identity, his or her sense of self and reality. This, in turn, negatively affects functioning, particularly interpersonal functioning. Narrative approaches to therapy directly target this area, but any approach that targets meaning construction processes, including EFTT, will address autobiographical memory and the narrative processes that were disrupted by trauma.

Interpersonal Problems

Most research suggests that the problems stemming from complex trauma during development are primarily interpersonal in nature (e.g., van der Kolk, 2003). These include difficulties with intimacy and trust, self-assertion, interpersonal boundaries, and setting limits in relationships, as well as marital and parenting problems and an overall sense of isolation and alienation. Limited awareness of one's own internal experience (e.g., as with alexithymia) translates into limited awareness of others' experience and a limited capacity for empathy. Supporting evidence for this comes from research findings that indicate maltreated children were less aware of the meanings associated with others' facial expressions (During & McMahon, 1991). Even so, in contrast, survivors who are externally focused and attuned to signs of danger can be overly vigilant and highly attuned to the needs of others. Some research (Pollak, Klorman, Thatcher, & Cicchetti, 2001) also suggests that maltreated children are especially sensitive to anger cues, the kind of information that is particularly relevant in a threatening family environment. Although the capacity to detect anger quickly is likely adaptive in such environments, this bias could be detrimental to interpersonal relationships outside of the maltreatment context.

In sum, the personality structure and the core sense of self for individuals exposed to complex interpersonal developmental trauma centers around feelings of anger, fear, and shame and difficulties regulating these experiences. Thus, problems with self-esteem, trust, impulsivity, and maladaptive avoidance of internal experience are all prevalent in this population.

Marital Distress. As we have seen, trauma can disrupt an individual's capacity for interpersonal connectedness, intimacy, and secure attachment— that is, the capacity to provide and respond to comfort, safety, and support. This is observed, for example, in combat personnel with symptoms of PTSD who, through exposure to extensive and extreme trauma, understandably feel isolated and alienated from civilian society. In their marital relationships, these individuals can be distant or angry and may experience guilt and intrusive symptoms such as flashbacks. Marital distress also can be a result of earlier attachment traumas that have disrupted the individual's capacity for intimacy and trust.

Emotion-focused therapy for couples (Johnson, 2002) is based on attachment theory and has been applied to marital distress resulting from unresolved trauma. When one partner in the relationship is dealing with the effects of trauma, his or her capacity for secure attachment may be seriously compromised. The goal of marital therapy with traumatized couples is to help each partner reconnect with his or her own and the partner's emotions and attachment needs that are being defended against through anger and distancing behaviors. Many clients in individual therapy for trauma also experience marital distress, and resolving their own attachment injuries and trauma can generalize to improving a marital relationship. Still, emotion-focused therapy for couples is an important additional resource.

Transgenerational Transmission of Trauma and Parenting Difficulties. The relationship between unresolved childhood trauma and parenting difficulties is well documented. There is some evidence, for example, that unresolved trauma in the mother, assessed using an Adult Attachment Interview, predicted disorganized attachment in her infant (Main, 1991). Caregivers who did not receive adequate parenting themselves, have unmet attachment needs and unhealed attachment injuries, and have not adequately developed the capacity for secure attachment seem to have difficulty providing adequate parenting. Studies indicate that women with these issues tend to misinterpret their infants' and their children's behavior by attributing malicious intent. Moreover, they have been found to overstimulate and frighten rather than sooth distressed infants and are not appropriately responsive to their children's emotional needs (Landy & Menna, 2006). Similarly, maternal depression, which is highly correlated with unresolved trauma, is associated with the neglect of children. The traditional intervention approach to this problem has been to teach parenting skills. However, helping these parents resolve their own personal trauma and attachment injuries also can contribute to improved parenting behavior. Indeed, it is revealing that the motivation for seeking therapy for many clients in EFTT is to become better parents and to stop the cycle of abuse and neglect.

Emotion Regulation Difficulties

Affective disruptions, including underregulation and overcontrol of emotion, are at the heart of disturbances stemming from trauma, particularly complex trauma. Affect dysregulation problems in childhood can interfere with core developmental tasks and become habitual ways of dealing with affective experience. Moreover, dysregulations of this kind can result in long-term impairments in functioning, including chronic depression and anxiety; difficulties recognizing and describing emotional experience (alexithymia); numbing of affective experience; anger control problems; and the self-esteem and interpersonal difficulties already noted above.

According to Schore (2003), secure attachment facilitates the experience-dependent maturation of the right brain that is centrally involved in adaptive regulation of motivational states, including aggression. Severely traumatic attachments result in structural limitations of the early-developing right brain; functional deficits include an inability to regulate emotional states (both fear/terror and aggression) under stress. Numerous neurobiological studies have documented the effects of sustained trauma exposure on the developing brain. The prefrontal cortex and parts of the limbic system, a brain area that participates in the processing of emotion, are particularly vulnerable to stress during childhood development (Teicher et al., 1997). Magnetic resonance imaging studies (Stein, Koverola, Hanna, Torchia, & McClarty, 1997) have found smaller hippocampal volume in women who had been severely sexually abused during childhood. The same study demonstrated that more dissociative symptoms also were associated with smaller hippocampal volume.

From a social developmental perspective, parents' responsiveness to their children's feelings and needs and parents' emotion coaching (accurate labeling and appropriate expression) teaches children affect regulation skills (Gottman, 1997). This includes the capacity to access the full range of emotional experience, to modulate the intensity of emotional experience, and to appropriately express one's emotions and associated needs (Gross, 1999). Through empathic responsiveness, children learn to dampen or intensify emotion in particular situations, and negative feelings, such as anger or fear, are associated with improvement and positive outcomes, such as problem solving or receiving support. However, in violent, abusive, and neglectful environments, there are limited opportunities to communicate, receive support for, understand, and appropriately express emotional experiences, in particular negative ones. In the absence of suitable emotional coaching and support, children learn to rely on avoidance to cope with the powerful feelings generated in response to their maltreatment. Often emotional overcontrol is a strategy for coping with high levels of internal distress, and the individual may alternate between the two extremes of under- and overregulation.

Effects of Underregulation of Emotion

The chronic threat of violence can result in extreme emotional arousal that is embedded in memory (van der Kolk & McFarlane, 1996). Automatic alarm reactions continue to be inappropriately triggered by current stimuli that resemble past experiences and activate the fear memory. This is evident in the intrusion and arousal symptoms of PTSD. The overwhelming emotions generated by the environment have a disorganizing effect on thought and behavior and interfere with learning, performance, and social relations.

Among adult survivors, underregulation problems include intense alarm, rage, or shame responses and a pervasive sense of self as insecure or worthless, as well as chronic "bad feelings" such as anxiety, depression, and irritability (Herman, 1992). Dissociation and behaviors such as substance abuse and self-harm can be reactions to overwhelming affect. Anger regulation problems and aggressive behavior also are highly correlated with unresolved trauma (i.e., irritability, the hyperarousal symptom cluster of PTSD), particularly with exposure to physical violence; this can have profoundly deleterious effects on interpersonal relations. There is strong evidence linking early exposure to domestic violence with later interpersonal violence (Wolfe, 2007) and with high prevalence of extreme anger and aggressive behavior among combat veterans (Novaco, 2007). Problems with anger and aggression are discussed further in chapter 10.

Effects of Emotional Overcontrol and Inhibition

Avoidance of trauma feelings and memories is a feature of PTSD and a strategy for coping with symptoms of intrusion and hyperarousal. Trauma survivors often wish they could excise the feelings and memories associated with traumatic events, but avoidance means that a person is incapable of benefiting from past experience. Furthermore, if avoidance is complete, these individuals do not understand their perceptions and reactive behavior. This is consistent with the perspective that internal experience and emotions are valuable sources of information.

Various forms of experiential avoidance, such as refusing to think about a bad situation or using distraction, predict negative outcomes for substance abuse, depression, and the effects of child sexual abuse (see Hayes, Strosahl, & Wilson, 1999, for a review of the literature). In addition, chronic inhibition of feelings associated with upsetting or traumatic events results in tension that contributes to maladaptive, underregulated anxiety or rage (Barlow, 1988) and the fear of emerging emotional experience. The fear of emerging anger, in particular, is a commonly observed underlying determinant for some forms of anxiety (Bourne, 2003). Pennebaker and colleagues (1997, 1999, 2000) reported the results from numerous studies of diverse populations that link the chronic inhibition of feelings concerning upsetting or traumatic events to negative health outcomes. According to inhibition theory, the chronic inhibition of trauma feelings and memories contributes to immune system breakdown (Pennebaker & Campbell, 2000) because deliberate suppression of the thoughts and particularly the feelings associated with upsetting events requires system energy (i.e., traumatic events are unforgettable). Such suppression over a prolonged period places added stress on the organism, which eventually contributes to immune system breakdown. This is consistent with the somatic complaints that are part of a DESNOS diagnosis.

Chronic inhibition of thoughts and feelings associated with traumatic events also is thought to perpetuate PTSD symptoms and interfere with recovery (Foa, Riggs, & Gershuny, 1995). Traumatic experiences and associated meanings thus are unprocessed, remain "frozen" in memory, and continue to negatively influence current perceptions of self, others, and reality. Core internal experiences that are suppressed remain "unfinished business" pressing for integration and intruding on current awareness (Paivio & Greenberg, 1995). Similarly, the strategies such as dissociation, disavowal, and overcontrol used by child abuse survivors to manage painful affect cut them off from the information associated with emotional experience that might otherwise aid in adaptive functioning. Consequently, survivors frequently are unable to assert themselves, establish appropriate interpersonal boundaries, or grieve and heal from important losses. This has additional disruptive effect on their everyday functioning.

These difficulties are evident in alexithymia that involves deficits in the capacity to recognize and describe emotional experience. Currently accepted social developmental theories suggest that these deficits originate from poor emotion coaching during childhood. As a condition, alexithymia has been associated with somatization, depression, social anxiety, and poor social support (Taylor et al., 1997; Turner & Paivio, 2002). Alexithymia also was found to mediate the relationship between childhood maltreatment and self-injurious behaviors (SIBs) such as self-cutting or burning (Paivio & McCulloch, 2004). Furthermore, it is widely accepted that SIBs (and other self-destructive behaviors) frequently are used to regulate affective states, particularly anger (Linehan, 1993). These findings suggest that a history of maltreatment seems to be, in part, causally related to difficulties identifying emotional experiences, and this, in turn, can lead to self-destructive behavior.

Specific Effects of Different Types of Trauma in Development

The most pervasive long-term effects of exposure to trauma are associated with cumulative and complex trauma, particularly interpersonal trauma during development. In terms of the effects of childhood abuse, overall, there are more commonalities than differences across different maltreatment subtypes (Mullen, Martin, Anderson, & Romans, 1996). Co-occurrence of multiple types of abuse in the same family partly accounts for the limited differential effects of different subtypes. This is consistent with findings that family environment accounts for significant variance as found in a meta-analytic study of the effects of child sexual abuse (Rind, Tromovitch, & Bauserman, 1998). Furthermore, a history of more types of abuse is related to greater psychopathology.

Although few unique effects have been identified, to avoid overgeneralizing, we briefly summarize findings on differential effects of abuse subtypes. These can have implications for effective treatment. Literature on the effects of childhood maltreatment has focused mainly on female sexual abuse, with the balance of work focusing on physical abuse. To date, there is little research on the long-term effects of emotional abuse and neglect, possibly because of a lack of standard definitions (Jellen, McCarroll, & Thayer, 2001).

Definitions of emotional abuse include assaults on a child's sense of worth or well-being, or any humiliating, demeaning, or threatening behavior directed toward a child by an older person. These experiences can be subtle, and it is this subtlety that can be most problematic for victims. These individuals can be unsure whether what they experienced was "abuse" and therefore may discount the effects. In our experience this type of emotional abuse frequently is associated with self-critical processes, fear of negative evaluation, and social anxiety in adulthood. These observations have obvious implications for the therapeutic relationship and participation in key treatment interventions.

Emotional abuse can also include witnessing violence perpetrated against loved ones, cruelty to pets, threats of harm to self or others, and being disciplined with weapons. Some of these experiences involve terror and horror and thus qualify as capital "T" trauma. Although exposure to family violence often is lumped with emotional abuse, at least some of the effects of these experiences appear to be similar to those of direct physical violence. For example, Wolfe and colleagues have repeatedly shown that growing up in violent family environments is associated with violence in adolescent dating relationships (Wolfe, Welkerle, Scott, Strautman, & Grasley, 2004). Our experience with these clients in EFTT also suggests their susceptibility to depression, that is, a collapse in face of their powerlessness and helplessness to protect loved ones.

Childhood physical abuse frequently involves a combination of physical danger or terror as well as distrust and has been hypothesized to be particularly detrimental to self-development and self-regulation (Ford, 2005). A review of the research shows correlates with a history of childhood physical abuse that are similar to those also documented for sexual victimization, which are described below. However, the distinct effects of physical abuse center on anger control problems and aggressive behavior, particularly among males. Scoboria et al. (2006) found that anger dysregulation was the only symptom of complex developmental trauma that was more severe for persons who had experienced physical victimization but not sexual victimization. Symptom scores were also more severe for those who had experienced physical victimization in childhood compared with those who had suffered it in adolescence or adulthood.

Sexual victimization appears to have pernicious effects, not only on sexuality and sexual development but also on development and self-regulation across the range of affective, physical, cognitive, and social domains (Beitchman et al., 1992; Mullen et al., 1996; Romans, Martin, & Mullen, 1996). The distinct features of childhood sexual abuse center on sexuality and bodily experience. These include sexual dysfunction (e.g., avoidance, promiscuity), shame (including body shame), somatization, stigmatization, and vulnerability to revictimization. Sexual trauma at any age predicted greater sexual dysfunction, whereas an earlier age of sexual trauma predicted greater overall severity in complex trauma symptoms as well as health problems (Scoboria et al., 2006).

Another important distinction is that between abuse, discussed above, and neglect. Emotional neglect refers to the failure of caregivers to provide a child's basic psychological and emotional (attachment) needs, such as love, encouragement, belonging, and support (Bernstein & Fink, 1998). This form of harm entails sins of omission (what was absent) rather than commission (the presence of negative events). The effects of neglect are insidious, even more so than for emotional abuse, because it is more nebulous. Researchers (Gauthier, Stollak, Messe, & Arnoff, 1996) have found more reported adverse effects for neglect compared with abuse. For example, among those with a history of neglect, Zlotnick et al. (2007) found higher levels of alexithymia, which, as we have seen, is associated with multiple areas of dysfunction. In our research on EFTT, we have observed that, at first blush, clients with a history of emotional neglect frequently appear to be socially anxious and emotionally constricted. But more important, these clients also possess an underlying lack of clarity or uncertainty about internal experience and looking to others, including the therapist, for direction. The implication here is that these individuals will need more support in terms of labeling and using their internal experience for direction.

When it comes to cumulative trauma, the specific effects for refugee trauma survivors, for example, include stresses from relocation and loss and adjustment concerns that may take precedence over resolving the trauma. Negative effects from cumulative trauma are exacerbated by, if not a result of, sociopolitical factors, and most experts agree that applying a psychopathology model to this client group frequently is inappropriate. For these individuals, a treatment focus on current struggles as well as client strengths and resilience is particularly crucial.

TREATMENT IMPLICATIONS

Large numbers of individuals seek therapy to address the effects of complex interpersonal and cumulative trauma. With the increasing numbers of asylum seekers worldwide, the need for trauma-focused psychological services also is increasing. The more complex and long term the traumatic events, the more complex are the disruptions. A comprehensive treatment is required that addresses this multifaceted array of disturbances. EFTT concentrates on the commonalities across different types of complex trauma, abuse, and neglect, with attention to individual client needs. This treatment also draws on the strengths of other approaches, particularly in terms of addressing cultural adjustment, affect management, and behavioral problems.

Experts agree that recovery from PTSD requires exposure to experiences that directly contradict the emotional helplessness and physical paralysis of trauma (Ford, 2005). In EFTT, these contradictory experiences take place through the therapeutic relationship, imaginal confrontation of offenders, and a focus on accessing adaptive anger and sadness and associated healthy resources. Symptom reduction occurs from an experience that "remembered" in therapy is not the same as one that is experienced in real life, and from coming to accept the event as part of one's personal history. Critical steps in treating PTSD and complex PTSDs include establishing safety, anxiety management, emotional processing, and integration of the experience into current meaning systems. This entails putting the event in perspective by articulating what happened; what led up to it; one's own contributions, thoughts, and fantasies during the event; its worst parts; one's detailed reactions, including perceptions of self and others; and the effects of these on one's current sense of self and relationships. This is what constitutes meaning and construction of coherent narratives in EFTT.

Interventions are required that evoke the experiential system. Interventions that involve emotion, body, somatic and sensory activation, and bilateral information-processing mechanisms can functionally counteract the effects of trauma (Fosha, 2003). EFTT interventions and procedures, such as evocative empathy, promoting experiencing, experiential focusing, imaginal confrontation, and other enactments, serve this function. These interventions foster right-brain, bottom-up processing (e.g., reliving, picturing). Techniques also are required that access and promote the processing of intense emotion. Accessing core emotion accesses the information associated with emotional experience, which includes split-off, dissociated, and ignored aspects of self, as well as healthy resources that guide adaptive functioning. Autobiographical information and self-reflection are important in constructing more coherent narratives. In addition, interventions are required that address self-related and interpersonal problems and change internal "object relations." EFTT is such a comprehensive treatment. The following chapter presents the theoretical model and outlines how EFTT addresses the effects of complex trauma.

2

EMOTION-FOCUSED THERAPY FOR TRAUMA TREATMENT MODEL

The purpose of this chapter is to present how emotion-focused therapy for trauma (EFTT) conceptualizes and addresses the disturbances produced by trauma that were outlined in the preceding chapter. As described in the introduction, EFTT has been developed and refined through a program of research that has included numerous process and outcome studies, spanning more than 15 years and across three clinical research settings, and has involved the treatment of several dozens of clients. This program of research and development began with clinical observation and later process analyses of emotion-focused therapy (Paivio & Greenberg, 1995) with clients who were specifically dealing with issues of child abuse trauma. Several key features of EFTT emerged from these observations and analyses.

First, participation in the primary exposure-based procedure used in therapy seemed more difficult for clients who were dealing with issues related to trauma. The *imaginal confrontation* (IC) procedure is a central component of EFTT and is introduced later in this chapter and discussed more thoroughly in chapter 7. The IC procedure requires clients to imagine perpetrators of abuse in an empty chair and to express their thoughts and feelings directly to them. When this procedure was first introduced in therapy, some clients became panicky, others were horrified at the thought of the perpetrator being in the room, and still others refused to participate. Subsequent work with IC required exploring and addressing these difficulties. For example, when the client Monica, whose mother had committed suicide, was asked to imagine her mother sitting in an empty chair, Monica became panicky, clutched at her blouse, and had difficulty breathing. The procedure evoked the pain and horror of finding her dead mother. Interventions helped her manage this distress while at the same time confronting her imagined mother with the pain and resentment she felt about that suicide.

Other processes that consistently emerged for clients dealing with child abuse trauma were shame and self-blame about the trauma, which frequently manifested as depression. Working through these issues was a key component of therapy with Monica: Although she had not been abused, per se, she felt "tainted" by her mothers "atrocity," feared that she and her siblings were somehow to blame for her mother's suicide, and felt that she could not have been very important to her mother to have been abandoned and traumatized so horrifically. Interventions helped her to work through this shame as well as her fears and longing for assurance that she had been loved.

We also observed that clients who were dealing with childhood abuse did not want to express vulnerable feelings, such as sadness, to imagined others who were perceived to be cruel and abusive. In these instances, work with these emotions involved clients disengaging from the IC procedure and instead expressing these feelings to the therapist, who was able to provide the necessary compassion and support. Vulnerable feelings were expressed during IC to those imagined others who were perceived to be capable of responding compassionately. In the case of Monica, although she felt abandoned and betrayed by her mother, she did not perceive her to be cruel or abusive and was able to express her pain and sorrow directly to her imagined mother using the IC procedure. She was able to do this more fully after expression of, and feeling entitled to, her anger about the devastating impact her mother's actions had had on her and her family.

Finally, we observed two different pathways to resolution. First, for some clients, increased acceptance and warmth toward offenders, particularly those who were primary attachment figures, was an important outcome. For Monica, healing the relationship with her internalized mother was a primary goal of therapy. Resolution involved holding her mother accountable for the harm she had caused and then imagining that her mother would be remorseful and take full responsibility for that harm. Monica thus was able to forgive her mother.

Other cases present a slightly different pathway to resolution. Although clients resolved issues with offenders and felt more autonomous and separate from them at the end of therapy, they typically did not feel more accepting and forgiving. Again, this was particularly the case when the offender was seen to be cruel and unrepentant. In these instances, the client feels more detached from the other, who is still perceived as despicable but is now seen as less threatening and perhaps "sick" or pathetic. The suitability of each of these pathways toward resolution is not prescriptive; preference for one or the other becomes apparent over the course of treatment and is entirely based on the client's idiosyncratic processes and interpretations.

THEORETICAL FOUNDATIONS

EFTT is an integrative approach that applies emotion-focused theory to the area of complex trauma. EFTT is grounded in current theory and research on experiential therapy (e.g., Greenberg & Paivio, 1997; Greenberg, Rice, & Elliot, 1993; Paivio & Greenberg, 1995) and shares features with behavioral (e.g., Foa, Rothbaum, & Furr, 2003), cognitive–behavioral (e.g., Resick, Nishith, & Griffin, 2003), and attachment-based psychodynamic approaches (e.g., Fosha, Paivio, Gleiser, & Ford, 2009) to the treatment of trauma-related disturbances.

General Theory of Functioning

The general emotion focused theory of functioning draws on the principles of attachment, experiential therapy, and emotion theories. These principles are delineated in the following sections.

Attachment Relationships Are Crucial to Development

Emotion-focused therapy emphasizes the centrality of early attachment experiences in the development of self and the expectations of others. From a humanistic perspective, this has its origins in Rogers's (1959) view of the importance of unconditional positive regard in self-development. This approach lays particular emphasis on the developmental importance of affective experiences in the context of attachment relationships. Accordingly, healthy attachment relationships are seen as providing a sense of safety and security that fosters exploratory behavior, a sense of self as worthwhile and competent, and a sense of intimate others as supportive and trustworthy (Bowlby, 1988). In addition, through appropriate emotion coaching from attachment figures (Gottman, 1997), children learn to regulate emotional experience and soothe themselves in times of distress.

Internal Experience Is a Source of Information

A fundamental assumption underlying all experiential therapies is that verbally symbolizing current subjective experience (feelings and meanings) is the primary source of new information used in construction of meaning. Again, this has its origins in traditional client-centered and experiential approaches (Gendlin, 1996; Perls, Hefferline, & Goodman, 1951; Rogers, 1957). More recent articulations draw on current narrative and constructivist perspectives (e.g., Neimeyer & Bridges, 2003; J. Pascual-Leone, 1991). The fundamental assumptions of these perspectives include the primacy of personal meaning, the social construction of identity, and coherent and flexible life narratives. Emotion-focused therapy theory states that conscious meaning is constructed from several sources of information but primarily involves the synthesis of information from both experiential and rational/linguistic systems (Greenberg & Paivio, 1997). Conscious meaning requires that internal experience is deliberately and sequentially processed and symbolized in words. Conversely, optimal functioning requires that rational knowing and language are anchored in the experiential system.

Affective Experience Is Central to Functioning

Experiential therapies place particular emphasis on affective processes and meaning. The importance of affective experience in human functioning is supported by emotion theory and research and recent developments in affective neuroscience (e.g., Damasio, 1999; Doidge, 2007; Fridja, 1986; Izard, 2002; Ledoux, 1996). Accordingly, emotions are associated with a network of multimodal information (e.g., thoughts, images, feelings, desires, somatic and sensory experience) or meaning system. Once an emotion is activated, the meaning system it embodies influences current perceptions, motivation, and behavior and is available for continual modification through the integration of new information. Furthermore, specific emotions are associated with specific areas of brain activation and specific information. The information associated with basic emotions aids in adaptive functioning. Anger, for example, helps in assertiveness, self-defense, and interpersonal separation, whereas sadness facilitates grieving and acceptance of loss, self-soothing, and moving on to other concerns.

Theory of Dysfunction Specific to Trauma

The theoretical concepts discussed here are particularly relevant to the area of trauma. The EFTT view of trauma-related dysfunction is based on material presented in the preceding chapter. In brief, first, unresolved traumatic experiences are encoded in memory and activated in response to current stimuli that resemble the trauma (van der Kolk et al., 1996). This is evident, for example, in the reexperiencing symptoms (e.g., nightmares, flashbacks) of posttraumatic stress disorder (PTSD). Second, prolonged and repeated exposure to trauma at the hands of caregivers has particularly devastating effects. These experiences can result in negative self–other representations that continue to influence current self-concept and close interpersonal relationships. Third, complex trauma in early development has a particularly detrimental effect on the development of emotion regulation capacities. Children learn to rely on avoidance to cope with the painful, powerful, and confusing feelings generated by these experiences. When experiential avoidance is chronic, it is associated with a number of disturbances, including substance abuse, self-injurious behavior, interpersonal problems, and impoverished social support (Paivio & McCulloch, 2004; Turner & Paivio, 2002). Moreover, chronic avoidance is thought to perpetuate trauma symptoms, interfere with recovery, and contribute to immune system breakdown (Foa, Riggs, Massie, & Yarczower, 1995; Pennebaker & Campbell, 2000). Traumatic experiences, attachment injuries, and associated meanings remain frozen in memory and continue to negatively influence current functioning. Recovery from complex trauma therefore requires reducing symptoms of PTSD, changing maladaptive perceptions of self and others, and reducing experiential avoidance.

Theory of Change in EFTT

The two posited change processes in EFTT are providing a safe therapeutic relationship and working with memories. In terms of the therapeutic relationship, a fundamental assumption underlying most experiential therapies is that therapist compassion, genuineness, and empathy are necessary (if not sufficient) ingredients for change. In EFTT, the relationship functions in two ways to promote change. First, an empathic and collaborative therapeutic relationship supports client engagement in reexperiencing procedures. In this sense the relationship is the sine qua non medium that allows for other change processes. Second, this relationship quality helps to counter the empathic failures of previous attachment relationships. Experiences of safety and support are internalized, promote self-development and interpersonal trust, and generalize to other relationships, thereby helping to restore the capacity for interpersonal connectedness that was disrupted by trauma. Thus, EFTT shares features with both cognitive–behavioral therapy (relationship as "anesthetic") and relational psychodynamic (relationship as directly curative) perspectives on the functions of the therapeutic relationship.

The second posited change process in EFTT is memory work. Most trauma experts agree that recovery from trauma requires reexperiencing trauma feelings and memories in a safe environment so that information is available for emotional processing, that is, exploration and modification through the admission of new information (Foa, Huppert, & Cahill, 2006). From a behavioral perspective, emotional processing primarily involves desensitization processes such that individuals learn that they can tolerate trauma material without being destroyed by it. From an EFTT perspective, emotional processing involves a more complex set of processes that will be explicated in chapter 3. Emotional processing of complex trauma involves not only desensitization to painful feelings and memories but also active construction of new idiosyncratic meaning, that is, a more adaptive and coherent view of self, others, and traumatic events. Furthermore, processing of trauma memories requires the application of rational/linguistic processes to trauma material that is encoded in the experiential system but has remained unprocessed or has been processed incompletely. An indicator of resolution, therefore, is that trauma narratives become more coherent, personal, affectively focused, and self-reflective. These qualities are reflected in the construct of experiencing, which is the focus of chapter 4.

In sum, affective disruptions are at the core of disturbances stemming from interpersonal developmental trauma, and EFTT is exceptionally well suited to address these difficulties. Clients learn to rely on interpersonal support so that they can tolerate previously avoided material and develop a more adaptive understanding of self, others, and traumatic experiences. These features of EFTT theory are consistent with other well-established therapies for adult survivors (e.g., Herman, 1992; Pearlman & Courtois, 2005). However, EFTT also makes a number of distinct contributions to the conceptualization and treatment of complex PTSDs.

DISTINGUISHING FEATURES OF EFTT

The following subsections outline the features that are characteristic of EFTT and distinguish it from other approaches.

Focus on Health and Adaptive Resources

Although EFTT includes attention to modifying maladaptive emotions, such as fear and shame, it explicitly emphasizes client strengths and resilience, as well as accessing previously inhibited adaptive emotions as healthy resources. Again, accessing anger at violation helps to counteract powerlessness, victimization, and self-blame, whereas experiencing sadness accesses compassion for self and self-soothing resources that aid in grieving losses and moving on. EFTT interventions direct clients' attention to these adaptive emotions and associated resources. This emphasis on adaptive resources is consistent with the recent interest in the concepts of trauma resilience (Harvey et al., 2003) and posttraumatic growth (Tadeschi, Park, & Calhoun, 1998). The latter involves areas of reported growth (e.g., increased spirituality or awareness of personal values) that are beyond pretrauma functioning and directly attributable to wrestling with the trauma. Psychopathology and resilience/growth are not mutually exclusive. Furthermore, recovery involves the use of strengths in some domains to help in others. To this end, it is important to identify the resilience capacities of individuals early in the recovery process and use these to promote recovery. Harvey et al.'s (2003) study found that factors such as connections with others over time, group membership, success experiences (e.g., work, parenting), self-care, and attributions of responsibility or choice were associated with client resilience. EFTT interventions explicitly highlight and direct clients' attention to these and other personal strengths and resources as a way of strengthening the self.

Reliance on Therapist Empathic Responding

All effective psychological treatments rely on therapist empathic attunement to client feelings and needs. This is the basis for treatment goals. However, experiential approaches have paid particular attention not only to attunement but also to advanced empathic responding and have developed a taxonomy of empathic responses and associated functions (Bohart & Greenberg, 1997; Elliott, Watson, Goldman, & Greenberg, 2004). Empathic responding to client feelings and needs is the primary intervention used throughout EFTT. This is used particularly to address the emotion regulation deficits described in the preceding chapter that are so central to complex trauma (Paivio & Laurent, 2001). Accordingly, accurate empathic responses can enhance the emotion regulation capacities identified by Gross (1999): that is, help clients access, identify, and accurately label the full range of emotions and associated meanings, modulate the intensity of emotion (up-regulate and down-regulate), and teach appropriate emotional expression.

Imagery and Enactments

In trauma work, techniques also are required that access experiential memory and promote the processing of intense emotion. Interventions that involve emotion, somatic, and sensory activation foster right-brain, bottom-up processing. EFTT draws on a long experiential/humanistic tradition and well-developed technology for overcoming experiential avoidance, evoking affective experience, and promoting experiential awareness. These, coupled with verbal symbolization, can help reverse the effects of trauma. Evocative empathy, experiential focusing, and gestalt-derived procedures involve imagery and multimodal enactments that quickly evoke core processes (i.e., trauma material encoded in experiential memory), making them available for exploration, integration, and change.

Marker-Driven and Process-Directive Intervention

A major contribution of emotion-focused therapy to the treatment literature is the idea of *marker-driven* intervention. This involves the identification of different types of emotions and associated processing difficulties (Greenberg et al., 1993; Greenberg & Paivio, 1997) as in-session markers for initiating specific therapeutic interventions. This "if–then" approach proposes that, within the broader context of understanding a particular case, "if the client presents marker X, then the therapist should do intervention Y." In the interventions to be discussed in later chapters, facilitating moments of productive process in this way are themselves considered mini-outcomes. These include, for example, accessing primary adaptive emotions, exploring and changing maladaptive emotions, and resolving complex difficulties, such as self-criticism or attachment injuries. These difficulties cut across and are more informative than global diagnostic categories in terms of intervention. For example, unresolved attachment injuries and self-critical processes can be at the root of either PTSD or major depression, but not all clients with PTSD have attachment issues, and not all major depressions are generated by self-criticism.

The emphasis on moment-by-moment processes has resulted in exceptionally specific and well-articulated guidelines for implementing interventions (Elliott et al., 2004; Greenberg & Paivio, 1997; Greenberg et al., 1993; Greenberg & Watson, 2006). EFTT draws on these guidelines. EFTT therapists make use of an ongoing process diagnosis, in which they monitor and attend to the client's unfolding affective state and level of readiness for potential interventions. Being familiar with the client markers of productive, as contrasted with relatively unproductive, modes of processing moment-by-moment can help orient therapists to a client's emerging patterns of change (Pascual-Leone, 2009). Moreover, these markers can help therapists with process-based choices for intervention, for example, "The client has already superficially identified an emotion and keeps going in circles, what might help her go deeper?" "When the issue arises, would it be more productive to help the client explore the subjective experience of a transgression or the motivation of the perpetrator?" and "The client makes progress but then always ends up feeling hopeless, is this productive?" By increasing their awareness of client shifts in experience and familiarizing themselves with productive patterns of processing, therapists can increase the precision of their interventions. These are the skills required in effectively using the process models that are the basis of EFTT (e.g., steps in the process of resolving attachment injuries; Greenberg & Foerster, 1996). These models, in turn, guide intervention and move the client closer to resolution.

Focus on Resolving Issues With Particular Attachment Figures

Most other treatments for complex trauma focus on skills development and changing current self-related and interpersonal problems (e.g., Chard, 2005; Cloitre, Koenen, Dohen, & Han, 2002). Even relational psychodynamic models identify maladaptive interpersonal patterns and provide a corrective experience with the therapist to change these patterns (e.g., Fosha et al., 2009). EFTT, in contrast, conceptualizes the adult disturbances associated with childhood maltreatment as largely involving unresolved issues with particular individuals, typically, attachment figures. Clients not only are distressed by current difficulties but also continue to be distressed by powerful unexpressed feelings, unmet needs, and disturbing memories concerning these individuals. From an attachment perspective, they are unable to separate, let go of unmet needs, and move on until feelings are expressed and processed and past experiences are satisfactorily resolved. The client Monica, for example, was plagued by feelings of confusion, shame, and anger about abandonment and unmet needs for "mothering" her entire life. The IC procedure used in EFTT is designed to resolve issues with these particular individuals. Together with the therapeutic relationship, resolving these issues is analogous to transforming internal object relations. This generalizes to other relationships and increases the capacity for interpersonal connectedness that has been disrupted by the trauma.

Empirical Support

Although there are a handful of stand-alone outcome studies supporting individual therapies for complex trauma (e.g., Chard, 2005; Cloitre et al., 2002; Resick et al., 2003; Talbot & Gamble, 2008), EFTT is the only treatment of this type that is based on a systematic program of process and outcome research. EFTT is based on an empirically verified model of resolving unfinished business with significant others using an empty-chair technique (Greenberg & Foerster, 1996; Greenberg & Malcolm, 2002) similar to the IC procedure described earlier. Particular steps in this process that empirically discriminated clients who resolved interpersonal issues from those who did not included expression of adaptive emotion and associated needs, entitlement to unmet needs, and changed perceptions of self and others. Clients who resolve these issues shift to a stance of increased self-empowerment and self-esteem, develop a more differentiated perspective of target others, and appropriately hold them (rather than self) accountable for harm.

An early outcome study (Paivio & Greenberg, 1995) supported the efficacy of individual therapy based on the above model with a general clinical sample. Clients made large gains in multiple domains that were maintained at follow-up. The sample included a subgroup of clients who were dealing with child abuse issues. Subsequent analyses of 72 sessions of therapy with these individuals led to the development of EFTT specifically for resolving child abuse trauma. Refinements to the original model included more attention to secondary issues of avoidance and self-blame, a longer course of therapy to address these issues, and reframing the empty-chair intervention in terms of an exposure-based or reexperiencing procedure. The term *imaginal confrontation* was adopted because it better captured this emphasis on trauma-related processes.

Outcome research supports the efficacy of EFTT with IC (Paivio & Nieuwenhuis, 2001), whereas process–outcome research supports the therapeutic relationship and emotional engagement with trauma material during IC as mechanisms of change (Paivio & Patterson, 1999; Paivio, Hall, Holowaty, Jellis, & Tran, 2001). Results of a recent clinical trial (Paivio, Jarry, Chagigiorgis, Hall, & Ralston, in press) evaluated two versions of EFTT with or without the use of the IC procedure. Results indicated that clients in both conditions made large and clinically significant gains on multiple dimensions, and these were maintained at 1-year follow-up. The average pre–post effect size across 10 dependent measures, which included symptom distress (PTSD, depression, anxiety), self-esteem, interpersonal problems, and resolution of issues with specific abusive and neglectful others, was 1.3 standard deviations. This far exceeds the American Psychological Association's recommended criteria (0.8 standard deviations) for effective therapy.

Broad Applicability Across Gender, Severity, and Type of Abuse

To date, EFTT (Paivio et al., in press; Paivio & Nieuwenhuis, 2001) is the only evidence-based individual therapy for both men and women who are dealing with different types of child abuse trauma (emotional, physical, sexual). Until recently, most published studies were group approaches for women with histories of child sexual abuse (e.g., Morgan & Cummings, 1999; Saxe & Johnson, 1999). The handful of published individual treatments (e.g., Chard, 2005; Cloitre et al., 2002; Resick et al., 2003) have also focused almost exclusively on women diagnosed with PTSD with histories of child sexual abuse. However, experiences of maltreatment are not unique to women or confined to sexual abuse experiences. As noted in the preceding chapter, few differential effects have been identified for different types of abuse (Scoboria, Ford, Hsio-ju, & Frisman, 2006). Furthermore, there is recognition that many individuals who have experienced complex and cumulative trauma seek therapy for a variety of disturbances besides PTSD (van der Kolk, 2003). EFTT addresses a constellation of trauma-related disturbances that are common across men and women and multiple types of maltreatment experiences. At the beginning of therapy, clients are asked to identify the type of abuse experiences and abusive/neglectful others they want to focus on in treatment. Protocol is sufficiently flexible to address individual client processes and treatment needs, and, in the end, resolution of these core issues generalizes to current areas of functioning.

DISTINCTIONS BETWEEN EFTT AND THE GENERAL MODEL OF EMOTION-FOCUSED THERAPY

It is useful to identify the features of EFTT specifically for trauma that distinguish it from the general model of emotion-focused therapy (Elliott et al., 2004; Greenberg & Paivio, 1997; Greenberg & Watson, 2006) and other current experiential therapies. As noted earlier, these distinct features emerged in the context of therapy with a subset of clients (including Monica) who were dealing with complex trauma. These distinct features derive from several sources, including the nature of the population and problems that therapy was designed to address, the research context in which the approach was developed, and a deliberate emphasis on integrating the guidelines and strengths of other approaches to the treatment of trauma (e.g., Pearlman & Courtois, 2005).

To begin, Elliott et al. (2004) specified the tasks that are prototypical of emotion-focused therapy in general. The following tasks are particularly relevant to trauma work in EFTT. First, *empathy-based tasks* include communicating compassion for client struggles and suffering and paying particular attention to markers of vulnerability (e.g., fear and shame about emerging experience) that frequently emerge in therapy with this client group.

Second, *relational tasks* include attention to attachment issues that are the sources of disturbance (e.g., feelings of worthlessness, insecurity, distrust) and addressing client anxiety about the therapy process. The latter partly can be accomplished by validating clients' anxiety, providing information about trauma response and recovery as well as clear expectations about therapy processes and client and therapist roles, and monitoring and addressing client difficulties with other types of tasks used in therapy (e.g., experiencing, enactments).

Third, *experiencing tasks* generally involve helping clients explore the meaning of affective experience. This can be particularly challenging for many trauma survivors who have difficulties identifying and labeling feelings (alexithymia) and have learned to rely on avoidance as a coping strategy. Specific experiencing tasks therefore frequently include directing clients' focus of attention when they are confused, overwhelmed, blank, or numb; when they present with feelings that are unclear or abstract; or when they are externally focused on situations or behavior. Experiencing tasks also are appropriate when clients have difficulties answering questions about and identifying and exploring feelings and their meanings.

Fourth, *reprocessing tasks* in EFTT that involve revisiting trauma feelings and memories can be particularly terrifying, painful, and difficult. This can include not only experiencing horrifying images and physical pain but also reexperiencing oneself as unloved, worthless, dirty, or negligible and attachment figures as malevolent. Thus, EFTT may involve focusing on intensely frightening and painful experiences to an even greater extent than in emotion-focused therapy for other client problems.

In addition, EFTT may be more structured and content-directive than emotion-focused therapy for other disturbances. For example, therapists deliberately instruct clients to disclose trauma memories rather than simply respond to markers of their emergence. They also may make connections between current concerns and past situations that could be considered interpretations, and may use confrontation, for example, to address maladaptive behaviors. Finally, therapy frequently includes the use of management strategies for clients with severe affect dysregulation problems or who engage in self-destructive behaviors, such as substance abuse or self-injury.

THE TREATMENT MODEL

EFTT is a semistructured approach that typically consists of 16 to 20 weekly 1-hour sessions. However, the exact length of therapy is based on individual client processes and treatment needs. In cases of greater severity and duration of trauma, as well as repeated victimization, therapy likely will be more long term. In particular, more time could be required to establish safety and trust, reduce dissociation and maladaptive avoidance, and develop more effective emotion regulation capacities. In our most recent work with refugee trauma survivors, EFTT includes more supportive and present-focused work on identity and adjustment issues.

Phases and Tasks of EFTT

EFTT is not a stage or linear model, but particular processes typically are dominant during particular phases of therapy. Clients can circle through aspects of several phases in a single session and vary in terms of the time needed to progress through particular phases.

Phase 1: Cultivating the Alliance

The first three sessions are exclusively devoted to cultivating a secure attachment bond and collaborating on the goals of therapy and how these will be achieved. A secure attachment bond primarily is created by establishing client safety and trust. Safety and trust, in turn, primarily are fostered by communicating genuine compassion for clients' past and current suffering and their struggle to cope (e.g., the therapist might say, "It's terrible that a child be exposed to such ugliness. I feel bad that you had to go through all that, especially alone"), and by empathically responding to painful feelings and needs for comfort, control, justice, and so on. This will foster further disclosure and begin to reduce isolation. Collaboration involves clients agreeing on the importance of reexperiencing trauma feelings and memories and understanding how this will help them accomplish their goals (e.g., to be free of trauma symptoms and emotional baggage, change maladaptive behavior, feel better about self, have healthier relationships). The rationale for memory work and a focus on feelings must be tailored to the individual client's goals and treatment needs.

Resolving attachment injuries is the primary task of therapy, and IC is the procedure most frequently used to accomplish this. Successful task collaboration during the initial IC requires monitoring the client's capacity to regulate emotions and to engage with trauma material and the procedure. For example, the client Monica entered the third session complaining about yet another incident in which she wished her mother could have been available for support and was not there. This was an ideal marker for asking Monica to imagine her mother in the empty chair and tell her about her resentment. This evoked panic and difficulty breathing. The therapist empathized with Monica's vulnerability and distress, coached her in breathing, and invited her to disclose what was going on (reduce isolation and fear). Monica disclosed horrifying images of all the blood, trying to wake her dead mother, and her mother in the coffin, as well as more detailed accounts of the circumstances surrounding these events. The therapist provided a brief rationale for engagement in IC and collaborated with Monica on a strategy for engaging in the procedure without the visual imagery. The therapist provided guidance, reassurance, and support throughout the process. For clients who cannot or will not participate in IC, intervention can switch to processing material exclusively in interaction with the therapist. The important point is to continue to focus on trauma material and follow the steps in the model of resolution. Clinical judgment will determine whether to initially confront more or less threatening others. This is discussed further in chapter 7. The introduction of IC and activation of core processes mark the transition from Phase 1 to Phase 2 of EFTT.

Phase 2: Reducing Fear and Shame

The second phase of EFTT focuses on reducing self-related processes that are barriers to resolving relational trauma and attachment injuries. These processes include lack of clarity about internal experience, fear and avoidance of affective experience, and self-criticism and self-blame. Self-related problems also frequently include depression or anxiety and the associated core sense of self as vulnerable, insecure, or defective (weak or bad self). For example, Monica feared she would be judged by others and stigmatized on account of her mother's behavior, and this became her "ugly secret." She also felt victimized and deficient. Other clients have internalized a "bad parent" such that these become self-inflicting intrapsychic processes. Two-chair dialogues, experiential focusing, and empathic exploration are used in conjunction with IC to explore and resolve these difficulties. Interventions are aimed at strengthening the client's sense of self by accessing alternative healthy resources (self-protection, self-soothing) and changing maladaptive avoidance behavior.

Phase 3: Resolving Trauma and Attachment Injuries

The third phase of EFTT focuses on resolving issues with specific abusive and neglectful others and involves accessing adaptive anger and sadness and associated meanings. For clients like Monica, this takes place in the complex context of grieving traumatic losses that had been interrupted. Her profound anger at having been traumatized and abandoned and the years of chaos, suffering, and responsibility had never been validated and continued to eat away at her. Therapeutic goals included the expression and validation of her anger, allowing her anger to run its course and the full experience and expression of sorrow and grief.

The uninhibited experience and expression of adaptive emotion is the catalyst for resolving traumatic attachment injuries in Phase 3 of therapy. As avoidance and self-blame are reduced, clients gradually are better able to confront imagined abusive and neglectful others. Interventions encourage the client to articulate the full impact of the abuse on him or her. It also is critical to elicit the imagined perpetrator's response to the client's confrontation. This captures the client's view of the other's capacity for understanding, empathy, and regret. For example, over time, Monica came to believe that her mother would profoundly regret what she had done and take full responsibility for the harm she had caused. Enacting her mother elicited assurance, in this role, that she has been loved and accessed memories of happy times and loving interactions with her mother (e.g., she remembered brushing her mother's hair). In response, Monica stated that she felt warm and loved for the first time in her life since her mother died.

One goal is for clients to arrive at a more differentiated perspective of abusive and neglectful others. In cases like Monica's, the other (in this case, her mother) is seen as more complex and human. If the client can see the other as repentant, the client is able to feel more compassionate and loving toward the person. In alternate cases, the other may be seen as pathetic and incapable of understanding. Either way, the offending others are seen as more life-size and less powerful. Having the client enact or imagine the other also can elicit client empathic resources, for example, Monica sensing some of the desperation her mother must have felt. This can be particularly important in healing attachment relationships, for instance, coming to understand that one or both of her parents also were victims or had limited resources.

Phase 4: Termination

The final phase of EFTT focuses on integration of therapy experiences and termination. In the last few sessions, a final IC is introduced to assess and consolidate changes. Clients are asked to compare their current experience of imagining the perpetrator(s) with their experience during the initial dialogue. For example, Monica shifted from feeling tied up in knots, victimized, and deficient to viewing herself as a strong survivor. She also shifted from the angry rejection of her mother and from seeing her mother as superficial and self-centered to viewing her with compassion. She came to see her mother's suicide as an act of desperation, a terrible tragic mistake that her mother would undo if she could. The termination phase also involves processing the client's experience of therapy (difficulties, successes, helpful aspects) and mutual feedback. Discussions also focus on and support the client's plans and goals for the future.

Basic Intervention Principles (Therapist Intentions)

Intervention principles are like therapist intentions that can be realized through a number of response modes, including empathic responses, questions, directives, and so on. EFTT intervention principles most frequently used throughout therapy include the following (examples in parentheses are the therapist's responses):

- Directing client attention to internal experience using simple reflections (e.g., "That must have been so painful") or questions (e.g., "What was going on for you on the inside?")
- Directing expression of experience to the therapist or imagined other (e.g., "Tell me/him/her what it was like for you")
- Promoting ownership of experience (e.g., use of "I" language)
- Evoking distal or recent episodic memories (e.g., "Do you remember a time when . . . ?" or "Let's go back to that time . . . bring it alive for me")
- Modulating emotional intensity—reducing it through empathy, validation, and reassurance or increasing intensity through evocative empathy (e.g., "You must have been so starved for

attention" or "How dare he!") and directives (e.g., "Say that again/louder")

- Establishing intentions, desires, wants, and needs (e.g., "What you needed as a child was . . ." or "So you are no longer willing to put up with . . .")
- Verbally symbolizing the meaning of emotional experience (e.g., "So the worst part about that was . . ." or "There is something so important about that?")

For clients with severe emotion dysregulation problems, such as panic or dissociation, commonly used anxiety management strategies, such as attention to breathing, relaxation, and present-centeredness, are incorporated while exploring trauma material.

Directing attention to internal experience, directing expression of experience, and exploring the meaning of experience are the "meat and potatoes" of experiential therapies. Directing attention is the foundation of all these intervention principles. Attentional processes are central in determining what people experience and in generating truly novel experience and performance. Attending to new features of experience, which previously were minimized or glossed over, will produce new awareness and new meaning. By directing client attention and posing the right exploratory questions, new information becomes available. Bottom-up processing (i.e., attention to perceptual–emotional data vs. concepts) is more conducive to discovery of new information as contrasted with prior knowledge and expectations, which is more conducive to pattern recognition (Pascual-Leone & Greenberg, 2006). Novice therapists who over emphasize expression skills often neglect directing attention. However, authentic expression emerges from the inside out, from attending to internal experience.

Exploring meaning is a core process, and establishing intentions is a critical subset of this process. Responses explicitly highlight client wants, needs, desires, and longings (e.g., wanting so much to please or be treated with respect; starving for attention). When therapist responses do this, they reinforce clients' motivation, promote growth, and help move the process forward.

Promoting ownership of experience is important when clients are vague or impersonal about their experience or externalize (i.e., just the facts). It is also useful when clients blame and complain about another. To shape more assertive client responses rather than the client blaming and complaining about another or assuming a victim stance, therapists can use responses such as, "So, it hurt your feelings" or "Try saying 'I'm angry at him [you] because' . . . ."

In terms of *memory evocation*, the important features of episodic memories are that they are specific, autobiographical, and affective in nature (Greenberg & Paivio, 1997). This is relevant to the encoding of trauma material in experiential memory. Specific and detailed memories of the concrete features of real autobiographical events provide more alternatives for further processing than general abstract memories. Self-related (autobiographical) and affectively charged events are more memorable because they elicit more attention allocation and increased sensory experience.

Specific Interventions and Procedures

A number of therapeutic tasks and specific procedures will be discussed in detail throughout the book. Although these are specifically defined, it is important to use them flexibly rather than adhering rigidly to a given protocol or procedure. Being familiar with the underlying principles of particular interventions and the treatment as a whole allows therapists to initiate, modify, and sometimes switch or change tasks in a manner that remains consistent with the spirit of treatment and empirically derived guidelines. In what follows, we outline four of the primary tasks and procedures used in therapy.

Empathic Responding

Empathic responding is the primary intervention used throughout EFTT. It is used as a standard intervention as well as an active and deliberate intervention, either alone or in conjunction with all other procedures. There is increasing recognition of the importance of "unflinching empathy" as the foundation of therapy with trauma survivors (Marotto, 2003). Paivio and Laurent (2001) delineated how empathic responses are used in EFTT to cultivate the therapeutic relationship, reduce client avoidance and self-blame, and explore and resolve complex trauma. This will be elaborated in specific intervention chapters.

Empathic attunement to client vulnerability and arousal levels is particularly critical in trauma therapy because of the risk of retraumatization. Furthermore, there are particular interrelated advantages to empathic responses in therapy for child abuse (Paivio & Laurent, 2001). First, empathic responding that mirrors or follows client processes rather than directing, teaching, or interpreting the client's experience from an expert stance is minimally hierarchical, maximizes client control over the process, and thus increases the client's sense of safety and control. Second, empathic responding ensures accurate understanding of the client's struggles, concerns, and goals that is essential for effective collaboration. Collaboration, in turn, additionally contributes to the client's sense of safety and control. Third, empathic responses, by definition, communicate understanding, acceptance, and support and thus minimize the defensiveness that can be elicited by questions, challenges, and interpretations. Social anxiety and fear of negative evaluation are common among child abuse survivors, and this aspect of the therapeutic relationship provides corrective interpersonal experiences. Fourth, empathic responses (that are appropriately tentative), unlike direct questions or directives, implicitly teach accurate labeling and description of emotional experience. As noted in the previous chapter, the use of language is thought to be essential to the integration of traumatic experiences (van der Kolk, 2003)), and many individuals with a history of child abuse lack these skills. Fifth, empathic responding models emotional authenticity, openness to experience, and compassion, which helps to minimize anxious self-monitoring commonly observed among child abuse survivors and increases the capacity for spontaneity. Finally, by responding empathically, therapists allow themselves to be touched by the client's pain without being overwhelmed by it, thereby modeling effective emotion regulation and increasing intimacy and trust.

In addition to the aforementioned advantages, there are three interrelated functions of therapist empathy that contribute to client emotional self-control and reprocessing of trauma material. These functions correspond to the criteria for healthy emotion regulation (Gross, 1999) described in the preceding chapter on trauma and are summarized below.

Increase Awareness/Understanding of Emotional Experience. Empathic responses are a form of implicit emotion awareness training. Again, many survivors of child abuse have learned to be externally vigilant at the expense of attention to their own internal experience and have difficulties recognizing and describing their feelings. Poor awareness of internal experience limits the individual's capacity for emotional self-control. Empathic responses increase awareness by focusing attention on internal experience, helping clients accurately label feelings, and helping them articulate the meaning of emotional experience.

The first way empathic responses contribute to self-awareness and emotion regulation is by focusing attention on client internal experience by communicating interest and that the person and his or her feelings and perceptions are worthy of attention. This helps to counteract learned evaluation of one's thoughts, feelings, wishes, and needs as bad, dangerous, invalid, or unimportant. Attending to internal experience also is necessary before one can exercise emotional self-control. Empathic responses that serve this function usually are brief statements made by the therapist that encourage the client to pay attention to a particular aspect of internal experience that could be adaptive (e.g., "That must have been so scary") or maladaptive (e.g., "Sounds like you feel it's not okay to be needy").

Teaching accurate labeling of emotional experience is the second major way in which empathic responses contribute to client awareness and effective emotion regulation. The capacity to verbally describe internal experience helps people to make sense of their experience, which simultaneously reduces arousal and improves interpersonal connectedness. The therapist's tentatively phrased empathic responses (e.g., "That must have been so humiliating") again minimize the defensiveness, withdrawal, and shutting down that can be elicited by questions and directives. This is particularly so among clients who do not know what they are feeling (i.e., alexithymia) or who fear negative evaluation (i.e., social anxiety).

The third way in which empathic responses contribute to self-awareness and emotion regulation is by helping clients to symbolize or articulate the meaning of their emotional experience. Emotional meaning derives from the needs, concerns, perceptions, beliefs, action tendencies, memories, and images associated with one's feelings. Empathic responses by the therapist refer to these implied aspects of emotional experience, highlighting the gist, central concern, or most poignant aspect of what the client said (e.g., "So, what hurt so much was the idea that your own mother *wanted* to hurt you"). Empathic responses also invite elaboration (e.g., "Something about that look on her face . . . ?") and conjecture about client experience. For example, in response to a client's description of his own passive–aggressive behavior, the therapist stated, "I guess you want to hurt her as much as she hurt you." Empathic responses symbolize in language both adaptive (e.g., a need for comfort associated with sadness) and maladaptive aspects (e.g., self-critical thoughts that generate shame) of emotional meanings.

Modulation of Emotion Experience. Empathic responses can both reduce and increase emotional intensity. They can reduce arousal by providing understanding, acceptance, and support. From a relational perspective, therapist empathy is the vehicle for establishing a secure attachment bond. Accordingly, painful and frightening feelings are easier to bear in the presence of an emotionally responsive attachment figure. This function of therapist empathy is particularly important when clients are reexperiencing trauma memories. Empathic responses that affirm the client's vulnerability (e.g., "I know it's hard to talk about this"), cued by indicators of client fragility or embarrassment, can reduce anxiety about being judged and help the client to allow and disclose painful and threatening experiences (Elliott et al., 2004). Another important function of empathy is to validate or normalize experience. A response such as "Yes, it must be scary to think about getting close to those feelings that you've worked so hard to keep away" conveys understanding of fear, affirms the client's emotional reality, and normalizes avoidance as a coping strategy.

Therapist understanding and responsiveness gradually are internalized by clients, strengthening their capacity for self-soothing, self-support, and self-acceptance, which increases their capacity to manage intense emotion. Empathic responsiveness to clients' feelings and needs also fosters interpersonal trust. Clients learn that they can rely on another person to help manage intense affect, and this can generalize to relationships outside of therapy. Seeking social support when needed is a vital emotion regulation skill.

Empathic responses not only help to reduce anxiety but can also be used to increase the intensity of emotional experience when needed. In the early phase of therapy, many clients will disclose horrendous episodes of abuse but are not experientially in touch with their feelings. Evocative words and phrases (e.g., "outraged," "how dare he," "tears you apart") can heighten arousal and activate emotional experience and memories, making them available for exploration. Responses that refer to the client as a child can be particularly evocative. Evocative responses also can help to promote client entitlement to unmet childhood needs and thus foster self-empowerment (e.g., "insistence" on respectful treatment, "refusal" to accept maltreatment).

Therapists can also use evocative empathy to exaggerate and thus increase awareness of the internal messages that contribute to anxiety, rage, shame, or emotional overcontrol. These processes can be explored in two-chair enactments. Responses such as "Somehow, if you remember what happened, you will die or go crazy" amplify, rather than directly challenge, the extremity of the client's position. This can evoke a reaction in the part of the self that does not quite believe the catastrophic expectations. These reactions act as healthy internal resources that help the client manage and allow negative emotion. Finally, empathic responses used in conjunction with explicit intensification directives to "say that again" or "say it louder" can contribute to the effectiveness of these interventions. They ensure accurate understanding of the client's experience, model emotional intensity coupled with emotional self-control, and support intense emotional experience such as deep grieving (e.g., "So many tears . . . let them come").

Appropriate Expression of Feelings, Meanings, and Concerns. Empathic responses also implicitly teach communication skills. Difficulties identifying and communicating feelings (alexithymia) reduce the capacity for intimacy and leave people isolated and lonely. Similarly, the feelings of alienation frequently associated with traumatic experiences and PTSD are partly a function of difficulties communicating extreme experiences that are beyond the realm of most people's experience. Empathic responses that model accurate labeling of feelings, verbal symbolization of meaning, and appropriately regulated affective material obviously improve the client's capacity to communicate and help to restore interpersonal connectedness, first with the therapist and then outside the therapy session.

Imaginal Confrontation Procedure

The IC of abusive and neglectful others is the primary vehicle used for resolving trauma and attachment injuries. Resolution and changed perceptions of self and these specific others generalize to other relationships. The procedure is introduced as early as possible in therapy (typically during Session 4), after establishment of safety and trust in the therapeutic relationship. This quickly evokes core processes, including fear and shame, making them available for exploration. Therapist operations during IC have been delineated (Greenberg et al., 1993; Paivio et al., in press) as follows: (a) promote psychological contact with the imagined other (e.g., vivid descriptions of the other, use of "I–you" language in dialogue with the imagined other); (b) evoke episodic memories associated with abuse; (c) explore and help clients overcome blocks to experiencing; (d) differentiate feelings (e.g., anger, sadness) and associated meanings from global distress and upset; (e) promote expression of unmet needs and entitlement to these needs (e.g., for protection, love, justice); and (f) explore shifting perceptions of self and imagined others. The therapist also maintains a balance between following client moment-by-moment experience and directing the process. The IC intervention is used judiciously throughout therapy according to individual client processes and treatment needs. Results of a recent study (Paivio et al., in press) indicated that, on average, five sessions in a 16-session therapy contained substantial IC work, and this ranged from two to eight sessions.

Empathic Exploration of Trauma Material

An alternative to using IC is the empathic exploration intervention, which was developed as a less stressful procedure for clients who are unwilling or unable to engage in the intended imaginal task. Like many reexperiencing procedures, confronting perpetrators of harm can be too evocative and potentially overwhelming. Clients with a fragile sense of self (ego strength) may prefer to maintain eye contact with the therapist rather than engage in a dialogue with an imagined other, and clients with performance anxiety may find it too anxiety provoking. Empathic exploration of trauma material is identical to IC described above in terms of the model of resolution and intervention principles. However, empathic responding to client feelings and needs is the primary therapist operation used to explore and construct new meaning regarding self, others, and traumatic events. Clients are encouraged to vividly imagine abusive/neglectful others and traumatic events in their mind's eye and express their thoughts and feelings to the therapist rather than engage in a dialogue with an imagined other. Research findings support the view that this procedure is less stressful than IC. Process analyses (Ralston, 2006) found lower levels of emotional arousal during empathic exploration, and results of a recent clinical trial (Paivio et al., in press) indicated a significantly lower dropout rate in EFTT with this procedure compared with the standard EFTT that used IC. These findings are discussed further in chapter 7 in the context of addressing client difficulties with the IC procedure.

Experiential Focusing and Two-Chair Enactments

Other experiential and gestalt-derived procedures are used to explore and reduce self-related difficulties, such as confusion about internal experience, fear and avoidance of internal experience, and shame and self-blame. Guidelines for intervention have been clearly delineated elsewhere (Elliott et al., 2004; Greenberg & Paivio, 1997; Greenberg et al., 1993). Focusing involves attention to and verbal symbolization of bodily felt or somatic experience. Two-chair enactments involve a dialogue between two parts of self, for example, the self-critical part and the part that feels demeaned. Goals are to increase awareness of maladaptive processes and agency in contributing to bad feelings and to access alternative healthy resources to challenge these feelings. The most frequently observed types of intrapersonal conflict in EFTT are between the dominant conceptual and weaker "experiencing" self. The process of change involves explication and integration of these self-organizations.

Clients with lingering bad feelings and unresolved issues with specific others are good candidates for the IC procedure. In cases in which the trauma does not involve unresolved issues with specific significant others, therapy will focus more on reducing self-related disturbances, such as fear and shame. For clients who are resistant or reluctant to engage in imaginary dialogues, all interventions described above can be carried out exclusively in interaction with the therapist. It is the intervention principles that are important, not the specific techniques. As we have seen from the overarching spirit of treatment, the two constructs of emotional processing and experiencing are central to all of the processes. These constructs are the foci of the following two chapters.

3

EMOTION ·

In discussing emotion-focused treatments, one risks inadvertently conveying that emotion, is the focus of treatment, which it is not. Emotion is perhaps best thought of as valuable insomuch as it is a vehicle for accessing implicit information and tacit meanings. Moreover, raw affect is only one aspect of experiential memory associated with trauma, along with thoughts, images, and somatic and sensory experiences. Exploring feelings and meanings (experiencing), not simply the expression of emotion, is the primary source of new information and the way by which new meaning is constructed in emotion-focused therapy for trauma (EFTT). In short, when it comes to therapeutic process—and this is true for all phases of EFTT—emotion is the means and deeper experiencing is the ends.

Nonetheless, we begin with emotion for a couple of reasons. First, as detailed in chapter 1, emotion and emotional processes are central to complex relational trauma that involves the full range of emotional experiences, affective disruptions, and emotional processing as primary mechanisms of change. Second, emotions and emotional processes are obvious targets for trauma therapy. People come to therapy to change "bad feelings" and not to modify maladaptive cognitions or working models of self and others or construct new meaning. This chapter places EFTT in the context of current interests in affect and reviews fundamental concepts used throughout the chapters to come. Our goal in this chapter is not to present a comprehensive theory of emotion but to review key constructs in emotion-focused therapy (e.g., Greenberg & Paivio, 1997; Pascual-Leone & Greenberg, 2007) as they apply to EFTT for complex trauma.

REVIEW OF EMOTION-FOCUSED THEORY OF EMOTION

The following sections review key constructs, present a taxonomy of different types of emotion and associated emotional-processing difficulties, as well as intervention principles for addressing these difficulties. Moreover, we review subtypes of change processes that constitute the emotional-processing construct and inform productive intervention.

The Role of Emotion in Adaptive Functioning

First, the emotion system is an adaptive orienting system. Discrete basic emotions are associated with specific information. This includes specific neurological activity, expressive motor patterns, and dispositions for action that motivate specific goal-directed behavior important in survival. Thus, second, emotions are both action dispositions and motivators. Emotion also helps people to survive by providing an efficient, automatic way of responding rapidly to important situations. It is well established that affect is processed faster and requires less mediation (fewer levels of processing) than cognition (LeDoux, 1996). Consequently, cognitive goals are given impetus by the orienting and action functions of affect.

Third, emotions organize systemic priorities through their salience. Negative emotions, for example, can orient the attention system to incongruence and incoherence. Negative emotional responses, such as anger or sadness, signal and are related to the experience of specific unmet needs. The assumption here is that there is a basic need or drive for internal coherence, compelling maladaptive emotional processes to be resolved. This is the assumption also underlying constructs such as cognitive dissonance and narrative coherence. One's sense of self has a predisposition to be internally coherent (Angus & Bouffard, 2004; J. Pascual-Leone, 1990). Positive, negative, adaptive, and maladaptive emotional experiences inform us about the degree of this coherence and the need to resolve inconsistencies. The integrating function that emotion plays in the brain is the neural substrate of this idea (Schore, 2003).

Fourth, emotions are associated with a network of cognitive, affective, motivational, somatic, behavioral, and relational information that is encoded in memory. Emotional experience and responding are mediated by the activation of this associative network. These networks or mental structures are dynamic and continually elaborated by new experience. Thus, emotion combines with cognition and these other elements to provide information about the idiosyncratic meaning of events, including one's values and concerns. In this way, emotion can be understood as a highly complex meaning system that is able to integrate all relevant facets of one's circumstances into an overall visceral experience. Thus, emotion provides information about the self and, at the same time, directs the self toward some implicit or explicit goal. The experience of emotion involves accessing a need and is an appraisal of that need (Frijda, 1986; Lazarus, 1991).

Finally, emotions are an interpersonal communication system telling others to draw closer or back off. Experience and appropriate expression of emotion increase the likelihood of getting interpersonal needs met. In sum, experiences such as complex relational traumas, which disrupt the adaptive orienting system, result in a host of impairments in adaptive functioning.

Emotion Structures or Schemes

Emotional memory consists of a multimodal associative network of information or meaning system. The term most frequently used to refer to this system is the behavior construct of an *emotion structure* (Foa, Huppert, & Cahill, 2006). From this perspective, traumatic experiences are encoded in emotion structures centered on the experience of fear. Current stimuli that resemble the trauma can activate feelings of fear and helplessness, associated somatic experience, the desire to escape the danger and avoid harm, and beliefs about self and the situations formed at the time of the trauma. Exposure procedures are intended to activate this fear structure so that maladaptive components are available for modification. Activation takes place through attention to sensory and somatic aspects of the trauma memory.

Emotion-focused theorists prefer the term *emotion scheme* (Greenberg, Rice, & Elliott, 1993; Pascual-Leone & Greenberg, 2007) to refer to this complex system of information. For many clinicians, the distinction between mental structures or schemes may appear to have little relevance to clinical formulation or interventions. The purpose of briefly introducing this concept here is to highlight how it informs the principles of working with emotion in clinical practice. Because emotion is so integral to goal-directed behavior, emotion schemes, unlike structures, are at once representations of experience and at the same time plans of action or intentions. Consequently, articulating an emotional experience implies a need or intention that organizes the client to carry out those intentions in the environment. EFTT therapists emphasize and explicitly help clients attend to and articulate this aspect of emotional experience and affective meaning, which helps to activate client goal-directed behavior.

Another set of terms used to refer to these mental structures derives from attachment theory—terms such as *object relations* or *internal working models* of self and others. These complex meaning systems are comprised of feelings, images, memories of needs met or unmet, and implicit or explicit beliefs and expectations about self and intimate others formed in the context of attachment relationships. Again, the entire network or meaning system can be activated in current situations (e.g., transference reactions). Although some theories emphasize the representational and conceptual aspect of the meaning system, it is universally recognized that these mental structures are formed in the context of affectively charged experiences with attachment figures. Obviously, relational context and emotion are interdependent, but EFTT focuses on emotion as the entry point for activating affective meaning concerning self and others, so this affective meaning is the target of intervention.

EFTT also draws on a constructivist understanding of multiple selves and self-organizations whereby an individual has different cognitive–affective–behavioral aspects of self in his or her repertoire, and one aspect may be most prominent at any point in time or may be generally prominent over time and across situations. Even so, except in the most extreme cases, other generally less salient self-organizations are available for awareness and integration into emerging experience. Prominent self-organizations resulting from complex trauma typically center on feelings of vulnerability, worthlessness, inferiority, and incompetence. The terms *emotion scheme* and *self-organization*, rather than structure or representation, emphasize the target and entry point for therapeutic intervention and also capture this dynamic nature of psychic organization (Pascual-Leone, 2009).

All that having been stated, and at the risk of glossing over subtle but important theoretical distinctions, we use the terms *emotion scheme* and *emotion structure* interchangeably, with the understanding that we emphasize emotion as a dynamic action plan rather than a static representation. We also use the terms *self-organization*, *internal representation*, and *object relations* as descriptors that refer to the core affective meaning systems formed in the context of affectively charged experiences with attachment figures and activated by current affective experience.

Types of Emotions: What to Look For

One of the hallmarks of the general model of emotion-focused therapy is a highly differentiated perspective of emotion. Greenberg and colleagues (Greenberg & Paivio, 1997; Greenberg et al., 1993; Greenberg & Safran, 1987) introduced to the field a taxonomy of different kinds of emotion and associated emotional-processing difficulties. This is not intended to describe facts about emotion but rather as a useful heuristic that can guide appropriate intervention. Clinical judgment about which emotional process to focus on is determined by empathic attunement to the client's moment-by-moment experience as well as knowledge of a particular client, personality styles, and disorders. This taxonomy is the basis of emotion assessment and intervention in EFTT.

Primary Emotion

The first type of emotion is an immediate and direct response to the environment that is not reducible to or mediated by other cognitive–affective components. Primary emotion corresponds to the limited number of discrete basic affects, including anger, sadness, fear, shame, joy, and curiosity/interest, that emerge across cultural groups at predictable developmental stages (Eckman & Friesen, 1975). Thus, in emotion-focused theory, primary emotion represents the initial underlying reaction to a presenting circumstance. Depending on the circumstances, the intensity of that emotion (arousal level) and the tacit meaning it might engender based on an individual's learning history, primary emotion can be either adaptive or maladaptive (Greenberg & Paivio, 1997). For example, under normal circumstances, fear in the face of danger is a highly adaptive experience. However, a person's history of physical or sexual abuse can lead to experiencing fear when shown love and affection or in response to benign disagreements. Thus, feelings can be both a source of difficulty for clients and a potentially guiding referent for self-development.

Primary Adaptive Emotion. Primary emotional responses that are adaptive function to mobilize healthy resources and action. Assertive anger at interpersonal violation, for example, mobilizes self-protective resources and action. Similarly, fear of imminent danger mobilizes action to avoid a threat, and sadness at separation or loss mobilizes withdrawal or seeking contact and comfort to promote healing. Processing difficulties concerning primary adaptive emotion involve problems with modulating its intensity that result in either underregulation or overcontrol. In either case, the information associated with the experience is not readily available to guide adaptive action. Survivors of complex trauma may feel overwhelmed by anger or sadness, for example, and may chronically avoid these feelings. The latter can result in a pervasive sense of victimization and powerlessness, self-blame, recurrent bouts of depression, and difficulties with assertiveness and with establishing appropriate interpersonal boundaries.

Primary emotional experiences, such as the sadness about loss or the shame of rejection, frequently are avoided because they are painful. This type of *emotional pain* is more complex than basic emotions but is nonetheless adaptive because it informs the individual that damage to the self has occurred. These painful emotions need to be allowed and fully experienced so that information can be integrated into current meaning and sense of self. In general, appropriate intervention for primary adaptive emotions that are inhibited or dysregulated involves either increasing or reducing arousal. The purpose of this is to access emotion and the associated adaptive information, as well as promote appropriate expression of the experience.

Another area that is less often discussed in the literature is that of *positive emotion*. Emotions such as curiosity and joy are considered primary adaptive experiences that serve the function of broadening and building on healthy experiences (Fredrickson, 2001). In addition to this, attachment, which is a fundamental process in human development, is driven by an affective system that (among other things) orients one to seek out positive warm relationships that provide the individual with associated positive feelings. Complex relational trauma disrupts the individual's capacity for positive affect and healthy attachments, and EFTT explicitly and implicitly aims at restoring these capacities.

Primary Maladaptive Emotion. Primary emotions that are maladaptive also are immediate and direct responses, yet they do not serve an adaptive function. These are often conditioned maladaptive responses. One obvious example is overgeneralized fear that is associated with posttraumatic stress reactions. Intervention in these cases could involve integration of emotion-focused therapy and cognitive–behavioral therapy (CBT) procedures that include counterconditioning of the maladaptive response (creating new associative links) and, at the same time, validating clients' feelings and focusing their expression toward specific sources of trauma or actual harm.

In many cases of complex trauma, the person's core sense of self is constructed around primary maladaptive emotions, particularly fear and shame, that result in crippling collapse or withdrawal. A holistic and pervasive experience of self as insecure or unacceptable is automatically activated in current situations. Even though this core self-organization comprises cognitive, affective, somatic, and behavioral dimensions, the experience of vulnerability or shame is not obviously caused or preceded by other underlying cognitive–affective processes. Self-criticism, especially when delivered in a harsh affective tone, can reflect a deeply rooted hostility or contempt toward the self. This self-critical process can be understood as resulting from the activation of a core sense of self as shamefully bad or broken and therefore deserving of criticism. Appropriate intervention requires processes similar to those used in the counterconditioning of primary maladaptive fear. This involves accessing a core maladaptive sense of self (typically through memory evocation) with its constituent thoughts, feelings, somatic, and sensory experience, and then simultaneously accessing more healthy resources (e.g., adaptive emotion) to create new associative links and thereby restructure the sense of self.

Secondary Emotion

Secondary emotions follow or result from more primary cognitive or emotional processes that are readily observable in the session. These forms of emotional experiences are longer lasting rather than immediate and fleeting responses to one's presenting circumstances, as in the case of primary emotion. One processing difficulty occurs when emotion is a secondary reaction to maladaptive self-statements or cognitions. Examples frequently observed in posttraumatic stress reactions are anxiety resulting from catastrophic expectations, or depressive symptoms resulting from shame-inducing self-critical statements (e.g., a client might say, "What an idiot I am! I should have known better."). Although self-criticism sometimes embodies deeper primary maladaptive processes, at other times these harsh self-criticisms are better understood as learned injunctions or incorrect/inappropriate negative beliefs. The resultant secondary emotions need to be explored to promote awareness of and modify the maladaptive cognitive–affective processes, or otherwise said, to change the maladaptive meaning that gave rise to them. Self-critical clients need to become aware of both the content and harshness of their negative self-statements and the experiential impact of these statements on self. This experiential awareness can help activate a more self-affirming stance, often based on primary adaptive anger at harsh or unfair self-statements.

In other instances, the emotion is secondary to and masks more core emotional experience. Trauma survivors can be afraid of or feel guilty about anger they may harbor toward a parent, or they sometimes respond angrily to their own more vulnerable feelings of fear or shame. Secondary or defensive emotions such as these should be bypassed to access the more core emotional experience and the information associated with it. For example, the client who routinely expresses anger at signs of interpersonal slight needs to gain access to underlying feelings of hurt or sadness. Similarly, the client who collapses in tears at memories of maltreatment and violation needs to gain access to more powerful feelings of resentment and anger.

Depression and anxiety are examples of *complex secondary emotions* that frequently are associated with posttraumatic stress reactions. Feelings of powerlessness, defeat, or emptiness associated with depression are complex "bad feelings" that are generated by cognitive–affective sequences or the activation of a core maladaptive sense of self, yet they are global and nonspecific. A depression, for example, could be comprised of unresolved sadness at the loss of a relationship, coupled with shame at having been rejected; a core sense of self as basically unlovable, which includes self-contempt for being "such a loser"; beliefs that one is doomed to be alone; and a collapse into powerlessness and despair. Here, as with other secondary emotions, the intervention strategy is to access the core sense of self and explore the underlying cognitive–affective components to arrive at more adaptive resources, such as suppressed anger at violation and sadness at loss.

Instrumental Emotion

The third broad category is instrumental emotion that is used, consciously or unconsciously, to manipulate or control others. Classic examples include crying "crocodile tears" or raising one's voice in anger as ways of influencing others. These types of expressions may or may not be accompanied by genuine emotion. However, instrumental emotions are not necessarily false; they can entail very real affective experiences with genuine arousal, and in many instances individuals may be unaware of the way they are using emotion. For example, a man with a history of having angry outbursts when his demands are not met is likely to be having genuine experiences of anger and frustration. However, the fact that his outburst usually results in him getting his way provides repeated reinforcement for his angry behavior. These types of emotions need to be changed. Intervention involves confronting and interpreting the instrumental function of the emotion being used and teaching more adaptive ways of getting one's needs met.

Both secondary and instrumental emotion can be problematic at the level of intensity, and in these instances, intervention needs to include emotion regulation strategies. All of the aforementioned emotion types can be problematic at the level of chronicity or frequency such that anger, fear, or sadness is an overdominant emotion experienced or expressed. In these cases, individuals can have limited awareness of and access to other feelings, so intervention consists of implicit emotion coaching or explicit emotion awareness training. Table 3.1 summarizes all the different kinds of emotion, their associated difficulties, and their intervention principles. Intervention for each of these types of emotion is designed to activate particular change processes or types of emotional processing. These are the focus of the following section.

CHANGE PROCESSES: EMOTIONAL PROCESSING IN EFTT

There is widespread agreement that avoidance of trauma feelings and memories can perpetuate disturbance and that clients need to confront these painful experiences in order to heal (Foa et al., 2006). Outside of the area of trauma, the notion that exploring bad feelings makes one feel better has been a widely held belief among several schools of psychotherapy (e.g., Freud, 1933/ 1961; Perls, Hefferline, & Goodman, 1951; Rogers, 1951). Nevertheless, leading clients into feeling bad in order to feel good is certainly counterintuitive and can be an obstacle for clients and clinicians alike. More recently,

TABLE 3.1
Types of Emotion, Associated Difficulties, and Intervention Principles

Type of emotion	Difficulties	Intervention principles
Adaptive Primary	Dysregulation or overcontrol (e.g., fear of actual danger)	Reduce or increase arousal
	Inappropriate expression	Model/teach expression skills
Painful emotions	Avoidance (e.g., anguish of loss)	Allow and explore
Maladaptive Primary	Overgeneralized response (e.g., fear in posttraumatic stress disorder)	Validate, countercondition
Core sense of self	Activated across situations (e.g., self as worthless)	Access and restructure
Secondary	Reaction to maladaptive cognitions (e.g., anxiety from catastrophic expectations)	Explore and modify cognitions
Defensive	Masks more core emotion (e.g., anger covering shame)	Bypass and access core emotion
Complex "bad feelings"	Activated across situations (e.g., powerlessness)	Attend to and explore
Instrumental	Used to control others (e.g., anger or tears)	Confront, access needs, teach better ways to get needs met
All maladaptive	Dysregulation	Reduce arousal
	Chronicity/frequency	Increase access to other emotions

Note. From *Working With Emotions in Psychotherapy* (p. 36), by L. S. Greenberg and S. C. Paivio, 1997, New York: Guilford Press. Copyright 1997 by Guilford Press. Adapted with permission.

there has been wide interest in the puzzle of what exactly "emotion processing" is and how it occurs. Answers to this puzzle are important when clinicians of virtually all theoretical orientations find themselves sitting across from a distressed client who is unable to surmount or push through intensely painful emotions.

In general, emotional processing refers to the process of change whereby emotion structures or schemes are activated in therapy so that the network of information can be exposed to new information. The means of activation, targets of change, and sources of new information vary across approaches. In CBT, for example, imaginal exposure procedures are used to activate the fear structure and constituent maladaptive associative links, reactions, and faulty attributions, such as self-blame. The sources of new information include new learning through habituation, challenging maladaptive cognitions, and psychoeducation about trauma. In relational psychodynamic approaches, traumatic experiences are more typically explored in the context of the therapeutic relationship; maladaptive elements include defensive processes and interpersonal patterns; and the primary source of new information is therapist interpretations.

Emotional processing is thought to be the primary mechanism of change in exposure-based therapies (Foa et al., 2006), and recently this construct has been incorporated more explicitly into other approaches. Emotional processing is described as a central process in integrative approaches to short-term psychodynamic psychotherapies (e.g., Fosha, 2000; McCullough et al., 2003) and in cognitive–behavioral formulations (e.g., Borkovec, Alcaine, & Behar, 2004; Samoilov & Goldfried, 2000). For example, there is increasing emphasis on accessing "hot cognitions" or thoughts in the context of exploring affectively charged experience (Safran & Greenberg, 1987). This is based on the recognition that maladaptive thoughts accessed in this way are more idiosyncratic and personally meaningful, relevant, and memorable. Recent theory has recognized the importance of exploring both affect and meaning construction and have integrated these into new cognitive models.

Emotional processing in EFTT is understood more specifically than in most psychodynamic therapies. It is also a more multifaceted construct than change-by-habituation, as described in the behavioral literature. In EFTT, meaning construction is seen as central to emotional experiencing. This is partly because trauma, particularly complex trauma, involves more complex emotions than just fear. Common exposure-based interventions are designed for reducing fear but have not been found to be effective in modifying other emotions such as sadness, anger, guilt, or shame.

Ultimately, the goal of an emotion-focused approach is to expand the experiential repertoire of an individual. Trauma and childhood abuse adversely affect individuals such that they experience their world in restricted and maladaptive ways. Thus, the aim of EFTT is to increase the range, depth, and meaning associated with clients' feelings. An emotion-focused approach helps promote emotional competence through a number of processes that are subsumed under the broader term emotional processing. These subprocesses and the particular emotions they target are the topics covered in the remainder of this chapter.

Different Emotional Change Processes in EFTT

How to best work with a presenting emotion depends principally on the nature of a client's presenting concerns and the short- and long-term goals of the treatment. Therefore, the most essential task in working with emotion is assessing what kind of processing is most useful when the client expresses a particular emotion. Most therapists will have had an experience in which a client presents several emotions that emerge in rapid succession. For instance, a client complains bitterly about the constant criticism of her mother, expresses contempt for her mother's self-centeredness and immaturity, collapses into tears and weeps, "It's hopeless, she will never change," then shifts to feeling conflicted about wanting to cut the mother out of her life but needing the mother's financial support, and finally worries about her own financial security. All of these are important issues and processes. Therapists might find themselves asking: What do I focus on? Which emotion is most important? How do I figure out what the client needs to do to continue processing emotion?

In a review of emotion research in psychotherapy, Greenberg and Pascual-Leone (2006) identified four major ways of productively working with emotion, all of which describe different subtypes of emotional processing that are relevant to trauma therapy and EFTT. These four ways are (a) emotional awareness and arousal, (b) emotional regulation, (c) reflection on emotion, and (d) emotional transformation, in which one aroused emotion (e.g., fear) is transformed by the emergence of another different, and usually incompatible, emotion (e.g., anger).

Awareness and Arousal

Insight-oriented therapies are founded on the assumption that increasing client awareness of emotional experience—usually the origins, meaning, and consequences of maladaptive emotion—is an important change process. Increasing awareness often requires a certain degree of arousal and immersion into bad feelings and emotional pain. Again, this is fundamental to the effectiveness of exposure-based procedures. This also is the assumption underlying posited change processes of emotional insight and challenging hot cognitions. Irrespective of intervention style, the deliberate immersion into feeling bad is difficult for clients, and when client arousal increases in session, therapists who are not specifically trained to engage affective arousal can become anxious and abandon the task. This, in turn, can be perceived by clients as invalidating and can reinforce their avoidance of affect.

EFTT therapists should facilitate client arousal and awareness from the beginning of therapy. Clinicians need to be selective about which experience to attend to in order to promote further processing. Any time clients become emotionally aroused and elaborate on their experience of trauma, there are several possible facets of that experience (assertion, hurt, disgust, hopelessness, and so on) on which a therapist might choose to focus. However, not all facets of that experience have equal potential for client progress.

Emotions associated with trauma frequently are suppressed or avoided, such that clients feel flat or numb. In these instances deliberately increasing arousal is productive. This is not for cathartic purposes but rather to activate the emotion structure and thereby increase awareness of the information associated with emotional experience. Although arousal of emotion is clearly important, several studies have shown that purging or venting emotion is not a productive process (e.g., Bushman, 2002). Rather, emotional processing is mediated by arousal such that it is the deep experiencing of emotion plus expressed arousal that is most indicative of progress (Greenberg, 2002). In short, arousal plays a critical role for ushering in and vivifying awareness.

When a client approaches any emotions that are not defensive or secondary reactions, it is productive to increase emotional awareness. Feelings of assertive anger, grief, or nonblaming expressions of hurt are all primary and adaptive emotions that are meaning laden and, to a useful end, can be explored and experienced more deeply. True to an experiential approach, the primary intervention for doing this in EFTT is empathic exploration. Empathic responses are used alone or in conjunction with other procedures, as was presented in the preceding chapter.

The EFTT therapist ("T" in the dialogues below) will deliberately guide the client's ("C") attention and awareness particularly toward those facets of emotion that are newly and spontaneously emerging. This process is exemplified by a client who had become estranged from her family and most recently had a falling out with her sister. She stated to the therapist:

C: I'm so fed up with her behavior. I'd be very happy not to have to see her again, ever!

T: What happens inside you when you say that?

C: [*Sighs*] Oh, I don't know, just a feeling of sadness.

T: Sadness.

C: Yes, because I remember happy times, summers at the cottage, our kids playing together. The thought of never having that again . . .

T: So it's like sadness at losing her?

C: [*Tears well up in her eyes*] Yes, very sad at losing her, her more than anyone.

Increasing awareness and arousal also is an important change process in working with primary maladaptive emotions that are central to the client's sense of self. Clients exert great efforts to get rid of and ignore feelings of vulnerability and worthlessness, and therapists may be reluctant to approach and intensify these experiences. Nonetheless, these experiences need to be activated in session to increase client awareness of the associated information. This can be accomplished by evoking and exploring memories of situations (traumatic events) in which the core sense of self is developed or by exploring current situations in which it is activated. For example, one client was recounting for the first time the experience of being raped by her father when she was a child. These memories had always been highly distressing and the only part she had been able to recall of her own experience was fear and the pain, which she would quickly shut out of her mind. The therapist validated this and queried for more.

T: Yes, it must have been so painful. Can you get past that? Was there anything else going on in your little mind as a child?

C: [*thoughtful*] I remember him saying, "Daddies do this to their little girls."

T: Stay with that. What did you think when he said that?

C: At the time I was so confused. I remember thinking I must have done something wrong, that my mother would be angry at me. But I couldn't figure out what I had done.

T: So somehow *you* were at fault, a bad girl?

Here, by increasing arousal and activating trauma memories, the client clearly accesses information that was not previously available, that is, core maladaptive shame and associated maladaptive beliefs about self formed at the time. These now are available for exploration and change. How shame can be transformed is another change process that is discussed below.

Emotional Regulation

The above example of exploring trauma memories illustrates that there is a delicate balance between facilitating emotional arousal in the service of awareness and managing very intense emotion. It is clear that there is a range of optimum arousal in evoking trauma memories, and both the therapist and client must develop a sense of what the most productive level is. Generally, it is most productive when clients are able to take a reflective stance regarding their emotions, allowing the feelings to be active yet sufficiently regulated to be useful in the exploration and creation of new meaning.

Emotion regulation and associated self-soothing are essential processes in all trauma therapies. In current CBT approaches for complex trauma (e.g., Chard, 2005; Cloitre, Koenen, Dohen, & Han, 2002) as well as eye movement desensitization and reprocessing (Shapiro & Maxfield, 2002), emotion regulation strategies are taught in the early phase of therapy before trauma exploration. In current experiential–dynamic approaches (e.g., Fosha, Paivio, Gleiser, & Ford, 2009), emotion regulation is part of the overall fabric of therapy and is accomplished largely through provision of a safe and empathic therapeutic relationship. This relationship provides a suitable context for processing painful traumatic experiences.

Therapists should be mindful of clients' capacity for emotion regulation in Phase 1 of EFTT, when painful emotions are explored for the first time. Later, in Phase 2, clients will often need to be coached through self-soothing and regulation strategies to both tolerate and work through painful emotions. Facilitating regulation is important when clients are overwhelmed by global distress, by secondary emotions such as rage, or by primary maladaptive emotions such as shame or fear, as in panic attacks (see top of Figure 3.1). The short-term goal of emotion regulation is to gain psychological distance from these experiences, to help clients turn down the intensity. Until this happens, painful emotions not only remain unarticulated in the moment but also are not experienced in detail (Pascual-Leone, 2005; Stern, 1997) and therefore cannot be useful sources of information or guide adaptive action.

Therapist interventions in EFTT that facilitate emotion regulation will vary depending on the client's level of dysregulation. Explicit use of skills training exercises, similar to those used in CBT, will be presented in chapter 8 on fear and avoidance. The long-term goal of facilitating emotion regulation in these instances is to help the client develop a repertoire of strategies for coping with intense feelings. At other times, however, clients may be experiencing intense and painful emotion but it remains bearable, at least for the time being. This was the case with the client described above, who was remembering the rape by her father. Distress that is intense yet bearable is a marker for

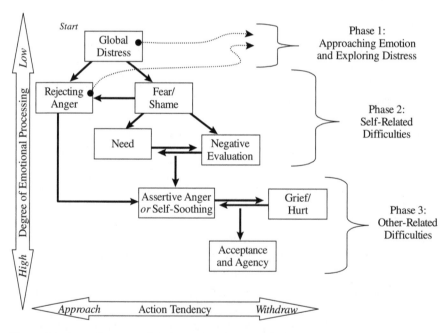

Figure 3.1. A nonlinear model of emotional processing and treatment phases of emotion-focused therapy for trauma. From "Emotional Processing in Experiential Therapy: Why 'the Only Way Out Is Through,'" by A. Pascual-Leone & L. S. Greenberg. *Journal of Consulting and Clinical Psychology, 75,* p. 877. Copyright 2007 by American Psychological Association.

empathic affirmation of client vulnerability, followed by helping the client to articulate the meaning of emotional pain. The long-term goal of this empathic and dyadic regulation of affect is to help clients develop their capacity to calm and comfort themselves by internalizing the soothing responses of the therapist, as well as by constructing meaning that makes distressing experience more comprehensible and manageable (Greenberg & Pascual-Leone, 2006; Paivio & Laurent, 2001).

As an example, a client who had suffered physical and emotional abuse as a child and is in Phase 2 of EFTT describes his feelings of shame in social settings. Although the client becomes highly distressed, his therapist joins him in empathically exploring the meaning entailed in this very painful emotion.

> C: Umm. Everything I say is just a bit off, you know. . . . Off of how other people see or . . . talk about things [*His voice cracks and he breaks down sobbing heavily.*]
>
> T: It's just really . . . it hurts to say that. . . . Can you say what hurts so much?
>
> C: [*He sniffles. There is a long pause.*]
>
> T: It's just a feeling of inadequacy that gets pulled . . . or . . . ?
>
> C: Well, yeah, I have to monitor everything I say, even while I'm saying it because I'm . . . I know, or feel that everything I say is just a little bit off, just doesn't . . . You know, people will just do a double take or disregard me as a nutcase.

In this example, instead of deflecting emotion or breaking down into despair, the client begins to follow the therapist's attentive and empathic initiative and begins to articulate the meaning of his feelings. In so doing, the dyadic process serves to regulate his arousal from sobbing back into a productive range.

Reflection on Emotion

The process of reflecting on emotion results in increased self-awareness. Clients use narratives to explain their experiences and why emotion is aroused (and in awareness) or not. Research has shown across a number of contexts that being able to symbolize and explain traumatic emotional memories promotes their assimilation into a coherent personal narrative, which in turn promotes healing (Angus & McLeod, 1999; Pennebaker & Seagal, 1999). In the context of traumatic events, individuals sometimes make appraisals about themselves, others, or the nature of events that are later shown to be untenable. For example, a woman who recalled how her parents "helped" her with homework during grade school described her emotionally volatile mother leaning over, screaming at her as she struggled with home-work late at night. She also recalled the periodic beatings by her father that followed any wrong answer during these late homework sessions. As an adult in treatment, she remembered weeping as a child, feeling exhausted, and thinking how she was obviously unintelligent and unable. However, after reflecting on the terror she felt, she eventually concluded that any child, or even any adult, would have had difficulty performing under those conditions and that perhaps she was not given a fair chance. From a cognitive perspec-tive, reflecting on emotion can be understood as a way of changing a client's assumptive framework (Beck, Freeman, & Davis, 2004).

All types of emotion are suitable targets for reflection; this will also be an important process in all phases of EFTT. Reflecting on secondary emotions when individuals are not actively in a position of defensiveness can help them become aware of the reactive nature of some of their feelings. Similarly, con-sidering the context and long-term meaning of primary adaptive emotions, such as assertive anger, can help a client focus on the importance of setting boundaries rather than letting anger become too diffuse when it is highly aroused in the moment. Finally, it also can be useful to reflect on primary mal-adaptive emotions and consider them from a certain psychological distance, at which point they are not as difficult to manage or endure. This can allow clients to take a bird's eye view of themes or patterns in their life.

Consistent with an experiential/humanistic position, emotion-focused therapies view the client as the agent in the development of new insight. So, one intervention in EFTT for facilitating reflection on emotion is to explore with clients any problematic reactions they may have to situations they have encountered. When clients express confusion or describe having felt puzzled by their own emotional reactions in a given situation, this is a marker to facil-itate reflection on that experience. Overall, reflection on emotion and the details of its circumstances can help clients with the narrative restorying of the traumatic events they have lived.

Insight is a classic form of reflection on emotion. A traditional psycho-dynamic intervention is to communicate to the client an interpretation in the hopes of facilitating insight. An interpretation is usually based on the therapist's appraisal of core themes relevant to the client (e.g., "This seems a lot like the kind of powerlessness and depression you used to experience with your father. Rather than experiencing your rage, you collapse."). Therapists in EFTT might guide the client process but do not presume to be experts of the client's experience or dynamics. Following this position, therapists are in the role of encouraging the client to articulate insights as they emerge from the client's perspective. Finally, reflection on emotion also is facilitated by mod-eling a discovery-oriented approach in which therapist and client alike are trying to understand the client's story of emotion (e.g., "Somehow you collapse into feeling like that powerless little boy. How does that happen? What goes on for you on the inside?").

Emotional Transformation

In the effort to facilitate emotional change, therapists must help clients to first access primary adaptive emotions for them to be strengthened and supported. Moreover, primary maladaptive emotions must also be accessed, explored, and specified, albeit for a different reason (Greenberg & Paivio, 1997; Pascual-Leone & Greenberg, 2007). Only when the core concern of emotional suffering, that is, primary maladaptive fear or shame, is differentiated can one reorganize the wounded or maladaptive facet of experience. Existential clarity is needed before emotional healing can begin. If global bad feelings and maladaptive emotions are not differentiated, the presenting state of suffering, potent and overwhelming as it is, often remains too nebulous and evasive to be grappled with. Consequently, superficially engaging negative emotions only leaves the client disoriented and often despairing. Thus, although emotions that emerge in Phases 1 and 2 of EFTT (global distress, fear, shame, rejecting anger) may not be curative in and of themselves, unpacking and exploring such emotions will yield both clarity about concerns and an opportunity to reorganize toward healthy, more productive ways of being.

Not only is the process of emotional transformation about generating new experiences in therapy, it is also about using facets of another, already present, maladaptive emotion. As we know from the discussion of emotion schemes, there can be coactivation of adaptive along with and in response to maladaptive emotion. One of the principles in EFTT, then, is to empathically respond to distressing, even maladaptive emotion, while continually supporting the tentative emergence of adaptive emotional responses. In this way, bad feeling is not purged or vented as such, nor does it attenuate, but rather another feeling is evoked in parallel and in contrast to the maladaptive feeling (Pascual-Leone & Greenberg, 2006). Although adaptive emotions are not necessarily enjoyable, this transformation of emotion is due in part to the fact that key components of "positive" emotions are incompatible with "negative" emotion as demonstrated by Fredrickson's (2001) experimental research.

The initial targets of emotional transformation and intervention in Phase 2 of EFTT (see Figure 3.1) are primary maladaptive fear and shame. These are complex and dysfunctional affective-meaning states that tacitly embody a sense of being incompetent, bad, and unlovable. These are embodied preverbal experiences that are not easily amenable to logical or rational change. In the example of the client who had been raped by her father, she states, "I know that he was the adult and I was just a child, but I still *feel* like I was responsible." Another client said, "I know in my mind that I'm successful—

I have a PhD for God's sake! But I still always have this sense that there's been some misunderstanding or clerical error." The fact that these feelings defy rational thinking makes it difficult to change maladaptive emotion directly.

In short, primary maladaptive emotion is transformed by accessing and evoking primary adaptive emotion. This process occurs toward the end of Phase 2 and throughout Phase 3 of EFTT (see Figure 3.1). Although this transformation process cannot be applied formulaically because it is contingent on the personal experience and idiosyncratic meaning of each individual, there seem to be some prototypic pathways that are supported by process research (Pascual-Leone & Greenberg, 2007). Maladaptive fear, for example, about being preyed upon by potentially abusive others, can be transformed by supporting the simultaneous emergence of assertive anger in which the client actively defends her boundaries and dignity. Similarly, shame that involves feeling bad, damaged, and unlovable can be transformed by simultaneously accessing emotions of compassion and love and acting soothing toward oneself. Shame and maladaptive self-blame associated with trauma also can be transformed by accessing justifiable feelings of anger at the actual perpetrators of harm.

Therapist interventions that facilitate emotional transformations in EFTT have been studied in detail (e.g., Paivio, Hall, Holowaty, Jellis, & Tran, 2001). Enactment tasks and imaginary dialogues are effective ways of activating contrasting emotions while at the same time keeping emotions symbolically and experientially delineated. Thus, in the context of unresolved feelings toward others, imaginal confrontation is a principal way of facilitating emotional transformations. In the context of self-related difficulties, two-chair enactments between different and incompatible parts of the self are useful. However, ultimately these enactments are built upon the experiential bedrock of evocative elaboration. To move through an emotion, clients are encouraged to "stay with the feeling." Therapists are empathically attuned and gently guide the client's attention to facets of his or her experience that may only be in the periphery of awareness.

In the following excerpt from therapy, a woman diagnosed with depression describes her relationship with her father who emotionally abandoned her as a child after her mother had died. The client begins in a state of maladaptive shame, feeling as though there was something about her that deserved to be rejected. As she explores this feeling, there is a sense of anger. After noticing this, the therapist guides the client's attention toward those aspects of the unfolding experience, thereby transforming her sense of worthlessness into more powerful self-assertion.

C: He was never there for me. All the suffering I put myself through—
    I guess I have only myself to blame.

T: So, there's this sense of somehow not deserving love . . .

C: [*Tears fill her eyes*] I feel I've had too many losses in my life. It seems so unfair. I had to deal with so much on my own. I hate him for what he did.

T: Tell him what he did. [*Points to empty chair*]

C: I don't think you realize . . . All my relationships, everything has been so much harder . . . because of the way you treated me. Every single day I've had to fight through that . . .

T: What do you resent? Tell him . . .

C: I resent that you didn't love me. I hate you for being so selfish, inconsiderate, and dismissive of me and . . . and . . . [*long pause*] . . . for just never putting me first. [*Pause*] Not that I needed that always . . .

T: What just happened there . . . something changed?

C: I'm feeling sorry for myself.

T: OK. Try not to go there, stay with your resentment for now . . . I know it's difficult but tell him more about your resentment.

C: It's hard for me to confront you but this I must say: You were not a decent father to me. You abandoned and neglected me . . . for most of my childhood . . . and I'm angry at you for that.

In this example, maladaptive shame undergoes a microtransformation as subdominant feelings of anger and healthy entitlement are brought to the foreground. Through this process the client eventually expresses adaptive assertive anger, which is supported by the therapist over the course of therapy until it becomes a new healthy part of the client's repertoire.

MODEL OF CHANGE AND PHASES OF EFTT

Recent qualitative and quantitative research has helped articulate concrete examples of different types of emotion and change processes that are central to the phases of EFTT. This research (Pascual-Leone, 2005, 2009; Pascual-Leone & Greenberg, 2007) described moment-by-moment processes in therapy using a sample of individuals who suffered from depression and longstanding emotional injuries, including childhood trauma, abuse, and neglect. The sample included therapy with the client Monica presented earlier whose mother had committed suicide. This research helped operationalize emotion types in concrete observable terms and provided empirical support for the emotional change processes that have been described. The body of Figure 3.1 shows key findings regarding clients who start a session with nonspecific emotional distress and productively process that distress. Empirical support for this model indicates that when in-session emotion events result in productive outcomes, key phases of emotion are likely to emerge in a sequential pattern. Identifying these subtypes of emotion is important for therapists because these will be the targets of specific emotional-processing interventions. Moreover, the model of emotional processing corresponds to the model of resolution that is the basis of EFTT and can be used to illustrate different phases in the EFTT treatment model.

It is important to remember that at the starting point (global distress) of this model, the client is already emotionally aroused and engaged. From then on, the path toward emotional processing is nonlinear and reveals that there is more than one way in which clients process emotion. However, each of the target emotions is best described as a necessary stepping stone toward emotional processing. Getting stuck in any of these states during therapy is what makes for disordered regulation and inadequate processing.

The theory of primary (adaptive/maladaptive) versus secondary emotion that underlies EFTT provides a context to differentially apply facets of emotion processing, depending on the client's presenting emotion. Although phases of EFTT presented in chapter 2 are associated with certain target emotions (see Figure 3.1) and certain subtypes of emotional processing, clients and their feelings operate as dynamic systems. Therefore, there cannot be rigidly delineated phases of emotional processing. The experiential process typically is cyclical and reiterative, in which clients oscillate between emotional progress and collapse (Pascual-Leone, 2009). As a result, all emotional-processing subtypes will be useful at different moments throughout treatment. Heightening emotional awareness and maintaining adequate emotional regulation, for instance, are processes that apply to any point in treatment. Nonetheless, different phases of treatment do lend themselves to different emphases in emotional processing.

According to this model, clients who begin an emotional event in a state of global distress (highly aroused with low levels of idiosyncratic meaning-making) must initially work through particular reactive feelings that are undifferentiated and insufficiently processed. The undifferentiated nature of this distress is characteristic of secondary emotion (Pascual-Leone, 2005). In Phase 1 of EFTT, clients identify target complaints and in so doing begin to approach particular emotional content. They begin exploring, sometimes for the first time, personal distress related to traumatic experiences. Secondary and global feelings of distress are engaged and differentiated into more primary underlying feelings that are the core issues (see top of Figure 3.1). The two types of emotional processing that are most useful in accomplishing this are emotional regulation, on the one hand, and emotional awareness, on the other.

Therapy with the client Monica can be used to illustrate this process. She had been unable to make sense of and get over the suicide of her mother and was tormented by painful feelings and memories. She entered therapy in a highly distressed state that included secondary (and primary) anger at her deceased mother as the source of this distress. At the end of Phase 1, confronting her imagined mother during imaginal confrontation evoked gruesome memories of her death and in-session reactions of panic and fear. Emotional processing was accomplished by helping Monica manage distress while confronting these painful memories and simultaneously explore and unpack her feelings so she could begin to make sense of them.

Phase 2 of EFTT addresses self-related difficulties, in which clients are grappling with feelings of primary maladaptive fear, shame, and sometimes rageful, rejecting anger. Fear and shame (middle of Figure 3.1) represent one of the later states in the model of emotional processing. These experiences are characterized by a deep, enduring, yet familiar painful state, which is highly idiosyncratic and often anchored in generic autobiographical narratives. Variations of fear and shame of this kind are primary maladaptive emotions and are typified by the maladaptive fear in posttraumatic stress disorder or the sense of being shamefully defective and "bad" inside. Clients at a comparable level of processing also can enter a state of rejecting anger (which is usually, but not always, a secondary emotion) for which the reactive action tendency is to angrily create distance from or destroy the source of distress.

Having emotional awareness and symbolizing these feelings, as well as articulating unmet interpersonal and existential needs, are critical to working through this second phase of treatment (middle of Figure 3.1). At a deeper level of processing, articulating a core negative self-evaluation is contrasted to an existential need, and this serves as a pivotal step in change, occasionally producing a client experience of relief. In addition, emotional transformation is a type of processing that helps facilitate change moments in working through these issues and in developing new positive evaluations and experiences of self.

In the case of Monica, all her life she had felt deep shame about her mother's suicide and hid this from the world. Her worst fear was that her mother really had not loved her—why else would she abandon her and cause her so much pain? A pivotal change moment in therapy came when she expressed this fear and a heart-felt need to feel loved to her imagined mother during an imaginal confrontation. She imagined that her mother, if she could, would respond with reassurance, nurturing, and love, and she felt comforted by this.

These sequences are followed by advanced states in emotional processing (bottom of Figure 3.1) that largely involve primary adaptive emotions. On one hand, clients can enter a state of hurt/grief, in which they are able to acknowledge personal losses without complaint or self-pity. On the other hand, clients will become mobilized through assertive anger, in which they proactively affirm healthy entitlement to experiences of fair treatment, worth, and/or connection with others. Similarly, clients can enter a state of compassion for self and self-soothing as a way of directly attending to their existential needs rather than through explicit assertion. Just as clients in hurt/grief can move to assertive anger or self-soothing, they can just as easily move back again into hurt/grief. Here, individuals come to terms with themselves.

Phase 3 of EFTT, in which the treatment focus shifts to resolving past interpersonal issues, is characterized by the emergence of primary adaptive emotions. Therapists help clients deepen their awareness of assertive anger, in which offenders are held accountable for harm, and primary adaptive grief, in which clients acknowledge, without protest or self-pity, the losses they have endured (bottom of Figure 3.1). As they confront the reality of their trauma history, clients can access and develop adaptive resources of self-soothing and self-nurturing in the face of primary and nonblaming emotional pain. As in Phase 2, clients eventually let go, forgive, or move on from these interpersonal issues by way of another emotional transformation. Phases 2 and 3 of EFTT (self-related and other-related difficulties) also tend to make special use of reflection on emotion as clients begin to process their feelings by constructing new personal narratives about self and other. With this, a synthesis of adaptive emotions leads to a resolved state of acceptance, letting go of the past, and gaining personal agency.

Again, if we think of Monica, in Phase 3 of therapy she moved back and forth between anger and hurt/grief over her mother's suicide. Over time she was able to assertively express and feel entitled to her anger at the damage and destruction caused by her mother's actions. This helped to strengthen her sense of self. She also was able to fully acknowledge and grieve the enormity of the many losses she had endured. She was able to feel compassion for herself and view herself not so much from a position of deficiency but as a strong survivor. Monica now imagined her mother as more vulnerable and remorseful ("If she could undo the past, she would") and remembered her mother as having been nurturing and loving to her when she was a child. She was able to forgive her mother and let go.

Finally, in Phase 4 of EFTT, clients such as Monica process emotion in several of the same ways as they did in earlier phases, as they revisit the difficulties and issues explored in the treatment. Processing therapy termination is most productive when it highlights emotional awareness of relational events in the dyad as well as an overall reflection on the meaning of emotional experiences during therapy. In the following chapter we focus on the relationship between emotion and emotional meaning, or client "experiencing," as the basis for EFTT.

4

EXPERIENCING

In the preceding chapter we discussed the importance of emotion and emotional change processes in trauma therapy and the unique contribution of emotion-focused therapy for trauma (EFTT) to this area. One of the central tenets of EFTT is that attention to emotional experience is important because it is a source of information and meaning. Generally speaking, the term *subjective internal experience* refers to the contents of emotion structures or schemes, the associated feelings, thoughts, images, bodily sensations, and so on. The term *experiencing,* on the other hand, refers to the process of exploring and verbally symbolizing those contents and constructing new meaning from this process. Of course, a focus on meaning construction in trauma therapy is not unique to EFTT. Different treatment approaches emphasize different aspects of meaning and different meaning construction processes, such as insight into maladaptive interpersonal patterns, restructuring of pathogenic beliefs, rescripting narratives, and deepening experience.

This chapter presents the unique perspective provided by the experiencing construct and the particular advantages of this perspective in terms of trauma recovery. We begin by defining experiencing in the context of EFTT and by outlining the historical roots of this construct. In doing so, we highlight some of the similarities and differences between EFTT and other approaches with respect to experiencing. Next, we describe the measurement of experiencing and give an overview of key research findings that have implications for trauma therapy. We end the chapter by outlining the role of experiencing in major tasks of EFTT, which will be discussed in further detail in the chapters to come.

DEFINITION OF EXPERIENCING

The following subsections describe features of the experiencing construct that are relevant to all trauma therapies and those that are specific to EFTT.

Experiencing as a Common Change Factor

There are three features of experiencing that are relevant to all trauma-focused therapies. First, there is agreement across theoretical orientations that the capacity to attend to and explore trauma feelings and memories is central to recovery from trauma. The process of reexperiencing trauma memories involves emotional engagement, that is, telling the story with attention to personal and affective material rather than simply the facts of the story itself. Thus, to some extent, all exposure-based procedures are designed to promote experiencing, which is part of emotional processing.

Second, there is agreement across theoretical perspectives that emotional processing of trauma memories and recovery involves constructing new and more adaptive meaning. Maladaptive meaning can include the view that trauma memories are intolerable and the sense that one is to blame for one's own victimization. In instances of complex interpersonal trauma, maladaptive meaning concerns fundamental views of self and others. Exposure-based procedures are designed to activate the core emotion scheme or fear structure associated with the trauma and the associated network of information so that it can be exposed to new information. But of course, as discussed in the preceding chapter, new information and meaning can come in many forms and through a variety of qualitatively different experiences. Treatments also use a variety of strategies (e.g., cognitive restructuring, psychoeducation, interpretations of maladaptive interpersonal patterns). Nonetheless, helping clients construct a new and more adaptive understanding of themselves, others, and traumatic events is the common goal.

Third, there is considerable agreement that constructing new meaning requires integration of information from the experiential (affective, sensory/somatic) and conceptual/linguistic systems. A number of major psychological theories have posited the existence of two separate knowledge systems (see Epstein, 1994, for a review). The experiential system involves right-brain processes, is holistic, and comprises sensory/somatic information, whereas the conceptual system involves more left-brain processes, is more linear, and comprises rational and linguistic information. In the area of cognitive psychology, for example, the dual coding theory of memory (A. Paivio, 2007) posits an imagery/sensory system grounded in experiential reality and a conceptual/linguistic system that is more procedural. There is considerable research supporting the postulate that optimal learning involves the integration of both of these systems. Freud (1933/1961) similarly distinguished between emotional and intellectual insight and maintained that enduring therapeutic change requires the linking of these two sources of information. This distinction between the "felt" and the "known" is one that has been emphasized by all leading experiential theorists.

These concepts are particularly relevant to trauma because traumatic experiences appear to be largely encoded holistically in right-brain experiential memory (Lanius et al., 2004; van der Kolk, 2003). Moreover, individuals with unresolved and unprocessed trauma (e.g., with symptoms of posttraumatic stress disorder [PTSD]) cannot make sense of and often do not have words for these experiences. This is evident in the impoverished quality of their trauma narratives. It is widely believed that recovery from trauma requires articulating the meaning of traumatic events, which occurs through the linking of the experiential and linguistic systems. Thus, although the means vary across treatment orientations, experiencing always involves verbally symbolizing the meaning of traumatic experiences and as such is considered a core change process.

EFTT Definition of Experiencing

The distinct EFTT perspective on experiencing is based in the extensive writing on this construct by current emotion-focused therapy theorists (e.g., Elliott, Watson, Goldman, & Greenberg, 2004; Greenberg & Paivio, 1997; Pascual-Leone & Greenberg, 2007). Experiencing in EFTT is both a change process and a key intervention principle. Procedures for promoting experiencing in EFTT target the experiential system (emotion, sensory, and somatic information) and help clients to verbally symbolize the meaning of that internal experience. Experiential processing focuses primarily on the moment-by-moment emotional experiences of individuals. Client experience is viewed as an ongoing dynamic synthesis that is created and recreated by active engagement with the internal and external environments. Emotional experience is "produced" by a progressive construction that emerges out of sensorial and cognitive/affective experiences that are interpreted through self-reflection and narrative.

Therefore, experiencing is tacitly constructed using both top-down and bottom-up information-processing strategies. On one hand, bottom-up processing begins by exploring with the client individual idiosyncratic details of internal experience. These are eventually combined to create a larger unit of general meaning, perhaps a maladaptive sense of being a "bad person" or an adaptive sense of being in tune with one's life. On the other hand, in a top-down strategy the client begins with an overall verbal formulation, such as the identification of a general theme occurring across situations (i.e., "I'm the type of person who . . ."), which is followed by the elaboration of details. Experiential theorists have stressed that bottom-up processing is most favorable to high-quality emotional processing and experiencing. Clients are directed to slow down and adopt an internal exploratory stance rather than hastily explaining how they already understand themselves.

However, emotion-focused therapy theorists recognize that the influence of a client's a priori conceptual vocabulary and sociocultural filters on personal reality is always present as the top-down contribution to emerging experience. In fact, it is the dialectical synthesis, that is, the integration, of these two ways of knowing oneself that makes up the process of creating personal meaning (Pascual-Leone & Greenberg, 2006). Experiencing requires both attending to an embodied felt sense and interpreting that emerging feeling in the context of a client's expectations, language, and self-concept. Thus, in a recursive manner, language plays an essential role in constituting one's emotional experience, but how one verbally formulates one's feelings, in turn, also influences those feelings. Symbolization, then, is not just encoding and retrieving experiential information; it involves a dynamic and constructive process of continuously synthesizing information from a variety of different sources and deliberately symbolizing it to inform an emerging subjective reality.

Although other treatment approaches may also rely on principles of reexperiencing, memory work, meaning construction, and verbal symbolization, EFTT defines experiencing more broadly by encompassing all of these as specific processes, or facets, of the process. Moreover, because deepening client experiencing is one of the two central aims in EFTT, the treatment offers particular expertise in promoting these different facets of the process, using them in ways that are more specific than most other treatments. Constructing new meaning in EFTT can occur through the following: (a) searching experiential memory and accessing previously unavailable aspects, for example, reexperiencing one's powerlessness to protect oneself (or a loved one) from harm; (b) accessing and explicitly questioning core beliefs formed at the time of the trauma (e.g., a client says, "It's as if I felt responsible for my mother's happiness, but I was just a child . . . I was the one who needed caring for!"); (c) experiencing a corrective interpersonal experience with the therapist, that is, by feeling and disclosing painful material in a safe and empathically responsive relationship; and (d) receiving feedback from the therapist in the form of information about human functioning or trauma, for example, or observations about client's in-session processes (e.g., the therapist might say, "Somehow it's hard for you to stay with those angry feelings"). The following section outlines key features of the experiencing construct as it is used in EFTT.

Experiencing and Emotional Arousal

Because emotion is a vehicle for quickly accessing an associative network of information or meaning system, it can be used as an entry point to deeper experiencing. Moderately high arousal activates the system, and then the therapist must help modulate the client's arousal in order to explore the system. Thus, the important feature in activating and exploring the information network is to create an optimal state of arousal. When arousal is too high, the affective charge can be overwhelming, and this blocks attention and learning. When arousal is too low, the emotion structure is not activated, and the associated information is not readily available for exploration and change. Exploration without sufficient arousal tends to be superficial and either externally focused or abstract and intellectual. Clients may feel lost, stuck, and uncertain of themselves, or they may feel that the session is unproductive and they are going around in circles. When this happens, therapists may also feel disoriented about what to do and sometimes have difficulty connecting with their clients or feel distant, frustrated, or bored.

Research supports this relationship between experiencing and emotional arousal. The model of resolution on which EFTT is based (Greenberg & Foerster, 1996), for example, uses extensive observation of the process of resolving attachment injuries. Accordingly, when client arousal peaks, meaning exploration is low, but when arousal decreases to a moderate level, productive experiencing or meaning exploration occurs. A study of EFTT (Ralston, 2006) found that the highest levels of arousal in treatment (and moderate experiencing) occurred during Phase 2 of EFTT, when clients were accessing trauma experiences, whereas the highest levels of experiencing (and relatively lower arousal) occurred during Phase 3, when clients were exploring their understanding of self, others, and traumatic events.

Experiencing as Process

One distinguishing feature of EFTT is the recognition of two fundamental levels of processing traumatic experiences and the distinction between trauma narrative (content) and the narration process. One way in which clients make sense of their feelings is through the *told story*, which unfolds through clients interpreting themselves in the context of cultural, familial, and personal narratives. Telling the story of traumatic experience is an important therapeutic process in all treatment approaches. But the told story is only one part of how people understand themselves and their experiences. The other part of the process is the *lived story*, which is a biological, perceptual, felt sense of how people experience themselves in the moment. People have a feeling of who they are and a "feeling of what happens" that evolves moment by moment through a dynamic and creative process (Damasio, 1999). EFTT therapists make use of this process to facilitate the exploration of feelings and meanings in psychotherapy.

The first aspect of client engagement with trauma material during EFTT involves telling the story of what happened. Trauma material is revisited as the client remembers him- or herself as a child, for example, feeling alone, terrified, and powerless, and concluding that "I must have done something bad to make my mother angry." Maintaining moderate levels of client experiencing while exploring trauma memories requires keeping the focus of attention on personally meaningful, affectively charged material, as opposed to on the description of overt behaviors or events. This type of experiencing typically takes place during Phase 1 in the initial sessions of EFTT. If this narration is a new experience, as it frequently is for many clients in therapy for complex trauma, new information comes from learning that they can tolerate the painful memories (desensitization) and from receiving comfort and support from the therapist (corrective interpersonal experience). This aspect of client engagement with trauma material, however, does not require deliberate self-examination.

The second aspect of client engagement is attending to and examining internal experience as it unfolds. This is the *lived story*, and it is typically explored from the second session in Phase 1 onward. This later target for client experiencing involves exploring what happens internally when one reexperiences painful and traumatic events. This type of engagement is exemplified when a client says something like, "I feel sad now, thinking about the innocence I lost." This second aspect of engagement exposes the client to new internally generated information. It involves deeper levels of experiencing than the narrative of memories themselves. Engagement on this level requires deliberate self-examination by attending inward and searching the contents of one's experience, that is, memories, images, beliefs, feelings, desires, values, or bodily sensations. More important, verbally symbolizing these aspects of experience helps integrate them into the client's current subjective reality, thereby constructing new meaning.

Of course, different levels of experiential awareness and meaning elaboration need to be distinguished from behavioral change proper. Experiencing should be thought of as an initial step that can lead toward new existential choices and living out other more transformational changes (Pascual-Leone & Greenberg, 2006). Once a new experiential awareness has taken place and one understands something differently (e.g., that one's treatment as a child has led one to close off for fear of disappointment), the subsequent change may still require that one respond differently. To open up and express one's need, for example, requires more than experiential awareness and insight. We communicate this point to clients in EFTT. For example, in introducing the imaginal confrontation (IC) procedure, we emphasize that its purpose is to help clients clarify things for themselves (see chap. 7, this volume). Once clients are clear on where they stand, they are in a much better position to choose how they want to behave in real life and to behave in self-enhancing ways.

Experiencing and Emotional Competence

Complex relational trauma during development negatively affects emotional competence, which, in turn, is associated with a host of well-documented problems in functioning. Other approaches to therapy for complex trauma recognize these deficits and teach emotion awareness skills (e.g., Cloitre, Koenen, Dohen, & Han, 2002; Linehan, 1996). In EFTT the process of experiencing is itself an important emotional competence skill. Labeling and symbolization in words create distance from and enhance regulation and understanding of experience. Clients with symptoms of complex PTSD, for example, consistently report themselves as being at the mercy of their feelings, often with little sense of their meaning. Symptoms such as depression, anxiety, dissociation, and interpersonal problems are related to deficits in processing internal experience. Experiencing is a process skill that can be developed by systematically directing an individual's attention to the internal sensations that accompany her or his feelings while deliberately attempting to articulate their significance (e.g., the therapist may ask, "What is that clenched fist [tone of voice] saying?"). Helping clients connect their affective experiences with personal meanings gradually transforms their experience of self, others, and the world.

The process of experiencing increases clients' awareness of and confidence in their internal experience—their perceptions, feelings, beliefs, and values—and thereby also contributes to self-development. Clients are better able to rely on their own subjective reality rather than external sources as a guide to problem solving, decision making, and behavior. Research on neuroplasticity suggests that the ability to generate personal meaning creates neuronal changes that help clients solve problems, which in turn alters the experience of future adverse events (Doidge, 2007). In addition, the experiencing process involves deliberately focusing on and exploring particular aspects of internal experience to understand them better, and observing the resultant internal changes as they unfold in the moment. This process skill increases emotion regulation capacities as well as client agency and self-control. Clients learn to observe, understand, and manipulate the internal processes that contribute to and generate their experience, both bad feelings and good feelings. Thus, clients learn not only the what but the how of experiencing. At the end of EFTT we routinely ask clients to describe the changes they observed in these capacities.

Returning to our discussion of alexithymia (from chap. 2, this volume) offers a useful point of comparison here because it describes the antithesis of productive emotional experiencing. Our research on trauma narratives demonstrated that the severity of alexithymia was only indirectly related to emotion word count; however, it was directly related to depth of experiencing (Le, 2006), that is, to impairments in complex meaning. This suggests that a focus on promoting experiencing in therapy, as done in EFTT, may be more effective than other existing approaches that focus on the accurate labeling of feelings per se. Furthermore, our research indicated that 83% of clients entering EFTT met criteria for alexithymia and this rate was reduced to 26% at the end of therapy (Ralston, 2006). Given that alexithymia is characteristic of shallow levels of experiencing and that EFTT aims to deepen experiencing, these reductions likely occurred through improvements in clients' capacities for experiencing.

HISTORICAL ROOTS OF EXPERIENCING

Several theorists in the experiential/humanistic tradition have made essential contributions to the experiencing construct that are relevant to EFTT. Rogers's (1951) client-centered approach emphasized the therapeutic relationship as a corrective interpersonal experience and developed a method (empathic responding) for exploring feelings and meanings. He saw self-relevant affective meaning as a guide to healthy functioning, authenticity, and personal growth, which is consistent with the current view of emotion as an adaptive orienting system. Rogers also emphasized process over information or content as such, so that experiencing involved a kind of meta-awareness of one's own internal search process. Thus, experiencing was more about the narration than the narrative. This emphasis on the moment-by-moment process of exploring affective experience and constructing new meaning from this exploration process is the foundation of all experiential approaches to therapy, including EFTT. In addition, empathic responding to feelings and meanings, mastered by Rogers, is the primary means of promoting experiencing and meaning construction in EFTT.

Later developments in client-centered therapy (e.g., Rice, 1974) drew on cognitive psychology and framed experiencing more explicitly in information-processing terms. Particular features of evocative empathic responses (personal, specific, connotative) were thought to be effective because they activated core emotion schemes, making the network of information encoded in memory available for therapeutic exploration. Rice also introduced a systematic approach to memory exploration that involved reexperiencing the internal and external aspects of a troubling situation. This allowed the client to make connections between these two spheres of experience and thereby make sense of troubling personal reactions. Obviously, both of these constructs are relevant to treating trauma. EFTT incorporates these concepts and procedures to activate emotion structures so they are available for exploration and to help clients make sense of their involvement in traumatic events (e.g., "I can't understand why I never told anyone" or "Maybe I did something to bring it on?").

Gendlin (1996) elaborated on the construct of experiencing. He deemphasized emotion in favor of meaning and explicitly emphasized bodily experience (the bodily felt sense) as well as the importance of language. For Gendlin, experiencing comprises two components: (a) making contact with a preverbal, bodily felt, and implicit meaning; and (b) articulating that meaning using words, images, and concepts. Thus, meaning is constructed through the integration of experiential and linguistic systems. Once inner experience is put into words, it can be owned, examined from a distance, and integrated into existing meaning systems. This is especially relevant to the treatment of complex trauma, in which traumatic memories are largely encoded in experiential memory and isolated from available meaning systems.

The bodily felt sense, as Gendlin (1996) described it, is a holistic and highly contextual sense of a situation, a kind of gut-level knowing that can be either adaptive or maladaptive. The experience of being "a loser," for example, is more than a disembodied thought; it is embedded in a complex set of experiences that exist at a nonverbal and nonconceptual level. Similarly, traumatic experiences and painful memories might not be verbally articulated but can be embodied. Difficulties articulating upsetting and traumatic experience mean that these experiences remain incomprehensible, and this contributes to distress. Finding the right words, or "handle," to describe the bodily experience begins to make it comprehensible. Gendlin's method for helping clients find the right words to describe painful but implicit and incomprehensible embodied experience is a part of the technical repertoire of EFTT and will be presented in chapter 6.

Other important contributions to the construct of experiencing as it is used in EFTT come from gestalt therapy (e.g., Perls, Hefferline, & Goodman, 1951). These contributions include explicit emphases on the role of emotional arousal, on bodily experience, and on the adaptive, organismic wants and needs associated with emotional experience as motivators of action. Gestalt theorists understood avoidance of emotional experience as the "cornerstone of pathology" (Perls et al., 1951). Psychological disturbance included client internal conflicts between the dominant socially desirable self or the "top dog" (e.g., "I should never have let him in the apartment. I have no right to complain.") and the weaker experiencing self or "underdog" (e.g., "I feel ashamed. I have no one to blame but myself."). Disturbances also resulted from suppression of authentic feelings and needs regarding significant others or unfinished business. These experiences remained frozen in memory, pressing for expression, completion, and resolution. This gestalt formulation is remarkably similar to current understandings of the role of avoidance in perpetuating trauma symptoms. As mentioned earlier, gestalt therapy also introduced interventions—two-chair enactments—designed to resolve these conflicts. The purpose of enactments is to increase clients' arousal and thus awareness of self-damaging processes, and to strengthen the experiencing self as an alternate self-organization.

More recently, Greenberg and colleagues integrated client-centered and gestalt approaches to therapy and placed traditional views of experiencing within a contemporary conceptual framework (Greenberg & Paivio, 1997; Greenberg, Rice, & Elliott, 1993; Greenberg & Watson, 2006). This framework understands experiencing in terms of both current cognitive psychology (i.e., a constructivist view of information processing) and developments in emotion theory and research that were presented in the preceding chapter (i.e., emotions are sources of information that aid in adaptive functioning). An integration of these views means that evoking emotion in therapy is explained, again not as catharsis but in terms of activating the meaning system associated with emotional experience, making it available for exploration, and the subsequent construction of new meaning.

The emphasis in all these experientially oriented therapies is to increase clients' awareness of what they are experiencing in the moment as well as a meta-awareness of the experiential process itself and how they influence it. Moments of deep experiencing in these therapies are essentially unconcerned with the question of why, and this contrasts with psychodynamic approaches (Pascual-Leone & Greenberg, 2006). Instead, discovering what one feels and does, as well as how one does what one does, is considered essential to clients' control over their internal processes, how they contribute to their own bad feelings or pain, and permanent change.

The goal of experiential approaches is to help clients explicate an implicit felt sense of self in the world. Over many years of research and practice, the emotion-focused tradition has developed a sophisticated technology (e.g., focusing, experiential search, evocative empathy, two-chair enactments) for promoting that process. Interventions make use of emotion's power to catalyze change, and to restructure core maladaptive emotion-based structures or schemes. This access to new internally generated information and synthesis of old with new self-organizations is viewed as central to change and is the chief purpose of deepening personal experiencing in EFTT.

EFTT COMPARED WITH OTHER PERSPECTIVES ON EXPERIENCING

As discussed earlier, there is universal agreement in insight-oriented trauma therapies that attention to and verbal symbolization of internal subjective experience are essential to change. These are the processes of reexperiencing and meaning construction that are common across theoretical models. There also is increasing interest in the construct of experiencing. However, the contents that are emphasized and the means of achieving high-quality experiencing differ across perspectives.

Traditional psychodynamic therapies, beginning with Freud, have always focused on affective experience and emphasized emotional insight. Psychodynamic theory has also always emphasized client reliance on authentic internal experience as a sign of maturity and healthy functioning. Clients must attend to and actively experience painful feelings, make visceral contact with these in a session, and explore their cognitive meanings (Vaillant, 1994). Current object relations and interpersonal/relational theories (e.g., Luborsky, Popp, Luborsky, & Mark, 1994; Mitchell, 1993) focus on current experiential meaning that is available to consciousness. In these approaches, promoting experiencing typically is achieved by therapists through questions (e.g., "What does his leaving mean to you?") and interpretations about the links between experiences in the present or past (e.g., "Feeling abandoned by him [or me] is a lot like what you used to feel with your father"). Thus, deeper levels of experiencing are characterized by the client exploring the similarities between current experience and other situations, and identifying maladaptive patterns and themes across situations. Accelerated experiential dynamic psychotherapy (AEDP; Fosha, Paivio, Gleiser, & Ford, 2009) is perhaps most akin to the experiential process as it is described and facilitated in EFTT. AEDP emphasizes the client's moment-by-moment experience of the empathically responsive therapeutic relationship and how this differs from early negative attachment experiences.

In EFTT for interpersonal developmental trauma, we also link current painful feelings and needs to childhood experience. However, like AEDP, we primarily emphasize bottom-up, data-driven processing (moment-by-moment) rather than generalizations across situations, which run the risk of becoming overly intellectual. This involves exploring a single experience or event in all its detail or "to the edges" (Rice, 1974) rather than making connections across events or identifying themes. Thus, therapists remain as close as possible to the concrete experience of those key themes (e.g., the therapist might say, "So this oh-so-familiar feeling comes up again . . . stay with that feeling . . . somehow you don't matter?"). Once material is experienced in the moment, clients frequently spontaneously make links to the past on their own without the assistance of an interpretive reflection. This is because the emotion scheme or relevant associative memory network has been activated. For many clients, recognizing these patterns of repeating the cycle of violence and abuse is one of the things that brought them into therapy in the first place (e.g., the client may say, "I see myself behaving just like my mother and I don't want to do that"). In any case, knowledge that is attained through one's own efforts is always well timed and more likely to be retained than if it has simply been conveyed.

Current behavioral and cognitive–behavioral therapy (CBT) approaches to trauma also have some relevance to the construct of experiencing. These models (e.g., Foa, Huppert, & Cahill, 2006; Foa & Kozak, 1986) assume that trauma recovery requires clients' emotional engagement with trauma memories and use techniques to facilitate this process. In traditional exposure procedures, new meaning comes from a new "experience" of being able to tolerate trauma feelings and memories and from accessing new facets of the traumatic experience that were previously unavailable. For example, a client might recall that she tried her best to fight back during a rape, which could then contribute to reducing her self-blame. Recent CBT approaches for complex trauma (e.g., Chard, 2005; Cloitre et al., 2002; Resick, Nishith, & Griffin, 2003) integrate exposure with techniques for accessing and restructuring pathogenic beliefs typically associated with trauma (e.g., faulty attributions of self-blame or danger). So, when CBT attends to internal experience, the focus of that approach is on assumptive processes. Erroneous assumptions are challenged rather than explored in an open-ended manner. This is a top-down rational process.

Similarly, in eye movement desensitization and reprocessing (EMDR; Spates, Koch, Cusack, Pagoto, & Walter, 2009), clients are encouraged to focus on disturbing aspects of the trauma memory, including thoughts, feelings, or images, and to free associate. This is a private experiential search process with the therapist guiding the process at regular intervals by directing the client to attend to aspects of the memory that remain troubling. The theory of EMDR is that by reviewing aspects of the trauma memory with bilateral stimulation and in a safe therapeutic environment, clients create new associative links, and trauma material is thereby reprocessed.

However, the above approaches do not explicitly and deliberately facilitate client experiencing in the sense of open-ended exploration of the idiosyncratic and personal meaning related to one's subjective reality. In contrast, EFTT helps clients to explore or "taste" specific situations in depth (the associated thoughts, feelings, images, desires, bodily sensations, and so on), to discover what they are in fact experiencing rather than whether it makes sense or not. Moments of awareness or meaning construction are "lived" insights that are anchored in a specific situation (bottom-up) and only later may be extended to a broader context (Greenberg et al., 1993). Furthermore, EFTT explicitly focuses on increasing client awareness of the complex repertoire of affective experience and meanings associated with trauma, not just changing maladaptive meaning.

Recent cognitive constructivist and narrative approaches to therapy are similar in many ways to EFTT, especially in their focus on meaning exploration rather than the veracity of people's construals (Neimeyer, 2006). In constructivist approaches to the treatment of complex trauma, the focus is on shifting from content themes that center on deficiency and victimization to themes that center on strength and survival. Intervention involves deliberate reframing of content themes, for example, by focusing on client strengths and resilience that emerge in their personal narrative. However, unlike EFTT's experiential focus, the primary concern of constructivist and narrative approaches is more with cognitive content and narrative quality (e.g., coherence) rather than with affect or arousal or the narration process.

We include a discussion of mindfulness here because of its current popularity, relevance, and applicability to the treatment of trauma and its surface-level similarity to the experiencing construct in EFTT. Mindfulness derives from Buddhist philosophy and has been adapted to Western culture and psychology (Kabat-Zinn, 1990). The current interest in mindfulness attests to the increasing recognition across theoretical orientations that allowing and accepting experience is often more appropriate and valuable than efforts to change it. The practice is largely being used as a skill for "allowing and attending" to the flow of moment-by-moment experience and as a method for modulating emotion, that is, by creating psychological distance or a momentary detachment from presenting problems. Mindfulness is a core skill taught in dialectical behavior therapy for borderline personality (Linehan, 1993) and is an important addition to cognitive therapy for depression (Segal, Williams, & Teasdale, 2002), as well as acceptance and commitment therapy (Hayes, Strosahl, & Wilson, 1999) for unremitting problems, including complex trauma.

A central tenet of mindfulness-based practice is to adopt a nonjudgmental stance and acceptance of the flow of internal and external reality. However, although the process of focusing on internal experience highlights an affinity between the practices of mindfulness and experiencing, they have different aims. The ability to allow and attend to experience as well as to modulate intense feelings is a prerequisite to experiencing, but it is not synonymous with it. The aim of mindfulness is to facilitate a focused but detached awareness of ongoing experience without committing to any single aspect or course of it; in this sense, mindfulness is "content free." In contrast, experiencing is content focused and content specific. The aim of experiencing is to deliberately delve into the ongoing flow of visceral experience in a concerted effort to symbolize and capture that experience in words as a way of understanding its meaning. Mindfulness practice helps clients avoid heightening arousal by directing their attention, in a detached manner, to the flow of emotional pain, for example, among other experiences. When clients' arousal is more manageable, however, experiencing would focus clients' attention on the personal and idiosyncratic nature of their emotional pain, for the purpose of symbolizing it in words and making it more palpable. It is clear that deep experiencing is not the intervention of choice for clients who are feeling overwhelmed and disorganized by negative affect, but it could be the intervention of choice for clients who feel stuck, lack direction, or are at a loss to make sense out of their experience. In some sense, mindfulness is the skill of "moving out" while experiencing is the skill of "moving in."

MEASUREMENT OF EXPERIENCING

The construct of experiencing has been behaviorally defined in the Client Experiencing Scale (Klein, Mathieu-Coughlan, & Kiesler, 1986). This scale originally was intended as a research tool, but EFTT therapists generally are familiar with the essential features of the scale and are able to use it as a tool in clinical practice. Therapists use the Client Experiencing Scale to help track client process and guide intervention (see Appendix A). The aim is to assess the quality of client experiencing and use interventions aimed at improving or deepening it.

The Client Experiencing Scale measures (on a 7-point scale) the degree to which clients orient to their internal experience and use this felt material as information to resolve their problems. At low levels of experiencing, clients talk about external events with behavioral or intellectual descriptions or self and others. For example, "We were in the kitchen, it was dark, he hit me so hard my nose began to bleed, the police came, my mother was crying." Low-level experiencing of this sort generally has been regarded as poor process, and although it may be useful as part of an initial disclosure, this type of process is not predictive of good treatment outcomes. This observation is consistent with trauma theory and research, suggesting that only emotional engagement with trauma material is predictive of outcome (Jaycox, Foa, & Morral, 1998).

As clients move to moderate levels of experiencing (i.e., Level 4), the communication concerns feelings and events told from the internal and personal perspective. The manner is self-descriptive and associative in an effort to paint a portrait of the client's internal state. This marks a turning point and is indicative of more productive therapy process. However, although clients create a personal and affective account of events, these accounts are not yet used for self-examination. For instance, a client describing a sexual assault said,

We were alone in the upstairs bedroom and I was afraid someone would walk in so I tried to be very quiet. When it was finally over I felt devastated, ashamed. So, well, I just went to sleep and tried not to think about it.

At high levels of experiencing (i.e., Level 5 and above), clients explore and work through problems, propositions, or questions about the self and experiences (e.g., "I don't understand how I could have kept it a secret for so long" or "Maybe I'm just not a very trusting person"). Feelings and meanings connected to events in clients' lives are elaborated and explored to resolve current problems. For example, a client exploring the death of his sister said, "For some reason, when she died I felt completely betrayed. When I think back, I think her death actually made me angry, I distrusted everything and everyone around me. I pushed everyone away." Notice that in this example the client's elaboration functions to expand his awareness of his experiencing. In this way, the self-reflection opens up a new conversation about the problem imbued with new meaning.

At other times a high level of experiencing is a synthesis of accessible feelings and experiences, and this emerging content is used to resolve issues that are personally significant. Content aside, the manner with which clients engage in high-level experiencing is integrative, and content is presented in a conclusive or affirmative fashion. The following is an example of a client discussing her feelings toward her younger brother:

C: Being with him makes me feel anxious.

T: Anxious?

C: Yes, I love him, but it's like I sometimes feel angry or something . . . And I don't like feeling like that.

T: Angry, like you resent something?

C: Yes, like I see he has everything, all the things I never had . . . [long pause]. Maybe I'm just jealous. I guess I would love to have all that and I just know it will never happen . . .

Notice how in this example emotion is vividly and freshly experienced in the moment. The new experience is unfolding right here, right now. There is also a new understanding of personal concerns that adds depth of meaning to the experience and sometimes leads to feeling differently about a situation.

RESEARCH ON EXPERIENCING IN THERAPY

In-session client experiencing has been used in research as a predictor of outcome for over 35 years (e.g., Kiesler, 1971). More important, experiencing is an in-session change process that has been shown to predict good treatment outcome across all major schools of psychotherapy, including client-centered (Kiesler, 1971), cognitive–behavioral (Castonguay, Goldfried, Wiser, Raue, & Hayes, 1996), psychodynamic (Silberschatz, Fretter, & Curtis, 1986), and emotion-focused therapy (Pos, Greenberg, Goldman, & Korman, 2003). This suggests that the experiencing construct may represent a common factor that helps explain change across approaches (Bohart, 1993). Furthermore, some studies have shown that high experiencing ratings have predictive power that goes over and above the therapeutic alliance (Pos et al., 2003). This is strong evidence that client experiencing does not represent a single or exclusive humanistic framework but rather a more wide-reaching framework.

Studies of experiencing have focused on the importance of client depth of experiencing during specific key episodes or themes in therapy. For example, Goldman, Greenberg, and Pos (2005) found that client depth of experiencing while they were discussing core themes was predictive of good outcome in emotion-focused therapy for depression. Similarly, a study of EFTT (Robichaud, 2005) found that client depth of experiencing while exploring trauma material in early sessions predicted some dimensions of client change.

Pos et al. (2003) extended this methodological approach by comparing moments of client experiencing that were identified as "on-theme" (i.e., issues related to the target concerns and the treatment focus) with moments of experiencing that were identified as emotional (i.e., when clients discussed emotional content). Identifying thematically versus emotionally relevant segments occasionally coincided, but not always. Although clients were sometimes emotional when discussing issues that were on-theme, at other times they also became emotional when discussing issues that were clearly off-theme and seemingly unrelated to the treatment focus. As one might expect, when clients were on-theme and reached deep levels of experiencing, this was predictive of positive treatment outcome. More intriguingly, however, emotional segments at a deep level of experiencing also were related to positive therapeutic outcome, even when the issue being discussed was clearly off-theme. In fact, deep experiencing during emotional episodes turned out to be an even better predictor of overall outcome than deep experiencing during on-theme episodes of therapy. As Pos and colleagues argued, this suggests that emotion points the way to an overarching or meta-theme. This idea is also supported by Pascual-Leone and Greenberg's (2007) emotional-processing model presented in the chapter 3. Findings such as these suggest that therapists would do well to be guided by clients' affect when deciding where and when to deepen experiential process. In this way they can capitalize on the power of emotion to orient clients to core content and facilitate healthy change. This has obvious relevance for exploring trauma-related feelings in EFTT.

Indirect support for the value of the experiencing construct in EFTT comes from a number of other studies. For example, Holowaty (2004) found that higher ratings of experiencing were characteristic of those therapy episodes that clients also identified in posttreatment interviews as having been most helpful. Furthermore, a process–outcome study on therapist skills in EFTT (Paivio, Holowaty, & Hall, 2004) indicated that therapist adherence to EFTT intervention principles predicted client change and that the two most frequently used intervention principles were directing attention to internal experience and symbolizing the meaning of experience. This supports the value of a sustained focus on exploring the meaning of experience (or experiencing) in EFTT. Finally, both client emotional arousal and experiencing (i.e., engagement) with trauma memories during the IC procedure (see chap. 7, this volume) was associated with the resolution of target issues related to abusive and neglectful others (Paivio, Hall, Holowaty, Jellis, & Tran, 2001).

Although the Client Experiencing Scale actually has no reference to discrete emotions or affective states per se, emotion-focused therapies (including EFTT) specifically emphasize the exploration of emotional experience. This emphasis, based on emotion and trauma theory and research, helps to guide the content of the experiential process to the elaboration and transformation of specific emotional states, particularly those that are central to trauma. In short, emotion provides an initial window through which one can access and explore internal experience and the associated idiosyncratic and personally relevant meaning.

EXPERIENCING IN THE MAJOR TASKS OF EFTT

Symbolizing the meaning of affective experience and deepening experiencing is a change process and intervention principle used throughout EFTT. How this is concretely accomplished will be discussed in detail in the remaining chapters of the book. However, the following sections provide an overview by summarizing the role of experiencing in the major tasks of this therapy.

Cultivating the Alliance

From the first session, symbolizing the meaning of experience is part of implicit emotion awareness training or coaching. When clients are discussing the past and present issues that brought them to therapy, they are directed to attend to and verbally articulate the feelings associated with those troubling situations and events and implicitly or explicitly invited to elaborate. The therapeutic relationship itself, particularly issues of trust, may be the focus of exploration. Clients are invited to explore their experience of difficulties in the relationship in the moment (e.g., the therapist might say, "I sense that something gets in the way of your being able to relax and just be yourself with me. Can we talk about what it is like for you being in therapy?"). The objective is to increase client capacity for, and increase the client awareness of, an authentic interpersonal encounter, in which client and therapist feel that they are able to "be real with each other." For many survivors of complex relational trauma, this may be a new experience.

Clients also are encouraged to discuss and explore their hopes and fears of being in therapy in general. Many clients enter therapy with fear and ambivalence about approaching and disclosing painful and traumatic experiences, for example, and may have learned to avoid their internal experiences as a coping strategy. Throughout Phase 1, EFTT therapists collaborate with clients to establish the overarching goal of emotional meaning exploration, which is always in the context of a supportive relationship. Above all, therapists must create an environment that is conducive to deep experiencing and reflection. They establish safety through empathic responsiveness, use of a quiet and soothing tone of voice, and slowing down the pace, for example, by saying, "These things are not easy to talk about. We can take all the time you need."

As discussed, optimal arousal facilitates productive experiencing. However, a client's level of arousal may be unproductively low through experiential avoidance, intellectualization, or worry, in which case the relationship may be used to empathically evoke and thereby heighten arousal and then invite further exploration. For example, a therapist might say to an emotionally constricted client, "It's like you're trapped inside your own head, a prisoner . . . how lonely."

Increasing Emotional Awareness

The transition from Phase 1 to the middle phases of EFTT follows the introduction of the IC procedure during Session 4. This can be extremely evocative for clients because the process involves reexperiencing painful feelings and memories and exploring them in depth while confronting an imagined perpetrator. Difficulties that interfere with client engagement in this procedure include lack of experiential awareness, fear of approaching and allowing emotional pain, self-critical processes, and a core shame-based or insecure sense of self, which become the focus of intervention in Phase 2. Helping clients symbolize the meaning of these experiences and deepening their experiencing is central to interventions designed to address these difficulties. The intervention principle for promoting deeper experiencing is to focus, above all, on exploring the meaning derived from the client's subjective internal experience, rather than challenging or explicitly trying to change maladaptive processes, content, or narratives. Effective interventions explicitly or implicitly communicate the message, "What you just said is important, and means a lot to you. Say more."

Given that many survivors of complex trauma have difficulties identifying, labeling, and articulating the meaning of their feelings, deliberate strategies are used in EFTT to promote and improve these capacities. In these instances, experiencing is thought of as a skill that needs to be taught and practiced in sessions (see chap. 6, this volume, on promoting experiencing). Emotion awareness also is increased by helping clients to attend to certain aspects of their ongoing experience that may otherwise go unidentified (e.g., the therapist might say, "Something in her tone of voice shuts you down. What happens for you on the inside when you imagine hearing that?"). At other times clients' experiences are deepened by encouraging them to explore and "re-own" aspects of how they experience themselves, which have thus far remained unaddressed or warded off (e.g., the therapist may say, "It's as if you have no right to complain, like 'You made your bed now you must sleep in it'?").

Reexperiencing Trauma Feelings and Memories

In Session 4 of EFTT, in-depth exploration of painful and traumatic experiences usually begins. Over the course of therapy, this can take place in the context of the IC procedure or through memory work and focusing-type interventions. The intervention principle involves reexperiencing both internal and external aspects of an event, at a slow and deliberate pace and in minute detail. This accesses previously unavailable information that helps clients to make sense of their reactions and also can correct erroneous assumptions. Fear during traumatic experiences and the stress of dealing with the aftermath sometimes overwhelm the system and interfere with information processing, thereby producing confusion and memory gaps. These gaps are a source of uncertainty and further anxiety for clients, which can result in faulty conclusions, for example, about being personally responsible. Reexperiencing and attending to the thoughts and feelings one had at the time of a traumatic event as well as to the contextual circumstances of the event help clarify one's motives, reactions, and behaviors. For example, reexperiencing one's powerlessness and revulsion at molestation can alleviate self-blame, such that a client begins to conclude, "I was an innocent, so small . . . I hated it but didn't know how to stand up to him." This deeper level of experiencing has clients deliberately explore their construals and interpretations at the time of traumatic events, thus sensing how a given experience is generated.

Complex trauma during development all too often results in pervasive feelings of worthlessness, or feeling dirty or responsible for the abuse, despite intellectually knowing this is not true. It also often produces chronic feelings of insecurity and collapses into feelings of powerlessness and depression. This is much more than a simple cognitive–linguistic distortion. It is an experiential reality that represents an implicit, holistic, and preverbal sense of self and internalized object relations, one that guides perceptions and behaviors. Interventions used to address this explore childhood experiences and the specific events in which that core sense of self was formed or current situations in which that sense of self is activated. Once they have been engaged, these experiences then can be clarified and examined.

Resolving Intra- and Interpersonal Conflicts

In Phases 2 and 3, two-chair enactments are used in EFTT to explore intrapersonal conflicts and to imaginally confront perpetrators of abuse and neglect. Although there are differences in terms of techniques and goals, these processes always involve conceptualizing and concretely addressing a conflict between two parts of the self—a client's dominant maladaptive part of self (e.g., self-critical, anxiously overcontrolled) or internalized negative other (e.g., "She [mother] was always putting me down, nothing I did was ever good enough") and a client's weaker or subdominant part of self that embodies authentic feelings, needs, and healthy resources. However this conflict presents itself, the intervention principles are to (a) increase arousal to activate the core emotion structure and (b) support the weaker experiencing self, giving that part of self a voice. In Phase 2, intrapersonal conflicts typically are enacted in a dialogue between the conflicting aspects of self or self-organizations. The dominant critical or controlling side of self initially is used strictly as a stimulus to increase arousal and evoke a response in the experiencing side of self, the side that feels oppressed, defeated, guilty, or ashamed. Here, therapist interventions help clients first to become aware of and enact how they contribute to their own bad feelings (e.g., therapist asks, "What do you say to tear yourself down?"). Clients then are encouraged to articulate their experience of being on the receiving end of that criticism or oppression and to articulate the meaning of this experience—the effect of feeling ashamed, oppressed, or defeated all the time, as well as the associated (albeit unfulfilled) needs for self-respect, acceptance, spontaneity, and so on. The latter, nascent feelings act as healthy resources that can be used to challenge or help clients stand up to the dominant self. As clients get closer to resolution and the two aspects of self become more integrated, deeper levels of experiencing help them further articulate core feelings, values, and goals and thereby develop confidence in these and a stronger sense of self.

The principle is the same for the IC procedure, which is used in conjunction with other procedures (e.g., two-chair dialogues between parts of self) during Phase 2, and is the primary intervention used during Phase 3. At the beginning of the procedure, imagining the negative other is used strictly as a stimulus to activate the core emotion structure (object relations) and evoke a felt response in the experiencing self. The client is encouraged to express her or his thoughts, feelings, and needs concerning the offending other that previously have been inhibited or suppressed and symbolize the meaning of painful traumatic experiences concerning the other. Experiencing involves exploring the importance of particular cherished beliefs that have been shattered, needs that were unmet, and the trauma's impact on the self and others. This is especially important with respect to all aspects of recovery from trauma but is most salient when it applies to issues with attachment figures. Here deeper levels of experiencing can help clients articulate the meaning of experiences of maltreatment, injustice, violation, and abuse. This can strengthen clients' sense of self and help them appropriately hold abusive others responsible for harm. Deeper experiencing also helps clients develop appreciation for the significance of their losses, as well as compassion for self and others and self-soothing resources.

If we think back to the client Monica, it was only through fully appreciating the meaning and significance of her mother's suicide—the devastation it caused to herself and others and the effects of this ultimate abandonment and betrayal on her sense of self and her relationships—that she was able to accept the reality of these losses, grieve, and move on, eyes wide open, to forgiveness.

This concludes Part I on trauma and EFTT theory. In Part II, we focus on each of the four phases of EFTT that promote client experiencing and meaning construction to address the different areas of concern in complex trauma.

II
INTERVENTION

PHASE ONE OF EFTT

5

CULTIVATING THE ALLIANCE

The primary task in Phase 1 of emotion-focused therapy for trauma (EFTT) is to cultivate a safe and collaborative therapeutic relationship. This is the exclusive focus of the first three sessions of therapy. The therapeutic relationship or alliance is a universal change factor across treatment approaches and client groups (Horvath & Symonds, 1991) and is considered the foundation of therapy with survivors of child abuse trauma (Herman, 1992; Pearlman & Courtois, 2005). A compassionate, empathic, and collaborative therapeutic relationship has two primary functions. First, it provides clients a safe environment for reliving painful material; a safe context counters beliefs that feelings and memories themselves are dangerous. Second, this relationship quality can be a new interpersonal experience that helps client to correct the effects of early attachment injuries and empathic failures.

In this chapter, we define alliance quality, describe the fundamental intervention principles for cultivating a strong alliance, discuss the goals of alliance development in Phase 1 of EFTT, and provide specific guidelines for conducting the first three sessions. The chapter concludes with a section on addressing alliance difficulties and the therapist errors that most frequently can occur during this phase of therapy.

EFTT defines alliance quality in terms of both bond and collaborative elements. We use the short version of the Working Alliance Inventory (WAI; Horvath & Greenberg, 1989; see Appendix B, this volume) both in our research and as a guide for clinicians to cultivate a strong and productive alliance. The attachment bond refers to affective aspects of the relationship, that is, mutual liking and trust. Collaborative elements refer to agreement on the goals of therapy and the in-session processes or procedures that will be used to accomplish these goals. In EFTT, relationship tasks always take precedence over other tasks, regardless of the phase of therapy. However, unlike psychodynamic approaches, in which the relationship and transference issues are the focus of therapy (see Kudler, Krupnick, Blank, Herman, & Horowitz, 2009, for a review), in EFTT, transference issues become the focus of therapy only when they interfere with other therapeutic processes—in instances of client distrust, hostility, or boundary violations, for example. Working through issues with the therapist is deemphasized in favor of resolving issues with particular abusive and neglectful others or attachment figures.

INTERVENTION PRINCIPLES FOR DEVELOPING A PRODUCTIVE ALLIANCE

The intervention principles or therapist intentions that are most relevant to the initial phase of therapy with trauma survivors include the following: empathize and communicate compassion, understanding, and nonjudgmental acceptance; validate client perceptions and experience; provide information about trauma and the process of therapy; define therapist and client roles; make process observations; provide reassurance and hope; and foster realistic expectations. The sections below elaborate on these principles.

Empathize

Empathic responding is the primary intervention used throughout therapy to realize all of the above principles or intentions and is particularly important in developing the therapeutic relationship in the early phase. As discussed in chapter 2, the two main functions of therapist empathy with traumatized individuals (Paivio & Laurent, 2001) are (a) modulating emotional intensity and (b) increasing client awareness and understanding of their emotional experience and processes. These processes contribute to client self-development and emotional control, and strengthening these client capacities, in turn, strengthens the therapeutic relationship.

To review briefly, in terms of emotion modulation, empathic responses by therapists can reduce distress and isolation by communicating understanding, acceptance, and support (e.g., "I know how difficult it must be to get in touch with how profoundly victimized you were"). These empathic responses also can reduce anxiety about being judged and thus foster interpersonal trust. Empathic responses that affirm client vulnerability help them to allow and disclose painful and threatening experiences. In contrast, *evocative* empathic responses by therapists (e.g., "Yes, how painful—treated like you were some kind of vermin!") can be used to deliberately increase emotional intensity and activate emotional experience and memories, making them available for exploration. Sharing emotional experience with a responsive therapist and collaborative exploration of that experience strengthen the bond.

In terms of increasing emotional awareness, a therapist's simple empathic responses (e.g., "You must have felt so resentful") can direct clients' attention to and help them accurately label emotional experience. These responses, when tentatively phrased, can be particularly helpful for clients who do not know what they are feeling and who fear negative evaluation. Empathic responses also help clients to articulate and communicate the meaning of their emotional experience; this not only increases understanding but also fosters interpersonal connectedness. At other times, therapist empathic responses highlight the gist, central concern, or most poignant aspect of what the client said (e.g., "So, what hurts so much is this feeling of being completely invisible"). Still other statements invite elaboration or conjecture about client experience based on knowledge of the client and human experience in general. For example, in response to a client's description of collapsing into powerlessness and depression, the therapist stated, "I guess you end up feeling like that powerless little girl all over again." These kinds of responses strengthen the therapeutic bond and agreement on the value of emotional exploration as a therapeutic task.

Validate Client Experience

Validating responses also are important in reducing client anxiety, promoting client self-development, and fostering interpersonal trust in the early phase of therapy. Validation is distinct from empathy but requires empathic understanding. Whereas empathic responses communicate understanding or promote exploration, validation is a type of reassurance or a confirmation of reality in context. Validation of client experience is offered in response to client expressed or implied insecurity about whether the client's experiences or perceptions of a particular situation are accurate, legitimate, or normal (e.g., the client may say, "I'm probably weird" or "I don't know why I think that, it's probably nothing"). Validating responses by therapists (e.g., "It's no wonder . . . , of course . . . ," "That makes complete sense," "I think most people would see it that way," or "That's a part of having posttraumatic stress disorder") reduce anxiety and fear of negative evaluation by normalizing clients' feelings and perceptions and help them to trust their own experience.

Linehan (1993, 1997) has written extensively about the curative role of validation in therapy for borderline personality disorder, which is strongly associated with a history of child abuse trauma. Her model of dysfunction posits invalidating environments and client vulnerability as the primary factors contributing to borderline processes. Many individuals were repeatedly told they were stupid, crazy, or exaggerating and thus have internalized these messages and learned to distrust their own healthier feelings and perceptions. Therapist validation helps to correct the effects of this early learning so that clients are better able to trust their internal experience as a source of information that can guide decision making and adaptive functioning. It is important to notice that validation is not the same as simple agreement with client opinions and perceptions or approval of their behavior. It is possible for therapists to communicate, for example, that substance abuse and self-cutting are understandable attempts to escape from overwhelming pain and, at the same time, emphasize the importance of learning less destructive ways of coping. Similarly, it is possible to validate clients' need for strict emotional control and, at the same time, challenge this need as excessive and not in their best interests.

Provide Information

Relationship development goes beyond empathic mirroring. In the beginning of therapy, it is particularly important to provide information about trauma and the process of recovery (resource materials are provided at the client's request), therapist and client roles, and clear expectations about the processes of therapy in EFTT. These, combined with provision of structure, help reduce client uncertainty about treatment.

Responding with an appropriate level of information when clients are feeling confused, distressed, or are misinformed is itself an expression of empathic attunement. Some theorists working with difficult populations have referred to this as *functional validation* (e.g., Linehan, 1993). The following concrete pieces of information should be communicated to clients, with appropriate timing and according to their needs.

- Traumatic events are so horrible people want desperately to forget them, but by definition they are unforgettable. The more clients try to forget, the more they force themselves into awareness. Perseverating on traumatic experiences is a way of trying to make sense of and integrate the trauma into existing meaning systems.

- Clients need to remember, tell the story over and over again in a safe environment, to work it through. Clients need to process all the details with another person who can provide guidance, feedback, and support. When clients are able to come to terms with traumatic experiences without professional help, these resources generally have been available to them through family or friends.
- When trauma feelings and memories are chronically avoided, clients become stuck in the feelings and perceptions formed at the time of the trauma. If that happens, a part of the client usually remains fearful, powerless, angry, or ashamed, and this part gets activated at current reminders of the trauma.
- Powerful emotions are at the core of trauma—both the recurring bad feelings that clients want to change and healthy feelings such as sadness and anger that usually were suppressed because there was no support for their expression or they were punished. These feelings need to be expressed and understood.
- A therapeutic focus on past trauma is hard work, takes courage, and could temporarily activate symptoms and increase distress. Clients should be reminded that therapy will incorporate strategies to keep this manageable and will balance a focus on the past with attention to present concerns.
- Clients also need to be assured that they will have control over the process and pacing of trauma exploration. Together, the therapist and client will monitor the client's level of distress and tolerance for trauma exploration and adjust the process accordingly.

Define Therapist and Client Roles

On one hand, the client is the expert of his or her own experience. On the other hand, the therapist is an expert in the area of trauma and in observing and responding to client in-session processes ("holding up a mirror"). In other words, therapists are experts in effective procedures, even though interventions are cued and guided entirely by client processes. This complementary relationship with respect to tasks is the very essence of a marker-based approach and a hallmark of all emotion-focused therapies (as discussed in chap. 2, this volume). At the same time, however, the therapist's job is to encourage clients to push their limits and to provide clients with the necessary guidance and support to make this possible. This is the dialectic of unconditional acceptance of clients as they are and of promoting change (Linehan, 1997).

The client's role is to explore her or his internal experience (feelings and meanings) and share that experience with the therapist, including any concerns and difficulties with the actual process of disclosure. Clients need to take risks and push their boundaries and at the same time set their own limits. Therapists can explain these roles to clients as follows:

> We are not going to hammer away at your traumatic experiences session after session. I am interested in you as a whole person. You are in the driver's seat. We will explore both past and present concerns, whatever is most important to you at the time. My job is to ensure your safety and, at the same time, to support and promote your growth. Of course, that will mean helping you get in touch with painful stuff so you can work it through, here, in this safe environment, and at a pace you can handle. Your job is to let me know what you can and cannot handle.

At the beginning of therapy, clients can be asked to specify the problems they want help with in therapy, identify their goals, and discuss how therapy might help with these problems. This helps to clarify expectations about the therapy process. Most processes in EFTT are fluid and responsive to situational cues so that information is provided in the context of exploring individual client's needs and concerns. For example, when a client complains about feeling like a frightened little girl in current situations, the therapist might empathize and state:

> It sounds like part of you is kind of stuck in the old childhood script. From what you told me, you have never had a safe place to open up, to explore these experiences so they can evolve. That's what we are going to do here.

Make Process Observations

Therapists provide feedback about client processes that are observed during sessions, and this can be thought of as a subset of providing information, for example, "I notice that you kind of withdraw whenever we start talking about your father." These communications are distinct from interpretations because no inferences are drawn from the client's behavior; rather they are empirically based observations at a low level of abstraction. Nonetheless, the purpose of doing this is to invite exploration of the underlying internal processes. These observations need to be offered at a time and in a way (e.g., preceded by an empathic response) that does not increase client self-consciousness, defensiveness, and withdrawal. Moreover, process observations provide a rationale for intervention and goals for sessions and therapy. For example, the therapist might tell the client, "Judging yourself so harshly, it must be so hard to hold your head up high. We want to change that and help you find a way to stand up to that internalized critic."

Provide Reassurance, Encouragement, and Hope

Reassurance is intended to assuage feelings of despair and hopelessness and to maintain motivation. Most trauma survivors have repeatedly tried to get over their trauma, sometimes having participated in other therapies to no avail, and consequently they enter therapy despairing and hopeless. They also are afraid of dredging up painful feelings and memories and fear the impact this might have on their current lives. Again, the therapist needs to reassure the client that, together, they will monitor distress and coping and that the client will have maximum control over the process and pace of therapy. Encouragement is provided by genuine statements such as, "You're not alone, I'll help you do this" or "It's OK, you're doing fine."

Providing hope also is considered a critical aspect of therapy for complex trauma (Pearlman & Courtois, 2005). This can be accomplished in part through information about the contribution of memory work to change and about the efficacy of EFTT. For example, a therapist might say, "Although there never are guarantees and there are individual differences in the degree to which people benefit, most people with similar problems to yours have benefited from this type of therapy. There is every reason to be optimistic." Thus, clients need to be reassured that with appropriate guidance and support, people can heal the wounds of the past and move on to live meaningful lives. Clients need to feel confident in the therapist's expertise, that the therapist understands and can guide them through the difficult and painful process of therapy. This reduces clients' anxiety and increases their sense of safety so they can disclose painful material and experience the relief of unburdening and receiving comfort. Hope also comes through attention to client strengths, accomplishments, resilience, and internal and external resources.

Foster Realistic Expectations

Of course, therapists need to help their clients develop realistic expectations for change. A short-term therapy, of necessity, has a circumscribed focus and cannot solve all of the client's problems. However, clients can reasonably expect to make significant progress in one or two identified areas of concern.

GOALS OF ALLIANCE FORMATION IN PHASE 1 OF EFTT

The features of alliance development in EFTT are not significantly different from those in the general model of emotion-focused therapy (Elliott, Watson, Goldman, & Greenberg, 2004) except that alliance formation particularly emphasizes establishing a secure attachment bond and attention to emotion regulation difficulties. These goals are interrelated and are explored in the sections that follow.

Establish a Focus on Trauma

Our work on EFTT primarily has involved clients who contact our clinic specifically to work on issues related to child abuse trauma. Most often, however, current issues will be integrated into EFTT, and clients should be assured that therapy likely will move back and forth between past and present concerns. However, many individuals who have been exposed to childhood abuse are primarily concerned with present difficulties. Other clients may want to resolve past trauma but are unable to focus on a circumscribed issue from the past because of multiple ongoing stressors and severe impairments in current functioning. A decision to focus on traumatic experiences therefore is based on the client's desire and capacity to do so or task markers that indicate unresolved trauma is at the root of a presenting disturbance.

Establishing a trauma focus in EFTT also involves identifying the specific abusive relationships that will be the focus of therapy. Most clients in our clinic have experienced multiple forms of trauma, abuse, and neglect at the hands of multiple perpetrators. This is consistent with the prevalence of revictimization cited in the trauma literature (van der Kolk, 2003). Nonetheless, a short-term therapy requires establishing a circumscribed focus. The client, therefore, is asked to identify which issues and relationships (one or two is ideal) she or he finds most troubling and would like to focus on in therapy. One of these should be the direct perpetrator of abuse, and the other typically is a neglectful or nonsupportive other, such as a mother who did not protect the child from abuse. Recently, we have been extending EFTT to work with refugee trauma survivors. In these instances, establishing a particular relational focus will not be a goal, or there may be an impersonal relation to a collective other (e.g., the government), a political leader, or a particular individual (e.g., jail guard) who is the focus of client distress.

Establish a Secure Attachment Bond

Establishing a secure bond between therapist and client is the fundamental task of the early phase of EFTT and is the cornerstone for the remainder of therapy. From a developmental perspective, an attachment figure is an older, gentler, wiser, stronger person to whom one can turn in times of vulnerability or distress (Fosha, 2003). Bowlby (1988) emphasized that attachment needs persist throughout the life span, and adult attachment relationships serve much the same function they do in childhood. Thus, we rely on adult attachment figures to provide safety, security, support, comfort, and soothing in times of stress or distress. The therapeutic relationship meets these needs in the context of the client disclosing and exploring trauma material. The client is not alone with painful feelings and can rely on the therapist to be supportive and responsive to his or her feelings and needs. Therapy for interpersonal trauma that occurred during childhood development is a type of reparenting process. Thus, a secure attachment bond in the therapeutic relationship can help to establish or rebuild the capacity for interpersonal connectedness that was disrupted by trauma.

It is paramount to understand that EFTT is conducted in the context of a genuine and "real" relationship between adults. Traditional psychoanalytic distance and neutrality are not appropriate in this approach to treatment. When viewing videotapes of EFTT sessions, one is struck by the quality of intimacy in the interactions: Therapists not only directly communicate compassion for their clients' fears, struggles, suffering, and pain but may also explicitly communicate that they feel sorry that clients have suffered so much in their lives.

Many clients who enter EFTT are disclosing victimization and abuse for the first time and fear that they are exposing themselves as defective or they are being judged by the therapist and thereby will be further humiliated and victimized (this is characteristic of shame–anxiety). Other clients have disclosed to people in the past but have had their experiences invalidated and the harm that they endured minimized. Therapist validation of experience (e.g., "Of course, that makes sense") and empathic affirmation of vulnerability (e.g., "I hear how hard this is") therefore are important responses. For example, one client ("Alan") who we will refer to in later chapters told the story of his drunken father first breaking all the toys his mother had bought him for his birthday and then beating him for crying. The therapist's response was, "So cruel, and so sad that a young boy should be treated like that by his own father, the person whose love he needed the most." For many clients, this may be their first experience of receiving this type of validation and compassion, and these new interpersonal experiences in therapy are what constitute corrective emotional experiences in EFTT. In the end, therapist empathic attunement and responding strengthens the bond for both parties. In other words, as clients feel understood and cared for, therapists feel closer to their clients as well, which in turn facilitates deeper understanding and connection, a primary goal of early alliance formation.

This is an area in which a focus on positive affect can play an important role in strengthening the attachment bond. Positive affect in this case is related to the experiences of joining, sharing, explicitly discussing feelings of connection, and celebrating client successes throughout the therapy process. Survivors of abuse and/or neglect not only have endured negative interactions with attachment figures but also have frequently missed out on positive inter-actions that are the bread and butter of healthy relationships (Frederickson & Losada, 2005). On that account, therapists provide and model shared positive experiences by acknowledging interpersonal connectedness, by using humor, and by modeling playfulness.

Begin Emotion Coaching and Awareness Training

While the first core feature of alliance development in the early phase of EFTT is to establish a secure attachment bond (as discussed above), the sec-ond is increasing clients' awareness of their emotions and emotional processes. Increasing emotion awareness is closely related to attachment processes because one of the primary functions of an adult attachment figure is to help a child contain, label, and make sense of affective experience (Gottman, 1997). This emotion coaching parenting style has been associated with many indices of superior interpersonal and academic functioning.

Emotion awareness training begins in the first session of EFTT and, in early sessions, is almost exclusively accomplished through empathic respond-ing to client feelings and needs. From the beginning of therapy with trauma survivors, problems are defined in terms of feelings. When clients talk about their week or past events, the therapist responds, not as much to the details of the story, but more so to their present emotional experience (e.g., "I hear what a struggle this is for you" or "So this is the worst thing in your life, the thing that still causes you so much pain"). Of course, therapists do respond to the content of trauma narrative and other material, but the focus is always on the internal experience rather than the plot and characters of what happened.

In early sessions, therapists are especially attuned and direct client attention to the core adaptive and maladaptive emotions and emotional processes (i.e., task markers) that will be the targets of therapy later on. Core adaptive emotions include unresolved anger at violation, betrayal, and mal-treatment; sadness at losses and neglect; and the associated longings, needs, and action tendencies (e.g., a therapist might say to a client, "Angry at the injustice, I'm sure you'd like to see him punished for his crimes" or "Such a huge loss, it must leave such a big ache inside"). Core maladaptive emotions include fear, anxiety, and shame as well as the associated beliefs about self and others (e.g., "So you're not sure you can handle dredging up all that pain" or "This is terrible—to walk around feeling like a loser"). Helping clients become aware of these emotional processes contributes to self-development and is the basis for developing a collaborative understanding of disturbance and the goals and tasks of therapy.

It can be particularly helpful to direct client attention to the bodily experiences associated with specific emotions (e.g., energy of anger, tension or trembling of anxiety, heaviness of sadness, hiding or slinking away in shame). Particularly in the early phase of therapy, this contributes to client recognition, self-monitoring, and self-control of emotion. As clients recount their reactions to situations, therapists can combine directives to attend to bodily experience (e.g., by asking, "What do you feel in your body as you think about that event?") with empathic responses that implicitly invite clients to articulate the meaning of their experience (e.g., "Butterflies—something scary about it?"). Doing this helps clients attend to their somatic and affective experience as sources of information that can guide them.

When necessary, EFTT also will include explicit teaching about emotions and emotional processes. This typically is integrated into the process of exploring current or past issues rather than presented as a separate exercise. For example, the early phase of therapy with one client included teaching him about the different types of anger. This was initiated at markers of defensive anger covering more vulnerable feelings of hurt and shame that the client was less aware of.

Because emotions are a source of vital information that aids in adaptive functioning, the concept of alexithymia, introduced in earlier chapters, is particularly relevant here. Helping clients find the right words for their feelings is essential to the goal of increasing emotional awareness, which, in turn, is an essential part of alliance formation in EFTT.

Begin to Address Emotion Regulation Difficulties

Emotion regulation problems include both underregulation and overcontrol of affective experience, and both of these generate secondary feelings of anxiety and fear. Typical client concerns at the beginning of therapy include the following: (a) shame–anxiety, that is, fear of negative evaluation by the therapist that results in fear of disclosure; (b) fear of their own painful experience and the impact that dredging up memories will have on their current lives; (c) fear of discovering something horrible about themselves or their histories; (d) fear of failure, that therapy will not help or that it will confirm their worst fears that they are a hopeless case; and (e) particularly for other clients with histories of emotional abuse and neglect, fear that their problems are not important enough, that they are exaggerating, or that there is something wrong with them for feeling so distressed (e.g., "I should really be able to get over it").

Therapists need to explicitly ask about client fears, acknowledge and validate that these concerns are normal, and then address them. EFTT therapists also observe the manner in which clients talk about themselves and traumatic experiences, their level of arousal, the degree of their openness and disclosure, their capacity for spontaneous elaboration, and so on. Once again, empathic responding in the therapeutic relationship is the primary vehicle for emotion regulation in EFTT rather than providing specific skills training. The soothing presence of the therapist, his or her empathic affirmation of client vulnerability, and ongoing validation help to reduce isolation and distress, all of which contribute to emotion regulation.

Intensifying emotional experience typically is not the focus of Phase 1 of EFTT. However, when clients are highly constricted and overcontrolled, therapists need to identify and address these processes (e.g., the therapist might say, "You can talk about these difficult experiences but it seems hard for you to actually connect with the feelings"). Part of dealing with avoidance involves providing information about trauma and recovery and a rationale for a focus on painful feelings and memory work that was presented earlier. Therapists also need to address misunderstandings and catastrophic expectations that clients have about emotions (e.g., when a client says, "If I start crying I will never stop") and to label these beliefs as essentially a fear of one's own feelings. Once these concerns are identified, therapists can emphasize how such fears "hold one hostage" and how they may be unrealistic given what is known about emotion, all the while providing a safe and empathic relationship.

In summary, client issues with both under- and overregulated emotion become apparent early in treatment. Addressing these interpersonally serves to strengthen the therapeutic alliance.

Collaborative Case Formulation

This aspect of alliance formation involves developing a mutual understanding of the factors contributing to disturbance. Such an understanding is the rationale for therapy and is essential to collaboration on the goals of therapy and the way by which these will be accomplished. This understanding is based on information about the client's trauma and attachment history, their current perceptions of self and others, their attitude toward their own internal experience, observable in-session processes and behaviors, and the interconnections among these factors.

First, it is useful to elicit client theories about their own problems. Clients should be encouraged to consider, for example: Why have problems persisted? Why do intrusive symptoms resurface? Why are angry feelings so pervasive and difficult to control? Why can't the client sustain long-term relationships or stand up to their mother even at age 60? Not only is this the first step in collaboratively arriving at an understanding of the problem, but it also flags possible alliance difficulties if clients have no theory or insight into their own problems, or if their theory is very discrepant with the treatment model. For example, clients might attribute their depression or anger control problems to external circumstances and other people and have no insight into how their own thoughts and feelings precipitate or exacerbate depressive or angry responses. Clients need to understand that internal thoughts and feelings contribute to their problems and agree that the specific goals for therapy are to address and change these internal processes. After all, clients need to know these are the areas over which they have some control.

Current Interpersonal Difficulties

During Phase 1, EFTT focuses as much on present concerns as unresolved past issues. Many clients are dealing with current interpersonal problems with employers, spouses, and children and are still in relationships with past abusive or neglectful others. For example, clients may be caring for an aging parent whom they hate and cannot forgive, are unable to set boundaries and stand up to the demands of an abusive parent (or employer), cannot be affectionate with their children, or generally have difficulties with trust and interpersonal connectedness. Not surprisingly, in the early phase of therapy, clients themselves frequently observe interpersonal patterns and draw connections between their past experiences and current problems. Therapists also make these connections between past and present, not so much as interpretations aimed at increasing client awareness, but more so because this is the rationale for a focus on resolving past trauma.

Self-Related Difficulties

Case formulation also involves developing a collaborative understanding of how clients have learned to view and treat themselves and the adverse effects these have on current functioning and trauma resolution. This is accomplished by highlighting and empathizing with problems related to self-identity, self-esteem, self-respect, and confidence. Problems include anxious monitoring and overcontrol of self, minimizing one's own feelings and needs, hostile self-criticism and loathing, perfectionism, or a pervasive sense of self as victim. The modification of these maladaptive self-organizations so that clients have an increased capacity for openness, spontaneity, and self-acceptance is a goal of EFTT and will become the focus in Phase 2 of therapy.

Attitude to Subjective Internal Experience

A key aspect of case formulation in EFTT is developing a collaborative understanding of the clients' approach to their internal experience. This client variable has implications for successful client engagement in the process of experientially oriented therapies such as EFTT. Clients may be open and attentive to their own feelings and needs, or they may be externally oriented, inattentive, defensive, intellectual, somatizing, or fearful of their own experience. As we have seen in the preceding chapter, research indicates that greater depth of experiencing is associated with better outcome (see Greenberg & Pascual-Leone, 2006, for a review). Thus, a severely limited capacity for experiencing means a poor prognosis in EFTT because attention to and exploring feelings and meanings are the primary sources of new information, and all procedures are dependent on this client capacity. That said, many clients who are cognitively oriented, intellectual, reserved, cautious, or slow, and who at first have difficulties with experiencing, will eventually demonstrate some capacity to explore their subjective experiencing. In fact, studies indicate moderate levels on the Client Experiencing Scale (i.e., Level 4) in the early phase of EFTT (Ralston, 2006; Robichaud, 2005). Clients also can learn to increasingly value their own experience over therapy.

From the beginning, interventions are geared toward exploring present subjective experience in current troublesome situations (e.g., the therapist might ask, "What happens to you on the inside when she criticizes you?" or " . . . you walk into a room of strangers?"). This exploration of current concerns strengthens the attachment bond (e.g., "I want to know you as a whole person"), increases awareness of emotions and emotional processes, and develops a collaborative understanding of the internal processes that contribute to disturbance and inform the goals and tasks of therapy.

Identify Task Markers

The notion of client markers that cue specific therapist intervention was introduced in chapter 2. In brief, task markers are the in-session behaviors that indicate the specific underlying cognitive–affective processing difficulties that contribute to disturbance and need to be targeted in session. Identifying task markers, then, plays an important role in collaborative case formulation. Markers include lingering bad feelings (hurt, anger, resentment, sadness, fear, shame) toward abusive or neglectful others from the past and intrusive symptoms that require reexperiencing and emotional processing. Markers of client self-blame for victimization (e.g., "I should have told someone about the abuse") or self-critical processes indicate a need to explore these internalized messages and access alternate healthy resources to challenge them and thus strengthen self-esteem. Markers of avoidant processes by the client indicate a need to approach and allow emotional experience to disconfirm maladaptive beliefs, increase one's sense of agency, and strengthen self-confidence. A client's lack of clarity about internal experience indicates a need to slow down, to focus on bodily experience, and to verbally symbolize the meaning of experience.

EFTT therapists direct client attention to these task markers (through process observations) and explicate the underlying processing difficulties. The first step in collaboratively identifying tasks is for clients to agree that their own internal processes are contributing to disturbance and that these are the areas over which they have most control, rather than external circumstances or other people. Promoting clients' self-control over their internal processes is an essential part of self-development and self-esteem that begins in the very first session.

Finally, arriving at a mutual understanding of underlying determinants may require explicitly educating clients about emotions and the effects of child abuse and trauma and providing a rationale for therapeutic intervention. For example, a client ("Paul") whose case we will refer to again in chapter 10 was asked about his understanding of his anger control problems. Paul stated that his physically abusive father was "a bad example" and also that he used anger to protect himself from ever being hurt again. This was an opportunity to validate the client's perceptions, educate him on different types of anger, and collaborate on the goal of bypassing secondary anger and accessing underlying vulnerable feelings in an effort to expand the client's emotional repertoire. After this, whenever Paul reacted to painful material by lashing out, this served as a mutually recognized marker for the therapist to validate, for Paul to dampen his anger, and for both Paul and the therapist to explore more deeply.

Collaborate on the Goals and Tasks of Therapy

Asking clients about their motivations for seeking therapy aids in the formulation of treatment goals. Repeated references to what clients want, what is important to them, and their values and standards help in maintaining motivation throughout therapy. Many adult survivors of child abuse and other forms of trauma have lived for years with recurring trauma symptoms and other adverse effects. Many have previously participated in therapies that focused on current life issues (e.g., marital distress, depression, substance abuse) but not explicitly on resolving past trauma or abuse. The motivation for seeking therapy explicitly to resolve trauma/abuse issues typically is triggered by distress about one's current circumstances. These triggers frequently involve significant life changes and events, such as the birth of a child, a fear of repeating patterns of abuse or neglect with one's own children, marital distress, divorce or maybe starting a new relationship, and dealing with an aging parent whom one hates or fears. Some of the hopes people have for therapy are to improve current relationships by resolving past issues. In our clinic, whenever we have advertised the beginning of a treatment program, clients frequently report that they see this kind of treatment as an opportunity to put past issues to rest.

In the initial sessions, therapists also explicitly elicit client goals for therapy—what they want to change or hope to accomplish. For example, clients may wish to be free of intrusive symptoms or free of chronically underregulated anger or depression. They may wish to have better relationships with their spouses, children, parents, or members of the opposite sex in general. Other clients simply wish to be more in touch with their feelings and connected to life. It is important to help clients be specific about how these problems interfere with their lives and to envision how their lives would be better if they were free of such problems. Again, this contributes to motivation for change, is the basis for ongoing collaboration, and helps therapists stay on track in terms of client goals throughout therapy. It is essential to validate the importance of these healthy striving and assure clients that, as their therapist, you will do everything in your power to help them achieve these goals.

Identifying goals at the beginning of EFTT is a fluid and open-ended rather than a structured process. Because emotions are a source of information about values, concerns, and needs, they are directly related to goal setting. Empathic responses highlight the wants, needs, desires, longings, and action tendencies associated with client feelings and concerns. Goals (and more specific tasks) emerge from these personal details. For example, when a sexually abused client talks about feeling dirty, her therapist can respond to the pain of this, validate that it is not right to feel contaminated by another's actions, and state that an important part of therapy will be to help her feel better about herself. Similarly, the therapist response to a client who had never disclosed his abuse to anyone was, "That's a huge burden to carry alone, I do not want you to be alone with this stuff anymore." This strengthens the bond by offering support and highlights the implied goal of disclosure and mutual processing. Clients typically receive these responses with tremendous relief.

Goals also emerge from collaborative agreement about the underlying determinants of disturbance (e.g., the therapist might ask, "What has prevented you from connecting with others?") and from the assessment of client in-session processing difficulties, as presented earlier. Tasks are the therapeutic processes and procedures that will be used to address processing difficulties and achieve goals. So, working backward, task collaboration emerges from setting goals. Client and therapist need to agree about the most important tasks for the client to engage in, and the client needs to agree that these tasks will be useful in achieving his or her personal goals.

In Phase 1 of EFTT, the key tasks are to establish safety and trust so that clients can open up and disclose painful and personal material and to begin the process of experiencing, that is, attending to and exploring important feelings and meanings. Although in-depth work on changing maladaptive fear and shame, reprocessing traumatic experiences, and grieving losses does not begin until a later phase of therapy, clients nevertheless need to tentatively agree that engaging in these tasks will eventually help them achieve their goals. Collaboration takes place throughout therapy as new task markers emerge and new procedures for addressing these tasks are introduced.

CONDUCTING THE FIRST THREE SESSIONS

Because the first three sessions are critically important in setting the course for the remainder of therapy, the following sections provide guidelines for conducting these sessions.

Structuring the Initial Sessions

All the essential elements of EFTT are present in the first session. There is no distinction between assessment and treatment in terms of empathic attunement or in responding to client expressed or implied feelings and needs. Clients are informed that initial sessions will focus on both parties getting to know each other, feeling comfortable, and getting a clear understanding of the client's specific problems and what is contributing to them. Clients also are told that later sessions will focus explicitly on addressing these identified problems and any others that emerge in the course of exploration. Typically, clients are told that later sessions will focus on helping them feel better about themselves and work through traumatic experiences so they are no longer haunted by them, can feel more at peace, and can get on with their lives.

On a practical note, the gender of the therapist might be a concern for some clients. Female sexual abuse survivors, for example, often feel more comfortable with a female therapist, although many men also feel more comfortable opening up to a woman. Issues of gender (or age, ethnicity, sexual orientation, or any other therapist factor that potentially could be an issue) need to be brought out in the open by the therapist and discussed whenever relevant. As an aside, psychotherapy research generally has not shown matching on these therapist variables to be significant in predicting outcome (Beutler, Machado, & Neufeldt, 1994), but these are overall effects, which do not account for individual cases or the unique nature of relational trauma. In short, clients need to be given the opportunity to express their thoughts and concerns (if any) on this. Moreover, their concerns need to be validated, and, if possible, their preference in terms of therapist factors should be met. This is consistent with the principles of genuineness and openness and helps to avert possible alliance ruptures. In contrast to some other approaches, we do not advocate clients working with a therapist of the nonpreferred gender in the interest of providing a corrective learning experience (unless the client wants this), even though this has the potential to occur.

Another practical issue concerns the possibility of clients concurrently participating in other therapies. We do not advise simultaneous participation in another individual insight-oriented therapy for the usual reasons (e.g., conflicting goals, mixed messages, incompatible processes). However, we do advise that clients maintain their involvement in or seek support for behavioral problems, such as anger management, substance abuse, or eating disorders. It also may be to the client's advantage to concurrently participate in couples or family therapy, social skills training, or sexual assault groups.

In the case of antidepressant or anxiolitic medications, clients are encouraged to discuss continued maintenance or withdrawal from their medication regimen with their physicians. Psychopharmacotherapy can be extremely helpful for clients who are suffering from severe intrusive symptoms (Friedman, Davidson, & Stein, 2009). For example, one of our refugee trauma clients was so severely affected by nightmares that she would leave her children alone at night and wander the streets to try and calm herself. Children's Aid was brought in to help her with parenting practices suitable to North American society, and medication was helpful in alleviating her symptoms so that she could sleep and focus on adjusting to her new life in Canada. On the other hand, psychotropic medications are notoriously overprescribed (Kirsch, Moore, Scoboria, & Nicholls, 2002), and clients need to be informed that psychological interventions alone often can be effective for trauma-related disorders.

We begin the first session of EFTT by simply asking clients how they feel about being there. This "checking in" at the beginning of sessions, rather than asking clients about their week, focuses on present experience and concerns—a core intervention principle in experiential approaches such as EFTT. In the initial session, this also opens the door for discussing clients' motivations for seeking therapy and any hopes and fears about therapy. Again, hopes and motivations form the basis of therapeutic goals, whereas expressed fears and concerns provide the opportunity to clarify expectations and misperceptions and to address fears directly. Most clients are ambivalent about being in therapy, particularly trauma therapy, so it is important to acknowledge and validate this ambivalence. Even when clients do not admit to this, the therapist can tentatively suggest that they probably have some "mixed feelings" and nervousness about being there and suggest the types of anxieties that many clients have—for example, not knowing whether they can trust the therapist, disclosing personal and potentially embarrassing material, or being overwhelmed by painful feelings. Again, this is a way of opening the door for discussion, clarifying expectations, and addressing specific client concerns.

Sessions 2 and 3 typically begin with statements such as "How are your feeling about being here today?" "Have you had any thoughts about our last session?" "How would you like to spend your time today?" and "What seems like the most important thing to focus on?" Clients frequently begin talking about their week or their current concerns. Typically, the therapist also tentatively has particular session goals in mind that have emerged from the events of preceding sessions (e.g., to gather or clarify specific information), and she or he might address this immediately at the beginning of the session. However, it is important first to ensure that the client does not have some other pressing concern. Often, therapist goals or objectives for a session can be addressed in the context of client exploration.

Assessment

Assessment of client mental health and interpersonal history, as well as past and present functioning, also begins in the first session and can be approached in a semistructured interview format with content areas or themes that need to be covered in the first few sessions. However, instead of taking notes, which would change the relational tone, therapists give the client their undivided attention and are attuned to in-session indicators of cognitive–affective processing difficulties. Cultivating the relationship is the most important task at this point, so therapists should not be overly concerned about information gathering. Thus, it is important for therapists to make notes immediately following the session and identify goals for the next session in terms of filling information gaps or identifying and initiating particular processes.

An important part of the early phase of EFTT is to develop an understanding of current client problems or target complaints and to specify the situations in which these occur. In discussion, the therapist and client connect these problems to unresolved trauma, and the therapist explains how therapy can help. The latter is connected to client hopes for change and goals for therapy. In our clinic, the most prevalent target complaints have informed the treatment model and (in order of frequency) include (a) unresolved feelings (anger, fear, sadness, shame) toward perpetrators of abuse and neglect and attachment figures; (b) low self-esteem and self-confidence (i.e., depression); (c) poor self-identity and awareness of feelings; (d) interpersonal difficulties (e.g., nonassertiveness, social anxiety, chronic anger); and (e) specific trauma symptoms (e.g., nightmares and flashbacks).

It also is important to assess current symptom distress (e.g., posttraumatic stress disorder, depression, anxiety) and levels of functioning because information from global diagnosis, integrated with ongoing process diagnosis, has implications for treatment. For example, Phase 2 of therapy with a client who is depressed likely will focus on understanding and alleviating her depression. Our clinic is a research facility where administration of standardized measures is a part of the assessment procedure but, regardless of whether data from tests are used for research purposes, these can provide useful information to share with clients and form the basis of a dialogue about the items endorsed. It also is essential to assess clients' current strengths and resources (both internal and external). These will affect their capacity to cope with the stress of therapy, build self-esteem, and cultivate the therapeutic bond.

In the case of complex trauma, it is especially important to assess factors such as age of onset, duration, types of traumatic experiences (loss, abuse, neglect), as well as the resources and supports that were available while clients were growing up, because these have implications for treatment. For example, very severe abuse over a long period of time may be associated with greater disturbance and indicate a longer course of therapy, whereas the presence or absence of supports during a traumatic period can mitigate the extent of disturbance and therefore would have implications for a client's relationship capacity and treatment success.

During Phase 1 of EFTT, interventions also elicit client perceptions of those attachment figures who were perpetrators of abuse and neglect. This includes asking about a client's understanding of others' motives and behavior and their capacity to admit wrongdoing. Initially, client perceptions tend to be globally negative (i.e., referring to the "bad other") but become increasingly differentiated over the course of therapy. These initial perceptions are also a baseline for change and can indicate the client's capacity for empathy, which is thought to play a role in resolution. The issue of forgiving offenders also may emerge in the early phase of therapy, and it is useful to clarify what a client's definition or understanding of this is. In any case, EFTT therapists are interested in client's values, wishes, and desires in this area but are not advocates of forgiveness because it is not seen as a requirement for resolution (e.g., "My only goal for you is that you feel better about yourself and less torn up inside").

Particular interpersonal styles and personality pathologies also can pose challenges in terms of cultivating and maintaining a strong therapeutic relationship. Examples of relationship difficulties include extreme defensiveness and difficulties with trust, fear of negative evaluation by the therapist, performance anxiety during enactment procedures, hunger for intimacy and falling in love with the therapist, and high needs for therapist attunement and praise. Although abuse type and severity do not appear to be associated with outcome in EFTT (Paivio, Jarry, Chagigiorgis, Hall, & Ralston, in press; Paivio & Patterson, 1999), our research indicates that severity of personality pathology can have a negative influence on some dimensions of client change (Paivio et al., in press). Nonetheless, many clients with Axis II pathology are able to forge reasonable working alliances and significantly benefit from therapy. This is attributable to EFTT's unwavering emphasis on maintaining a strong therapeutic relationship, primarily by empathically responding to client feelings and needs. In the case of clients with long-standing and severe interpersonal difficulties, these feelings and needs could concern the therapeutic relationship itself.

Telling the Story

Within the relational context, the primary task during Phase 1 of EFTT is to help clients tell the story of their victimization. This topic is initiated directly (e.g., the therapist might ask, "I know some really bad things happened to you as a child, can you tell me about those?"). Although this is not a time for deepening experience, it is critical for therapists not to shy away from the client's emotional pain or from eliciting detailed information about the type and extent of trauma/abuse/neglect (e.g., "What exactly did he do? When did this begin? How long did it go on for? How often did this occur?"). The important thing here is to empathically respond to pain that the trauma has caused and the difficulty of dredging this material up in session with a perfect stranger, and to acknowledge the client's courage in doing so. The client's process of telling the story also provides an opportunity to assess relationship, emotion regulation, and experiencing capacities, as well as the client's capacity to focus on a circumscribed issue from the past and other aspects relevant to case formulation.

Telling the trauma story is a form of exposure, but the emphasis in EFTT is more on disclosure as well as affirming interpersonal support and acceptance rather than desensitization to the material. Again, the therapist responds to the clients' story with compassion for their pain and suffering, empathic affirmation of their vulnerability, and validation of their experience and perceptions (e.g., "This is terrible," "So sad," "What a shame," "That's not right"). These types of empathic responses strengthen the attachment bond and provide security and relief. Responses that highlight core adaptive emotions of anger or sadness, for example, begin to differentiate these from global distress or upset. This develops clarity about emotional experience and begins to counter prior invalidation or minimization of traumatic experience. Responses such as "It sounds like you missed out on so much" encourage elaboration and help clients symbolize the meaning of their emotion.

Empathic responses as clients tell their story also bring to light any problems with emotional underregulation. For example, the therapist might say to the client, "So you're feeling panicky remembering these things, like he can still hurt you. We need to help you feel less vulnerable." Or "Yes, it's so hard to talk about these things. That's OK, when you're ready, we can take all the time you need." This is similar for cases of emotional overcontrol. For example, a client felt guilty expressing her anger toward her mother for not protecting her from beatings, explaining that she did not want to blame her mother. Therapist interventions validated and empathized with her implicit desire to protect her mother and, at the same time, highlighted that, "in the process of protecting your Mom, you seem to squash your own feelings and needs." Two-pronged empathic responses such as this validate (and highlight) the negative impact of emotion dysregulation, while at the same time reflecting implicit wants and desires. Moreover, they keep the focus on client goals and help to maintain client motivation for change.

ALLIANCE DIFFICULTIES

This section outlines alliance difficulties and therapist errors that frequently occur in the early phase of therapy and provides suggestions for how to address them. Some of these (e.g., self-consciousness, task refusal, power and control issues with regard to the therapist, problems with attachment and collaborative issues) occur in many therapies. As such, established approaches to resolving similar alliance ruptures at any stage of therapy have been outlined by other experts (Elliott et al., 2004; Safran & Muran, 2000). In these approaches, markers for alliance ruptures tend to come in one of two kinds: clients confront the therapist directly (i.e., challenges, criticism, anger) or clients withdraw from the treatment process (i.e., passivity, nonengagement, distancing). In either case, the general process of resolving alliance ruptures begins with the therapist initiating a discussion of the difficulty and inviting the client to participate. This is followed by the therapist taking a nondefensive position while both parties present their side of the problem. Next, they arrive at a shared understanding of the difficulty and address any concerns that may have led to the rupture in the first place. In the last steps of this process, therapist and client identify relevant client needs that may have been at play in the rupture (i.e., needing more independence or more support) and then explore practical solutions to the problem, before moving on to productive work.

The following sections are organized in terms of difficulties with each of the components of alliance development that were specified in earlier sections of the chapter. We particularly focus on therapist errors that interfere with early alliance development.

Secure Attachment Bond Has Not Been Established

These difficulties primarily concern lack of warmth and intimacy in the therapeutic relationship. These can partly be a function of the client's attachment history and associated issues of distrust, hostility, defensiveness, or an externally oriented or intellectual stance that is devoid of feelings. However, difficulties establishing an attachment bond also can be a function of the therapist's style. The traditional cool, distant, and neutral psychoanalytic stance is not helpful with trauma survivors, particularly survivors of childhood maltreatment. Therapists may be empathically attuned to (aware of) client feelings and needs, but they are too much in the role of the objective observer and not emotionally involved and responsive enough. This observer stance is not conducive to a real relationship or intimacy. Neutrality heightens clients' anxiety, uncertainty, and the self-doubt in a way similar to what they experienced in childhood. Clients with trauma histories need to know where the therapist stands, which makes transparency and genuineness crucial to establishing safety and trust. In addition, helping clients articulate their experience when they are struggling to do so is an essential part of providing support. Traditional psychoanalytic reluctance in this regard is intended to promote client independence but can be perceived as withholding, especially by clients in this population who have a distrusting bias toward others, and is not conducive to a secure attachment.

Another therapist style to be wary of involves being overly directive. The problems of many trauma survivors stem from experiences of profound lack of interpersonal control. An empathically responsive, client-centered stance that is tentative when making process directions helps to restore a sense of control, reduces anxiety, and increases safety and trust.

Difficulties Related to a Focus on Emotional Processes

Client difficulties related to a focus on emotional processes include limited client capacity to attend to or regulate affective experience. Addressing these difficulties is the explicit focus of the second phase of EFTT and will be detailed in later chapters. Nonetheless, these client problems appear early in therapy and can interfere with the alliance and lead to retraumatization or dropout. Therapists therefore need to at least manage these difficulties early on. First, therapists should not be overly preoccupied with maintaining a focus on emotional experience but rather with being responsive to the client's main concerns. Any important concern is affective in nature. With clients who are more cognitively oriented and for whom a focus on feelings is foreign and awkward, responses such as "I hear how important that is to you" can be much more effective in building an alliance than responses that explicitly point at emotion (i.e., "sounds like you felt pretty hurt"). Optimal therapy is characterized by a therapist's flexibility in accommodating different client personalities and styles.

Therapists also can be too active and not give the client enough space to explore internal experience or can have a more expert rather than exploratory stance. Asking highly anxious clients about feelings or meanings instead of making tentative empathic responses can increase their anxiety, precipitate shutting down, and does not teach clients how to accurately label experience.

In terms of emotion regulation difficulties, at one end of the spectrum, client avoidance can be inadvertently reinforced by overly cautious therapists who tend to approach their clients with kid gloves. These therapists might avoid getting specific information about the type and extent of trauma/abuse out of their own timidity, for fear of overwhelming the client, or by being overly reverent in respecting client boundaries. This misguided reticence on the part of therapists in not asking about the details of abuse also tacitly communicates to clients that the content may be taboo. Therefore, it is best to adopt (and model) a matter-of-fact approach that helps to counteract the client's fear and avoidance. Although the early phase of therapy is not the time to deepen the exploration of trauma, therapists must generally take the lead in helping clients approach painful and threatening material.

On the other end of the spectrum, therapists who are not attentive or responsive to signs of client arousal and distress when those clients are disclosing painful material can contribute to client retraumatization. Consistent with the principles of systematic desensitization, it is crucial that clients begin to approach distressing trauma material in the early phase of therapy and that all efforts at approaching that material are success experiences by virtue of the safe and supportive context.

In sum, cultivating a safe and collaborative therapeutic alliance is the primary task and is the foundation of all other tasks and procedures in EFTT. Second to this, the other primary task is promoting client attention to, and exploration of, internal experience (experiencing) to construct new meaning. This is the focus of the next chapter.

6

PROMOTING EXPERIENCING

Disruptions in emotional competence and awareness are among the major long-term effects of complex relational trauma, yet recovery from trauma depends on these very client capacities. In addition, subjective internal experience, particularly affective experience, is the chief source of new information used in constructing new meaning in experiential therapies such as emotion-focused therapy for trauma (EFTT). Thus, the therapeutic relationship aside, all major procedures used in EFTT are dependent on a client's capacity to attend to and symbolize the meaning of affective experience (referred to as *experiencing*). Promoting as well as increasing client capacity in this area is the focus of this chapter. We describe the means by which therapists can facilitate the exploration of affective meaning at key moments from the beginning of therapy and through all of the phases of EFTT.

First, we describe the value and nature of deepening experience over the course of treatment, which provides a context for the dynamic process we are trying to foster. The chapter then outlines those qualities of the therapeutic environment that are most conducive to experiencing and identifies intervention guidelines for deepening the client's experiencing process. At the end of the chapter we describe a structured focusing procedure and then address common difficulties in promoting client experiencing.

RATIONALE FOR DEEPENING EXPERIENCE

As discussed in chapter 4, process and outcome studies have shown a strong relationship between in-session emotional experiencing, as measured by the Client Experiencing Scale (Klein, Mathieu-Coughlan, & Kiesler, 1986), and therapeutic gain in psychodynamic, cognitive, and client-centered therapies, as well as emotion-focused therapy for depression and trauma (see Greenberg & Pascual-Leone, 2006, for a review). Collectively, these findings suggest that experiencing is a common factor that helps facilitate change across theoretically different approaches. Other emerging research (Singh, Pascual-Leone, & Greenberg, 2008) has shown that therapists who consistently focus on deeper levels of client experience tend to elicit more shifts by the client among different emotion states (suggesting an increased emotion repertoire), as well as more meaningful types of emotional experiences (e.g., grief, assertion, self-soothing).

Experiential processing occurs spontaneously in some clients, and in these cases the therapeutic process proceeds with minimal intervention on the part of the therapist. The client Monica presented in earlier chapters was an example of such a case. For other clients suffering from complex relational trauma, however, difficulties with experiencing are part and parcel of the presenting concerns. In working with these individuals, therapists must continually highlight the experiential process, helping clients to experience, in session, new ways of being.

THE PHENOMENA OF DEEPENING EXPERIENCE

From an experiential perspective, clients' problems arise because affective information goes unrecognized or is restricted such that it is not available to inform and organize the individual adaptively (Greenberg, 2002). Awareness is increased through deliberate attention to and labeling of ongoing affective experience such that it becomes more highly differentiated and new emotion schemes are created and incorporated into one's repertoire (Pascual-Leone & Greenberg, 2006). The concept of experiential differentiation can be illustrated with the sensory example of wine tasting. To the uninitiated, all red wines taste more or less the same, perhaps only distinguishable from white wines, but as one is exposed to different wines, distinct features of flavor come to one's attention. With more and more exposure, the original monolithic experience of "red wine" develops into a variety of more subtly differentiated experiences of flavor that simply did not exist for the individual before. Moreover, this differentiation occurs in conjunction with, and partly as a result of, developing a more refined vocabulary for describing subtleties of flavor, for example, "dry" or "sweet" becomes more differentiated into "fruity," "earthy," "spicy," "smoky," and so on. The same process holds true for the experiential flavors of affect and meaning. Thus, a change in one's experiential landscape (J. Pascual-Leone, 1991) happens simply by virtue of it having been systematically explored and verbally articulated.

In exploring internal experience in a session, clients find themselves moving from one referent to another, and another. Each time the inward scene changes, new felt meanings are available for awareness. Thus, therapists must continually return to explore clients' feelings anew to make use of their expanding panoply of meanings. As a client's feelings are addressed and readdressed, they metamorphose and become more and more personally significant and tangible. The metamorphosis of that meaning structure occurs as if through the splintering of general schemes into more specific subschemes. The result is richer meaning and deeper feeling (Pascual-Leone & Greenberg, 2006; J. Pascual-Leone, 1990).

A therapist facilitates the client's elaboration of her or his ongoing experience through a progressive cocreation of meaning. For example, consider the client who was disciplined as a child by ridicule. Humiliation, sometimes sexual humiliation, was a way her parents used to control her behavior. Among her presenting concerns is that she feels anxious about interpersonal encounters. When her anxiety is first aroused in a session, the therapist encourages her to notice and describe, in the moment, the sense of nervousness inside her body and any thoughts or images to which it may be related. In doing this, the client begins to describe and experience the nervousness in slightly different ways. The act of attending to and describing the feeling changes it, and she reports that it becomes somewhat more about shame. As the uncomfortable feeling unfolds, the client continually symbolizes it in words:

> I'm uptight. I guess . . . I feel like I'm not very good socially and people will see that. I'm embarrassed . . . that I'm basically defective somehow, and I'm afraid that I will never be able to compensate enough for that. I'll just end up getting kind of ridiculed and rejected.

In this example, coming to symbolize new and more differentiated meaning is, in and of itself, an insight from emerging emotional experience. The initial vague sense of nervousness is not in itself productive, but it is elaborated into a personally significant, although painful, experience. The client comes to appreciate the core meaning that underlies her social anxiety. We return to this client example in chapter 9, when discussing shame.

It is critical to notice that the aim of facilitating experiencing is to produce deeper experience in the sense of more nuanced feelings and meanings, not necessarily more emotionally intense or aroused experiences per se. At times, it will be appropriate for therapists to support and facilitate client emotionality, for instance, when clients are disclosing painful material or in the early stages of confronting imagined perpetrators. However, as maintained in chapter 4, arousal is only an entry point for experiencing and frequently must subside somewhat in order for productive meaning exploration to occur. So, therapists need to acknowledge intense feelings but reduce arousal to open up the exploratory process (e.g., "I hear how absolutely beside yourself you are, it had such a big effect on you. Can you say more about how it has affected you all these years?"). Although emotion is fertile soil for meaning making, in the end, emotion plus meaning making is what leads to productive therapy, not simply the activation of affect on its own (Greenberg & Pascual-Leone, 2006).

THE VALUE OF DEEPENING EXPERIENCE OVER THE COURSE OF TREATMENT

Experiential interventions and the process of consistently promoting experiencing not only can lead to instances of insight or a fresh new awareness but also can produce a gradual shift toward a new way of engaging with self. Consider a client who came to treatment in the hopes of resolving issues related to physical and emotional abuse by his parents. Being disregarded and ignored had been commonplace in his childhood. When he got upset his feelings were minimized and ridiculed, and he was usually told he was overreacting. As the therapist and client explored key issues related to his childhood experiences, it became increasingly clear that, although distressed, the client was very uncertain about what his own thoughts and feelings about these events actually were. Similarly, in his adult life he was filled with doubts about his feelings and values, he often changed his mind, and he felt controlled by the demands of his elderly mother, his wife, and society at large. As he tried to appease these unrelenting demands, he was riddled with confusion and guilt about his own needs and desires because they conflicted with these external standards.

Therapists can help clients like this, who are self-effacing and who stifle their own experience, by redirecting them again and again to attend to and explore their internal experience. As a therapist encourages a client to attend to an internal referent, even one that is hardly there at first, it becomes elaborated and more salient. Cultivating this kind of inward awareness eventually provided the client with a reliable source of wisdom, an internal guide. The client in the above example began to more easily identify and have confidence in his gut feelings and opinions (e.g., "I do not want to spend the rest of my life doing a job I hate. It just feels like such a waste to me."). Practicing attention to and articulating the meaning of his affective experience in session both helped strengthen the client's sense of self and provided him with direction in the face of ongoing life events.

QUALITIES OF THE THERAPEUTIC ENVIRONMENT CONDUCIVE TO EXPERIENCING

Some qualities of the therapeutic environment are more conducive to the exploration of affective experience and meaning than others. Cultivating these qualities can be particularly important when working with clients who have learned to minimize or fear their internal experience, as is the case with many survivors of complex trauma. The following sections give guidelines for cultivating an environment that will facilitate deeper levels of client experiencing. This process begins in Phase 1 of therapy.

Maintain a Consistent Focus on Feelings

Promoting experiencing is an essential part of emotion coaching that begins in the first session of EFTT and was presented in the preceding chapter on alliance development. As such, responses that frame problems in feeling terms and communicate valuing of emotional experience and expression are the foundation for deepening client experiencing (e.g., the therapist might say to the client, "This must be so painful—it's like you are your own worst enemy" or "It must be so lonely to keep that secret all these years"). Responses that focus on affective experience implicitly and sometimes explicitly give permission to the client to experience and express what often are confusing, frightening, and intensely negative or painful feelings. Therapy, like any social engagement, is filled with subtle cues that indicate to clients what type of behavior and what tone are acceptable, desirable, or appropriate. Valuing and validating emerging feelings communicates to clients that the usual restrictive social norms concerning intense emotion do not apply in this context. For example, the therapist might say, "I understand part of you must really hate him for what he did," and the client might reply, "I do. I hate him. I used to wish he was dead and then I'd feel guilty." This is especially important in therapy with trauma survivors who fear that others will minimize, misunderstand, or negatively evaluate their feelings and/or may have internalized these attitudes themselves.

This focus on feelings not only is central to exploring affective meaning in EFTT but also is considered essential to the task of emotional processing of trauma memories in general. Research from a variety of theoretical perspectives has indicated that a cognitive emphasis is counterproductive to emotional processing of trauma memories. In a meta-analytic review, Foa, Rothbaum, and Furr (2003) concluded that when exposure therapy was augmented with other cognitive–behavioral interventions (e.g., cognitive restructuring), the combination can actually decrease the effectiveness of treatment with respect to emotional processing. This suggests that a cognitive emphasis can be an impediment to working through difficult emotion perhaps because it serves as a distraction from affect.

Another line of research has argued that worry is distinct from and antithetical to the "working through" necessary for emotional processing (Borkovec, Alcaine, & Behar, 2004). Worry is understood by these researchers as a cognitive response that orients individuals to a threat while at the same time insulating them from the immediacy of emotional experience. The cognitive, verbal-linguistic behavior of worry suppresses potentially evocative imagery, underlying meanings, and even somatic activity. In this way, rumination can block the natural course of experiential processing. Thus, EFTT interventions direct clients' attention to exploring the core emotional processes that underlie chronic worry (e.g., a core sense of self as inadequate, fragile, or flawed).

Ensure Optimal Arousal

Very high levels of arousal interfere with the capacity to explore meaning. Clients who are processing a profound loss, for example, may need to have "a good cry," but arousal must diminish before they can really explore the meaning of the loss in their lives. Even so, arousal must be sufficiently high to activate relevant emotion structures so that meaning is available for exploration. Thus, to promote experiencing, interventions need to help clients modulate levels of arousal.

Cultivate a Client's Attitude of Curiosity and Exploration

Interventions that encourage clients to pay careful attention to their feelings, needs, concerns, and perspectives promote an attitude of interest in, respect for, and valuing of self. The therapist can make this an explicit part of collaborating on the task of exploring affective meaning (e.g., "Let's try and understand how this works for you, how you always end up feeling like the bad guy" or "Somehow it's hard to believe you deserve better?"). Clients need to be aware that experiencing is both discovering and creating meaning and that answers to their problems do not exist a priori. This helps to promote tolerance for ambiguity as well as client agency in solving emotional problems.

Create an Environment Conducive to Internal Focus

Clients in trauma therapy frequently are tense and focused on describing external situations and the behavior of negative and abusive others, or they may talk continuously so it is difficult for the therapist to intervene at all. The therapist's interventions in these instances need to help the client relax and slow down the process (e.g., "Wait, wait, so, all this was going on and I'm wondering—What's it like for you to tell this story? This is worth slowing down for. Take a minute . . . What's going on inside?"). The aim is to help clients become introspective and self-reflective, and learn to be comfortable with a pensive silence so they can hear their internal processes. This is similar to an environment that would be conducive to mindfulness meditation.

Maintain Interpersonal Contact

Experiential processing takes time, and clients vary in the amount of time they need to symbolize and fully process a given experience. Productive silence can occur naturally when the client is searching internal experience. Therapists would do their best to attend to these moments and resist "filling in the spaces." However, silence should not go on for too long because clients can easily lose focus or direction. The principle here is to respect the client's need for silence and at the same time maintain contact. Therapists need to periodically invite clients to share what they are experiencing (e.g., "Can you tell me what you are thinking/feeling right now?"). Constructing meaning in EFTT is not a solitary but a collaborative process. When processing is productive, clients typically will simply share their experience (e.g., "I was just thinking how strange it is that I have let this go on for all these years, sad really").

Explore Positive Experiences

Finally, it is important to differentiate and explore positive as well as negative and troubling experiences. We find that after teaching trainees how to use an experiential approach, they often become "negative-centric," as if there was no other experiential material to deepen when the client has nothing upsetting to talk about. However, successful therapy also includes recognizing, attending to, and exploring client accomplishments, successes, and pleasures, both past and present, and inside and outside of therapy. Thus, clients' positive feelings of pride, comfort, satisfaction, or joy are equally important targets for deepening experience. Doing this contributes to self-awareness and self-development and strengthens the attachment bond.

INTERVENTION GUIDELINES FOR PROMOTING EXPERIENCING

There are two stages to facilitating deeper emotional experiencing in EFTT. At the first stage, during exploration of trauma feelings and memories, the focus of attention is on personally meaningful and affectively charged material, not simply behavior or events. This is a requirement for moderate levels of experiencing. The second stage, however, is exposure to new information, which involves deliberate self-examination. This second stage consists of deliberately searching inward to access memories, images, beliefs, feelings, desires, values, bodily sensations, and so on, and then symbolizing these in words and concepts and integrating them into existing perspectives.

A client's level of engagement necessary for trauma work involves reexperiencing the narrated past (e.g., "I remember sitting alone thinking there must be something wrong with me"). At the same time the client must remain engaged with the present moment, which sometimes contrasts and at other times complements or informs the past narrative (e.g., "Now that I tell the story I feel angry at the betrayal and violation I suffered"). Productive experiencing is characterized by an internally focused vocal quality, indicating a reflection that is unrehearsed and searching. This is often characterized by pauses as the client concentrates and gropes toward new meaning (Rice & Kerr, 1986). These are indicative of good process that the therapist should encourage and support (e.g., "Stay with that, take your time" or "Keep your fingertip on that gut feeling, it's important"). Of course, externally oriented clients eventually return to the default of an external stance, but these repeated forays into idiosyncratic meanings and feelings facilitate experiencing.

Next, we provide general intervention guidelines for promoting deeper experiencing. These methods serve as the foundation for addressing client difficulties with experiencing and for the more complex tasks and interventions discussed in later chapters.

Empathically Respond Rather Than Ask Questions

As noted in chapter 2, tentative empathic responses by the therapist (e.g., "I imagine it must leave you feeling so wounded and betrayed") have advantages over direct questions about how clients are feeling because they serve both emotion regulation and labeling functions. These responses reduce anxiety because clients do not feel put on the spot, and they feel less isolated and understood. Also, the therapist who bluntly asks "What are you feeling?" presents the client with a difficult kind of recall/construction task, whereas the client might be better presented with a recognition task (i.e., "Is it something like this?"). In this way, when a client seems to have difficulty identifying an emotional experience, a therapist's empathic conjecture offers the client an opportunity to check his or her internal experience against a plausible example (e.g., the therapist might say, "I imagine you must feel quite resentful at times—like you can't count on her when you need her?"). Even if the conjecture is not accurate, so long as it is a tentative attempt, clients will modify or correct their therapist, which is easier than being asked to articulate or construct a symbolization from scratch. For instance, the therapist might ask, "Maybe you feel . . . resentful?" In reply, the client might say, "No, not really 'resentful' . . . but kind of 'let down,' I thought she was my friend, friends are supposed to support each other." This type of tentative empathic conjecture also models an exploratory approach in the experiencing process.

First Affirm, Acknowledge, or Validate, Then Explore

The overarching task of EFTT is to help a client fully appreciate an experience, including its various meanings and affective nuances, and then help that client further explore some implicit aspect of it. However, clients who are highly vulnerable, uncertain, or insecure about the value of their experience benefit from assurances that they have been heard and understood before they are able to move forward. In instances of extreme vulnerability, when clients are feeling nervous or ashamed about emerging experience— disclosing instances of sexual abuse, for example—their vulnerability needs to be affirmed (e.g., the therapist might say, "Yes, I understand, it feels like a tremendous risk even just to mention it"). Moreover, the sense of vulnerability will have to decrease before the experience can really be examined. Many survivors of complex trauma are uncertain about whether their feelings and perspectives are legitimate or normal. When this is the explicit or implicit client message, therapists need to validate their client's feelings or perspectives before inviting exploration (e.g., "Of course you're nervous—these things are very difficult to talk about").

After acknowledging or validating a client's experience, the therapist may have a sense of what might be particularly productive to explore more fully. This is especially important when clients themselves are unclear about their trajectory for self-exploration. Thus, following a validation with an empathic exploratory statement helps move the process forward (e.g., the therapist might say, "That sounds important, feeling 'invisible.' Can you say more about that?"). Once again, however, this requires a tentative stance, one that is exploratory rather than prescriptive. Clients are ultimately the experts of their own emerging experience. Thus, in facilitating experiencing, the client, not the therapist, is the original author of any insight or new awareness. In this way, therapists are left with the precarious job of helping their clients discover something that they, themselves, are not privy to (Pascual-Leone & Greenberg, 2006).

Differentiate Global Hurt, Upset, and Distress

Emotional experience needs to be sufficiently specific before the underlying experience can be put into words. The emotional-processing model presented in Figure 3.1 and the model of resolution on which EFTT is based (see chap. 3, this volume) suggest that when a client's experience is undifferentiated hurt, upset, or global distress, then the client cannot hope to articulate any specific meaning. Specific meanings emerge only from an increasingly specific emotional experience. Thus, differentiating global upset or distress into discrete emotions is a necessary step in promoting exploration of meaning and thereby moving the process forward. Again, this is because discrete emotions are associated with particular information used in the construction of new meaning: Adaptive anger at violation or sadness at separation and loss can help modify maladaptive meaning associated with fear and shame. Promoting experiencing thus requires exploring and integrating the context-relevant meaning associated with specific discrete emotions.

Explore All Facets of an Emotional Episode

Any important affective event is encoded as a multimodal network of information (i.e., an emotion scheme or structure), and experiencing entails activating the structure to deliberately explore its components. When a client definitively states that he or she feels a certain way (e.g., "Well, it's embarrassing, nothing else"), many therapists who are learning to work with emotion have difficulty knowing how to explore the issue further, and the therapeutic process can get stuck or redundant. However, labeling an emotion is only one part of the process. This is because most of the elements in an emotional experience are tacit. As discussed in chapter 3, emotions can be thought of as richly packed units of information, and helping to unpack or elaborate that information or meaning is what facilitates client experiencing.

In an effort to describe the components of an emotional experience in response to a given situation, researchers have developed the construct of an emotion episode (Greenberg & Korman, 1993; Pos, Greenberg, Goldman, & Korman, 2003). Although this was initially intended as a research tool, being familiar with the essential components of an emotion episode can provide direction for therapists intending to explore a client's feelings beyond simply labeling them. Accordingly, when a client refers to a particular feeling (e.g., sad, happy, afraid, embarrassed), the given emotion usually entails the five following elements or facets of experience, each of which might be points for exploration.

Situation/Interpersonal Context

This emotion context is typically the stimulus or circumstances of the emotion (e.g., a client says, "I have failed in yet another marriage" or "My mother left me alone while she went off with her boyfriend"). The situation/interpersonal context of an emotion episode may be presented as part of an external narrative—the plot and characters.

Action Tendency

Because one of the purposes of emotion is to organize a person for some response or behavior, emotional experiences are almost always accompanied by some kind of action or a will toward action. In fact, sometimes clients first present an action tendency (e.g., "I felt like kicking the door in" or "I wanted to just crawl into bed and pull the covers over my head"). From a purely behaviorist perspective, an action tendency is the operational definition of an emotion. From an experiential perspective, an action tendency is one facet of a complex experience that is laden with personal meaning to be explored. Specific emotions go hand-in-hand with certain action tendencies. For example:

- Anger organizes one to fight and defend one's boundaries.
- Fear organizes one to run, flee, and escape, possibly by freezing.
- Shame organizes one to hide oneself from the scrutiny of others.
- Sadness organizes one to seek comfort or to withdraw and conserve one's resources.
- Disgust organizes one to spit out or reject some noxious experience.
- Guilt organizes one to repair some situation.
- Love, happiness, curiosity, and other positive emotions organize one in different ways to reach out, share, celebrate, and explore.

Labeling the emotion and the associated action tendency helps root the client in the concrete meaning of an experience and opens the way to further elaboration (Greenberg & Paivio, 1997). Action tendencies also are the concrete manifestation of particular needs and serve a motivational function, which is discussed below.

Somatic Component

Emotions are "embodied." Just as a given feeling entails an action tendency, both of these facets will be related to some bodily experience. Anger involves adrenaline and energy, sadness involves sapping of energy, anxiety may be associated with tension in the shoulders or a knot in one's gut, and so forth. Unlike action tendencies, these somatic elements are not usually indicative of particular goal-oriented behavior, rather they represent a preverbal aspect of meaning that can be captured in a client's metaphors or images (e.g., "I have butterflies in my stomach" or "I feel warm inside, imagining her beside me"). Helping clients to describe their bodily experience is another way to solidify it and create an entry point for exploring meaning. As we will see, focusing (Gendlin, 1996) is a technique that can be especially useful for elaborating affective meanings via the somatic component of an experience.

Unmet Interpersonal or Existential Need

When emotions are differentiated enough, they organize a person for action toward some implicit goal. The fundamental need or wish that is central to any emotion is of primary importance in EFTT. Similarly, psychodynamic therapy has highlighted the importance of becoming fully aware of the "wish" that usually drives a client's core relationship theme (Luborsky, Popp, Luborsky, & Mark, 1994). Thus, therapists in EFTT need to be attuned to core interpersonal or existential needs. These drive affective and cognitive goal-oriented behavior.

Research on the process of resolving distress presented in Figure 3.1 (Pascual-Leone & Greenberg, 2007) has shown that in productive sessions, articulation of some unmet need typically is the bridging point between a maladaptive emotion (e.g., crippling shame, collapsing into fear) and emerging adaptive responses (e.g., assertion, self-soothing). Although clients may not be able to identify their needs as such, problematic experiences presented by clients are usually about unmet needs. This is especially the case in EFTT when client problems stem directly from unmet attachment needs in development. The verbal symbolization of existential or interpersonal needs related to complex trauma is pivotal in the full elaboration of the meaning of these experiences (e.g., a client might say, "I needed love, affection, even just some acknowledgment that I was there!" or "What he did was just wrong— we deserve justice!"). Thus, accessing and expressing these core needs is central to helping clients move through the phases of therapy and toward resolution of interpersonal trauma.

Concern Regarding the Self or Self-in-Relation-to-Other

Self-related difficulties observed in EFTT usually concern feelings of insecurity and worthlessness that stem from negative experiences with attachment figures. The articulation of these concerns usually emerges as the client explores the effects that traumatic experiences have on personal identity, hopefulness, and relatedness to others (e.g., "Maybe I'm just an angry person,

I wish I weren't like that"). Concerns about the self are usually relatively easy to access in clients who are already emotionally aroused; sometimes it is sufficient to guide a client from the situation and circumstances to focusing more on the personal ramifications. For example, a client might say, "She just stood there and watched him beat the crap out of me!" and the therapist might respond, "So, somehow that says something about both of you—the fact that she didn't intervene?" These concerns can be explored in interaction with the therapist, in two-chair dialogues between parts of the self, or in imaginal confrontation (IC) with an imagined other.

Recalling these five aspects of an emotion episode can be a useful strategy for deciding where or how to explore further when therapists feel stuck and clients present their feelings as deceivingly straightforward. Moreover, because these elements of an emotion structure are linked together in a network, elaborating one such facet of experience can lead to each of the others. Addressing each of these facets is a potential avenue for further exploration.

Move From Concrete to More Abstract Aspects of Experience

The principle of exploring all facets of an emotion scheme assumes that experience needs to be activated. To make an emotion episode vivid in a client's immediate experience, therapists could begin activating the network from any of the components described above. However, when clients are not aware of specific emotions, exploration moves best from concrete sensations (i.e., bodily felt sense, action tendencies, concrete images) to more complex and abstract aspects of experience (i.e., thoughts, feelings, desires, needs), not vice versa. In EFTT, just as in eye movement desensitizing and reprocessing or in anger management therapies, for example, clients are taught to use bodily experience as a source of information about emotion or arousal states. However, the aim of experiencing is to symbolize the meaning of affective experience. This is a higher level process or skill than just increasing an awareness of affective experience.

In contrast, if a client already can identify her feelings (e.g., anger), directing attention to her associated bodily experience typically will not move the meaning-making process forward. Similarly, if a client already knows what he wants or longs for (e.g., to be treated with respect) and the experience is vividly experienced in the moment, then directing his attention to embodied action tendencies (e.g., the impulse to fight back) will not usually move the process forward. In these situations, when clients are already aroused and in touch with the more complex and abstract aspects of their experience, it is more useful to move directly to helping them articulate the meanings associated with those feelings in the context of self, others, and interpersonal relatedness.

Listen for the Implied Message

Most training manuals on basic psychotherapy and counseling skills distinguish between the explicit and implicit aspects of a client's communication and emphasize the importance of responding to the implicit message. This has been called responding to the "leading edge" of experience (Gendlin, 1996) because responses that highlight this aspect of experience move the process beyond what is merely being stated. Thus, empathic reflections, directives, questions, or interpretations that focus on the implied message promote deeper experiencing. For example, the client says, "She's the adult, she should be looking after that, not me!" and the therapist responds, "I hear how much you resent being saddled with that burden, almost being *her* mother rather than the other way around. I imagine you would love some mothering of your own at times." The caveat is that the therapist is responding to a client's *intended* message, which is on the periphery of awareness, not to material that the client wants to keep hidden or private. Responding to the latter (e.g., confronting defenses) can evoke defensiveness and shame.

Therapists can respond to a client's implied message by making small inferences or attending to overt nonverbal cues. As clients explore, the focus of their attention shifts such that what was an implicit meaning in one moment may be made explicit in the next, dynamically moving the dialogue forward. Even so, some meaning is beyond the reach of the client's verbal symbolization. The client experiences this implicit meaning as a preverbal intuition, a "felt sense" to use the words of Gendlin (1996). Through lack of support and repeated experiences of invalidation, survivors of complex trauma frequently are unable to articulate their gut sense of how things were. Therapist responses that capture this aspect of experience will have to glean meaning from, say, the client's tone of voice, an unanticipated pause or pattern of speech, or incongruence in the implicit or explicit message. When a therapist is able to tentatively put words to this felt sense, clients often immediately recognize it as their own intended meaning. This process of tentatively offering the client meaning that may barely be out of reach provides a scaffolding and expands the client's horizon of awareness, thereby facilitating experiencing.

Attend to Subdominant Affect and Self-Organizations

Experiencing is a highly dynamic process. Whether an existing experiential state is an ephemeral one or is a stable feature of the client's personality, the most salient experience is always in dynamic competition with other lesser activated states. These potential states can be thought of as subdominant experiences that exist in the background yet bleed through and color the dominant affective-meaning state, sometimes in subtle ways (Greenberg & Pascual-Leone, 1995; A. Pascual-Leone, 2009). This is comparable with gestalt (Perls, Hefferline, & Goodman, 1951) ideas of conflict between the dominant "top dog" side of personality and the weaker experiencing self or "underdog" and with current constructivist views of multiple selves or voices working in harmony or disharmony (Hermans, 1996). From an EFTT perspective, subdominant experiences often characterize those more fragile parts of the self that embody authentic feelings and needs and adaptive resources, which have been squashed or damaged by trauma. Therapists looking to facilitate an emotional transformation in their clients by way of experiential exploration need to be attuned and responsive to these weaker subdominant self-organizations.

Consider a client whose core sense of self is that she is worthless or bad. This maladaptive state or emotion scheme is a network of feelings and meanings that gets activated across situations. Perhaps the sense of being bad is elicited in therapy by imagining an abusive and critical parent during IC. The client describes the most salient facets of her experience as fear of being berated by the parent. As she describes this experience, she sometimes lowers her eyes in what might be embarrassment or shame and sometimes grits her teeth in what seems like a flicker of anger. She describes wanting to freeze or hide and, as she says this, she tightly grasps the armrest of her chair. Unmet needs for security, safety, and protection are at the center of the maladaptive experience of fear. As these thoughts and feelings are activated in therapy, it leaves the client drained of energy and with a sinking feeling in her stomach. Part of the implicit meaning entailed in this state is captured by her thoughts of "I'm bad" (shame), "I'm going to get it!" (fear), and "There's nothing I can do about it" (powerlessness), but she also says "I hate him" (anger) when referring to the critical parent.

Therapists attuned to the nuances of experiential process notice signs of shifting affect and meaning in the form of nonverbal cues, fragments of meaning, or emerging incongruous emotion. In the above example, fear is the dominant aspect of experience, whereas shame and anger are subdominant. Therapist interventions could focus on either of these subdominant aspects depending on the intentions of intervention. In Phases 1 or 2 of EFTT, the therapist might want to focus on exploring underlying shame that prevents this client from holding the father accountable for harm. As therapy progresses, however, the therapist may want to increase the client's awareness of adaptive anger at maltreatment, and possibly help her express this to the imagined father in IC. In such a case, the therapist would be attuned to transient instances when the client grits her teeth, clenches her fists, deepens her voice, and feels anger toward her abuser. By drawing attention to these traces of anger, interventions orient the client's attention to a different set of affects and meanings besides fear such that they gradually move to the foreground. Any verbal or nonverbal sign of the subdominant emotion scheme could be used as a point of elaboration. For example:

C: [*under her breath, clenching her teeth*] I hate him.

T: Yeah, hate him, like he's a big bully, picking on you and scaring you. I'm sure you'd like to make him go away, leave you alone!

Or, T: Clench your fists some more. It's like you just want to fight back . . . does that fit?

Finally, facets of experiences that are attended to always become increasingly salient and, as the newly emerging process is symbolized in words, the once subdominant experiences of assertion and anger shift to the foreground and become dominant while the experience of maladaptive fear becomes background, at least for the time being. When anger is attended to and accessed, the client feels she wants to stand up and shout "Stop it!" at her imagined abuser. She feels mobilized to assert herself and has a sense of "I don't deserve this," "This is wrong," and "I'm OK the way I am." This particular manner of facilitating deeper experiencing is a central part of two-chair and IC interventions that we will return to in later chapters.

GUIDELINES FOR FOCUSING TO PROMOTE EXPERIENCING

Gendlin (1996) developed the focusing method for systematically helping clients to attend to and verbally symbolize the meaning of bodily felt experience. This is similar to the process of guiding clients, by empathic responding, to focus on personal aspects of their story, except that while the clients' personal narrative usually flows from the plot and characters of the story, focusing flows from bodily or visceral experience that is then translated into words and elaborated. In short, this is a specific task that follows the intervention guideline mentioned above: Move from concrete to more abstract aspects of experience. So, focusing is successful when clients synthesize various aspects of their immediate psychophysical experience with their linguistic-based understanding and are able to capture in words an aspect of their own subjective world that was previously unclear.

Gendlin (1996) described, from an experiential/humanistic perspective, specific sequential steps in this focusing process. Some cognitive–behavioral therapy approaches incorporate abbreviated or modified versions of this procedure as a way to reduce client confusion about their internal experience and thereby reduce anxiety (e.g., Bourne, 2003). All of the steps in the focusing procedure can be used systematically in EFTT as a way of teaching the skill of experiencing, or individual components of the focusing procedure (e.g., finding words to describe bodily experience) can be used piecemeal as needed in the process of therapy. The basic principles of focusing are implicitly incorporated into most of the major procedures used in EFTT. The chapters that follow have many examples of how these principles are incorporated into various other EFTT interventions.

Focusing is indicated when clients are unclear or confused about their feelings regarding some situation or circumstance. The problem situation could be past or present so that focusing could be incorporated as part of reexperiencing trauma memories. At a suitable moment, the therapist might explicitly identify the marker, then follow with an invitation to explore further to understand the experience. For example, when the client says, "I don't know, I just feel tense or something, I don't know what it's about," the therapist might respond, "Mmm, it's hard to put your finger on it. Let's take some time to help you get clear." The following sections summarize steps in the focusing procedure as used in EFTT.

Relaxation, Calming, and Freeing the Mind of Distractions

The first step is similar to the procedure of mindfulness meditation. Once clients agree to spend time understanding their experience, they can be guided through breathing or progressive muscle relaxation exercises (as needed) and encouraged to free their mind of distractions and gently focus their attention inward, with no pressure or forcing, just noticing (e.g., the therapist might say, "So, can you take a deep breath? [*Therapist models, client follows*] Right, so that's a big sigh. What do you notice inside?").

For clients who have difficulty regulating their emotions, learning to relax and free their mind of distractions may be an important treatment goal in and of itself. This is in line with the mindfulness-based practices in dialectical behavior therapy (Linehan, 1993). However, for clients who are sufficiently able to tolerate difficult or ambiguous feelings and for whom the goal is to facilitate deeper experiencing, the subsequent focusing steps will be useful in carrying the process forward.

Attending to Bodily Felt Experience

Individuals then are instructed to attend inward to "that place in your body where you feel your feelings" or to the particular sensation or felt experience they have identified. They are encouraged to attend to the entirety of the experience, "the whole of it," rather than to analyze the experience. Sometimes clients are only aware of feeling overwhelmed, "dead," or "blank" inside, but if they can patiently attend to the flow of this experience, things inevitably develop and one particular issue will become more salient. It is essential to help clients cultivate an attitude of gentle receptiveness, to let things naturally evolve, not to struggle to find answers or intellectually figure anything out. When clients feel overwhelmed by multiple issues, the therapist can encourage them to focus on one thing at a time (e.g., "Pick one problem for now and push the other issues aside, just for the time being").

Finding the Right Words

Once clients are directed inward toward an unclear felt sense, they arrive at the task of symbolizing it somehow. Therapists can help by guiding clients to search for and check potential descriptors for this experience (e.g., "What is the quality of that feeling/sensation in your chest? Is there a word, phrase, or image that seems to fit?"). However, in using bodily experience as an entry point for exploration, clients should be encouraged to avoid describing their experience from the outside looking in and to avoid interpreting or explaining their experience. Rather, they should speak from the experience. This is like gestalt interventions that encourage clients to be that aspect of self (e.g., the therapist might say, "If your gut (or fist) could speak, what would it say?" or "Put words to your tears"). This type of bottom-up processing is characterized by an internally focused rather than external vocal quality in which the client is immersed in the experience rather than describing it from a distance (Rice & Kerr, 1986).

Although, at first, the choice of words for an internal experience may seem limitless, there ultimately are only a few select descriptors that will seem adequate. This is like a tip-of-the-tongue experience and only the correct word, image, or handle will fit and, when found, it will be immediately recognized. Getting a handle on these newly emerging feelings and meanings eventually yields an experience-near insight (Pascual-Leone & Greenberg, 2006).

Therapist empathic responses that stay close to the client's words and avoid any form of interpretation will facilitate this process. Empathic responses maintain contact with the client, communicate understanding, and function like a mirror to promote reflective clarity. For many clients who were raised in abusive and neglectful environments, their perceptions of self, the world, and others were shaped by tacit meanings that they were unable to identify and articulate as children. Helping these clients find the right words can be difficult but pivotally important in personal development and therapeutic change.

The process of finding the right words involves shifting back and forth between the descriptor or image and the felt sense itself. This is a way of checking for the "fit" and making adjustments in an effort to improve the descriptor and create a match between the experience and the verbal or imagistic representation. Again, this is similar to the process involved in the tip-of-the-tongue phenomenon in which one tries out and rejects different words in an effort toward better symbolization through successive approximations. Once the correct descriptor is found, there is a felt shift (or a mini "Ah-ha!"), a bodily experience of fit that goes with a kind of relaxation of effort. Tentative empathic conjectures aid in this process as a client and therapist coexplore the client's experience. For example:

C: I don't know, it's just like this dark empty feeling.

T: Dark, empty, sounds kind of bleak or sad . . . ?

C: Something like that, more like just this dead zone, a lifeless feeling, or half alive.

T: Half alive, like something's missing . . . ?

C: Yes, a lot missing . . . joy, that's what's missing. There's no joy in my life. There hasn't been for years, and I just can't see any way of changing it.

In this example, the therapist tracks the client and they both grope for the right words until the client has a sense of having captured the new felt meaning.

Exploring the Experience

Once a client has tentatively symbolized an experience and it seems to capture the essence of that felt sense, interventions help the client explore further by contemplating the role of this experience with respect to the client's values, goals, or life. Gendlin (1996) referred to this step as *asking* because it involves contemplating exploratory questions that extend beyond the initial symbolization. Exploratory questions or exploratory empathic responses posed by a therapist nudge the client to expand his or her emerging awareness. For instance, in the above example, the therapist might say, "Something about feeling 'only half alive,' what would bring joy? What do you long for in your heart of hearts?" or "Trapped, something holds you back, keeps you locked up in that dreadful situation?"

Elaboration and Acceptance

The goal here is to expand the information network, to integrate the now-symbolized experience into existing perspectives, the broader context of the individual's life. Just as a well-attuned therapist closely tracks the process of the client, clients themselves must be encouraged to track their own evolving experience (e.g., the therapist might say, "Stay with that feeling, observe the flow") and then to communicate their emerging understandings to the therapist. Therapists' empathic responses, in turn, communicate understanding and encourage further elaboration. In another example:

T: So, it's about being alone, that's the main concern, like you can't handle it?

C: It's not, "can't handle it" exactly, but . . . lonely. I hate it.

T: OK, stay with that lonely feeling. It's uncomfortable, I know, but let's explore it a bit.

C: Like, I hate coming home from work, the apartment is so empty, we used to talk about stuff. She always seemed to understand, well, at least listen (*laughs*) . . . , like now I'm just floundering around . . .

T: Floundering, directionless. So, she was like your anchor, it's like you were so very attached to her.

C: Yes, I guess I was.

T: And now she's gone, you've become unattached, not only lonely but kind of insecure?

C: Yes, I do feel insecure, less confident, it's weird. I never realized how much I depended on her.

T: Say more, depended on her for what?

At times clients can feel uneasy or unwilling to acknowledge the reality of a tacit experience. The client in the above example never felt he could rely on others for support and had developed a fiercely independent style. So, he felt ambivalent about acknowledging this newfound sense of insecurity and neediness. Therapists must model and foster uncritical acceptance of the client's gut sense and the new experiential insight. Here it is useful to relate the "finding" of this process to the client's broader narrative as a way of both making sense of it and validating it.

Finally, even though there is naturally occurring variability in clients' capacities for experiencing, it is essential to treat experiencing as a skill that can be improved with practice—collaboration on skills practice is the first step. It is possible, for example, for the therapist to begin each session with some form of focusing on experience, either in a structured or open-ended format (e.g., "Let's take a couple of minutes to just focus inward and see what's the most pressing concern for you right now"). When clients find experiencing difficult, the therapist should enlist their permission to redirect their attention inward. Clients also can be encouraged to practice focusing at home.

ADDRESSING DIFFICULTIES WITH EXPERIENCING

The above sections have presented principles and strategies for promoting experiencing with clients who have at least minimal capacities in this area. As noted, research indicates that early in therapy most clients in EFTT achieve moderate levels of experiencing (i.e., a mode of Level 4) on the Client Experiencing Scale (see Appendix A; Holowaty, 2004; Ralston, 2006; Robichaud, 2005). This is characterized by exploration that is affective and personal. Sometimes, however, clients do not respond to therapist efforts and directives in this regard, and the experiencing process seems stuck at more external levels of processing. In these cases, the client repeatedly goes over the same material but the process itself seems stale and unproductive. Although material may be emotional in content, it is only contacted and engaged at a superficial or cognitive/intellectual level. As we shall see, some client difficulties with experiencing may be due to client factors, others are attributable to the therapist.

Unproductive Therapist Style

Unproductive therapist factors include frustration with and intolerance for the client's external style, as well as the therapist's own impatience or intolerance for ambiguity. Other impediments include a therapist attitude of "already knowing" rather than curiosity, or a focus on pathology and fixing problems rather than exploring experience. Sometimes therapists are simply pushing too hard. They may have unrealistic expectations for dramatic change (change usually occurs in baby steps), which goes along with an intolerance for backsliding (change usually moves in "two steps forward, one step back"). Counter to this, therapists need to encourage client patience, trust in the process, and discourage clients' effortful struggles to change or find quick answers. This is part of unconditional acceptance and fostering realistic hope.

On another note, consistency in focusing on affective experience is particularly important. Therapists not trained in emotion-focused therapies can unwittingly use language that connotes thinking rather than feeling. The difference here is subtle but often has an impact. This is consistent with the observation that clients pick up where therapists leave off. If therapists are subtly straying from the immediacy of emerging experience and arousal, then clients will follow their lead, and the discourse becomes more external or intellectual.

Assuming that the therapists' style is conducive to promoting experiencing, the following sections identify interrelated difficulties that are attributable to the client and offer suggestions for addressing them. Addressing all of these difficulties requires collaboration with the client about the nature of a difficulty and finding an appropriate intervention. For example, the therapist might say, "We seem to be going in circles here. We need to find a way to deepen the process, help you move forward."

Lack of Clarity or Confusion About Internal Experience

In these situations, clients might explicitly state that they are unclear or confused about their experience, that something is bothering them but they cannot clearly identify it. Alternatively, they are unclear about a focus for a session, or the session can be marked by unproductive silence and tense withdrawal in response to therapist invitations to disclose internal experience. In these situations, Gendlin's (1996) structured focusing procedure described earlier can be effective.

External Focus of Attention

Some clients not only have limited awareness of internal experience but also simply do not value it. This interferes with emotional processing of trauma material and with intimacy, including intimacy in the therapeutic relationship. The externally focused client who is in therapy to resolve trauma issues therefore is doubly handicapped. Markers of this difficulty appear in dialogue with the therapist and in the IC procedure where, despite therapist directives, the dialogue does not shift from blaming and complaining about the other's behavior and has a highly predictable, premonitored, "talking at" quality.

When client experiencing is externally oriented (i.e., Client Experiencing Scale Levels 1 and 2), the intervention strategy must move the client step by step to deeper levels of experiencing. This involves first helping the client tell a story that is more personal, beginning with the therapist making more references to self (e.g., "I guess *you* must have felt completely shut out"). If these efforts are fruitless, therapists need to be more directive and explicit in their intentions (e.g., "But what is it like for *you*, on the *inside*, when she turns her back on you like that? What were/are you thinking, or feeling in your heart, or in your body? Were you aware of saying anything to yourself?").

In these situations, it is important to have patience and realistic expectations. Attending to client markers of internal experience can momentarily shift them into a more internal mode. However, externally oriented clients typically will return to the less evocative, external narratives about plot and characters because it is familiar and less stressful. Even so, an experientially attuned therapist will attend to when clients make this type of deflection and then gently guide them back to feelings and meanings (e.g., the therapist might say, "Let's come back to what it was like for you, your perspective is so important here"). This will require agreement on the value of acquiring this skill of deeper experiencing and the use of intervention guidelines already described.

Difficulties Labeling Feelings

Some clients have noticeable difficulties when it comes to labeling feelings, which is one dimension of alexithymia. Interventions to address this include providing information about normal human emotions as well as skills training. Several principles apply here, including the use of empathic responses rather than questions to explore affective experience, and attention to bodily experience rather than emotions as entry points to deeper experiencing. The intervention process for clients who confuse emotional feelings with physical sensations is similar to focusing, except the internal referent is not so much an unclear or preverbal felt sense but rather a specific bodily sensation. In this way, the therapist can help clients to put words to their bodily experience (e.g., "This knot in your stomach, what is it telling you . . . this tight little ball?") and to identify the affective component of their concern (e.g., "So, you'll be lonely, or maybe afraid, on your own?").

Cognitive/Intellectual Style

Some social and cultural norms can be emotion-phobic, and emotional experiences and expressions can have all kinds of negative connotations, particularly for traumatized individuals. Clients can have a relatively restricted emotion repertoire and misconceptions about feelings (e.g., believing that feeling necessarily involves high arousal or weakness). Emotion coaching entails helping clients understand that their emotions are an important source of information about how to address their primary concerns. However, for some individuals who are more cognitively oriented or intellectualized, and who may not feel comfortable expressing feelings as such, helping to identify their values and concerns can serve as an alternative entry point for exploring affective experience. This is because values and concerns, even if they are expressed dispassionately, ultimately represent core needs that are central to emotional meaning; this is an approach of "digging where the ground is soft." Primary concerns related to self and self-in-relation-to-others (the focus of EFTT) are always affective in nature. For example, a highly intellectualized client struggled to identify his feelings about an impending separation from his girlfriend, even though he would only acknowledge that this was a source of "concern." The therapist helped him articulate the concern (e.g., "This is a problem, important to you because . . . ?") and, in the process, helped him identify the associated affective experience (worry, loneliness), which further opened up the process.

Silent Withdrawal

Difficulties with experiencing can result in unproductive silence during which clients are actually disengaging from the process. The silence may reflect clients' uncertainty about their internal experience, or clients may be safeguarding, perhaps feeling too vulnerable to continue. These silences are not just a lull in conversation; they have an awkward and tense quality to them. When therapists enquire, clients have difficulty articulating or seem reluctant to share their experience. Intervention involves collaboratively assessing the reason for the silence and drawing the client out, helping them reengage with the therapeutic process. Silences of this kind should be acknowledged or affirmed and are best addressed by the therapist tentatively reflecting the implicit meanings of the silence (e.g., "I get the sense you have withdrawn, moved far away from here [or me]" or "It seems like you've gone blank, like you've somehow shut down?"). This is a way of returning to productive processing in which the underlying issue itself (i.e., client reluctance to share experience) can be itself a topic of exploration.

As an example, one client was referred to EFTT by her psychiatrist whom she had been seeing with no progress for 5 years. Once in therapy, she was chatty and engaging when discussions concerned her daily life. However, she was completely silent in response to empathic exploration or questions that concerned the trauma (sexual abuse by several male relatives). This continued for the first 10 sessions. It took considerable patience on the part of the therapist and persistence in empathizing with how difficult engaging in therapy must be (e.g., "It must be very hard to talk about these experiences," "How lonely it must be for you to be shut up inside," "I imagine you wish the whole thing would just go away"). These empathic conjectures were important in building trust and initiating an exploratory attitude in session. Eventually the client began to open up, which then allowed for deeper therapeutic work.

In sum, this chapter on promoting experiencing and the preceding chapter on cultivating the therapeutic relationship have laid the foundation for EFTT. All major tasks and interventions used in therapy depend on these two fundamental processes. The following chapters focus on other major tasks and procedures.

7
THE IMAGINAL CONFRONTATION PROCEDURE

Once a secure attachment bond and a focus on internal experience have been established, it is time to begin in-depth trauma work with the introduction of the imaginal confrontation (IC) procedure. As noted in an earlier chapter, IC is generally similar to the gestalt-derived empty-chair intervention for resolving "unfinished business" that is described in other writings on emotion-focused therapy (e.g., Greenberg, Rice, & Elliott, 1993; Paivio & Greenberg, 1995). The new "IC" terminology places this procedure in the broader context of trauma therapies, emphasizes its affinity to other exposure-based procedures, and focuses on the confrontational nature of trauma exposure. As a quick overview: During IC the client imagines an offender in an empty chair and expresses evoked thoughts and feelings directly to this imagined other. The client is also encouraged to imagine or enact the other's reactions to the client's expressions and thereby to engage in a dialogue with the imagined other. In this context the client explores his or her own shifting perceptions of self, other, and traumatic events.

Introduction of IC usually takes place during Session 4. Research on emotion-focused therapy for trauma (EFTT) indicates that both emotional engagement with trauma memories during IC and the quality of the alliance early in therapy each independently contributes to client change (Paivio,

Hall, Holowaty, Jellis, & Tran, 2001; Paivio, Holowaty, & Hall, 2004). There is also a reciprocal relationship between these variables such that they overlap on the task agreement dimension of the alliance. The more clients agree on the value of core interventions, the better they are able to engage in them and vice versa. Thus, a strong alliance at Session 3 predicts productive engagement in IC at Session 4, which, in turn, strengthens the alliance and predicts the quality of subsequent trauma exploration and positive treatment outcome. Because of its critical importance to productive therapy, therefore, the present chapter focuses on how to facilitate high-quality engagement in the initial IC procedure.

In this chapter we outline the features and intervention principles relevant to IC, describe process measures that can be used to assess clients' progress through the resolution process, and review research on the client and therapist characteristics related to successful engagement in IC. This is followed by a detailed description of client processes and therapist operations during each step of the IC procedure, providing a roadmap of both short- and long-term goals. We also review those aspects of the therapeutic relationship that are critical to successful introduction and implementation of IC. The chapter concludes with a section on addressing client difficulties during IC and describes empathic exploration (EE) as an alternative procedure.

REVIEW OF THEORY AND RESEARCH ON REEXPERIENCING TRAUMA MEMORIES

Although trauma exposure can be stressful, through telling and retelling the story of their victimization, individuals learn that they can tolerate painful feelings and memories as well as develop a new understanding of traumatic events. Outcome research supports the efficacy of exposure-based therapies with diverse traumatized populations, including survivors of complex relational trauma (e.g., Cloitre, Koenen, Dohen, & Han, 2002; Paivio & Nieuwenhuis, 2001; Resick, Nishith, & Griffin, 2003). However, few studies to date have directly examined the benefits of exposure techniques.

Results of our research on EFTT (Paivio et al., 2001) indicate that emotional engagement with trauma memories during IC (assessed through observations of videotaped therapy sessions) contributed to multiple dimensions of client change and had independent benefits beyond alliance quality. When both the quality of engagement and the frequency of participation over the course of therapy were taken into account, IC was associated with a host of improvements, including reduced trauma symptoms, global symptom distress, and interpersonal problems, as well as improved self-esteem. Furthermore, among those clients who made clinically significant improvements, more were classified as being highly engaged during IC as compared with those who had low levels of engagement (71% vs. 39% recovered; 93% vs. 71%, reliably improved, respectively). The independent contribution of "dosage" of IC to outcome supports the posited role of this procedure in the emotional processing of trauma memories, where dosage is frequency of task by quality of engagement. Thus, the contribution of this dosage to reduced trauma symptoms is consistent with the effect of habituation processes cited in the literature. The additional contribution of dosage to reduced global symptom distress and interpersonal problems further suggests that the repeated confrontation of specific perpetrators of abuse or neglect generalized to more global dimensions of change.

THE IC FOR REPROCESSING TRAUMA MEMORIES

The following sections place IC in the context of other reexperiencing procedures and discuss the importance of the first IC dialogue.

IC Compared With Other Exposure-Based Procedures

Exposure procedures described in the literature range from clients simply telling their stories of victimization in client-centered and psychodynamic approaches (e.g., Fosha, Paivio, Gleiser, & Ford, 2009) to more structured approaches, such as eye movement desensitization and reprocessing (e.g., Shapiro & Maxfield, 2002) or cognitive–behavioral therapy (e.g., Chard, 2005; Cloitre et al., 2002), that incorporate aspects of prolonged exposure. Although specific techniques differ, in general, exposure systematically encourages clients to focus internally on troublesome aspects of trauma memories. When these stories are richly told, this facilitates attention to multimodal aspects of experience. Therapists monitor their clients' level of distress, acknowledging and accepting the emergence of any maladaptive beliefs or perceptions (e.g., self-blame). These continue to be processed until a shift occurs. Because traumatic events are thought to be largely encoded in experiential memory, reliving procedures used in all therapeutic approaches are intended to evoke experiential memories that include feelings, sounds, smells, images, and bodily experience. Once activated in therapy, this material is available for exploration, working through, emotional processing, and change.

The IC used in EFTT is one of these systematically implemented procedures; however, the manner of implementation and the frequency of client participation in IC vary depending on individual client processes and treatment needs. The process itself is based on an empirically verified model that identified steps in the process of resolving past interpersonal issues, particularly with attachment figures (Greenberg & Foerster, 1996; Greenberg & Malcolm, 2002). This model provides guidelines for directing the process of trauma resolution in EFTT. It is important to appreciate how IC is distinct from other approaches to systematic exposure by virtue of its emphasis on interpersonal processes, whereby the client (in the role of victim) imaginally interacts with a specific perpetrator of abuse and neglect. This enacted or imagined interaction can be thought of as a behavioral index of internal "object relations." Emotional engagement with trauma material during IC is consequently more complex than simply fear expression while reliving a traumatic event. It also follows that trauma recovery in EFTT is more than a simple desensitization to trauma material and the subsequent reduction of distress.

Recovery in EFTT primarily involves restructuring internalized object relations and constructing new and more adaptive meaning vis-à-vis both oneself and offending others. Object relations can be understood as the interpersonal component of an emotion scheme, activated either by others or by the internalized representation of others. Moment-by-moment experiential shifts during IC gradually contribute to developing adaptive relational changes of this kind. These changes include not only the attenuation of negative feelings (hurt, anger, fear, shame) concerning the other but also reduced self-blame, increased self-empowerment, separation from the other, letting go of the rigid hope that a specific other will meet one's needs, and more adaptive perceptions of abusive others as life-sized and human.

Importance of the Initial Dialogue

The goal of the IC procedure at this early phase of therapy is to begin the process of in-depth trauma exploration. This intervention quickly activates core emotional processes and clients' processing difficulties for their subsequent exploration and change. In this way, observing client engagement in the initial IC procedure helps with case conceptualization. Moment-by-moment observations of how a client experiences, regulates, and works with such emotionally evocative situations contribute to understanding the generating conditions of a client's disturbance and ushers in a collaborative discussion on the goals and anticipated tasks of therapy. Research across different approaches supports the importance of high-quality client processes and a good start early in therapy (e.g., Horvath & Symonds, 1991; Jaycox, Foa, & Morral, 1998; O'Malley, Suh, & Strupp, 1983). Productive engagement with trauma material in early sessions helps set the course for the remainder of therapy, allowing maximum time for exploring and reprocessing trauma feelings and memories. From a learning perspective, clients' initial experiences of confronting imagined perpetrators and accessing painful material should be successful and reinforcing.

Research on the effective use of EFTT (Paivio et al., 2001, 2004) indicated that the quality of clients' engagement during IC remained relatively stable from the initial to later sessions. Research also indicated that the first IC intervention can have a lasting positive influence on client change. In one study (Holowaty, 2004), the majority of clients who were interviewed at the end of therapy identified the initial IC as one of the most helpful events in therapy. Clients stated that what was particularly helpful was realizing, for the first time, and at a gut level, the impact that early experiences of abuse and neglect had had on them. It is likely that the novelty of the IC procedure played a role in the salience of these initial episodes. As noted above, a successful experience of confronting trauma feelings and memories in the presence of a supporting therapist also contributes to strengthening the therapeutic alliance—a finding that has important implications especially for clients who have suffered interpersonal trauma. Another study (Paivio et al., 2001) further indicated a significant association between the initial engagement of clients during IC and the resolution of their abuse issues at a 6-month follow-up. This suggests that engagement in the first IC intervention may have a delayed impact on resolution that did not appear immediately following therapy. People continue to process these experiences after therapy has terminated.

There is also an important clinical relationship between the quality of engagement in the initial IC and subsequent use of the intervention. Clients who were highly engaged in the first IC continued to be highly engaged in the procedure whenever it was used, and (unfortunately) clients who initially engaged at low levels similarly continued to engage only superficially. However, when it comes to participating in IC, the quality of engagement is independent of the frequency of participation. Thus, because dosage (quality × frequency) is the most predictive variable in terms of outcome, rather than quality or frequency alone (Paivio et al., 2001), clients who are only minimally engaged during the initial IC may need to be encouraged to participate in it more frequently so as to receive maximum benefit. Therefore, therapist observations of a client's processes during the first IC will have implications for the treatment plan of that client. In short, therapists should not refrain from repeatedly using the IC procedure with clients whose quality of engagement is moderate or low in the initial session.

INTERVENTION PRINCIPLES

The following intervention principles are particularly important in enhancing the quality of client engagement in the IC procedure: promoting ownership of experience, evoking memories, and balancing attending to and expression of emotional experience.

Promote Ownership of Experience

This principle of promoting ownership of experience involves shifting from a stance of victimization, reduced client minimization, and invalidation of their experience to a stance of client-assertive communication. This is accomplished in part by directing and redirecting client attention to their internal experience and modeling or encouraging the use of "I" language rather than focusing on events or the other's behavior or hurling insults at the other. For example:

C: He's such a disgusting pig!

T: Yes, I hear how angry you are. Tell him what makes you so angry.

Or, in another example:

C: I don't like to be angry at her, she had a hard life.

T: I hear that you don't want to blame but it's important not to discount your own feelings either, try saying that to her, "I don't want to blame you but . . ."

In essence, interventions like these promote a client's depth of experiencing, the goal of which is self-exploration that becomes increasing personal and affective in quality.

Evoke Memories

Trauma memories either spontaneously emerge in the course of imagining a confrontation with offenders or will be deliberately elicited by the therapist. A client's memories of concrete and specific events (e.g., "I remember the terror of hearing my parents fighting outside on the driveway") are more likely to activate core emotion and meaning structures than vague or generic memories (e.g., "I remember they used to fight all the time"). So, therapists aim to facilitate the former rather than the latter. Evocative empathic responses that are personal, concrete, and specific and that include the use of connotative or metaphoric language help activate this core material. For example, the therapist might say, "That must have been so frightening for you as a little girl, alone in your room, hearing them fighting, imagining . . . what? . . . that they were going to kill each other?"

Balance Attending To and Expression of Internal Experience

Subjective internal experience is the primary source of new information in EFTT, and so, as we have seen, one overarching treatment objective is to help clients articulate their subjective reality (promote experiencing). Thus, the therapist's interventions must balance directing attention to internal experience (e.g., "Sounds like you feel pretty resentful remembering what he did, stay with that") with directing expression (e.g., "Now, tell him what makes you so resentful, what a good father should have done"). In this effort, clients are regularly asked (a) to check how they are feeling "on the inside," (b) to deliberately put words to that experience, and (c) to direct expression to the imagined other. The general rule here is to explicitly direct clients to first attend inward, and then express.

The following are some additional general emotion-focused therapy intervention principles that are most relevant to implementing the initial IC procedure:

- Promote suitable emotion regulation: Reduce excessive (disorganizing) arousal through empathic affirmation, attention to breathing, and using a present-centered focus; and/or increase arousal to productive levels through evocative empathy.
- Help clients to symbolize the meaning of their experience, including unmet needs and the effects of trauma on self and relationships.
- Communicate observations about the client's process as an aid to task collaboration (e.g., the therapist might say, "You say the words but somehow it's hard to get in touch with those feelings?" or "I see that really touches you. Can you put words to those tears?").

THE PROCESS OF ENGAGEMENT IN IC

The following sections present an overview of the model of resolution shown in Figure 7.1 with an emphasis on the initial dialogue. Next, the Levels of Engagement Scale (LES; Paivio et al., 2001) is presented to help describe the features of high-quality engagement in IC. Finally, we focus on therapist interventions that promote client resolution at each step in the process.

Steps in the Process of Resolution

Figure 7.1 presents the model of resolution that guides the IC intervention in EFTT. Modifications to the original general model and the specifics of this task (Greenberg et al., 1993) include a central focus on trauma memories and on self-related disturbances. Thus, in the process of resolving relational

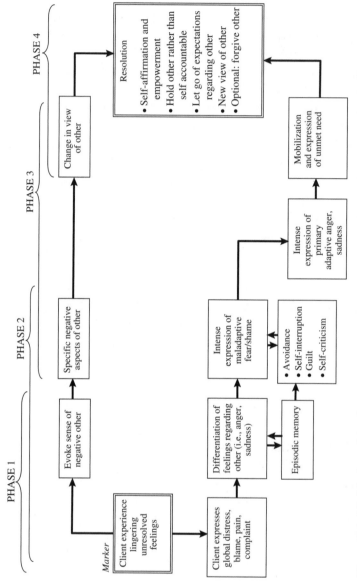

Figure 7.1. Model of resolving interpersonal trauma using imaginary confrontation or empathic exploration and the phases of emotion-focused therapy for trauma. From *Facilitating Emotional Change: The Moment-by-Moment Process* (p. 248), by L. S. Greenberg, L. N. Rice, & R. K. Elliott, 1993, New York: Guilford Press. Copyright 1993 by Guilford Press. Adapted with permission.

trauma, specific memories of trauma/abuse are explicitly evoked and explored. Furthermore, in the early stages of therapy with clients in this population, full emotional expression is typically blocked by secondary self-related disturbances (i.e., fear, avoidance, shame, self-blame). These difficulties are observed in the first IC, and they prevent the client from moving forward in resolving issues with abusive and neglectful others (see chaps. 9 and 10, this volume).

The IC procedure shown in Figure 7.1 requires following and directing client interaction between the self and the imagined other enacted in different chairs. In the early stage, the client feels victimized and the other is viewed negatively, as the internalized "bad object." Even when the imagined other is not enacted by the client, it is critical to track the client's evolving perceptions of the other throughout the process and over the course of therapy. Similarly, even when the IC technique is not explicitly used (this is described later in the chapter), steps in the model guide the process of intervention and resolution (Paivio, Jarry, Chagigiorgis, Hall, & Ralston, in press).

Research by Greenberg and Foerster (1996) and Greenberg and Malcolm (2002) has identified process steps in the original theoretical model that discriminated clients who resolved issues from those who did not. These core components are similar to those related to the process of resolving global distress that was discussed in chapter 3 on emotion and presented in Figure 3.1 (Pascual-Leone & Greenberg, 2007). The core components of resolution during IC are as follows:

- Identification of negative perceptions of the imagined other
- Intense expression of adaptive emotion (anger, sadness)
- Expression of needs and entitlement to unmet needs
- Changed perceptions of self and the significant other

Accordingly, clients who resolved issues shifted to a stance of increased self-affiliation, self-empowerment, and separation from the other. They also developed a more differentiated perspective of the other and held the other (rather than themselves) accountable for harm. In some cases, for example, when the imagined other is perceived as a remorseful attachment figure, resolution may include forgiveness. In other cases, where the imagined other is perceived as cruel or abusive, resolution most frequently involves eventually seeing the other as less powerful and perhaps "sick," disturbed, or pathetic. In either case, full resolution of relational trauma always includes appropriately holding perpetrators of harm accountable for the injuries they have inflicted.

The Degree of Resolution Scale

The Degree of Resolution Scale (DRS; Greenberg & Hirscheimer, 1994) in Appendix C assesses the degree to which clients have resolved issues with specific offenders who are the focus of therapy, according to steps spec-ified in the resolution model (Greenberg & Foerster, 1996). Although the measure describes hierarchically organized levels of process, working through relational trauma is not a linear process. The client may reach a particular level of resolution during a particular session (e.g., entitlement to unmet needs) but slide back to an earlier level (e.g., self-doubt and self-blame) in the next session. Even within the same session, clients cycle through the levels, gradually moving closer to full resolution. Moreover, this "two-steps-forward, one-step-backward" progression has been empirically demonstrated to be part and parcel of emotional processing in productive therapy sessions (Pascual-Leone, 2009).

Research on Levels of Engagement: How Do We Know When It Is Working?

At any point during the IC procedure, the quality of client engagement with trauma material is important, irrespective of the stage a given client may be at in the resolution process. All therapy approaches recognize the impor-tance of high-quality client processes during key interventions. The question is how do we know when the client is productively engaged in IC, what should we observe? Answering this question will inform clinicians about what they are trying to promote in the intervention so as to enhance good process and maximum change.

Clinical observation has indicated considerable variability in the qual-ity of client engagement during IC such that interaction with an imagined other can range from none at all, to a few tentative utterances interspersed throughout the session, to continuous and intense involvement that some-times lasts for the entire session. The objective of one study of EFTT (Paivio et al., 2001) was to behaviorally define this quality of client engage-ment, to measure its variability, and then to test whether better quality pre-dicted better outcome. *Engagement quality*, therefore, was defined in terms of process elements that are generally important in expressive and experiential therapies and of particular importance to therapy for trauma, as well as those features that are unique to this specific intervention. In the end, the quality of engagement was described in terms of three dimensions and included clients' (a) involvement in the therapy process, (b) expression and explo-ration of their affective experience, and (c) ability to maintain psychological contact with an imagined other in an empty chair.

On the basis of the above process dimensions, we developed the Levels of Engagement Scale (LES; Paivio et al., 2001) to assess client processes dur-ing IC. First, the dimension of involvement is closely related to the construct of client experiencing described in chapters 4 and 6. Criteria include a willing participation in the intervention rather than resistance (e.g., refusal to speak to the imagined other), expressiveness rather than withdrawal, and spontaneous elaboration and initiating dialogue with the imagined other rather than simple compliance with therapist directives. Second, criteria for emotional expressiveness include the client admitting feelings (e.g., "I feel so *angry* when I remember what he did to our family") and nonverbal indicators of arousal (e.g., vocal quality, facial expression, tears). Third, criteria for the dimension of psychological contact include descriptions of the imagined other, looking at the imagined other rather than the therapist, and use of first- and second-person pronouns (I, you) rather than third-person pronouns (he, she) while in dialogue with the imagined other. In brief, the client behaves as if the other were actually there rather than reporting on events.

In our research, ratings on the LES are based on the observation of videotaped therapy sessions, where high ratings indicate emotional engagement with trauma material during IC for an extended period of time. As expected, we found considerable variability in client engagement quality during the first IC (Paivio et al., 2001). However, most clients required considerable support and coaching from their therapist to confront imagined perpetrators for the first time. Furthermore, as we have discussed, for most clients the quality of engagement during the initial IC set a precedent for the rest of treatment; this underscores the importance of promoting the best processes possible.

Factors Related to Client Engagement in IC

Research on client engagement (Paivio et al., 2001, 2004) indicates that about one quarter of EFTT sessions contain substantial work using the IC procedure. In an attempt to understand the client characteristics related to participation and thereby explore the applicability of the procedure, we examined the relationship between engagement quality and a number of client variables. These included gender, type and severity of abuse, severity of current trauma symptoms, presence of Axis II pathology, and social anxiety. Prior research and clinical observation had already indicated a link between some of these factors and participation in other exposure-based procedures. For example, severe problems with emotion dysregulation (i.e., current trauma symptoms) have been associated with difficulties confronting trauma memories (Jaycox et al., 1998). Results of our investigations, however, have shown no systematic link between severity of trauma symptoms and engagement in IC. This is likely because therapists in EFTT collaborate with their clients on when, how, and how often they feel able to confront trauma memories. Moreover, during the actual IC procedure, therapists provide empathy, support, and guidance in response to individual client needs.

The only client characteristic we have studied that has interfered significantly with engagement in IC is the presence of Axis II pathology (Paivio et al., 2004). About one third of clients in our clinic have met criteria for some form of Axis II disorder, the most frequent being avoidant, narcissistic, and borderline personality disorders. The presence of Axis II pathology also predicted higher rates of therapist adherence to EFTT principles, in general, coupled with greater therapist competence in using the IC procedure. These findings likely reflect the fact that therapists were aware of client difficulties with therapeutic tasks and, therefore, pressed harder to implement the model and spent more time addressing client difficulties (one criterion for therapist competence during IC). In any case, these findings suggest that, in general, clients with personality problems may find it challenging to keep a sustained focus on disclosure and exploration of emotional processes in IC and in EFTT.

The IC procedure requires clients to express thoughts and feelings to an imagined other in the presence of the therapist. Clinical observation has suggested that severe client social or performance anxiety can interfere with engagement in enactments such as IC. Research on emotion-focused therapy with a general clinical sample found that client nonassertiveness and social anxiety were prognostic of poorer outcome (Paivio & Bahr, 1998). Considering the prevalence of shame, distrust, and fear of negative evaluation among survivors of child abuse, it is not surprising that, in some instances, a client's nonassertiveness and social anxiety interfere with adequate engagement in IC. However, observation also suggests that one of the best predictors of whether a client will engage in these enactments is simply the confidence with which they are introduced by the clinician. Therapists therefore must provide unambiguous instructions and ensure that a client's performance anxiety is not actually a function of their own lack of confidence or skill.

Overall, IC is designed to be flexibly implemented to accommodate individual client differences in terms of interpersonal and processing style and treatment needs. The procedure therefore is broadly applicable across men and women dealing with different types of abuse types and with a range of trauma and trauma symptom severity.

STEPS IN THE IC TASK AND CORRESPONDING THERAPIST OPERATIONS

While Figure 7.1 describes the client processes that lead to resolution, Exhibit 7.1 and the following sections summarize the steps and therapist operations that facilitate the IC task. In terms of the initial IC, the primary goals are to elicit client negative perceptions of the imagined other and begin to

EXHIBIT 7.1
Steps in the Process of Resolving Interpersonal Trauma Using Imaginal Confrontation (IC)

Phase 1
Predialogue Stage
1. Collaborate on the task and use of the IC procedure
2. Initiate and structure the IC procedure

Arousal Stage
3. Establish psychological contact with imagined other by (a) evoking the sensed presence and (b) accessing the client's feelings in response to the imagined other.
4. Differentiate feelings toward imagined other.
5. Facilitate enactment (or vivid experiential memory) of the imagined other.

Phase 2
Work with avoidance, self-interruption, guilt, and self-blame.

Phase 3
Expression and Exploration Stage
6. Promote full expression of primary adaptive emotion (anger, sadness) about other.
7. Facilitate expression of unfulfilled needs and expectations regarding the other.
8. Track evolving perceptions of self and the imagined other.
9. Support increased sense of client entitlement to having needs and expectations met.

Resolution Stage
10. Support emerging new understanding of both (a) self and (b) other.
11. Close contact with the imagined other appropriately.

Postdialogue Stage
12. Process client understanding of IC experience.

---

differentiate global distress and bad feelings into separate emotions (anger, sadness, fear, shame) and their associated meanings—unmet needs and the effects of these and the trauma on self.

Using IC in the Early Phase of EFTT

The following sections specify process steps in each of the stages during Phase 1 of EFTT as outlined in Exhibit 7.1.

Predialogue Stage

1. *Collaborate on the task and use of the IC procedure.* Two issues to be considered prior to the initial introduction of IC concern client preparation for trauma work and the choice of imagined other. In terms of preparation, we typically do not inform clients that in-depth trauma work (or use of IC) will be the focus of a particular session because, in our experience, the anticipation can increase client anxiety as they think about it between sessions, mentally

prepare, or come to the session with scripted material, all of which interfere with present-centeredness and spontaneity.

The decision regarding who will be the focus of the first IC (i.e., the imagined other) should be carefully considered by the therapist prior to the session. This decision can be based on in-session client markers (e.g., reports of nightmares or troubling encounters with perpetrators) or asking the client in session who they would like to focus on, or can be chosen by the therapist based on information about client processes and treatment needs. Sometimes it may be more effective to engage a less threatening other, for example, a parent who minimized abuse, rather than imagining a malevolent other with accompanying memories of severe violence and horror. The overarching goal in the initial dialogue is to ensure a successful experience in terms of engaging and processing trauma material at a deeper level as compared with previous sessions, without the client being overwhelmed.

Therapists should prepare for the first IC by imagining how they might introduce the procedure. They should develop a rationale that is tailored to their individual client, anticipate how the client will respond to the procedure, and consider problems that could emerge and how to address them. Of course, this planning in advance needs to be balanced with responding to the moment-by-moment client processes in a session. For example, the initial IC with one client began with the planned confrontation of her parents who minimized her experience of sexual abuse by her brother, rather than with the brother (e.g., the therapist said, "It's like they don't understand how devastating it was for you. Make them understand."). However, when the therapist noticed expressed markers of client anger toward her abusive brother, the confrontation with parents shifted to confronting the perpetrator (e.g., the therapist asked the client, "What would you like to say to your brother right now?").

Before actually introducing the IC procedure, the therapist and client need to agree on this task and intervention as a focus for the session. So, at the beginning of Session 4, the therapist asks the client whether there are any pressing issues the client wishes to discuss and, if not, suggests an in-depth exploration of trauma issues with a specific other person who has been the focus of therapy. (Of course, if the client does have another pressing concern, those take precedence.) The therapist asks the client what feelings and memories come up when the therapist suggests this focus. Whether the choice of imagined other is predetermined or emerges spontaneously, the therapist needs to elicit and/or confirm appropriate markers for beginning IC (e.g., the therapist might say, "Sounds like you are still very upset when you remember what he did?" and the client might reply, "Yes, I still can't get over it").

2. *Initiate and structure the IC procedure.* At this stage, the therapist suggests a dialogue with an imagined other as a way to deepen the process (not speaking *about* feelings but *from* feelings). The therapist also provides a brief

rationale tailored to the individual client (e.g., "You were always shut down. Here's a chance to say what you really felt.") and brief and clear instructions for participation (e.g., "Pay attention to what is going on inside, your thoughts and feelings, and put words to those. Speak from your heart/gut. Say them out loud, get it out in the open so we can look at it, so you can get some clarity. I'll help.").

To begin, after clients agree to participate in the task, the therapist places an empty chair in front of them, directing them to attend to their internal experience or reaction and express this to the imagined other in the chair. Client resistance, reluctance, or difficulties concerning performance anxiety, their current relationship with the offender, or the purposes of the procedure are validated and, if possible, either bypassed or quickly addressed. These issues are discussed in the last section of this chapter on addressing client difficulties.

When initially confronting the imagined other, the client typically feels victimized, expresses hurt, and blames the other. Clients also usually will describe external circumstances and the other's behavior (e.g., "They always defended him, like he was a little angel, but he was a devil. I can't believe they didn't see that, they were so blind!"). At this stage, depth of experiencing is low and the client's level of resolution corresponds to a Level 1 on the DRS. An important intervention principle in moving the client forward is to promote ownership of experience so that exploration becomes increasingly personal and affective in quality.

Sometimes clients are resistant because they feel it is pointless and hopeless to do a "pretend dialogue" to actually effect change (e.g., "I already said this and it didn't do any good, I know what he would say and it never changes!"). Interventions should validate that engaging with the other in real life, indeed, has been pointless and never helped, and the therapist should clarify that the purpose of the IC is to help clients resolve issues for themselves. Therapists further explain to clients, for example, that the other always shut them down in real life; that they never had their say and there was no one to witness this or help them express their truth; and that squashing down their feelings is what has kept them stuck.

Arousal Stage

3. *Establish psychological contact with imagined other*. Once clients have agreed to participate in the IC procedure, facilitating deeper engagement requires establishing psychological contact with the imagined other. Thus, the goal at this stage is to move the client to Level 2 on the DRS. This is characterized by an emotional reaction evoked in response to the imagined negative other and memories of traumatic events.

At this stage, episodic memories involving the other may spontaneously emerge, clients can be asked to recall a particular event, or the therapist can suggest an event based on information gathered in earlier sessions (e.g., the therapist might say, "Take me back to that time, you are coming home from school and see the ambulance outside your home. Bring it to life."). This focus on external details is balanced by directing client attention to their internal experience during the event (e.g., the therapist might ask, "What was going on for you on the inside—trembling, feeling scared, or . . . ?"). Typically, at this stage, the client also collapses into resignation or intellectualization, minimizes harm, blames him- or herself, or is overwhelmed by distress and shuts down. Arousal may be high, but depth of experiencing still remains low. In the pursuit of deepening experience, there are two facets to establishing psychological contact with the imagined other.

3a. *Evoke the sensed presence of the imagined other.* The client is asked to imagine and describe the other in the empty chair, for example, his or her facial expression, posture, or tone of voice. In the early phase of therapy, the other usually is seen as threatening, critical, invalidating, rejecting, indifferent, and so on. Clients might visualize the other as huge and scary, for example, and might want the chair moved further away. Interventions need to highlight the essential quality of the imagined other (e.g., the therapist might say, "Back turned to you, it's like he's shutting you out" or "That tone of voice, what's the message being sent?").

3b. *Access client feelings in response to the imagined other.* Once the presence of the other is clearly evoked, interventions then direct clients' attention to their internal experience in reaction to the other (e.g., the therapist might ask, "What comes up for you on the inside when you imagine him there, with that look on his face?"). This is followed by encouragement to express clients' reaction to the other. An important principle in directing the dialogue throughout is to balance directing client expression with directing client attention to internal experience.

During the early phase of therapy, the client still tends to respond to the imagined other from a stance of powerlessness and victimization and to focus on external circumstances and the behavior of the other. Responses commonly include distress, hurt, and blaming the other for maltreatment. Therapists' empathic responses at this point must communicate understanding, promote ownership of experience, and begin to help clients differentiate their feelings. At markers of hopelessness or resignation (e.g., when the client says, "What's the point, nothing will change no matter what I say"), interventions should again provide a brief rationale for confronting the imagined other (e.g., the therapist might say, "It's not for him, it's for you, this is a chance to finally tell your truth without being shut down or worrying about the right words. You've stuffed so much over all these years.").

Other common client responses include shame and embarrassment at evoked memories, difficulties disclosing details of victimization (e.g., sexual abuse), or extreme distress in response to memories of violence and horror. For example, the client Monica had difficulties breathing as she recalled finding her mother after she had shot herself. Another client collapsed into tears recalling her father beating her younger brother. In these instances, therapist interventions affirm client vulnerability, promote emotion regulation, and if necessary momentarily deflect from IC to encourage disclosure to the therapist (e.g., "It's important to get it out, tell me, don't let those things fester inside"). Therapists also provide feedback through the use of process observations (e.g., "He still has the power to shut you down, even here") and encourage the client to push through distress if possible and return to IC when he or she is calmer. It is most helpful for clients to express anger experience directly toward abusive others rather than indirectly to the therapist, because this facilitates self-empowerment (e.g., "He has caused you so much pain and suffering. Tell him how angry you are about that!"). In contrast, more vulnerable feelings such as fear, shame, or sadness require support, so these are expressed either to the therapist or toward an imagined other who is perceived as potentially responsive to the client's suffering.

Client responses during the first IC also can include intellectualizing, minimizing harm, and making excuses for the abusive other (e.g., the client might say, "I know she had a difficult childhood"). Again, interventions validate and redirect clients' attention to their own experience (e.g., "What do you feel in your heart/gut/body when you remember/imagine . . ." or "You are good at understanding her perspective but you don't want this to be at your own expense"). At the other end of the spectrum, clients get distressed and may shut down (e.g., dissociation). This could be so severe that they are unable to continue in a dialogue with the imagined other. Alternatively, some clients want to maintain contact with the therapist rather than an imagined other (e.g., the client says, "I would rather talk to you") or they resist engaging in the IC procedure for other reasons. These difficulties need to be explored and addressed. Sometimes trauma exploration can be discontinued altogether until other issues are resolved. In-depth exploration of persistent self-related difficulties will affect trauma exploration or IC participation and are the focus of later sessions during Phase 2 of EFTT.

4. *Differentiate feelings toward imagined other.* The immediate process goal at this stage of the IC process is to differentiate client global upset, distress, or blame into clear expressions of primary emotions to access the unique information associated with each (see Figure 3.1 in chap. 3, this volume). In terms of the mechanisms of change in EFTT, it is particularly important to differentiate primary adaptive anger and sadness from more complex emotions and from each other, such that the embodied meaning can each be explored in its own right.

The goal at this stage is to help the client move toward Level 3 of the DRS, which is characterized by assertive expression of healthy anger and sadness. Clients also can shift between anger and sadness. Interventions must validate both experiences as legitimate and important and encourage the client to focus on each, one at a time. The decision about which emotion to highlight in empathic reflections can be based on the presence of predominant markers for each emotion. Anger, for example, is associated with references to injustice and unfairness, whereas sadness is associated with deprivation, separation, and loss. This decision is also based on the therapist's understanding of the case. For example, in helping Monica grieve the loss of her mother, the therapist opted to preferentially reflect sadness when both anger and sadness were present. Alternatively, the client can be asked which emotion he or she is most in touch with at the moment. Monica angrily responded to the imagined mother's excuses by saying, "I don't accept those excuses!" Therapist interventions specifically labeled anger and helped Monica symbolize its meaning (e.g., "So you don't accept those excuses, tell her what you resent, the damaging effect her suicide has had on you all these years").

Similarly, adaptive anger and sadness can collapse into fear or self-blame, and therapists need to identify these and work with them separately. Depression, for example, is not sadness at loss but sadness mixed with powerlessness and fear or self-criticism and shame. Although these are apparent during the initial IC and therapists make note of their idiosyncratic nature, actually modifying these maladaptive emotions takes place during later sessions in Phase 2 of therapy.

5. *Facilitate enactment (or vivid experiential memory) of the imagined other.* When therapists vivify the client's experience of the other, the goal is to promote Levels 2 or 3 on the DRS. At these levels, the purpose is to intensify the stimulus function of the imagined other. Clients are asked to imagine how the other would respond to their expressions and might be asked to "switch chairs" and respond from the other chair. Markers for switching chairs are like normal conversational markers that call for a response from the other party (e.g., the client may say, "You should have . . ." or "I want you to . . ."). During the initial IC, the client may or may not enact the imagined other. In our experience, clients will not want to enact (or identify with) an imagined other who is seen as frightening, disgusting, or despicable. At this early stage in the process, it does not matter whether the other is enacted or not. The therapist's aim is to highlight, clarify, intensify, and perhaps exaggerate the core meaning of the other's response to evoke a response in the self. For example, a client imitated the screechy voice of her mother calling her father's name ("Frank!!"). The therapist echoed this vocal quality and asked the client to articulate the meaning ("Like a shrew . . . or a witch? How do you feel when you remember her voice?"). Again, it is critical to continually track

client perceptions of the other during IC because these shift over the course of therapy as the client's self-esteem and confidence increase.

Using IC in Phase 2 of EFTT

Clients commonly have self-related difficulties (i.e., avoidance, self-interruption, guilt, self-blame) that interfere with their engaging in IC. In Phase 2 of EFTT, those difficulties become the focus of therapy. Therapists provide process observations (e.g., "Even though you know you were just a child, somehow you still blame yourself") and a rationale for reducing these blocks—that they interfere with functioning and trauma resolution. The IC procedure is not entirely abandoned during this phase but instead is used in conjunction with other interventions for exploring and reducing these blocks. These are described in chapters 8 and 9.

Using IC in Phase 3 of EFTT

Once self-related disturbances are gradually worked through, the client will be increasingly better able to confront the imagined other during IC. The following steps in the resolution model begin with full experience and expression of anger and sadness, which are the catalysts for resolution. These steps, presented in Exhibit 7.1, are described briefly below to provide direction for later sessions, and they will be further elaborated in chapters 10 and 11. It is important to note that although the following steps are most typical of a later phase of therapy, they could occur at any time. No matter what phase of therapy the client is in or what degree of resolution the client has achieved, the goal is to help the client move, step by step, session by session, closer to full resolution, and to do so as quickly and efficiently as possible.

Expression and Exploration Stage

The expression and exploration stage is intended to facilitate higher levels on the DRS (see Exhibit 7.1). In Step 6 interventions promote full expression of anger and sadness to the imagined other. Increased arousal is accomplished by encouraging the client to approach painful or threatening emotion, as well as to adopt a body posture and vocal quality that are consistent with the focal emotion and through the use of emotion intensification techniques. In Steps 7 through 9, interventions facilitate expression of and entitlement to unmet needs. Here the client begins to define self in terms of legitimate wants and needs (e.g., for justice, attention, love). Arousal also decreases and experiencing increases, as clients explore the effects of having had their needs neglected.

Resolution Stage

During Step 10, interventions support the emerging new understanding of self and other. At this stage, the client no longer is seeking retribution or an apology ("It doesn't matter any more what *he* thinks, I know the *truth*"). Through enacting or imagining the other's reactions to the client's expressions, the client begins to see the other in a more differentiated fashion and, at the same time, begins to hold the other (rather than self) accountable for harm.

Whatever stage the client has achieved during a particular therapy session, one can skip ahead to ending the IC task for the time being. This takes place through Steps 11 and 12, which help the client close contact with the other and process the experience to date. This could include bridging to the next session (e.g., the therapist might say, "Okay, so you're not done, tell him you'll get back to him"), saying goodbye, or asserting expectations and boundaries in the current relationship (e.g., "Tell her you are only willing to see her when she's sober"). Here, processing also entails setting goals for subsequent sessions, ensuring client safety and emotion regulation between sessions, and providing reassurance and hope for resolution (e.g., "I know it's still not finished for you. We will continue to work on this, we have time."). Over time, processing the IC experience involves integrating it with other therapy experiences and with the client's current life.

RELATIONSHIP DEVELOPMENT TASKS IN THE INITIAL IC

Introduction of the IC procedure is a bridge between the first and second phases of therapy. Client self-related difficulties emerge but are not yet the focus of deliberate exploration and change. At the same time, IC introduces new elements into the relationship dynamic that the client needs to become comfortable with. It therefore is essential to pay particular attention to features of the relationship during the first IC. The following sections describe the components of alliance development that were presented in the preceding chapter as they apply specifically to the IC procedure. These features will remain important throughout the therapy process.

Establish a Secure Attachment Bond

Therapists ensure safety and support during IC by empathically responding to client processes, not just directing the process. This particularly includes providing empathic affirmation of client vulnerability and as much interaction with the therapist (as opposed to the imagined other) as is needed by the client. It is important to collaborate with clients about the procedure and to assure them that they ultimately have control over the process. The therapist's role is to guide the process, provide support, ensure there is adequate time for processing the IC experience, monitor client composure, and ensure that the client has adequate resources for coping after the session.

Provide Emotion Coaching and Awareness Training

Intervention principles that increase client awareness of emotional experience during the initial IC include directing client attention to internal experience, promoting ownership of experience, and helping clients accurately label their feelings and symbolize the meaning of their experiences. Ownership is accomplished through modeling and gradually shaping client behavior rather than explicit teaching. During the first IC, it is important to empathically respond to and validate a client's negative perceptions of the other and, at the same time, not to reinforce the client's victimization or intensify blaming. For example, when the client says to the imagined other, "You're so selfish!" the therapist may respond, "Yes, so very angry! Tell him more about what makes you so angry, the effect on you."

Promote Emotion Regulation

It is important to closely monitor client arousal levels during the IC procedure (e.g., the therapist asks, "What's going on for you right now?"). Therapist soothing responses, attention to breathing, and present-centeredness can be used to reduce distress, whereas evocative empathic responses (e.g., "So, you feel discarded, like a piece of trash") can increase emotional intensity to work past instances of avoidance. However, the initial IC is not a time for explicit emotion intensification strategies. Rather, avoidance processes are observed at this point in the treatment and, if they persist, become targets for intervention in later sessions.

Collaborate on Understanding the Generating Conditions for Disturbance

The first IC is an opportunity to observe client processing difficulties that have interfered with trauma recovery. Interventions that aid in developing a collaborative understanding of these difficulties include directing client attention to internal experience and process observations that have an exploratory quality and form the basis for further exploration (e.g., "It's like part of you is furious and the other part says 'it's not okay to feel that way'? Let's spend some time looking at that.").

Collaborate on Use of IC to Accomplish Client Goals

This entails providing a rationale for participation in IC that is tailored to the goals of an individual client. It is useful to highlight, for example, that standing up to a perpetrator in imagination can increase one's self-confidence, clarify feelings and needs so they can be met in one's current life, resolve "unfinished business," and reduce "emotional baggage" that interferes with current relationships. All of these reasons should be discussed with clients as they personally apply. Interventions also validate and explore the difficulties that clients have with IC. This includes providing alternatives (see below) and reassurance that alternatives also are effective.

The issue of forgiveness may arise in the early phase of therapy and may be an important goal for some clients. This can emerge, or can be elicited, in the initial IC particularly when the client is expressing anger at the other. The therapist can respond to client expressed anger with a statement such as "So you don't forgive him for what he did" to then assess the client's perspective. Such an intervention can elicit client clarification that the client may want to forgive but cannot, does not want to forgive, or finds the issue of forgiveness to be irrelevant. If the client explicitly states that forgiveness is a goal, it is important to discuss what this means to him or her. Forgiveness then can serve as an additional marker for assessing a client's degree of resolution. In any case, because research is mixed on whether forgiveness provides additional benefits for clients (see Chagigiorgis & Paivio, 2006), it is important to clarify that forgiveness is not part of the therapist's agenda and is only one of several viable solutions. The topic of forgiveness will be discussed in chapter 10 in the context of anger.

EMPATHIC EXPLORATION AS AN ALTERNATIVE TO IC PROCEDURE

The IC procedure is appropriate only when there is an identified other who is the target of the client's distress. In instances where this is not the case, trauma exploration can focus more on telling the story and on self-related disturbances. In other cases, there may be an identified other but the client declines to participate in IC, possibly because of performance anxiety or because imagining the other is simply too evocative and threatening. For this reason, we designed the empathic exploration (EE) procedure, which may serve as a less stressful alternative for the significant minority of individuals who cannot, or will not, engage in IC.

The EE procedure is based on the identical model of resolution (see Figure 7.1) and incorporates the same intervention principles and the same criteria for engagement as IC, only without the use of an empty chair (S. C. Paivio et al., in press). In EE, clients are encouraged to imagine perpetrators in their mind's eye rather than in the empty chair, and feelings and memories concerning abusive and neglectful others are explored exclusively in interaction with the therapist (e.g., the therapist might say, "Tell *me* [versus *her*] more. Her minimization of your pain must have been so devastating . . .").

Results of a clinical trial (Paivio et al., in press) indicated comparable efficacy of EFTT with EE alone, compared with EFTT with IC. Clients in EE made large gains on multiple dimensions, and these gains were maintained at 1-year follow-up. Research on the in-session processes (Chagigiorgis, 2009; Ralston, 2006) also revealed that both IC and EE interventions promoted moderate levels of experiencing, comparable levels of client engagement with trauma material, and comparable levels of client-reported distress (measured on the Subjective Units of Distress) that, as expected, diminished over the course of therapy (desensitization). Finally, observed levels of emotional arousal (which is distinct from global distress) were lower during EE (Ralston, 2006), and the dropout rate in EFTT with EE was 7% compared with 23% in the IC condition. The latter is comparable with rates reported for other exposure-based therapies (e.g., Chard, 2005; Cloitre et al., 2002; Foa et al., 2005).

Overall, the above findings support EE as an effective and less stressful alternative to the IC procedure. However, a number of factors need to be considered before a clinician chooses EE over IC. First, comparable efficacy for the two treatment approaches likely was due to a sustained focus on trauma work, comparable client and therapist expectancies regarding efficacy, and both the same underlying model of resolution and the specific steps guiding the process. Furthermore, the IC procedure includes greater structure, which may have advantages for both clients and therapists. It also has greater novelty, which may make it more memorable. In the end, the IC enactment is a more complex interactional process that likely evokes more multimodal experiential memories. Intuitively, it is more evocative and powerful to stand up to an imagined abusive other than to talk about these feelings with a therapist. Trauma work during EE may be less stressful, but it also is less evocative and less distinct from the rest of therapy. Effective processing of trauma material during EE, therefore, requires careful therapist attention to the use of evocative language, activating experiential memories, and deliberately tracking perceptions of self and other (e.g., "How do you imagine she would feel/respond, if she knew how you felt?").

For these reasons, and because most clients (about two thirds) are able to engage in IC (Paivio et al., 2001), we advocate the use of IC unless clearly contraindicated. A common therapist error in early sessions is shifting to EE too quickly in response to client difficulties with IC. Most clients are reluctant to confront imagined abusive and neglectful others. Therapists, therefore, should have realistic expectations for client engagement in IC and help clients persist despite their difficulties. In light of the evidence presented above that dosage of IC contributes to client change (Paivio et al., 2001), the only reasons for abandoning IC completely are clients' inability to manage distress, dissociation, and outright refusal to participate. Furthermore, these client processes in early sessions do not preclude reintroducing IC in later sessions once the client is stronger. Clients thus can move back and forth between EE and IC.

CLIENT DIFFICULTIES WITH THE INITIAL IC

Addressing client difficulties with IC first requires collaboratively determining the nature of the difficulty. This frequently includes providing a rationale that makes sense to a client and that increases her or his motivation to participate. Responding to markers of core "hot" internal processes always makes intervention using IC easier.

The Structure Is Not Conducive to Dialogue With an Imagined Other

Structural problems are the easiest to address. In terms of setting up the dialogue, if a therapist avoids being in the client's line of vision with the empty chair and is verbally less active, then it is easier for a client to engage with an imagined other. The therapist acts like a coach directing the process from the sidelines and provides only as much contact with the client as needed. The chairs should be arranged in a triangle so the client can look directly at the imagined other and easily move back and forth between the two chairs. This way the therapist also can lean back and out of the client's line of vision.

If this structure is in place and the client continues to speak primarily to the therapist, the therapist should encourage the client to speak directly to the imagined other using "I–you" language and provide a brief rationale (e.g., "That's important what your saying, I want you to try saying that directly to your father over there, it's *him* you're angry at. Now tell *him*."). Once the client complies with this, the therapist provides encouragement and directs the client's attention to her or his internal experience (e.g., "Good, what was it like saying that to him?"). Here, one wants the client to be aware of the increased experiential impact that making psychological contact with the imagined other has and to understand that pressing through the difficulty has value.

In instances when the client has difficulty imagining the other, it can be helpful to spend a short time evoking an image (too long and detailed and the immediacy fizzles out). Imagery refers not only to visual images but also to other sensory information encoded in experiential memory. Thus, clients can be encouraged to remember gestures, a tone of voice, a facial expression, or the size or smell of the other. Sometimes, however, the sensory images associated with traumatic experiences are too evocative and distressing, so the goal is to block out that material.

Client Is Unclear About the Task

Typical areas of client confusion are whether to focus on the imagined other from past or present and whether one would say this in real life. Lack of clarity can be due to absence of appropriate markers for the IC task so that the intervention does not make sense. The task is much easier to initiate at appropriate client markers of "unfinished business" with someone because these indicate a client's readiness to express what has heretofore been suppressed. If these markers have not emerged spontaneously, interventions must elicit them (e.g., the therapist might ask, "So, where are you at with your father?"). Again, therapists should keep their instructions short and simple (e.g., "Imagine your father in that chair—your young father, the one who beat you, not father as he is today. What do you see or sense?"). Clients also need to clearly grasp that the purpose of the intervention is not rehearsal for real life or to effect change in the real other but rather to achieve clarity and resolution for themselves. The therapist might say, for example, "This is for you, so you get clear, no censoring. What you do in real life or later is a different matter, and I can help with that too."

Client Experiences Performance Anxiety

When clients express feeling foolish or embarrassed, interventions should validate their concern but, if possible, bypass the difficulty. For example, the therapist might say, "Yes, it's a little strange at first, but most people get used to it. Let's give it a try because we know it can be really helpful. But if it's not for you, don't worry. We'll find some other way of working." Thus, one reduces clients concern that they are somehow a failure and that alternative procedures (e.g., EE) are inferior. As noted earlier, unless the client refuses to participate, do not abandon IC during a session, rather move back and forth between IC and EE, and briefly reintroduce IC (possibly without physically moving the empty chair) at markers of client expression of feelings, beliefs, or desires concerning the other.

Client Need for Interaction With the Therapist

When, despite directives to interact with the imagined other, clients say or imply (e.g., through eye contact) that they would rather talk to the therapist, the therapist should respond to this preference. At the same time, therapists may solicit clients' permission to periodically, at critical moments, direct their expression to the imagined other (e.g., "Standing up to her, even in imagination, even for a couple of seconds, will help you be more assertive in ways that talking to me will not"). Again, after clients express their thoughts and feelings to the imagined other, interventions should direct their attention to their own internal experience of doing this. This accesses information about the degree of resolution (e.g., the client might say, "It felt good" or "It's hard to believe my own words") for subsequent processing.

Client Has Difficulty Enacting the Other

A critical part of the IC process is to access client perceptions of the other. These perceptions are evident in the imagined response of the other to client expressions. Assuming clear instructions have been provided, clients' difficulty enacting the other can be due to difficulties imagining the other or an aversion to taking on the role of the other. The therapist's interventions support clients who do not want to enact the other (e.g., "That's okay, never mind. How do you *imagine* he would respond or react to what you just said?"). The point here is to elicit a client's perceptions of the other's character, not just of the overt behaviors. Effective interventions highlight the essential quality of the other to evoke a response in the self.

In addition to the above technical difficulties, many client processing difficulties also are observed in the initial IC. Addressing those difficulties takes place in Phase 2 of EFTT.

PHASE TWO OF EFTT

8

REDUCING FEAR, ANXIETY, AND AVOIDANCE

Phase 2 of emotion-focused therapy for trauma (EFTT) typically begins in Session 5 and concerns reducing self-related disturbances (fear, avoidance, shame, self-blame) that interfere with engagement in imaginal confrontation (IC) and act as blocks in resolving issues with perpetrators and attachment figures. This chapter focuses on reducing fear, anxiety, and avoidance of internal experience (specifically trauma feelings and memories), and the chapter that follows will focus on transforming shame. Disturbances related to fear and shame are interrelated and functionally equivalent (Pascual-Leone & Greenberg, 2007) in terms of the information they provide about a client's sense of self (i.e., insecure and vulnerable to harm and/or worthless and vulnerable to rejection and abandonment). Maladaptive fear and shame also each embody action tendencies of withdrawal or collapse, and they call for similar processes of change. Therapists and clients collaboratively determine which focus (fear or shame) will be most productive based on in-session markers of core underlying process.

The primary focus in EFTT with anxiety-related processes is to help clients allow and explore previously avoided or disavowed emotional experience. This is different from simply admitting to or labeling one's feelings, although those are necessary first steps. Many clients can name their feelings yet do not allow themselves to fully feel the depth, power, or intensity of those experiences. From an EFTT perspective, catastrophic expectations, anxiety about, and avoidance of feelings are all different forms of self-interruption of potentially healthy experience. The goal of this phase of EFTT is to help people reach a stage where they can choose to fully allow previously warded-off material. The distinction between admitting feelings and fully allowing their experiential impact was evident in a study described in earlier chapters that asked clients to identify the most helpful aspects of EFTT (Holowaty, 2004). The aspect clients most frequently identified as helpful was "fully allowing painful and threatening feelings."

In this chapter we compare EFTT with other approaches to working with fear and avoidance, provide clinical guidelines for distinguishing among the different types of fear observed in trauma therapy, and specify the relevant change processes and goals. The last half of this chapter focuses on intervention for the different types of fear that have been described. These include step-by-step guidelines for helping clients allow emotional pain and explore disavowed "bad feelings" such as hopelessness and despair. Finally, we provide guidelines for two-chair dialogues in challenging catastrophic expectations and reducing fear of internal experience and for memory work in restructuring a core vulnerable or insecure sense of self.

PERSPECTIVE ON FEAR AND AVOIDANCE: EFTT COMPARED WITH OTHER APPROACHES

By definition, fear is central to trauma. Posttraumatic stress disorder (PTSD) involves overgeneralized fear and anticipatory anxiety in response to stimuli that trigger feelings, memories, and bodily sensations that are reminiscent of the trauma. Accepted interventions for simple PTSD address these underregulated fear responses. Interventions for complex traumatic stress disorders additionally address difficulties with interpersonal fear and distrust. Moreover, as noted in several chapters already, it is universally recognized that relying on avoidance as a coping strategy can interfere with recovery from trauma. Essentially, when cues are avoided, the fear structure is not available for modification and the individual is cut off from key aspects of self.

Current cognitive–behavioral therapy approaches for complex trauma (e.g., Chard, 2005; Cloitre, Koenen, Dohen, & Han, 2002), as well as eye movement desensitization and reprocessing (EMDR; Shapiro & Maxfield, 2002), incorporate exposure procedures to promote habituation, skills training for managing distress, and strategies for challenging the catastrophic expectations associated with PTSD. Other cognitive and behavioral approaches incorporate acceptance-based strategies for reducing the avoidance of internal experience. For example, dialectical behavior therapy for borderline personality (Linehan, 1993), which is strongly associated with a history of child abuse trauma, balances "radical acceptance" of clients' feelings and perceptions with a focus on changing destructive behaviors (e.g., self-harm, substance abuse). Recent cognitive therapy for depression (Segal, Williams, & Teasdale, 2002) and other approaches (e.g., Hayes, Strosahl, & Wilson, 1999) similarly emphasize acceptance of, rather than efforts to change, distressing internal experience. Principles of exposure, promotion of emotion awareness, and nonjudgmental acceptance of internal experience are all part and parcel of EFTT. However, EFTT relies more on therapist empathy rather than skills training to help reduce client distress, and it focuses more on meaning exploration rather than habituation or simple acceptance of internal experience.

EFTT also shares features with recent psychodynamic approaches to trauma, such as short-term dynamic psychotherapy (McCullough et al., 2003), that focus on defensive covering of core affective experience, except that confrontation and interpretation of defensive processes are not part of the EFTT repertoire. Of these, attachment-based models (e.g., accelerated experiential dynamic psychotherapy; Fosha, 2000) are the most compatible with our approach. Thus, common ground would emphasize the provision of a secure attachment bond and empathic responsiveness to a client's feelings and needs as a means for reducing client defensive avoidance and to access core affect.

PROCESS DIAGNOSIS: DISTINGUISHING DIFFERENT TYPES OF FEAR AND ANXIETY

Appropriate intervention in EFTT requires accurate process diagnosis of different types of fear and anxiety and their associated processing difficulties, according to the typology presented in chapter 3. These difficulties are described in the sections that follow.

Adaptive Fear and Anxiety

Although fear and anxiety frequently are considered synonymous, the following sections describe their distinct properties and functions.

Fear

As a basic emotion, fear is automatically activated in response to a perceived imminent threat of harm. The action tendency is to escape or freeze to avoid the danger. Trauma-related problems with this type of adaptive fear concern a lack of awareness. For example, among child abuse survivors, vulnerability to revictimization is thought to stem, in part, from an inability to recognize or trust one's own perceptions concerning danger.

Anxiety

Anxiety is distinct from fear in that it involves anticipating a potentially harmful or threatening situation rather than being confronted with imminent danger. In moderation, anxiety can be adaptive by motivating strategies for coping with an anticipated danger as in seeking help to avoid an episode of domestic violence. Although its inherent meaning is not a source of difficulty per se, problems with adaptive anxiety occur when it is of very high intensity. When this happens, it interferes with information processing, learning, and ultimately with performance.

Maladaptive Fear and Anxiety

Problems with maladaptive fear and anxiety are easily recognized by therapists and clients alike. However, distinguishing among different types of these emotions is crucial to effective intervention.

Primary Maladaptive Fear

Primary maladaptive fear is an automatically activated and conditioned response to stimuli that have become associated with harm. This is the type of fear classically observed in PTSD reactions. For instance, a refugee from a country with a violent military may experience feelings of terror and panic at the sight of anyone in a uniform. Over time, this fear response can generalize to other stimuli and situations. The problem here is an overgeneralized fear and avoidance of situations that, in reality, are harmless.

A Core Sense of Self as Vulnerable or Insecure

This is a kind of hybrid of primary maladaptive fear/anxiety. This sense of self is organized around experiences of fear, dread, and chronic anticipation of danger that originated in attachment relationships and is activated in current interpersonal situations. This pervasive sense of vulnerability is activated as a holistic experience. Although anticipating danger and catastrophic expectations are both part of this complex self-organization and perpetuate feelings of anxiety, those cognitive processes do not precede or generate its activation. In this sense, the experience of vulnerability is distinct from secondary anxiety that will be described in the following section, and this distinction has implications for differential intervention. The problem here is that the activation of an insecure or vulnerable sense of self makes people feel fragile, powerless, helpless, or victimized and interferes with self-confidence, coping, and the capacity for interpersonal relatedness.

Another important point is that complex trauma in attachment relationships typically results in both chronic insecurity and feelings of worthlessness and inferiority. Thus, the sense of self typically is organized around experiences of both fear and shame. This is similar to the emotion-focused therapy conceptualization of depression as involving a core "weak/bad" sense of self (Greenberg & Watson, 2006). Complex PTSD is highly comorbid with depression, and the weak/bad and insecure/worthless self-organizations are central to an understanding of both disorders. Although traumatic experiences of fear on one hand, and shame and self-blame on the other, may coexist for an individual, one of these usually dominates as a more salient way of being in the world. The ramification of this in session is that interventions need to target the dominant experience.

Maladaptive Anxiety

Maladaptive anxiety is most often defined as a secondary emotional experience because it is preceded and strongly influenced by obvious maladaptive cognitions. These anxiety problems can entail the misattribution of danger and lead to inappropriate avoidance. Anxiety also can be secondary to other painful or threatening feelings, such as anger, neediness, embarrassment, or shame. Traumatized individuals, for example, experience anxiety about the emergence of feelings, memories, and bodily sensations associated with the trauma (similar to the anticipatory anxiety associated with panic disorder). This is the basis for the avoidance symptoms so characteristic of PTSD. The problem here is that maladaptive anxiety and the subsequent avoidance of trauma feelings and memories interfere with processing and change. Thus, chronic anxiety needs to be reduced, the associated maladaptive cognitions need to be changed, and the meaning of any underlying painful or threatening emotions needs to be explored.

Bad Feelings and Emotional Pain

In addition to the different types of fear and anxiety described above, the general model of emotion-focused therapy (Greenberg & Paivio, 1997) uniquely distinguishes between "bad feelings" and emotional pain. Both of these types of experiences are uncomfortable, and people make efforts not to feel them or try to get rid of them. However, for change to occur, both of these need to be experienced in session. Even so, they involve different change processes and call for different intervention strategies.

Maladaptive Bad Feelings

Feelings of hopelessness, helplessness, or despair are common among victims of trauma. These are complex secondary emotional reactions or products of the kind of core maladaptive emotion schemes or self-organizations discussed earlier. These sometimes vague, bad feelings need to be regulated, experienced, and explored, and the underlying issues related to a maladaptive sense of self-need to be addressed. In general, changing bad feelings of this kind involves complex processes that correspond to those outlined earlier in the general model of change and illustrated in Figure 3.1 (see chap. 3, this volume). This includes exploring the cognitive–affective constituents that generate the bad feeling, and then accessing adaptive emotions and associated healthy resources so that this information can be used to modify the maladaptive emotion scheme that underlies complex secondary feelings.

Emotional Pain

Complex relational trauma also involves intensely painful emotional experiences related to feeling unwanted, unloved, worthless, or inferior, or stemming from the loss of cherished aspects of self or the loss of or separation from loved ones. Painful experiences such as these pertain to primary adaptive emotions but differ from basic feelings such as anger or sadness in that they are more complex than any single emotion (Greenberg & Paivio, 1997). This type of emotional pain needs to be allowed to desensitize the individual to it and to acknowledge that damage to the self has occurred. Only after facing and acknowledging this damage can one integrate this painful information about self. Over time, this process of acceptance will lead to redefinition of self and the development of new values, concerns, and coping strategies.

CHANGE PROCESSES AND GOALS

The overarching objectives when it comes to addressing fear, anxiety, and avoidance in EFTT emerge from steps in the general model of change presented in Figure 3.1 (Pascual-Leone & Greenberg, 2007). These are to (a) access the underlying maladaptive emotion structure or scheme (i.e., fear, shame, etc); (b) explore the related cognitive, affective, and motivational constituents; (c) support the emergence of other, adaptive emotions and associated healthy resources; and (d) use these to modify the maladaptive emotion structure. Of course, at each of these steps, various forms of avoidance may continue to interrupt progress through later steps in the model and block the process of change. So, although all of the interventions presented below follow the general model, they address specific blocks that may occur at specific steps in the change process.

Addressing problems of underregulated fear and anxiety begins, by necessity, in the first session. However, explicit therapeutic work to reduce experiential avoidance generally begins only after a therapist repeatedly observes these processes in session and there have been unsuccessful attempts to bypass the problem. Sometimes bypassing the problem can be done, for example, by the therapist directing attention to the suppressed experience (e.g., "So hurtful, stay with that, tell me more") or through use of evocative empathic responses to access it (e.g., "So hurtful treated like a little nothing!"). Although EFTT focuses on reducing the fear and avoidance of both external and internal stimuli, it particularly promotes acceptance of internal experience. This therapy fosters a desire to know, respect, nurture, and protect, rather than reject or disavow, the part of self that has been injured. For example, the therapist might say to a client, "It's important, what you've been through, Paul—a profoundly meaningful part of who you are. I want you to learn to embrace and respect that part of yourself rather than pretending to be someone you are not."

The following change processes identified in the general model of emotion-focused therapy (Greenberg & Paivio, 1997) are particularly relevant to work with trauma. We begin with processes and goals related to the task of managing fear and anxiety, which is a prerequisite for other tasks. Many of these are similar to the strategies used in other treatment approaches.

Gradual Exposure

Examples of gradual exposure in EFTT include initially working with less threatening others in the IC procedure or expressing feelings simply to the therapist rather than starting with a direct confrontation of the imagined perpetrator. Therapists also can begin by deliberately using less evocative language to access threatening feelings (e.g., "You didn't like" as opposed to "You hated"). As a rule, clients decide in what manner and how often they confront trauma material.

Emotion Regulation

Although the therapeutic relationship is the primary vehicle for emotion regulation in EFTT, therapy also can use emotion regulation and distress tolerance strategies (e.g., Linehan, 1993; Najavitz, 2002) as well as mindfulness-based practices (Kabat-Zinn, 1990). These skills are typically enhanced in EFTT through experiential "hot" learning in the context of aroused feelings in the session, as opposed to "cool" learning in an instructional or tutorial context (Greenberg & Paivio, 1997). Whether by way of the relationship or by emotion regulation skills or both, the goal is to help the client manage distress and gradually approach the feared experience (e.g., the therapist might say, "It's okay. Breathe, take your time, tell me what's so difficult."). During this process the therapist functions as a secure attachment figure, like a soothing parent with a frightened child or a supportive spouse in emotion-focused therapy for traumatized couples.

Allowing and Owning Painful Experience

The important aspect of allowing previously disavowed painful experience is the experiential linking of information to the self. This is the first step toward motivating new ways of coping and new resources. For example, the client, Clare, whose parents minimized sexual abuse by her brother, eventually accessed intensely painful feelings of shame during IC ("I feel dirty"), which quickly shifted to sadness at her loss of innocence and self-respect. The therapist empathically responded to her vulnerability and validated her experience ("Yes, so sad that a little 3-year-old girl, you, should feel dirty, as if *you* were to blame"). Then, the therapist encouraged Clare to imagine herself in the empty chair and express what she needed as a little girl by asking, "Imagining yourself as a girl, what does that little girl need? What would comfort her?" This accessed compassion for herself and self-soothing, which quickly shifted to anger at her brother. Processing this experience at the end of the session, she remarked that, despite the pain, she felt hopeful for the first time that things could change.

Facing Hopelessness

Accepting irrevocable loss or damage and the futility of attempts to change circumstances or others is essential to letting go of past traumas, healing, and moving on. Clients need to face the painful fact that no matter how hard they try, they cannot get back what was lost or get an abusive parent or spouse to change, love them, apologize, acknowledge responsibility, or feel remorse. If one gives up struggling against the irrevocable truth, stops "wishing it were not true," and accepts realistic hopelessness or defeat, this will lead to giving up unattainable goals or unworkable strategies. This is the principle embodied in the Alcoholics Anonymous Serenity Prayer as well as the Buddhist and mindfulness principles of nonattachment. Peace and serenity can be attained by accepting life on life's terms and focusing one's energy on working with what is. The goal of EFTT interventions therefore is to increase client reflection on this (e.g., the therapist might ask a client, "What's it like to know that you can push, push, push and still not get what you want—

desperately hoping that one day he will see the truth?") and accept the painful reality of hopeless situations. Acceptance in this case must be differentiated from depressive resignation. We will return to this topic in chapter 11 in the context of sadness and grief.

Symbolization

Verbal symbolization reduces anxiety because it helps clients to make sense of traumatic experiences and gain a sense of control. The capacity to communicate deeply painful experiences to others also serves to reduce the sense of isolation that is characteristic of PTSD. The goal of intervention is to help clients articulate not only specific painful or bad feelings but also the meaning of the feelings and the internal processes that contribute to the experience. For example, the therapist might ask, "What was so hurtful about that for you? I know in a general sense how painful that would be, but it's important to say what exactly was so bad *for you*." This shift in focus, from the general case to that which is particular to the individual, is the essence of promoting experiencing.

Promote Agency

Increasing clients' awareness of how they create or contribute to their own anxiety is necessary for emotion regulation and permanent change. The goal is to help them recognize that it is "I" who is thinking, feeling, needing, wanting, or doing this. If clients experience themselves as generating their own feelings, then they begin to see how they can change them. For example, with a client who learned in her family to suppress her feelings, the therapist reflected, "It's as if you have taken over where your parents left off." This process observation is in the interest of promoting client awareness of personal agency (for better or for worse) rather than blaming. When maladaptive anxiety spontaneously occurs in session, EFTT interventions promote "hot" experiential awareness of agency.

INTERVENTIONS FOR MANAGING ANXIETY AND FEAR

In the face of evoked trauma feelings and memories, markers or signs of underregulated fear and anxiety include panic, dissociation, catastrophic expectations about current situations or internal experiences, or overgeneralized fear in current situations. For example, the client Monica who found her mother moments after the mother had shot herself felt panicky remembering this event. In her life, she was unable to attend funerals because of crippling anxiety and dreaded the anniversaries of her mother's death. These responses are addressed through repeated imaginal exposure, for example, in the context of IC or in conjunction with two-chair enactments (described below). When necessary, EFTT also uses the following standard skills training interventions for managing fear/anxiety and achieving appropriate distance from potentially overwhelming emotions.

Regulated breathing is important when clients are anxious, holding their breath, or hyperventilating while recalling traumatic experiences. Also, explicit attention to tensing and *relaxing muscles* during the session is a helpful skill. Spending a few minutes with breathing and relaxation can be useful before accessing memories of traumatic events or focusing exercises.

Attention regulation skills or "grounding" strategies (Najavitz, 2002) help people to focus on their internal sensory experience and external reality rather than on thoughts that escalate anxiety. Present-centered awareness counteracts ruminating and anticipating. These strategies are most appropriate for reducing PTSD-related intrusive symptoms and dissociation. In doing this, clients are asked to look at the therapist, feel their feet on the floor, and feel their bum in the chair, to focus their attention on present sensory reality.

To address dissociation, intervention additionally involves processing the experience and providing education about the actual function of dissociation. The longer term goal is to strengthen the self so that the client can handle a feared experience (e.g., the therapist might say, "We want you to no longer feel like that defenseless little girl, so you don't have to disappear, or go away like that"), which also involves developing more adaptive emotion regulation strategies. This is followed by a gradual exposure to threatening material. Therapists should not persist with IC if imagining the perpetrator was, in fact, the stimulus for dissociation. For example, one client psychologically escaped during sexual molestation by imagining herself as a "little angel" far removed from the experience. In our view, she would be unable to let this dissociative part of herself go until she felt strong enough to face those feelings and memories. Successful interventions involved brief confrontations of the perpetrator during IC and accessing and validating her disgust and anger toward him in efforts to strengthen self. Intervention also included two-chair dialogues between the terrified (and disgusted) little girl and the little angel parts of herself. These strategies finally ended with an imaginary dialogue in which the client thanked the little angel for having protected her all these years and then said goodbye to her.

Distraction techniques (Najavitz, 2002) are useful in cases involving intrusive memories of horror, terror, and physical pain. To that end, directing a client's attention to breathing can help manage distress while she or he is describing horrific and physically painful events, but the goal is not to help clients explore, as such, those aspects of the event. Rather, these interventions validate pain and distress while focusing attention on the cognitive–affective processes at the time. The goal is to access the core self-organization formed at the time of the event so that maladaptive aspects are then available for restructuring. Therapy with the client Monica, for example, involved helping her block out horrific images of her mother's death and focus instead on expressing thoughts and feelings about the effects of the event. In another example, the client described in an earlier chapter who was raped by her father at age 4 could only recall the excruciating pain. Her therapist validated the pain but asked her to attend to the thoughts and feelings at the time of the event and afterward rather than the pain.

Self-soothing skills that involve developing compassion and empathy for the self in distress also are taught, shaped, and encouraged in EFTT. It can be helpful to ask clients to imagine themselves as children or how they would soothe and comfort their own child or a friend. Clients may be encouraged to engage in soothing behaviors (Linehan, 1993), such as taking a walk or a hot bath, listening to calm music, or in some way taking care of themselves to help deal with bad feelings. Finding a "safe place" (Elliott, Watson, Goldman, & Greenberg, 2004) is one self-soothing strategy that is similar to that used in EMDR (Shapiro & Maxfield, 2002). Clients are instructed to imagine a place where they feel safe and calm, to vividly get in touch with all the sensory aspects of the imagined place (sights, sounds, smells, bodily sensations), and to practice accessing this experiential memory, at will, until distress declines. Finally, avoidance and shutting down may be reframed as strengths and useful skills that clients can learn to deliberately use when needed to regulate high levels of distress. This enhances client self-esteem and sense of control.

ALLOWING PRIMARY EMOTIONAL EXPERIENCE

The above section dealt with underregulated anxiety and fear. The following two sections deal with chronically overcontrolled and avoided emotional experience. First we focus on avoided or disavowed material that needs to be accessed for its adaptive information.

Addressing Difficulties Allowing Emotional Pain

The pain of rejection or loss can feel like it will destroy oneself and thus may be avoided as a self-protective strategy. Markers of avoided emotional pain are evident in session when clients have been exposed to some deeply painful experience but are unwilling or unable to express the depths of their pain, either to the imagined other during IC or to the therapist. They may avoid talking about this experience altogether, speak intellectually about the event, minimize the pain, or cover it with secondary anger. They also may admit to coping or distancing themselves from their pain through substance abuse, promiscuity, or excessive work. Approaching painful emotion requires gradually overcoming the fear of falling apart or being destroyed by it and a conscious decision to allow and engage it. This change process involves emotional processing of the pain. Activating the pain-producing emotion structure by way of exposure modifies a client's belief that she or he cannot handle the pain, which is then followed by meaning reconstruction.

The process of working through emotional pain in emotion-focused therapy has been studied from analyses of videotaped therapy sessions as well as from clients' descriptions of their experience of reliving this kind of emotional pain (Bolger, 1999; Greenberg & Bolger, 2001). The phases in the process roughly correspond to the phases in EFTT that (a) provide safety so clients can begin to explore painful experience; (b) access, explore, and work through fear, avoidance, and shame; and (c) resolve issues with perpetrators of harm. The last includes constructing more adaptive views of self and these particular others, which generalizes to healthier current relationships. The process of allowing emotional pain is outlined below in a four-phase process. However, it should be clear that this is a meta-task that, like EFTT itself, may unfold over many sessions and may incorporate other interventions and tasks.

1. *Approaching.* In the first phase, previously avoided experience is approached and talked about. For example, after several sessions, a client named "John" began to describe, in detail, the events surrounding the drug overdose and death of his mother—coming home from school and seeing the ambulance and police around his house. Interventions that facilitated John approaching such painful material included highlighting his strengths, resources, and resilience throughout the therapy process and using emotion regulation strategies. Therapists, above all, need to communicate compassion for the client's pain and validate how hard it is to approach these feelings (e.g., "It's terrible for a child to feel so alone and afraid, I know it must be so hard to feel that again"). Therapists must also communicate the importance of owning these experiences as part of self and provide support (e.g., "It's okay, John, let it come. It's so important. I'll help.").

2. *Allowing.* In the second phase, while reliving a traumatic experience, clients see and accept themselves as having been damaged by the trauma. John, the client mentioned above, saw himself as a defenseless little boy ripped away from his beloved mother when he was placed in an orphanage after her death. This step in the process involves a conscious decision on the part of a client to fully allow the pain of the experience, despite his or her fear. In this phase of working through emotional pain, one of the goals is to help clients tolerate the complex set of feelings and realizations that emerge in the process. For John, facing the pain of his mother's death and the subsequent

brutality and betrayal he experienced in the orphanage also involved facing his own rage, and the hopelessness and despair of knowing that he had never received the love and nurturing he needed. He also needed to face and accept his own history of coping through substance abuse, the wasted years, and loss of opportunity, and to forgive himself.

Evoking and allowing emotional pain in EFTT may take place in the context of IC, in which the client confronts transgressors. Gradually and with time, therapists' provision of comfort and validation and empathic affirmation of vulnerability during IC are internalized by the client. These, in turn, help to establish stability in the face of what was previously overwhelming and provides access to a more self-affirming stance. When clients are unable to allow and express painful feelings to an imagined other in IC, expression of feelings can be redirected to the therapist or to an imagined part of themselves in the empty chair. Imagining oneself as a child and fully experiencing the pain of being abused or unloved can elicit compassion for oneself along with nurturing, soothing responses.

3. *Exploration.* In the third phase, questions and doubts about the newly acknowledged view of self open the door to forays of self-exploration. This requires helping clients to stay with feelings of being shattered, fully acknowledge the harm that had been done to them, identify the cause of damage and the person(s) responsible, and allow and fully express (perhaps in IC) feelings of anger and sadness about traumatic events.

The IC with another client, "Martha," began with expressions of anger toward her husband who had abandoned her and her four children 30 years earlier ("I hate you for what you did to us. How could anyone be so heartless!"). This activated a shift for her into deep sobbing and fully experiencing the pain of her sadness and loss for the first time. The therapist's soothing responses (e.g. "So many tears. Let it come . . .") helped Martha sink into her vulnerability and weep for her own suffering. This process also accessed questions about herself that later could be explored:

C: How could I have put up with his crap for so long?!? Was I so desperate?

T: So, you were willing to accept anything he threw your way, desperate for . . . ?

C: His love, I guess. But he never loved me, was always putting me down, or going off by himself. I just didn't want to see it.

T: Didn't want to face the truth, it was too painful? Or threatening?

C: Devastating. I didn't think I could survive, literally. I felt like I might not survive.

T: Like your very life depended on him.

This exploration led to a shift in Martha's view of self from a vulnerable and victimized young mother to a mature woman who had survived and raised her four children on her own.

4. *Integration.* In the fourth and last phase of this process, the painful experience is accepted and integrated into the sense of self. Clients have a clearer view of themselves and how damaging experiences functioned in their lives, are able to clearly express feelings associated with damaging people and events, and possibly take responsibility for contributing to their own pain (e.g., "My anger has pushed others away"). Therapist responses that support this new sense of self (e.g., "It's like your entire life has been defined by that moment—abandoned, terrified, and alone") facilitate an increased sense of personal agency and control for clients rather than victimization. Fully allowing experience also mobilizes the associated needs that act to challenge maladaptive beliefs associated with the painful state. Knowing what one wants and needs empowers the individual to assert boundaries or seek out support and nurturing, either internally, in the form of compassion and self-soothing, or interpersonally, from the therapist or others.

Addressing the Self-Interruption of Adaptive Emotion

Sometimes clients prevent themselves, deliberately or not, from having feelings. Here we discuss the self-interruption that occurs when secondary fear and avoidance stifle the emergence of specific primary adaptive emotions, such as anger at violation or betrayal, sadness about neglect and loss, or fear of dependency and weakness. Thus, although self-interruption may be an automatic defense, the individual is cut off from the adaptive information associated with these emotions.

Markers for self-interruption frequently are found in the abrupt change or disappearance of emotion. An example is when a primary emotional experience (anger, sadness, vulnerability) is emerging in IC or empathic exploration (EE), and this is abruptly followed by a client's withdrawal or inhibition of the experience via some other secondary emotion (e.g., anger to cover fear or shame). Emotions also can be interrupted via client cognitions, including injunctions against feelings (e.g., "anger is a sin" or "crying is feeling sorry for oneself") and catastrophic expectations about emotional experience and expression (e.g., "If I start crying I will never stop" or "If I get in touch with my anger, I will go crazy or hurt someone"). In addressing these beliefs, it is important for the therapist and client to collaboratively assess the actual risk of harm (e.g., a client's history of violence or self-harm) and distinguish this from unrealistic expectations. Some clients also may believe that they have no right to feel angry (or sad) about victimization because they brought it on themselves.

In these instances, the core maladaptive processes are primarily related to shame, a topic discussed in the next chapter.

The goal of addressing self-interruption of adaptive emotion is to help the client accept the suppressed emotion, experience it in awareness, and express it. Subgoals are to increase client awareness of (a) how they interpret their own experience or contribute to their own fear and anxiety (the thoughts and feelings involved), (b) to show the negative experiential consequences of self-interruption, and (c) to motivate a desire to allow the interrupted experience. Again, understanding how one's thoughts and feelings contribute to one's experience strengthens self because it increases agency and control. Although the techniques differ, cognitive–behavioral therapy approaches also help clients understand the connection between their maladaptive cognitions and, for example, depression or anxiety.

The intervention strategy in EFTT is both to explore the interruptive process—the internalized messages, beliefs, fears, memories, and their impact—and to access the suppressed experience. In this model, self-interruption is viewed as a conflict between the part of self whose feelings push for expression and the part of self that squashes that experience. The traditional gestalt (Perls, Hefferline, & Goodman, 1951) conceptualization of the conflict between the "top dog" (the dominant controlling part of self) and the "underdog" (the weaker suppressed part) is a useful framework for understanding this intervention process. The therapist's job here is to support the underdog, the healthy part of self that is chronically squashed, and to help that part have a voice.

One strategy for addressing self-interruption of internal experience involves using a two-chair enactment. Many clients who find it difficult to engage in IC are better able to engage in two-chair dialogues between conflicting parts of the self. However, even when clients are unable to engage in two-chair work because of performance anxiety, for example, the general model can act as a guide to the intervention process. The general model for two-chair enactments applies not only to undoing emotional blocking but also to challenging catastrophic expectations about external situations and self-critical processes, which will be discussed in the next chapter.

When self-interruption of adaptive experience repeatedly interferes with a client's functioning and with the therapeutic process, particularly emotional expression during IC, the therapist must bring the process into awareness and then collaborate with the client to understand and resolve this block. Notice that the self-interruptive split only needs to be addressed if the emotional block seems impassable. If the client can be encouraged to express primary emotion with the support of empathy alone, the intervention will not be needed. For example, the therapist might say to a client, "I know you want to look 'put together,' but can you put that part of yourself aside for now, speak from the part of you that feels like you're falling apart?" However, for some clients, explicitly addressing self-interruption is a pivotal process in the larger effort toward trauma resolution.

The following description of a two-chair intervention for self-interruption is based on descriptions presented in other manuals of emotion-focused therapy (e.g., Elliott et al., 2004; Greenberg, Rice, & Elliott, 1993). We present it here in five steps.

1. *Collaborate on and structure the task.* The initial step involves identifying and separating the two sides of the self and establishing contact between them. The therapist observes both some emerging experience and the client pulling back (e.g., "You got in touch with some anger there, but something happens, somehow it's hard to stay with it"), and further observes that this process has occurred repeatedly in therapy. Upon reflection, the client recognizes this pattern and acknowledges that it is problematic. At this point, the therapist can guide the client to engage in the two-chair procedure (e.g., "Let's separate these two parts of yourself, spell out what you actually do or say to yourself to squash down your anger") to better understand the process and to eventually change it.

Structuring the procedure is the same as structuring the IC described in the preceding chapter except the client is enacting an internal dialogue between two parts of him- or herself. We have found it most helpful for clients to sit in their usual chair when they are speaking from the healthy part of self that is being interrupted or suppressed. This helps them identify with that part of self throughout therapy. They will sit in the opposite chair when speaking from the dominant suppressing part of self. It is most naturalistic and effective to begin the dialogue with the client taking the role of the dominant part of self (i.e., the therapist says, "Come over here and do that to yourself again, be the part of you that squashes your own feelings down. How do you do it? Squash her, shut her down . . ."). As in the early stage of IC, when the purpose of imagining the negative other is to evoke a response in the self, the purpose at this stage is to evoke a reaction on the part of self that is being suppressed, the healthy experiencing self.

If necessary, the therapist can reevoke markers of self-interruption by asking clients to recall a troubling situation that may have just been discussed and attend to and express their reaction to it. When clients again pull back, they are directed to attend to their internal experience and enact how they just stopped themselves from feeling (e.g., "What happened just there? What did you just do or say to stop yourself from being angry at her? Do that again. Stop her, this part of you that felt angry for a second."). Just as psychological contact between self and the imagined other is critical to the success of IC, contact between the two sides of self is critical to the success of two-chair enactments. This promotes clients' experiential awareness of agency and the role they themselves play in the self-interruptive process.

Once the client enacts her or his own interruptive process (e.g., the client, speaking from dominant part of self, says, "You shouldn't be angry at your mother, she did her best"), the client is directed to switch chairs and attend to internal experience in response to being shut down. The therapist's intervention couplet used here is to facilitate expression ("Say that to yourself again") and follow by directing the client inwardly ("What is it like being on the receiving end of that message?"). Clients frequently will collapse and bow to the suppression of their feelings, fearing, for example, that these feelings are dangerous. The therapist then heightens awareness of this process ("It's very hard to fight that message. What does it feel like in your body to stifle it? Tell her [points to interrupting chair].").

2. *Differentiate and intensify self-interruption.* During the second step, therapists ask clients to elaborate and express their position to the suppressed experiencing part of self. In the case of catastrophic expectations about emerging internal experience, clients are encouraged to specify the imagined dangers and enact how they make themselves feel afraid of their feelings. Therapists also could provide corrective information about emotional processes (e.g., that normal emotions do not persist; they are fleeting, run their course, and quickly shift).

Intensification interventions by the therapist (e.g., "Say that again, really scare her") and evocative empathy can be used to exaggerate self-interruptive messages. For example, a therapist might reflect, "So you're saying you should sacrifice yourself, keep all those feelings tightly bottled up inside, suffer in silence." This is intended to increase clients' awareness of the extremity of their position and evoke a challenging response in the experiencing self. Challenges also emerge as a result of increased experiential awareness of the negative impact of squashing the self (e.g., the client says, "I don't want to sacrifice myself" or "I hate feeling all bottled up inside"). This mobilizes healthy strivings for self-expression that function to challenge maladaptive self-interruption. This process is similar to cognitive interventions intended to increase awareness of irrational beliefs about the dangerousness of internal experience, except that challenges in EFTT are self-generated and emerge from the client actually experiencing the impact of squashing oneself in the session rather than from a rational/logical process.

3. *Identify the interrupted expression.* By creating awareness that there is indeed a self-interruptive process and precisely *how* that happens, clients gradually become aware of *what* is actually being suppressed. So, in this third step, the client gets in touch with the interrupted experience. Therapist empathic responses help the client identify and stay with the feeling (e.g., "It's

so important to feel entitled to your anger—you were treated very badly—not necessarily express it to your mother, but at least acknowledge it for yourself").

4. *Restructure by accessing healthy resources.* The fourth step is characterized by client assertion of his or her need to express authentic feelings and needs (e.g., "I don't want to sacrifice myself, spend my whole life locked up inside. I have a right to my feelings as much as anyone."). The therapist supports the client's emerging felt need and encourages her or him to experiment with the appropriate expression of feelings and associated needs.

5. *Reintroduce IC or EE.* Because interrupted feelings in EFTT typically concern perpetrators of harm, in this fifth and final step, it is a good time to direct the client to reengage in the IC procedure and to express the previously inhibited feelings to this imagined other. Once the client is able to fully express and explore the meaning of previously inhibited feelings, the task shifts and the client moves on to resolving issues with perpetrators. This is carried forward in the third phase of EFTT.

Catastrophic Expectations About External Situations

Experiences of trauma frequently result in unrealistic beliefs, not only about internal experience but also about the dangers of situations and consequent avoidance of these situations. In cases of complex PTSD, these perceived dangers and beliefs typically are interpersonal in nature (e.g., I will get hurt; I will be abandoned; I will lose my sense of self). The model of resolving self-interruptive processes described above can also be applied to reducing catastrophic expectations and anxiety about external situations.

For example, during Phase 2 of therapy with the client, Martha, who had been abandoned by her husband, the focus shifted from her past issues to the conflict between wanting companionship versus fear of entering into another intimate relationship. From the dominant fear-producing part of herself, Martha was asked to specify anticipated dangers that prevented her from entering into a new relationship ("I will become too needy and dependent, put up with anything, be devastated by another rejection"). This process activated the core emotion structure in the part of self sitting in the experiencing chair: pain and devastation at abandonment, and the belief that it was her own neediness that caused her abandonment and pain. Therapist interventions validated her need to protect herself, highlighted and exaggerated her anticipated dangers (e.g., the therapist said to her, "So you can't trust yourself, you will be so needy you will settle for anything, you will be blind to signs of danger, you will be destroyed so you better not get involved"), and then encouraged her to attend to her response to these internally generated warnings. It is important to note that these therapist highlights and exaggerations are not delivered as confrontations but rather as empathic reflections of implicit meaning.

As a result, this elicited sadness in the client at the prospect of remaining alone for the rest of her life and made her more aware of a desire for companionship and intimacy. Interventions supported the emergence of these healthy resources ("Say more about how important companionship is to you"), which, in turn, accessed challenges to catastrophic expectations ("Why should I be a lonely old woman? I'm not the vulnerable young mother I used to be, I've learned a lot in 30 years."). The therapist supported this self-affirming stance.

Secondary Emotions Covering Adaptive Emotions

Another form of avoidance consists of a simple sequence in which a primary emotion is quickly followed by another emotion that functions to regulate, distance, or protect the individual from the initial painful or threatening experience. In psychodynamic terms, these are considered defensive emotions. In these cases, where one emotion is dominant, clients usually have a limited emotional repertoire. Markers of secondary defensive emotions are evident when the client repeatedly expresses, for example, hurt, sadness, or fear concerning maltreatment but seems to have no access to anger. Alternatively, the client has been deeply hurt but only expresses anger. There may be brief and subtle verbal or nonverbal indicators of the underlying emotion but this quickly disappears. More complex sequences include the client experiencing primary shame, then expressing secondary anger at being humiliated, followed by feeling guilty or anxious about his or her anger.

At markers of any secondary emotion, the therapist can invite clients to examine what they are feeling (e.g., "Something about her rejection made you feel angry?"). This can open an opportunity to help the client access primary experience, in this case, hurt. Or the therapist can empathically inquire in a direct way about the experience that led to the client's secondary emotion (e.g., "Something must have hurt you deeply to be feeling so angry?"). Frequently, however, intervention also requires explicit process observations and discussions with clients that a particular experience seems to dominate their repertoire and possibly serves some protective function. This can be accompanied by providing information about normal emotional processes—distinguishing between adaptive and maladaptive emotion, for example—and collaborating on the goal of expanding clients' emotion repertoire.

In an example introduced in an earlier chapter, the client Paul had a history of anger control problems and a limited emotion repertoire dominated by anger. During one session he expressed anger at his wife for using his abuse as a child against him in arguments. Helpful interventions validated his anger at betrayal and directed his attention to more vulnerable experience (the therapist said, "I hear how angry you are. And at the same time, it must be so hurtful to have her take your trust and use it against you like that."). Paul then was able to acknowledge that he felt like his wife probably did not love him. This opened the door to exploring how his anger had pushed others away and deprived him of the connection and love he wanted. The therapist used empathic responses to evoke and support his sadness, loneliness, and longing for connection and love (e.g., "So, under all that anger is a sad and lonely man, hungry for love, and yet pushing others away for fear of being hurt"). Over the course of several sessions, the client was able to acknowledge his more vulnerable experience and receive comfort and support from the therapist. Interventions also validated his need to protect himself and addressed ways in which he could feel safe while expressing vulnerability outside of the session.

ACCESSING AND RESTRUCTURING BAD FEELINGS

In addition to avoiding potentially adaptive experience, trauma and abuse survivors often are plagued by feeling hopeless, powerless, victimized, alienated, and despairing. These feelings cause considerable distress; people work hard to keep them at bay and seek therapy to get rid of them. However, these bad feelings are not the same as avoided emotional pain; they have no adaptive action tendency, and as such they cannot really be worked through to completion. As we have seen, therapy with these processes requires a complex set of interventions that include regulation and restructuring, but the route to restructuring in EFTT is through acceptance, experiencing, and exploring bad feelings rather than a direct focus on changing them. Experiencing and exploring bad feelings are methods to access new information about the self, in the form of needs and goals, and they provide new learning that negative emotions are a normal part of life that can be tolerated and understood.

Once bad feelings have been accessed, the process of restructuring follows the general model of change presented earlier (see Figure 3.1; Pascual-Leone & Greenberg, 2007). This process involves the following four phases.

1. *Evoke bad feelings.* Feelings, such as resignation and powerlessness, can emerge in the IC intervention when the client is confronting imagined others or when the client is discussing problematic current situations, such as difficulties standing up to a domineering parent, spouse, or employer. Interventions in response to these markers include process observations, directing client attention to their internal experience (e.g., the therapist might say, "That was a big sigh, resignation, like 'what is the point of saying how I feel?'"), and encouraging the client to stay with the bad feeling just long enough to understand it.

2. *Explore bad feelings.* Complex feelings, such as resignation, powerlessness, or desperation, are composed of underlying cognitive–affective processes

that generally are evident in the session. For example, a client named "Kim" who had been molested by a babysitter over several years was in therapy to resolve issues with her alcoholic mother who did not protect her at the time of abuse. The mother was very demanding, and the client still could not stand up to her even as an adult, even though she knew the mother's current behavior was inappropriate. She felt resentful but acquiesced to her mother's demands because she was afraid of losing the relationship altogether. She frequently collapsed into powerlessness and despair. She felt trapped and plagued by these bad feelings.

3. *Access core maladaptive emotion structure*. The core emotion structure underlying bad feelings frequently is related to fear and/or shame. Intervention typically involves memory work to access and explore a recent or past event in which this emotion structure was activated or developed. An episodic memory is explored in detail to access the associated feelings and beliefs. Kim, for example, reexperienced a recent episode of acquiescing to her mother's demands. During this process, she accessed her core fear of abandonment, that if she "rocked the boat," she would lose "the only mother I have and the only grandmother my little boy has." Guidelines for this type of memory work are presented in a later section of this chapter.

4. *Access healthy resources*. New emotions, action tendencies, and associated desires and needs are accessed and used to restructure the core emotion structure. The basic needs in the situation, for example, for safety, protection, or reassurance, and adult resources for coping are identified. The shift in perspective that results from the client exploring core emotions often occurs spontaneously (e.g., "I hate her manipulating me to get what she wants") and then is supported by the therapist ("Yes, you must be very resentful at times").

Alternatively, the therapist can play a more active role by guiding the client's attention to the emergence of some new experience. The therapist might hear in the client's momentary expression of anger a sense of autonomy and then bring this to focal attention (e.g., "What are you feeling right now?" or "You sound pretty determined"). The client who previously had collapsed into powerlessness is able to assert herself and lobby for her own interests. A therapist's open-ended questions (e.g., "As an adult, how do you feel about a little child being so neglected?"), in response to the client's feelings of anger or sadness, can help access survival-oriented goals.

Restructuring a Core Vulnerable/Insecure Self-Organization

In many instances, bad feelings related to powerlessness and helplessness stem from the inconsistent availability of protection and support in times of distress and are rooted in the basic fear that one will be left alone and unable to cope. This is a core sense of self, organized around experiences of fear and the anticipation of danger. Many of the clients presented already, for example, felt defenseless in the face of childhood or adult trauma, and these feelings continued to be activated. Markers include chronic feelings of insecurity, fearfulness, and possible avoidance of close relationships; others include clients' inability to assert themselves in current relationships or to establish appropriate interpersonal boundaries. Clients usually are troubled and confused by their reactions and their inability to cope in current life situation, or they intellectually understand the connection to past traumatic experiences and the irrationality of their reactions (i.e., there is no real danger) yet are unable to change them. Clients also may be troubled and confused about their reactions in past traumatic events. For example, a client who powerlessly watched his mother being beaten by his father stated, "I don't understand why I just stood there. I should have done something, anything, to try and stop him." This client struggled with chronic depression and continued to be disturbed by his own "failure" to protect his mother even though intellectually he knew he had been just a boy.

In session, clients may repeatedly collapse into resignation or hopelessness when confronting imagined offenders in the IC procedure. Typically, they not only are afraid of and avoid the anger of others but also have limited access to their own appropriate anger that might mobilize self-protective resources. Although these clients chronically feel anxious (e.g., "I'm always waiting for the other shoe to drop"), feelings of vulnerability and insecurity are not preceded by obvious cognitive processes, and a focus on changing maladaptive cognitions, through two-chair enactments, for example, is not effective in bringing about change.

Therefore, intervention for restructuring a core vulnerable/insecure sense of self requires processes similar to those used in the counterconditioning of primary maladaptive fear. This is usually accomplished through evocation of recent or distal memories to activate the core emotion structure. This was the case with the client Kim, described above. This also is a key intervention strategy used in transforming shame and will be discussed again in the following chapter.

Guidelines for Memory Work

Memory work in EFTT involves attention to both the external details of situations or events and the internal experience in response to the events. External details are used as stimuli for evoking internal experience. Emphasis is placed on accessing and exploring this internal experience, particularly concerning self and others. These are core components of the maladaptive self-organization that needs to be reorganized. The following are steps in the intervention process.

1. *Bring the situation alive.* After identifying a situation and collaborating on the task of memory work to understand self and situation better, the therapist's goal is to bring the situation alive in the session. Here EFTT draws on an intervention approach called *systematic evocative unfolding,* which is used at markers of problematic or troubling reactions (Elliott et al., 2004; Rice, 1974) and involves the use of colorful, expressive language and evocative reflections. Facilitating this intervention with clients is like playing a movie in which you start at the beginning of a specific incident and slow down the playback so that it can be examined in detail. Interventions move back and forth between exploring both the external/situational and internal/experiential aspects of the situation. The therapist directs the client's attention to details of the situation (e.g., deadly silence, sarcastic and belittling tone of voice, looming presence of the other) and to internal reactions or experiences evoked in response to a situation or imagined other person (e.g., sense of panic, feeling small and powerless, desire to run away or hide, suppressed anger or resentment). These internal reactions are all aspects of the core self-organization.

2. *Examine feelings and beliefs from current (adult) perspective.* The goal here is to help the client examine and question aspects of self evoked in the situation. Standard EFTT interventions that promote experiencing help the client recognize and reexamine core feelings and beliefs, connect current reactions and behavior to past traumatic situations, recognize patterns of behavior (e.g., nonassertiveness, overcompliance, collapsing into tears), and then consider new options. If the situation entails childhood trauma, this will involve examining the related feelings and beliefs from the client's current adult perspective (e.g., "I am no longer that defenseless child. So what if she gives me a dirty look? It won't kill me. I can walk away.").

3. *Restructure sense of self.* The final goal is to restructure the core maladaptive self-organization that produces feelings of insecurity and vulnerability. This is accomplished by reentering a situation in imagination while simultaneously accessing alternative healthy adult resources. For example, one overly responsible client named "Stephanie" who suffered from chronic depression explored an episode in which she, as a child, was waiting for her physically abusive father to come home. She reexperienced her sense of dread, trying to be a "perfect little girl" to avert danger and to protect her mother and younger brother, but always failing to do so, leaving her feeling helpless and powerless. Stephanie also reexperienced hating her father for terrorizing her family, then squashing these feelings because "it is a sin to feel that way about your father," and then collapsing again into powerlessness. The client recognized this as the same feelings of powerlessness that were activated in many of her current life situations. Therapist interventions helped mobilize her adult perspective and healthy strivings ("How do you feel now when you think about him terrorizing your family like that?"). Acknowledging how much she hated his tyranny, as well as

recognizing her desire to feel safe, happy, and unburdened, helped motivate Stephanie's assertion. From this process, she then refused to put up with her father's ongoing rages, asserted stronger boundaries with him and others, and relinquished the excessive sense of responsibility she had in her caregiver role.

During memory work, clients also can be encouraged to imaginally reenter these difficult situations to comfort themselves or to retrospectively confront perpetrators in IC or EE. One client who found herself as an adult crying for her "daddy" whenever she felt threatened was asked to imagine such a situation and respond from her adult perspective. The therapist asked the client, "Get in touch with yourself feeling like a little girl. What is she feeling? What does she need? If she was your child, what could you say to calm or comfort her? How can you keep her safe?"

As always, challenges may emerge for the therapist when using the interventions for fear, anxiety, and avoidance as described in this chapter. These challenges are similar to those that emerge when working with shame and self-blame. Therefore, we will discuss these issues together at the end of the next chapter.

9

TRANSFORMING GUILT, SHAME, AND SELF-BLAME

The present chapter focuses on transforming guilt, shame, and self-critical processes as a continuation of Phase 2 in therapy. Clients cannot move forward and resolve issues with perpetrators and hold them accountable for harm until they stop blaming themselves; they cannot sustain healthy relationships in general until they feel more compassionate toward themselves. As discussed in the preceding chapter, fear and shame are closely related in terms of action tendencies and are considered functionally equivalent in terms of providing information about the client's core sense of self and the process of change (Greenberg & Paivio, 1997; Pascual-Leone & Greenberg, 2007). Therefore, many of the change processes and intervention principles and strategies presented in this chapter are similar to those presented in the preceding chapter. However, in cases of complex posttraumatic stress disorders (PTSDs) and in relational trauma, unlike simple PTSD, shame is typically more dominant than fear, and shame is also more central in the damage to a client's sense of self. Feelings of shame are extremely painful, frequently avoided, and difficult to access in therapy. This, in turn, makes these feelings notoriously difficult to change. Working with shame therefore presents unique challenges for the clinician.

This chapter is structured similarly to the preceding ones. We place emotion-focused therapy for trauma (EFTT) in the context of other approaches for reducing shame, describe different types of shame experience as observed in trauma therapy, and then describe the change processes and goals specific to our approach. The last half of the chapter focuses on intervention, and, again, many of the strategies parallel those described in the preceding chapter. Material that is uniquely relevant here includes working with adaptive shame about violating one's own personal standards, shame–anxiety underlying social phobia, and guidelines for changing hostile self-criticism and a core sense of self as defective or worthless. Some of this work is done in the context of using two-chair enactments and memory work. The chapter concludes with a section on addressing difficulties in working with the functionally equivalent emotions of fear and shame.

COMPARISON OF EFTT WITH OTHER APPROACHES TO WORKING WITH GUILT AND SHAME

Guilt, shame, and self-blame are recognized as the defining features of complex PTSD stemming from interpersonal trauma. There are several reasons for this. First, victimization—being rendered powerless and stripped of one's dignity—is profoundly humiliating. Victims frequently share the belief that people are entirely responsible for their own fates and circumstances, and they therefore blame themselves for their own victimization. Furthermore, complex trauma can include overt or implicit messages of blame and shame from the actual perpetrators that, over time, erode self-esteem (van der Kolk, 2003). It also has been suggested that self-blame provides an element of perceived control over otherwise random acts of violence. It may be less threatening for a child to blame him- or herself, for example, than to accept that an attachment figure, on whom they are completely dependent, is unreliable or dangerous (Winnicott, 1965).

Another reason for the centrality of shame in trauma is its prominence in many disorders that are comorbid with complex PTSD. Thus, shame has been called a transdiagnostic emotion. Shame is intrinsic to self-critical depressions, for example, as well as lingering depression at loss (Pascual-Leone & Greenberg, 2007). Accordingly, a history of rejection by attachment figures results in a core sense of self as defective and, therefore, vulnerable to abandonment. Adult experiences of actual loss or rejection later seem to confirm this shame-based sense of self. Similar processes are thought to be involved in particular types of personality pathology. Borderline and narcissistic rage, for example, is considered a defense against core feelings of shame, and avoidance of interpersonal contact, which is characteristic of avoidant personality, protects against morbid fear of rejection (projected shame-based sense of self). Likewise, social and performance anxiety can be rooted in a fear that others will see one's essential defectiveness. Sexual victimization is particularly stigmatizing. Victims of child sexual abuse not only are disgusted by perpetrators but are disgusted with themselves, feel contaminated, or "dirty." Behaviors such as substance abuse and self-injury can function to numb these feelings of shame, and engaging in these behaviors, in turn, can generate additional shame.

In terms of intervention, traditional cognitive and behavioral approaches focus on changing the self-critical thoughts associated with depression and the self-blame associated with trauma (e.g., Beck, Freeman, & Davis, 2004; Foa, Huppert, & Cahill, 2006). However, there is increasing recognition that shame, which in this case is rooted in early attachment experiences, can be difficult to treat with standard cognitive–behavioral therapy methods and can interfere with the therapeutic relationship (Courtois & Ford, 2009; Solomon & Siegel, 2003). Recent approaches to reducing shame target these more complex meaning systems. As discussed in the preceding chapter, for example, dialectical behavior therapy (Linehan, 1993) emphasizes the importance of therapist validation to reduce underregulated shame and promote self-development. Other approaches (e.g., compassionate mind training; Gilbert & Irons, 2005) use a variety of experiential tools to help clients explore and revise the inner dialogues they learned as they grew up and to develop self-soothing capacities. Although these approaches share similarities with EFTT, they are, in contrast, essentially skills training models. Although EFTT may incorporate skills training strategies, it relies primarily on therapist empathy, validation, and promoting client experiencing as the mechanisms of change.

Many psychodynamic relational models also understand shame as originating from a core sense of self that develops through negative attachment experiences (e.g., Benjamin, 1996; Fairbairn, 1952; Kohut, 1984). Current accelerated experiential dynamic psychotherapy (AEDP; Fosha, Paivio, Gleiser, & Ford, 2009) draws on Winnicott's (1965) views concerning the "true self" that embodies authentic feelings and needs and the "false self" that squashes authentic experience in order to secure approval. AEDP emphasizes provision of a secure attachment bond that helps clients to relinquish their defenses and access suppressed feelings and needs. These concepts are useful metaphors used in EFTT and have obvious similarities to Rogers's (1959) views concerning the necessary and sufficient conditions of change—the therapeutic relationship qualities that undo "conditions of worth" and help clients to access authentic experience. These views are particularly compatible with EFTT.

PROCESS DIAGNOSIS: DISTINGUISHING DIFFERENT TYPES OF SHAME EXPERIENCE

Just as with fear and anxiety discussed in the preceding chapter, EFTT distinguishes among different types of shame experience and these distinctions inform appropriate intervention.

Adaptive Shame

Shame is characterized by feeling exposed and condemned as lacking in dignity or worth, feeling looked down on or inferior in the eyes of others (Greenberg & Paivio, 1997). The capacity for shame develops with the capacity for self-consciousness around 2 years of age. Shame-related experiences include self-consciousness, embarrassment, humiliation, and a sense of worthlessness or inferiority. The action tendency associated with shame is to withdraw or hide so that personal flaws are not exposed. Shame reduces facial communication (Sedgwick & Frank, 1995) and involves lowering of the eyes, shrinking of the upper body, pounding of the heart, and blushing. Awareness of one's own blushing perpetuates it. The hiding response associated with shame is captured in expressions such as "losing face" and wanting to "crawl into a hole and die." The adaptive function of shame is to protect social standing and connectedness, to promote belonging and conformity to social standards among one's group. The public shunning practiced by certain cultural groups as a punishment for violation of social standards exemplifies this social function.

Maladaptive Shame

The following sections describe two types of maladaptive shame that, even more than fear or anxiety, define complex rational trauma.

Primary Maladaptive Shame

Abused and neglected children grow up with a sense of themselves as fundamentally flawed and bad and maintain this sense sometimes despite explicit beliefs to the contrary. For example, a client might say, "I know it's ridiculous to be so concerned about making small mistakes but I *feel* like it's terrible, almost like I'm a murderer." These individuals can feel that they were somehow responsible for their own maltreatment even though, intellectually, they know that children cannot be held responsible for such acts. As in the case of primary maladaptive fear, this sense of self is a holistic, implicit, and embodied emotion scheme or meaning system that is composed of thoughts, feelings, and somatic-sensory experience. When activated, this emotion scheme generates feelings of shame and may generate explicit critical self-statements, but not vice versa, as in secondary shame.

Secondary Maladaptive Shame

Secondary shame, on the other hand, is considered a response to self-critical thoughts and self-statements or to other feelings (e.g., jealousy or weakness) or is the result of a sequence of thoughts and feelings that characterize complex experiences, such as depression. Secondary shame typically is more circumscribed and less entrenched, and the accompanying hostile affect directed at self may be less harsh than in primary maladaptive shame. For these reasons, secondary shame also can be more amenable to change using two-chair enactments of self-critical processes. We will return to these distinctions between primary and secondary maladaptive shame in the intervention section of the chapter.

Shame and Other Emotions

In addition to the above subtypes, shame also is related to and frequently coexists with a number of other emotions. The following sections describe these distinct emotions and their relationship to shame.

Guilt

Guilt is similar to secondary shame that is associated with obvious self-critical thoughts. Unlike shame, however, guilt is always considered a complex secondary emotion that is the product of a client's learned injunctions against particular actions, behaviors, or feelings (e.g., "You *shouldn't* be angry at your parents") rather than referring to the whole person (e.g., "I am such a loser"). Guilt can provide adaptive information when it concerns real wrongdoing (e.g., perpetrating abuse or neglect), in which case the action tendency is to make amends or change the behavior. Maladaptive guilt associated with trauma, however, involves victims erroneously feeling responsible for their own or others' victimization. In-session markers of guilt are similar to those for secondary shame and include implicit or explicit "should" or critical self-statements. Another example of this is when witnesses of maltreatment suffer survivor guilt.

Shame–Anxiety

Social anxiety can be secondary to core feelings of inferiority (shame) so that people fear being exposed as such. This frequently stems from a history of being berated or humiliated for failures or shortcomings. Shame–anxiety involves overcontrol and overmonitoring the self and an inability to be spontaneous for fear of exposing defective aspects of self. Individuals who are plagued with shame–anxiety are vigilant for signs of disapproval, have difficulty asserting themselves or saying "no" for fear of rejection, and may engage in extraordinary efforts to please others. Shame–anxiety also is observed in the therapeutic relationship when clients fear disclosure and judgment from their therapist and can interfere with a client's participation in key interventions.

Anger, Contempt, and Disgust

Clients can feel disgust at thoughts, values, people, or anything else they view as offensive. Contempt can be thought of as a blend of cool anger and disgust; it is rejection that is haughty and superior. Disgust and contempt, when directed at another person, serve the same distancing function as anger. These feelings are adaptive when they are directed externally and in response to violations of one's physical integrity or rights and standards, but they are problematic when directed at the self. Anger, contempt, and disgust directed at self are the affective qualities that drive self-critical cognitions and statements. Together, these cognitive–affective processes are activated along with a core shame-based sense of self and can contribute to or perpetuate secondary maladaptive shame.

CHANGE PROCESSES AND GOALS

Transforming shame involves processes and goals similar to those involved in transforming fear, which are presented in the general model of emotional processing (see Figure 3.1 in chap. 3, this volume; Pascual-Leone & Greenberg, 2007). In brief, once shame is identified as the source of client distress, interventions access a client's specific negative self-evaluations ("I'm no good/I'm defective/I'm unlovable") and unmet needs (i.e., for self-respect, compassion toward self) that are part of the emotion structure. The exploration process then shifts to the client accessing healthy internal resources in the form of more positive self-evaluations and a sense of entitlement to unmet needs (e.g., "I deserved encouragement and support, not that constant criticism"). This, in turn, activates assertive anger at maltreatment or sadness about losses, both of which are associated with adaptive action tendencies. As such, these adaptive emotions help to counteract shame, an example of transformative emotional processing.

Just as in working with fear, one goal of EFTT with shame is to help clients allow previously avoided painful experiences of shame to integrate the associated information into the self. Change, here, necessarily involves gradual exposure to potentially overwhelming shameful experience and the incorporation of emotion regulation strategies. Strategies also help clients explore and construct new meaning concerning shameful traumatic experiences and promote client agency and self-control, particularly through awareness of how internalized self-critical processes contribute to undermining their own self-esteem.

INTERVENTION PRINCIPLES RELEVANT TO SHAME

In addition to the above change principles and goals, the following emotion-focused therapy intervention principles are particularly relevant to working with shame-related processes.

Affirming Client Vulnerability

Affirming client vulnerability is perhaps the most important principle related to therapeutic work with shame. Clients feel highly vulnerable disclosing embarrassing or humiliating experiences. Simple statements by the therapist (e.g., "Yes, I know it's hard to talk about this"), communicated with a quality of gentleness and compassion, are invaluable in reducing anxiety so that clients are willing to disclose hidden aspects of self. Of course, affirmation of vulnerability should precede attempts to explore shame-related experience. Markers of vulnerability include clients' overt expressions of shame or embarrassment, reluctance to disclose, expressions of self-doubt (e.g., "Maybe I'm making mountains out of molehills"), and a vocal quality of "confession" or revealing deeply held secrets. After affirming client vulnerability, therapists also can prompt for further disclosure through the provision of support (e.g., "I don't want you to have these dirty secrets festering inside anymore, it's important to get them out in the open—here, where it's safe").

Refocusing Client Attention on Internal Experience

Refocusing client attention is frequently necessary in shame work because deflections away from experiences of shame are intrinsic to the expression of this emotion. Clients can often talk about or around shame-inducing experiences but will avoid full engagement as a way of curtailing their discomfort. Interventions such as "Let's go back . . ." can refocus attention on core shame experience. Therapist interventions also can validate reactive anger as a coping resource and then follow by directing the client's attention to an underlying core experience of shame (e.g., "Can you *also* get in touch with that feeling of being used, that's the damaging part").

Being Present-Centered

Being "present" involves the therapist directing clients' attention to what they are experiencing in the moment (e.g., "What are you feeling right now as we talk about this?"). The difficulty with shining a spotlight on shame experience is that it risks increasing a client's self-consciousness and may thereby promote further withdrawal. However, one area in which this is essential is in increasing clients' awareness of their own agency in contributing to shame through self-criticism. In two-chair work, clients are encouraged to direct self-critical statements at themselves and then attend to the experiential impact of that criticism in the moment.

Analyzing Expression

This principle involves directing clients' attention to the vocal quality of contempt and disgust associated, for example, with self-critical statements and helping them articulate the meaning of these feelings. Expression analysis also can be used to help identify the origins of negative self-statements (e.g., the therapist might ask, "Whose voice is that? Is that you, or is that your father talking?") and can focus clients' attention on their own reactions as the recipients of harsh self-directed criticism. Client gestures, sighs, and vocal qualities can indicate feeling hurt, defensive, or bad about self in response to criticism. This increases experiential awareness of the negative impact of self-criticism and helps to mobilize those protective parts of self that do not believe these criticisms or do not accept such harsh treatment.

Promoting Agency

Ownership of experience or acknowledging agency occurs in two ways. First, clients are encouraged to enact how they make themselves feel ashamed to specify the beliefs they actually harbor about what is so deeply wrong with them. Therapists initially validate that there are interpersonal origins for these messages, but eventually clients must understand that they have come to believe these things as well. Second, once clients (ironically) perceive themselves as contributing to their own bad feelings, this opens the way to new adaptive experiences such as fighting back, assertion, and aspiring for change.

Intensifying Experience

During two-chair work, intensifying client experience lends impact to self-critical statements and reveals the implicit self-loathing, disgust, or contempt to activate the shame-based emotion structure. This, then, is available for exploration and change. When clients are resistant to focusing on shame experience, it can be helpful for the therapist to intensify the damaging effects of hiding and constant vigilance (e.g., "I know every fiber of your being wants to push it away, but that's such a strain—to be on guard all the time"). Intensification strategies similarly are used in memory work, to evoke core maladaptive emotion structures (as presented later).

Offering Process Observations

Offering observations to clients as feedback about their process is important because clients often are unaware of (through avoidance) or reluctant to acknowledge shame experience. Process observations help clients reflect on their core emotional state and contribute to developing a collaborative understanding of the generating conditions for disturbance. For example, a therapist might observe that a given client frequently has a belittling tone of voice when she talks about herself.

Evoking Memories

Strategies are used to access memories of experiences in which the client's sense of self as worthless or defective was formed, or present situations in which this sense of self was activated. Once activated, these memory structures yield new information about self and situations that is then available for exploration, emotional processing, and change.

INTERVENTION FOR REDUCING SHAME–ANXIETY

We begin this intervention section with shame experiences that sometimes are erroneously considered in terms of anxiety; when this happens, the change process is derailed. These experiences concern fear of negative evaluation in interpersonal relationships. From an EFTT perspective, these experiences are characterized by secondary anxiety about more primary shame, so that appropriate intervention must involve transforming the core shame.

Reducing Shame–Anxiety in the Therapeutic Relationship

Fear of negative evaluation in the therapeutic relationship was discussed in chapter 5 in the context of alliance development. We review it here briefly because of its fundamental importance in working with trauma survivors. Most clients are concerned about what to disclose and what to keep hidden or private in therapy (Greenberg & Paivio, 1998). However, shame and shame–anxiety are particularly prevalent in cases of complex trauma in which clients have been shamed by their attachment figures. These individuals are vulnerable to feeling incompetent or foolish when they experience difficulties engaging in the tasks of therapy (e.g., experiencing, enactments) or when they are misunderstood by the therapist. Furthermore, they are asked to disclose experiences of humiliation, rejection, or neglect that are difficult for anyone to acknowledge, even to themselves.

Transforming shame in therapy is entirely dependent on the therapist's genuineness, empathy, and unconditional positive regard. This Rogerian stance helps to reduce client fear of negative evaluation and disconfirms beliefs that their feelings and perceptions are unimportant or stupid. In cases of child abuse trauma, this stance can further help to counteract early learning experiences. The fundamental interventions here are validation and empathic responding to client feelings and needs, including feelings of vulnerability and needs to defensively withdraw.

Addressing Shame Underlying Social Anxiety

Initially in therapy, socially anxious clients might only be aware of their anxiety and are less aware of underlying core feelings of worthlessness or inadequacy. It also can be difficult for clients to admit that shame is the core issue—what amounts to their shame about being ashamed, and their secondary shame about the primary shame. The first step in intervention, therefore, is to arrive at a mutual understanding that social anxiety is driven by primary maladaptive feelings of shame.

In some cases, it is sufficient for intervention to focus on obvious negative self-statements. In other cases, it is necessary to access the core self-organization by activating formative emotion memories. For example, one anxious and avoidant client had chronic feelings of inferiority and worthlessness that were internalized from the abuse of a critical stepfather. He found it impossible to engage in two-chair work for fear of losing control and looking stupid, and he was extremely emotionally blocked. Therapy attempted to explore how the client made himself feel anxious, but again, anxiety interfered with the exploration process. Successful treatment first needed to reduce his anxiety in the session, for example, by providing structure. Only then could interventions focus on exploring memories of shaming experiences with his stepfather.

Another socially anxious client with a history of severe emotional abuse discussed receiving a promotion at work, then automatically feeling afraid that she would not be able to live up to the expectations, and then feeling anxious that her boss and coworkers would see her nervousness and evaluate her negatively. Her account reveals a sense of primary shame about her (felt) inadequacy and then her secondary anxiety about being "found out." EFTT intervention involved validating the secondary anxiety and redirecting the client's attention to and exploring primary feelings of incompetence. She had a sense that she could not possibly perform as expected, combined with a fear of disappointing others, and the belief that this was inevitable because she is fundamentally incompetent, inferior, and so on. Interventions included arriving at a mutual understanding that this sense of self is what needed to change. For example, the therapist said to the client:

> I know you don't like feeling so anxious in these situations, but my sense is that what's really going on is shame, a deep sense of yourself as incompetent or inferior. Your anxiety is the fear that others might see this "defective you" that comes from all those experiences of being humiliated as a girl. If we can change those feelings of defectiveness or inferiority, I think your anxiety will disappear. Does this make sense?

The client immediately recognized this as true. The focus of therapy then shifted to strengthening her sense of self through memory work rather than challenging the anxiety-producing cognitions.

INTERVENTION FOR PRIMARY SHAME ABOUT VIOLATING PERSONAL STANDARDS

This section addresses another area of possible confusion for clinicians, and that is the notion of adaptive shame. It is not uncommon for clients with histories of complex PTSD to engage in self-destructive behaviors as strategies for coping with emotional pain, including the pain of shame. Ironically, people also frequently feel ashamed of themselves for engaging in these behaviors, and self-condemnation can be accompanied by a fear of being found out, stigmatized, and rejected. Many trauma survivors also can feel responsible for causing harm or failing to protect others. Others feel ashamed about having participated in morally unacceptable behavior during their own sexual abuse, for example. Before deciding how to intervene in these cases, a distinction must be made between behaviors over which clients had or did not have control.

When clients feel ashamed about behavior over which they have control (e.g., substance abuse, neglecting one's children), the goal is to shift their overgeneralized shame and self-condemnation (e.g., "I am a despicable, bad person") to guilt and regrets about the specific behavior or mistake and then to mobilize a desire to make amends or change. In short, the aim of this intervention is to make use of the primary adaptive shame that clients have about violating their own personal standards. The first step is to acknowledge and empathically affirm the difficulty of facing painful and shameful memories, as well as acknowledge the client's courage in disclosure. Therapists communicate unconditional positive regard for the client, compassion for his or her suffering, and a matter-of-fact attitude toward the content. Intervention then involves exploring the client's values and increasing the client's awareness of the function of the shameful behavior, including the core needs and desires that it fulfils (e.g., the need to escape, to be free). Interventions also support appropriate acceptance of responsibility for the behavior and, at the same time, promote compassion toward self for imperfection and mistakes and acknowledge the coexistence of different aspects of self. In short, the goal is to change the formulation from "bad person" to "bad deed."

One example is a client who had been physically and sexually molested by multiple perpetrators, including her parents, and who was also riddled with shame for hitting and sexually experimenting with her younger brother. She felt a lot of pain for hurting him the way she had been hurt. She believed that she "should have known better" and initially was very reluctant to disclose details of her own abusive behavior. Therapist responses that highlighted her desire to be a loving sister and her deep regret helped to reduce anxiety. In addition, the therapist's reflection that "this is eating away at you" elicited weeping and further disclosure of what she had done.

Later, memory work was used to access this client's motivations, thoughts, and feelings as a child (i.e., promote experiencing to construct new meaning). She recalled her pain, anger, and confusion at the chaos in her life at that time and her struggle to handle those situations on her own. This accessed deep sadness and empathy for herself as a child. The therapist also asked how she would feel if her parents expressed regret for treating her the way they did. She acknowledged that she certainly would forgive them. This helped to mobilize self-forgiveness. Finally, she also was able to express regret in an imaginal confrontation (IC) with her brother.

Another example of this process was with a highly religious and emotionally constricted client who secretly visited massage parlors. On one hand, he enjoyed the "rebellion" against his church's moral proscriptions and control as well as the excitement of physical contact. On the other, he felt ashamed of "cheating" on his wife and exploiting young women ("They are all somebody's daughter"). Notice that this is different from self-critical processes because the shame is, in fact, adaptive; it tells him that he is violating important personal values and standards. Successful intervention, in this case, involved validating and helping the client acknowledge and explore his need for freedom and physical contact while also bearing in mind his values, and then searching for more personally acceptable ways to get his needs met.

INTERVENTION FOR TRANSFORMING PRIMARY
MALADAPTIVE SHAME

Besides shame–anxiety in the therapeutic relationship, the most frequently observed shame-related difficulty in therapy for complex trauma concerns a core shame-based sense of self. Survivors of sexual abuse, for example, feel "dirty" and that they must have been somehow responsible for disgusting acts over which they objectively know they had no control. Others feel they must have deserved physical abuse even though they would never beat their own children for similar behavior. In the case of emotional abuse, harsh verbal derogation by caregivers is internalized so the person comes to believe the criticisms. In cases of childhood emotional neglect, people have internalized a sense of self as negligible and not worthy of care or attention.

Again, these experiences of self are difficult to change because they are difficult to access in therapy and because the person often has limited access to alternative healthy self-structures; there is no healthy pretrauma self. For example, when asked, a client who had been incessantly ridiculed by his mother could not say how he would have preferred her to respond to him because he had no experience with nurturing responses. Clients like this, who have limited experience receiving compassion or soothing from an attachment figure, may have limited compassion toward themselves and a limited capacity for self-soothing in times of distress.

Markers of primary maladaptive shame in therapy include chronic feelings of worthlessness and inferiority (sometimes despite intellectual awareness to the contrary) or chronic depression generated by this "weak/bad" sense of self. In cases of social anxiety and avoidant personality, markers for primary maladaptive shame are intense fear of negative evaluation and frequent self-consciousness and embarrassment across situations. Other examples include excessive anger at perceived slights, as in narcissistic rage, and rage at the threat of abandonment as seen in people with borderline personality.

The intervention strategy for changing primary maladaptive shame is similar to that for changing primary maladaptive fear described in the preceding chapter. It involves accessing the core sense of self and restructuring it by simultaneously accessing alternative healthy adult resources. This is typically accomplished by activating episodic memories of recent or past situations in which the shame-based sense of self is activated or was formed. However, accessing and disclosing shameful and humiliating experiences are more often than not accompanied by intense feelings of vulnerability and emotional pain, and so intervention must be more delicate and will be more complex than doing memory work with fear.

Transforming Shame Through Memory Work

Memory work to access new information is particularly suitable with clients who have been profoundly neglected as children. Neglect, unlike abuse, involves the absence of responsive information. Neglected children grow up with the implicit sense that there must be something wrong with them but are unclear what this might be, and they are constantly searching to figure it out. In therapy, these clients can be cautious or inhibited, have difficulties with experiencing, and often look to the therapist for guidance. However, unlike social anxiety from emotional abuse, which primarily concerns fear of an anticipated negative evaluation, the experience of neglected individuals tends to be one of uncertainty about internal experience and what is expected of them. Therapist interventions provide the emotion coaching and mirroring they did not receive in childhood. These include offering tentative guesses or conjectures about a client's experience while exploring episodic memories until the client can recognize his or her own self-experience.

Of course, abuse and neglect frequently co-occur as is the case for John, the client who grew up in an orphanage following the death of his mother and subsequently suffered repeated physical and sexual abuse. A prominent focus of therapy with John was shame and self-blame. For example, he recounted an incident in which he ran away from the orphanage and then was molested by a stranger in a movie theatre.

C: I don't know why these things kept happening to me!

T: When you think about it, what answer comes? How do you explain it to yourself?

C: [*pause*] I don't know.

T: Let's stay with this a bit. You seem to be saying it was something about you. Something about you made you profoundly vulnerable to being victimized over and over again?

This led to interventions that included John reexperiencing himself as a boy, alone in the movie theatre—young, scared, unprotected, needy, and alone. Intervention with this client also included explicit education about predators and child abuse to promote understanding of his vulnerability to victimization. In these ways, the therapist was able to help John increase experiential awareness of his own vulnerability and underlying feelings of shame. Doing so reorients a client in such a way that shame can be accessed and responded to, paving the way for the transformation of this maladaptive shame.

Another example is a socially anxious client, "Helen," who recalled coming home from school with her report card and being ignored by her cold and silent father, then going up to her room and sitting alone on her bed wondering what was wrong with her. The therapist's intervention first directed the client's attention to the external details of the situation (e.g., "Can you imagine the look on your fathers face; his tone of voice; details of your bedroom as you sat there alone?") to bring the situation alive. This evocative function of concrete external descriptors is similar to the function of initially imagining the other in the IC intervention. The goal is to activate the primary emotion scheme and associated core sense of self that developed through repeated similar experiences. Once the memory was activated, successful interventions helped the client explore her subjective internal experience as it was at that moment. The therapist began with a reflection ("Proud of your report card. You must have been disappointed by his reaction? Slinking off to your room and sitting by yourself . . .") and then explored details about tacit meanings (e.g., "What was going on in your mind? How did you feel . . . confused, or sad, maybe angry? What was your understanding of why he behaved that way? Somehow it was something about *you*—what did you imagine was wrong with you? How did you cope with those painful thoughts and feelings?")

This is the process of promoting experiencing with the goal of increasing understanding and constructing new meaning. In Helen's example, she recalled feeling so disappointed, sad, alone, and confused, trying to figure out what was wrong with her that her father was so disinterested. She thought she was somehow boring or weird, but there was no clear answer, just a perpetual feeling of inadequacy and uncertainty about who she was and how to behave appropriately to get the attention and recognition she desired.

Change occurs first through accessing core maladaptive beliefs (e.g., "I must be weird") followed by alternative healthy resources. For Helen, change eventually occurred through emergence of speculative questions ("Maybe there was *nothing* wrong with me, maybe it was just *his* weirdness. . . . Hmm, I don't think I did anything to deserve his coldness"). Following this, Helen shifted to feelings of sadness via the emerging awareness of unmet attachment needs ("More than anything I wanted his approval. I feel so sad that I never got that. I was such a confused little kid, trying so hard to figure out how to please, always failing, always disappointed. That's how I've lived my life.").

Shift to Enactments

Just as with using memory work to transform insecurity, once an emotion is activated and the client is in a position of self-reflection, it can be particularly powerful to ask clients to imagine themselves as children and to ask what they needed or wanted and, from their current adult perspective, then have them respond to that need. As with the client Helen whose father ignored her (and her report card), when clients reexperience their hurt, need, longing, and vulnerability, it can elicit deep sadness and compassion for the self and anger at the other. This is the new information that emerges bottom-up from the experiential process.

Clients also can be directed to imagine themselves as adults revisiting the past situations and consider how they might now respond. For example, the client described earlier in this chapter who felt anxious about receiving a promotion at work recalled being cruelly degraded and humiliated by her father and not protected by her mother. She was asked to reenter a particular situation and imagine herself as that little girl and then to consider what she could say to herself or to her mother (e.g., "Help your mom be a good parent. How would a good parent talk to a frightened child?"). In this process, the client suddenly felt sorry for herself, was able to clearly articulate what she needed as a child (and as an adult), and felt entitled to having those needs met. It is important to help clients articulate and enact the exact soothing, protective words and gestures (e.g., "You're a smart, beautiful little girl") that emerge from this experience. The aim is for clients to feel the impact of this new meaning, so the therapist might ask, "Imagine hearing that, what happens on the inside?" Thus, these new protective or soothing resources are integrated at an experiential level.

For clients whose sense of shame is deeply entrenched or who have never had an experience of nurturing, therapist interventions may need to explicitly model these more adaptive responses. In another case, for example, a client described a childhood incident of being publicly humiliated by his mother for having his shoes on the wrong feet. He could not identify what response he would have wished for because he had no saliently positive childhood experience to draw on. Responding to this lack of experience, the female therapist assumed the position of a gentle, nurturing mother ("I guess a 'good' mother might have said . . ."). Thus, she responded as someone who would have found her boy's mistake funny and cute, and she offered to help him out rather than criticize. The client's eyes welled up with tears, "If my mother had ever talked to me like that . . . ." The therapist acknowledged how touched her client was, and this became a shared positive attachment experience. In this way, the intervention increased the client's awareness of an unmet need and helped him internalize the therapist's soothing response.

The process also can shift from self-related work to confronting imagined others in IC or emphatic exploration (EE), sometimes bridging the transition from Phase 2 to Phase 3 of EFTT. Markers for shifting to IC include client expression of healthy anger, indignation, resentment about the shaming experiences or messages, identification of personal strengths ("I was a good kid, I bent over backward to please him"), and a client's emerging awareness of a need for and entitlement to self-respect, acknowledgment, soothing, and support.

For example, after the client Clare was encouraged to vividly engage memories of sexual abuse at the hands of her brother, she accessed feeling dirty, and then felt sad for herself as a little girl. The therapist brought the empty chair closer (to increase intimacy and connection) and asked what she would like to do or say to that little girl who feels dirty. This elicited self-soothing responses by the client ("You're innocent, you deserve to feel good about yourself, about your body"), which quickly shifted to anger at her brother ("I've been ripped off, deprived of my childhood innocence. That's huge, I hate him for doing that to me and I hate my parents' refusal to talk about it, making me suffer through this alone. I need them to be outraged with me."). Following this shift, in an attuned fashion, the therapist pushed the chair further away (to create distance and separation) and encouraged her to express that anger directly to the imagined brother. For the client, this was only a few clear statements, but it was followed by turning attention to how good it felt to stand up to and assert against him.

Transforming Self-Blame

Obvious markers for this type of memory work include client distress, confusion, and self-blame concerning the traumatic event (e.g., "Why didn't I tell anyone [about the sexual abuse]?" or "Why didn't I try to stop him [from beating my mother]?"). One of the functions of exposure-based procedures is to access information about the trauma that has been blocked through avoidance. Similarly, memory work in EFTT can be used to promote client understanding of their own behaviors and reactions that cause them shame, and thereby reduce maladaptive self-blame. Again, details of the shame-producing event are relived and used to elicit clients' internal experience during their reaction to the situation, thereby promoting understanding and constructing new meaning.

This intervention strategy was used in therapy with a client who had been molested by a priest for a period of 3 years starting at age 11. This case also illustrates the difference between memory work as contrasted to working with self-critical processes (described below). The client could not understand and blamed himself for not avoiding contact with the priest and not telling anyone about the abuse. Intervention initially focused on self-critical processes and the client's belief that he "should" have been able to avoid the abuse or at least tell someone about it. However, after a number of sessions exploring his beliefs and his dilemma as a child, nothing had shifted; he kept coming up against the same block ("Why did I keep going back?"). His confusion and self-blame intensified further when he came to the conclusion that his mother probably would have believed him and probably would have done something to stop the abuse.

Ultimately, memory work offered the effective intervention that was needed. Following emergence of the client's puzzling reaction ("Why didn't I quit the church?"), therapist and client agreed to engage in memory work for the client to understand himself and his reactions better. Intervention involved reevoking specific events, starting at the beginning, slowing down the process, and attending to his thoughts and feelings at the time. During one session, the client recalled preparing to go to church, dreading seeing the priest, making futile efforts to avoid contact, contemplating leaving the church, but fearing this would draw negative attention.

The next step in the process involves exploring possible connections between the situation and the reaction, behavior, or decision, to make sense of this. This client recalled thinking that there was no way he could stay away from church—he would be found out, questioned, and doubted. He also recalled wanting to tell his mother, but given her devastation after the recent death of his father, he feared he would wound her further by disclosing the abuse. This helped to explain the client's decision to handle it secretly and on his own. During another session, he recalled going to a neighborhood park after being with the priest, sitting alone and trying to figure our how to deal with the situation, and deciding that his only option was to continue to avoid and resist the priest as much as he could. He felt completely powerless and trapped. This is a good example of the close connection between primary fear and shame, where highlighting primary adaptive fear (and the need to escape) helps to counteract maladaptive shame and self-blame, particularly in a context where one is essentially powerless. This systematic and evocative exploration helped this client to consider new options for interpreting the events ("I was in an *impossible* situation as a kid, I wish I could have told someone but I made the best decision I could at the time"). Reexperiencing in an emotionally alive way helped the client understand his dilemma and decision at a gut level and have compassion for himself as a powerless boy rather than blaming himself.

INTERVENTION FOR REDUCING SECONDARY SHAME

In the above sections we described primary maladaptive shame as it is best addressed through memory work. In the following sections we discuss guilt and shame that are associated with obvious critical self-statements and how they are effectively addressed through two-chair enactments. We also discuss shame that is secondary to other feelings (e.g., anger, weakness, jealousy) or the result of a complex sequence of thoughts and feelings, as in depression.

Reducing Secondary Shame Associated With Self-Critical Processes

Criticism related to traumatic events can be internalized from significant others or from society. What is so painful and damaging about this is that negative self-evaluations are accompanied by hostility, contempt, and disgust directed at the self. Self-criticism, then, generates feelings of guilt and shame and can perpetuate these feelings once a core shame-based sense of self is activated. Markers of guilt and secondary shame are obvious or implied in a client's self-critical or "should" statements (e.g., "I should have known better, how could I be so stupid!"), accompanied by a vocal quality and/or facial expressions indicating hostility (i.e., sneer, curled lip, haughty arrogance). The goal is to strengthen the demoralized part of self so the client can stand up to such harsh criticism. The intervention strategy involves first highlighting hostile affect, specifying the negative self-evaluations, and heightening experiential awareness of the pain of guilt and shame. Then intervention highlights the client's own agency in producing this pain and supports the emergence of healthy parts of self, which do not believe or accept the criticism. This strategy is similar to that used for reducing self-interruption (see preceding chapter), and both are examples of promoting emotional transformation (Greenberg & Pascual-Leone, 2006).

In instances of secondary shame, part of the self negatively evaluates and feels contempt or disgust toward another part of self and rejects certain feelings, behaviors, or characteristics. The part of self that is the recipient of criticism and hostility, in turn, feels demoralized, defensive, and ashamed. Examples are when clients fail at things they believe they should be competent at, such as relationships and careers. Other examples are when clients believe they should have been able to stop or control some terrible event, such as a rape, abuse, or accident. Failure in these instances implies to the client some personal shortcoming or defect.

Self-critical processes also can emerge as projections, whereby clients believe that others are criticizing them. For example, the client Clare who had been sexually abused by her brother was angry at her parents for minimizing the abuse ("They think I'm exaggerating, making a big fuss over nothing!"). Although it is important to validate a client's sense of invalidation by significant others, the core issue was her own (internalized) minimization and her consequent desperate need for parental affirmation in order to accept herself. In cases such as this, it may or may not be useful for the therapist to tentatively point out the projection ("It seems that your parents' invalidation brings up your own insecurity, a part of you that fears that maybe you are exaggerating"). In a given moment, the client may or may not accept such an interpretation. In time, the client will come to experientially understand that it is her own internalized shame that makes her vulnerable to the real or imagined negative evaluations of others. Regardless, the goal in the moment is for the therapist to help the client clearly articulate the imagined criticisms ("What do you imagine they are saying or thinking about you?"), direct these at the self with associated hostile affect, and elicit the client's reactions to these condemnations.

Because criticism hurts, a need for comfort and support emerges in reaction to the experienced condemnation. Attention to and exploration of the authentic feelings and needs in response to harsh criticism help activate internally generated challenges to this self-denigration. As in memory work, described above, access to healthy resources is easier if the person has had prior life experiences of compassion, nurturing, and pride. When clients are unable to feel the experiential impact of their own criticism or healthy resources do not spontaneously emerge, interventions need to facilitate the process. The therapist can ask, for example, how a child or a friend might feel hearing such criticism and what the client would need to hear instead, or how the client would feel if she or he heard support from a friend. Again, the process is one of accessing new information through imagined experiencing.

The following six steps in the *two-chair intervention for resolving self-criticism* parallel those for resolving self-interruption, as outlined in the preceding chapter.

1. *Work together to structure the dialogue.* After confirming a marker for a self-critical split (e.g., the therapist might say, "So, one part of you says there's something wrong with 'Kathy' and the other part ends up feeling bad or defective"), the therapist separates the critical and the experiencing parts of self by enacting them in separate chairs, each in turn. One should inform the client that the intervention is aimed at strengthening the weaker, demoralized part of self so the client can learn to stand up to his or her own criticism. Next, one promotes contact or dialogue between the two parts of self (in the two chairs) and asks the client to start by enacting the internalized critic.

2. *Access core self-critical statements and accompanying affect.* Interventions encourage clients to tell themselves what is required to be more acceptable ("should" statements). It is also useful to highlight the contempt or disgust (i.e., in vocal quality) that clients feel toward themselves. Research on self-criticism has demonstrated that it is a criticism's affective tone rather than its content, per se, that is most related to psychopathology (Whelton & Greenberg, 2005). Thus, clients can be reminded that it is not so much what you say, but more how you say it that counts.

It requires considerable trust for clients to reveal what they believe to be their deepest flaws, and therapists need to provide guidance and support in this process. This includes the therapist giving examples, suggesting possibilities so clients may recognize themselves (e.g., "What are you saying . . . that you deserved the punishment?"), and helping clients clearly articulate their specific criticisms. Clients who blame themselves for their own trauma, for example, need to specify what they feel it says about them as a person that they did not or could not stop it (e.g., the therapist might ask, "So what are you saying? 'I was so weak, stupid, I must have asked for it'—is that it?").

3. *Access a reaction to criticism.* The goal here is to help the client feel the painful impact of his or her own harsh criticism and communicate this to the critical part of self. Interventions, first, may need to heighten arousal to increase awareness of bad feelings and then evoke a reaction in the experiencing self. This can be done by the therapist exaggerating the content and/or the vocal quality associated with specific criticisms (e.g., "So you tell this part of yourself that she's not desirable? My guess is you're pretty mean to her. What do you say? 'You fat slob'? 'Who could love such a fat slob?'"). Once a response is evoked (e.g., the client's eyes well up in tears at being hurt, or anger at unfairness), the therapist can help the client express the effect of this criticism ("Tell the other part of yourself how bad you feel. What it's like to be put down like that? Make her understand.").

4. *Restructure by accessing healthy primary experience.* Resolving self-criticism can take one of two paths (see Figure 3.1 in chap. 3, this volume; Pascual-Leone & Greenberg, 2007). In one path, resolution occurs through a full experience of the self as defective, which activates hurt/sadness and the associated needs for compassion, support, and soothing. In the other path, the client rebels against the criticism, feels angry at its unfairness, and accesses associated needs for dignity and respect. In either case, therapist interventions highlight these needs (e.g., "Yes, it would feel so good, make such a difference, to get that kind of respect. Can you get in touch with that? Say what it would mean to you?") and help the client feel entitled to having these needs met. Positive self-evaluations are activated along with the sense of entitlement. Interventions support the emergence of these alternate realities (e.g., the therapist might encourage the client, "Tell her about your good qualities, what she should respect. Make her understand.").

5. *Softening of the critical aspect of self.* Through this dialogue, the judgmental part of self begins to understand the position of the other and takes a more benevolent, empathic, compassionate stance toward the more vulnerable part of self. Therapist interventions support this process (e.g., "Can you hear her position, how hard it is for her, how much she needs your support and encouragement?"). Negotiation between the two aspects of self is now possible, which, in turn, leads to the dialectical construction of something new from disparate or opposite aspects of self. Negotiation can involve exploring the intended function of a criticism; for example, to motivate or protect the self from failure or disappointment, or to ensure that values and standards are adhered to. In two-chair enactments, the critical part of self also may be hesitant to soften, for fear of annihilation or abandonment because this part has often served to protect the client through trauma and crises. Negotiation with oneself and resolution in these instances involve respecting the intention of and reassuring the critical part of self.

T: She [critical self in other chair] is afraid that you don't appreciate how she kept you safe all these years, afraid that without her you will get hurt . . . How do you respond?

C: I do appreciate you [critical self], I really needed you to push me to survive, but now it's not working. I need something else, more encouragement.

6. *Switch to IC or EE.* As in memory work, this dialogue can switch to an interpersonal process, that is, a dialogue with a critical other. The client may spontaneously recognize the origin of critical messages or the therapist may ask, "Whose voice is that?" The spontaneous emergence of a client's challenges to his or her own self-criticism is a good marker for switching to the confrontation of shaming others in IC or EE (e.g., the therapist might say, "So it's not true what your father said about you. Tell him [imagined father] what's good about you."). This shifts the treatment into Phase 3, where the focus is on resolving issues with perpetrators. This is an organic and fluid process, and IC with critical others also could shift back to two-chair exploration of self-criticism.

Reducing Secondary Shame About Internal Experience

Another type of secondary shame results from feelings or a complex sequence of feelings and thoughts about some other deeper feelings, for example, shame of feeling vulnerable or needy when one believes that neediness is unacceptable. This can be closely related to avoidance of neediness or vulnerability that was discussed in the preceding chapter. Obvious markers are explicit self-consciousness, embarrassment, or efforts to hide or avoid particular experiences. A common example is clients' shame about their own trauma symptoms, their level of distress, or not being able to get over it. Intervention with disavowed experience typically involves exploring maladaptive beliefs and/or empathic affirmations to help the person face the disavowed state. In the example of shame about trauma symptoms, interventions also may include education about the nature of trauma and the difficulty of recovery. This is especially useful in the context of a client's limited social support and any societal attitudes the client may have internalized, such as having little tolerance for prolonged grieving over the loss of loved ones.

DIFFICULTIES WITH PHASE 2 INTERVENTIONS

In this section, we present strategies for addressing client difficulties with two-chair enactments and memory work for addressing both fear and shame.

No Contact Between Parts of Self

In two-chair enactments, when clients continue to have difficulty maintaining contact between the parts of self, despite clear directives, therapists must first collaborate with them to understand the reason for this difficulty. It could be due to structuring problems, lack of clarity about the task, performance anxiety, or a client's need for contact with the therapist. Again, as in the IC procedure, optimal EFTT intervention means providing as much support and contact with the therapist as the client needs. The intervention principles underlying two-chair procedures are used almost identically even when most of an interaction is directly with the therapist. In these instances, only pivotal statements that indicate the emergence of healthy resources are directed at the other chair. To maintain contact with "hot" processes, this is done quickly, without an elaborate rationale and without moving the client to the other chair.

No Conflict Between the Two Parts of Self

There are two common difficulties when trying to maintain the dialectical tension between two parts of self. One is lack of activation—the two-chair enactment never really takes off (and this is not due to technical difficulties). The other is when the client agrees with the dominant part of self and there no longer is a split. In both instances, intervention requires the reactivation of the enactment and conflict. The goal is to increase the emotional impact of messages coming from the dominant self. This is accomplished by specifying and intensifying those messages. The contempt of the critic, for example, must be directed at the more vulnerable self to elicit a reaction (e.g., the client says [as self-critic], "You need to be accepted so badly that you're blind to reality!").

Therapist Is Reluctant to Activate Painful Feelings

This difficulty applies to both two-chair enactments and memory work. Therapists who are reluctant to promote and intensify negative feelings, particularly painful feelings of shame, tend to focus instead on changing these feelings. However, because change is contingent on evoking core maladaptive emotion structures, the client must feel afraid, dirty, or unlovable, in the session. Furthermore, EFTT requires a therapist stance of exploration rather than a focus on change. Exploration requires trust in the client's healthy processes. This trust is based on knowledge, training, clinical experience, and an assessment that these resources, indeed, are available to the client. Caution is necessary when clients have histories of severe affect dysregulation with a risk of self-harm.

Client Directs Extreme Hostility Toward Self in Two-Chair Enactment

It can be especially alarming when clients direct extreme hostility at themselves and feel destroyed by the hostility, agree with it, or both. The purpose of increasing anger, contempt, and disgust toward the self is to increase a client's awareness of agency and to activate material that is not fully in awareness. However, it is not appropriate to promote or encourage client self-destructive tendencies, just as it is not appropriate to intensify rage at others. Just as interventions are used to shift aggression to more assertive expressions of anger, here, it is appropriate to acknowledge negative feelings but to reduce, rather than increase, arousal. In two-chair dialogues, for example, interventions can direct the client to specify his or her perceived defects and focus more on feelings from the more vulnerable part of self. If hostility does not decrease, the therapist needs to explicitly tell the client that self-destructive hostility directed toward self is not healthy and collaborate to change it. The therapist can switch to empathically exploring client hostility toward self or can reframe the purpose of the enactment, for example:

> Okay, but this isn't about true and false, is it? . . . who's right or not? The point is, how does being on the receiving end of that kind of criticism make you feel? It must leave you feeling so . . . what? . . . Hurt? Squashed? You seem so deflated, so crushed down.

Orienting toward the vulnerable experience highlights an unmet need, which then leads to more adaptive activation. Notice that reframing the intervention in terms of "what this process does to you" rather than the rational or irrational nature of a belief makes it markedly different from cognitive–behavioral therapy interventions that encourage clients to examine evidence for and against a belief.

Client Has Difficulties Reexperiencing Memories

Difficulties reexperiencing memories could be a function of emotion regulation problems (see the preceding chapter) or the therapist spending too much time on the situational details. In EFTT, the function of these details is to evoke internal experience, which is the source of new information and change. Interventions need to heighten the stimulus value of the external situation (e.g., loud harsh voice) and connotative aspects of internal experience (e.g., cowering in the corner like a frightened little animal).

In the case of shameful material, interventions need to balance respect for the client's need for privacy with promoting disclosure. In cases of sexual abuse, for example, therapists may need to provide considerable guidance, use a matter-of-fact approach to embarrassing sexual material, explicitly ask about sexual pleasure and orgasm, and provide education about normal sexual response. Interventions also need to highlight the maladaptive consequences of hiding (isolation) and the healthy human needs for validation, comfort, and support.

Once clients are able to allow painful experience, feel more self-confident, and be less self-blaming, they are better able to express feelings and needs to imagined perpetrators. This marks the transition to Phase 3 of EFTT, which is the focus of the next two chapters.

PHASE THREE OF EFTT

10
RESOLUTION THROUGH ANGER

The preceding two chapters dealt with strengthening clients' sense of self by helping them work through fear, avoidance, and shame during Phase 2 of emotion-focused therapy for trauma (EFTT). This is necessary before clients can hold offenders accountable for harm, fully grieve losses, and thereby resolve their issues with offenders and attachment figures. This chapter marks the beginning of Phase 3 of EFTT, which is defined not by a particular session number but by establishing a more sustained focus on resolving interpersonal issues. The catalyst for resolution in this phase is full experience and expression of previously inhibited adaptive anger at maltreatment and sadness at loss, which lead to meaning exploration and change. Once these emotions are accessed, the process of resolution typically moves forward relatively quickly, and as such, this arousal and resolution phase of therapy may take only a few sessions.

The process of interpersonal resolution in EFTT is based on steps in the model presented in Figure 7.1 and introduced in chapter 7. This resolution process also parallels the general process of change shown in Figure 3.1 of chapter 3 (Pascual-Leone & Greenberg, 2007). In both of these figures, we see that one pathway to resolution and change is through anger. Global distress shifts to rejecting anger (e.g., blame, complaint) expressed toward the imagined other in imaginal confrontation (IC), which then is differentiated and directly transformed into more assertive and adaptive anger expression. Alternatively, adaptive anger and associated healthy self-protective resources are accessed in the course of allowing emotional pain or addressing fear and shame (described in chaps. 9 and 10, this volume). At the emergence of these resources, clients are encouraged to reengage in the IC procedure and express anger directly to the imagined other in the empty chair. Again, the relatively uninhibited expression of adaptive emotion to imagined offenders in IC marks the shift into Phase 3. Although resolution through anger does not necessarily occur before the grieving of losses, the strength that comes with anger often helps clients allow the vulnerability of facing devastating loss.

Promoting anger experience and expression in therapy is controversial. Anger is a powerful emotion, and when accompanied by aggressive behavior, it can have destructive personal, interpersonal, and societal consequences. Moreover, most research has demonstrated that although increasing anger arousal (venting or catharsis) can produce immediate relief, it does not reduce anger in the long term (Novaco, 2007). The vast majority of treatments for anger, therefore, focus directly on its reduction. However, EFTT distinguishes among different types of anger and specifies criteria for adaptive anger experience and expression, as well as the circumscribed parameters under which anger intensification in therapy is appropriate. These points are discussed in the present chapter, along with research supporting the benefits of healthy anger expression in EFTT. This chapter also describes intervention principles and strategies, first for reducing maladaptive anger, then for accessing adaptive anger in response to maltreatment during the IC procedure. We review the model of resolution presented in chapter 7, Exhibit 7.1, with a special focus on anger expression and the later steps in the model. We begin with a review of current literature on the resolution of interpersonal trauma and the centrality of anger in trauma across different theoretical perspectives.

REVIEW OF THEORY AND RESEARCH ON
THE RESOLUTION OF INTERPERSONAL TRAUMA

Repeated betrayal and maltreatment at the hands of caregivers and loved ones typically cause a more complex array of disturbances (complex posttraumatic stress disorder) than exposure to a single traumatic event (Courtois & Ford, 2009). With respect to treatments, EFTT is distinct in its emphasis, not only on reducing current symptom distress and self and interpersonal problems, but also on resolving past issues with particular attachment figures (and offenders) that continue to be sources of distress.

EFTT Definition of Resolution

Above all, resolution of relational trauma in EFTT involves developing increased emotional competence and more adaptive views of self and specific others (i.e., perpetrators) who are the focus of therapy. More adaptive emotional processes include reduced negative feelings concerning the other (e.g., hurt, fear, shame, anger, sadness) and an increased ability to acknowledge and attend to one's own needs. When the client continues to be in a relationship with past offenders, this also could mean letting go of the hope that these specific individuals will meet their needs (e.g., for attention, approval, respect) and letting go of expectations that the other will acknowledge responsibility for harm, apologize, or change. Thus, healthy personal needs are met in new ways: by asserting or soothing oneself, for example, or by reaching out to the therapist or current loved ones for support. Clients do not give up on their own needs but rather become more autonomous and let go of the longing or insistence that their needs be met by unresponsive or even abusive attachment figures.

Resolution also includes increased self-esteem, despite the other's opinions; reduced self-blame for one's victimization; increased ability to assert and stand up for oneself; and increased detachment/separation from the other and the traumatic events. Changes in client perceptions of the other include a shift from globally negative views of the other (the "bad object") to a more differentiated and realistic perspective, a better understanding of the other's position and actions toward the client, and clearly holding others responsible for the harm they have caused rather than erroneously blaming oneself. The client may or may not feel more positively toward the other or feel forgiving. The relationship between resolution and forgiveness becomes important here and will be discussed in the following section. Resolving issues in relationships with attachment figures, together with forging a strong therapeutic relationship, generalizes to reduced symptom distress, increased self-esteem, and reduced general interpersonal problems. These changes help cultivate or restore the capacity for interpersonal connectedness that all too often was shattered by the trauma. As cited in chapter 2, there is a body of research supporting these mechanisms of change. This definition of resolution in EFTT shares features with the construct of posttraumatic growth (Tadeschi, Park, & Calhoun, 1998). According to this idea, as a result of struggling to come to terms with traumatic experiences, people report personal growth that exceeds their pretrauma levels of functioning. Thus, out of the devastation of trauma, there is the possibility of constructing something new. These new (rather than simply recovered) benefits include increased personal strength, greater clarity about values (e.g., the importance of relationships), closer connections with family and loved ones, and a generally stronger sense of spirituality or personal meaning in life.

The process of interpersonal resolution in Phase 3 of EFTT develops from the process of resolving self-related disturbances (fear and shame) in Phase 2 of EFTT. For example, intervention for allowing emotional pain involves helping clients to fully acknowledge the damage and harm—the scars—that has been done to them. It also helps these clients to clearly identify the cause of damage and the person(s) responsible (e.g., "His rages terrified me, destroyed my mother, ruined our family, made me take on a responsibility for the family that was way beyond my years"), and to allow and fully express feelings of anger and sadness about the other and traumatic events (e.g., "I hate him for what he did to me and my mother" or "I feel so sad that we all missed out on so much"). Again, this can be done by directing and redirecting clients to confront transgressors in the IC procedure. Similarly, following the emergence of healthy rebellion against self-criticism (i.e., internalized criticism from attachment figures) during two-chair enactments, clients can be encouraged to shift to the IC procedure and stand up to the unfair criticisms of imagined significant others.

Forgiveness

The construct of forgiveness in EFTT overlaps with, but is not identical to, resolution and is particularly relevant to resolution through anger. Facilitating forgiveness is controversial partly because it sometimes comes with moral and religious imperatives that may seem distasteful to some individuals. It also is unclear whether forgiveness is appropriate in situations of extreme cruelty and childhood abuse, and whether forgiveness, as a therapeutic outcome, affords additional benefits beyond other forms of resolution (Chagigiorgis & Paivio, 2006). However it may be, forgiveness does not involve condoning the behavior of offenders and bypassing anger but rather acknowledging offenses and working through anger.

Widely held definitions of forgiveness suggest that it requires both psychological separation from and increased affiliation toward offenders. An analysis of posttherapy interviews with clients in EFTT indicated that although most clients (82%) reported resolving issues with perpetrators, only a small portion (23%) of those who resolved also reported forgiving (Chagigiorgis & Paivio, 2006). Furthermore, clients more often forgave neglectful as opposed to abusive others. These neglectful others tended to be nonprotective mothers. As a case in point, recall that the client Monica was able to forgive her dead mother by the end of therapy. This suggests that clients may be more motivated to forgive primary attachment figures and, because more time in treatment was spent focusing on issues with primary attachment figures (e.g., as opposed to estranged abusive fathers or nonfamily members), forgiveness may be a function of more time spent on task. Research on forgiveness also indicates that people's motivation to forgive is a function of many factors, including religious or moral beliefs, and the belief that forgiveness will reduce personal distress (for a review, see Chagigiorgis & Paivio, 2006). Moreover, Woldarsky and Greenberg (2009) found that clients in emotion-focused therapy for couples were more likely to forgive a romantic partner when they believed that partner truly regretted and felt shame about the transgressions. As we shall see, this finding likely also applies to forgiveness of perpetrators in EFTT.

Therefore, as noted earlier, EFTT does not advocate forgiveness as a treatment goal but rather leaves this up to the individual client. If forgiveness of the other has been an appropriate and desired goal for the client, then this issue will surface again during Phase 3 of therapy, as the client moves closer to resolution. Issues of forgiveness also could emerge for the first time during this phase as perceptions of self and other evolve. In either case, tracking clients' perspectives on this issue may be a key part of the resolution process.

ANGER AND TRAUMA ACROSS THEORETICAL PERSPECTIVES

There is abundant literature documenting the centrality of anger in trauma. Anger at violation and maltreatment is a healthy emotion that motivates self-defense but becomes problematic when it is overgeneralized, under-regulated, used to cover more vulnerable emotional experience, or turned against the self. Because areas of the brain that are responsible for affect regulation develop in the context of secure attachment relationships, failure of brain development may account for the hair-trigger anger response observed in many survivors of child abuse trauma (Ford, 2005; Schore, 2003). Anger and aggression also are learned responses and ways of coping. There is considerable evidence supporting a link between both childhood physical abuse and exposure to violence with aggressive behavior later in life (Wolfe, 2007). Anger dysregulation is a particular problem among war veterans who have been exposed to prolonged and extreme violence (Novaco, 2007). Dysregulated anger is also a feature of borderline personality disorder that is associated with a history of childhood abuse.

With few exceptions, reducing maladaptive anger is the focus of most approaches to trauma therapy when anger is identified as a problem (e.g., Linehan, 1993; Novaco, 2007; Zlotnick et al, 1997). However, some recent cognitive–behavioral therapy (CBT) approaches to therapy for complex trauma (e.g., Cloitre, Koenen, Dohen, & Han, 2002) also acknowledge fear of anger as a problem among clients who have been exposed to violent childhood abuse. So, these approaches also include training in emotion awareness and assertive communication skills. Criteria for the healthy expression of adaptive anger in EFTT (described below) are compatible with principles that would be applied in CBT assertiveness training (Kubany et al., 2004). However, EFTT focuses more on exploring the personal meaning of disavowed anger experience rather than on skills training.

Traditional psychodynamic approaches also focus on the meaning associated with defensive anger, or "anger turned inward," and help clients acknowledge the underlying feelings or to express anger at the appropriate source. Meanwhile, some current psychodynamic models (e.g., Davanloo, 1995) emphasize increasing arousal as a means of increasing awareness of suppressed anger and unconscious impulses. EFTT includes anger intensification strategies under specific conditions—increasing arousal is only appropriate for accessing inhibited adaptive anger so as to access the associated adaptive information. Paradoxically, healthy anger experience can sometimes facilitate forgiveness. For example, Monica had been unable to forgive her mother, who had committed suicide, largely because her own anger had been invalidated and suppressed for so many years. Once one's anger has been acknowledged, validated, assertively expressed, and understood, people feel stronger and more self-confident, and they are freer to focus on, empathize with, and forgive others.

Several research studies support the benefits of adaptive anger expression in EFTT and similar approaches. First, indirect support comes from the results of outcome and process–outcome studies that support the treatment model, in general, with its emphasis on adaptive anger expression (Hall, 2008; Paivio & Greenberg, 1995; Paivio & Nieuwenhuis, 2001). Similar results were reported for comparable emotion-focused therapies for depression (Pos, Greenberg, Goldman, & Korman, 2003; Watson, Gordon, Stermac, Kalogerakos, & Steckley, 2003), in which expression of inhibited anger in loss-related depressions was a key therapy process. Direct support for the benefits of anger expression comes from two studies that specifically examined the role of anger in EFTT.

In one study (Holowaty, 2004), 50% of the episodes identified by clients as helpful had anger as the most predominantly expressed emotion (followed by sadness, fear, and shame). Furthermore, results indicated that the level of emotional arousal was significantly higher in helpful episodes compared with a group of control episodes. Ralston (2006) similarly found that higher arousal during both IC and emphatic exploration (EE) predicted outcome in EFTT, and again, the dominant emotion during these episodes was anger. Furthermore, anger expression in EFTT does not appear to be simply a function of clients' compliance with their therapists' directives and the treatment model. At pretreatment, 64% of clients identified anger-related problems among the three target complaints they wanted help with in therapy. Of these, the most frequently identified were unresolved anger toward perpetrators of abuse and difficulties stemming from limited access to anger experience (e.g., powerlessness, nonassertiveness). Thus, it is clear that many victims of complex trauma entered therapy with a limited capacity to access anger and its associated healthy strivings.

Another study more directly examined the contributions of anger expression to the resolution of child abuse trauma in EFTT (Paivio & Carriere, 2007). Client dialogues during the IC procedure (99 videotaped episodes for 33 different clients) were analyzed using criteria for healthy anger expression (presented below). The results indicated a moderate relationship ($r > .30$) between healthy anger expression and the resolution of abuse issues as well as interpersonal dimensions of change, particularly at 12 months after treatment. Together, these results provide some support for the assertion that healthy anger expression during IC can have a beneficial effect on psychotherapeutic outcome in EFTT, particularly on interpersonal dimensions of functioning.

PROCESS DIAGNOSIS: DISTINGUISHING DIFFERENT TYPES OF ANGER

Anger is a powerful emotion that has a profound influence on self-organization and interpersonal relations. There are important societal implications concerning displays of anger and its connection to aggressive behavior that account for the existing emphasis in the literature on anger regulation (e.g., see Cavell & Malcolm, 2007). Anger involves surges of adrenaline, a loud firm voice, erect body posture, and direct eye contact with the target, all of which ready a person to thrust forward and attack.

Adaptive Anger

The following sections describe anger that has an adaptive function and specify criteria for healthy anger expression in therapy.

Primary Adaptive Anger

Like other basic affects, adaptive anger is an immediate and direct response to real environmental threat that is not preceded or mediated by obvious cognitive or other affective components. Anger at interpersonal violation and maltreatment quickly mobilizes self-protective resources and action. It provides energy and a sense of power and readies the individual for self-defense or to protect one's integrity and boundaries. Interpersonally, anger signals others that an offense has occurred, creates separation and distance, and signals them to back off. Difficulties here concern modulating its intensity, which can result in either dysregulation or overcontrol. In either case, the information associated with the anger experience is unavailable to adequately guide adaptive action. The negative consequences of overwhelming anger are obvious. Negative consequences of anger avoidance include a pervasive sense of victimization, recurrent bouts of depression, difficulties with assertiveness, and problems with establishing appropriate interpersonal boundaries. Chronic suppression of anger can also result in hypertension and instances of "bottle up–blow up" (Novaco, 2007).

Criteria for Healthy Anger Expression

EFTT defines healthy anger expression according to specific criteria (Paivio & Carriere, 2007) that are consistent with the above mentioned definition of primary adaptive emotion. These criteria inform and guide interventions intended to promote anger expression, for example, when confronting perpetrators of harm during IC. Criteria for healthy anger expression are as follows. First, the anger must be directed outward toward the perpetrator rather than inward toward the self, and it must concern actual and specific harms, transgressions, or violations. Second, the anger must be differentiated from other emotions, such as sadness, guilt, or fear. Anger expression mixed with tears or fear, for example, does not allow the individual full access to the cognitive, motivational, or somatic information specifically associated with anger experience. Third, the anger is expressed assertively with ownership of experience rather than aggressively, passively, or indirectly. For example, clients use "I" statements rather than referring to themselves in the third person or rather than blaming and complaining, or attacking or hurling insults at others. Anger that is inappropriately expressed does not have the desired effect on the environment, and consequently adaptive needs for respectful treatment or distance are not met. Fourth, the intensity of anger expression must be appropriate to the situation. Intense emotional expressions that are a catalyst for change are not the same as catharsis, although relief and release of tension can play a role in both of these. Appropriate intensity is assessed through verbal and nonverbal indicators of arousal, including body posture, vocal quality, and facial expressions that are congruent with anger and the situation. Inappropriate anger intensity includes both rage that is overwhelming and anger that is lacking in conviction or energy. Again, in both instances, the associated adaptive information is neither available to guide one's action nor a clear social message of assertion communicated to others. Finally, anger expressions must include some elaboration and exploration of meaning. Healthy anger is not a verbal tirade but rather involves working with anger in an attempt to understand it. This is consistent with the fundamental principle underlying EFTT that client experiencing is the primary source of new information used in promoting resolution and change.

Maladaptive Anger

Most therapeutic approaches focus on reducing maladaptive anger but typically do not distinguish among subtypes. The following sections describe clinically relevant distinctions among subtypes of maladaptive anger.

Primary Maladaptive Anger

In general, most forms of maladaptive anger are inappropriate to the situation and long-lasting rather than immediate, fleeting, and precise responses to violation. Primary maladaptive anger is an immediate but overgeneralized response to perceived environmental threat and frequently is associated with posttraumatic stress reactions. A rape victim, for instance, might react with rage at being touched by men, or a survivor of child abuse, whose trust has been betrayed, might react with anger to others' displays of affection.

Secondary Anger

Secondary anger is a response to maladaptive cognitions that produce, perpetuate, or escalate the anger (e.g., erroneous attributions of malicious intent or dwelling on revenge fantasies). Alternatively, secondary defensive anger masks more vulnerable core emotion, such as sadness, fear, or shame. Obvious examples are anger and aggression in response to the shame or fear of abandonment, as observed in some clients with borderline personality (Linehan, 1996) or some male perpetrators of intimate violence (Holtzworth-Munroe & Clements, 2007). In these instances, secondary anger serves the maladaptive function of momentarily alleviating painful feelings of vulnerability, and this is reinforcing when it is repeatedly successful.

Instrumental Anger

When anger is used, consciously or unconsciously, to manipulate or control others, it is instrumental. Thus, the social impact of angry-aggressive behavior can act as a means for attaining a desired interpersonal goal (i.e., control). This too can be a reinforcing pattern of behavior. Aggression without affect is a similar but more highly antisocial behavior.

Complexity of Anger Processes

The same individual can experience and express different types of anger. The complexity of anger experience and its accurate assessment are illustrated in the client Paul who was described in earlier chapters. He had been physically abused by his father and sexually molested by a male relative, and he frequently experienced adaptive anger as well as secondary defensive anger covering shame. Paul also had a history of using anger and aggression to control others and prove his masculinity. Moreover, he often felt betrayed and insulted by his wife and held cultural beliefs that children should respect their parents, blowing up at perceived signs of disrespect. Finally, he also had difficulty acknowledging feelings of anger about his father's abuse of him because he feared this would jeopardize the current relationship he had with his father, which he had worked so hard to achieve. Each of these distinct anger processes required different intervention strategies.

Feelings of contempt and disgust, discussed in the preceding chapter, are also related to anger experience. Like anger, these are maladaptive when directed at the self but can be adaptive when they are directed at others in response to legitimate moral transgressions and despicable behaviors (e.g., sexual abuse). Contempt involves looking down on an object with a sneer or curled lip of distain ("You worm!"), whereas disgust involves wanting to rid oneself of the object by revulsion or throwing up ("You make me sick!"). Although similar principles apply, accurate intervention with anger, contempt, and disgust involves accurate perception and empathically responding to the nuances in meaning associated with these different emotions.

INTERVENTION PRINCIPLES

Many of the intervention principles discussed in earlier chapters also apply to working with anger. In the following sections, we present examples of the particular ways in which these principles are implemented in the context of this specific emotion.

Regulation

Clients may inhibit their legitimate anger toward abusive or neglectful others for a variety of reasons, including fear of losing control, fear of being like the offender, or concern about unfairly blaming the other. In these cases, EFTT interventions validate client concerns and, at the same time, promote acknowledgment of legitimate angry feelings and model, shape, and teach appropriate and assertive expression of these feelings.

Sometimes, anger can be the dominant emotion to such a degree that the client does not have access to emotions that indicate vulnerability. This interferes with optimal functioning. For example, the client who expresses anger in place of hurt, sadness, or fear when perceiving a potential abandonment will have difficulty getting his or her needs met for contact, comfort, and support. Similarly, anger that is underregulated does not serve an adaptive function, even if the anger itself is a legitimate and adaptive response to harm. High levels of arousal overwhelm both the angry individual and the person being confronted with that anger.

Gradual Exposure

When clients are afraid of, deny, or believe that anger is socially unacceptable, the change principle is similar to that of gradual exposure to other threatening experience. Intervention involves successive approximations to the experience (e.g., moves from "feeling annoyed or resentful" to "feeling angry" to "feeling outraged and furious"). When clients deny feeling angry at situations that normally would evoke anger, therapists must use empathic responses, questions, or challenges to elicit a reaction or open a door for acknowledging the experience (e.g., "Sounds like you thought that was pretty unfair" or "Did you like what she did?" or "I would have been so pissed off!"). Here, clients also are implicitly learning the range and appropriate modulation of anger experience, which helps to challenge maladaptive beliefs that all anger is too intense and dangerous. At other times, intervention can focus on client actions that emerge spontaneously and then encourage clients to put words to these actions (e.g., "What does that type of voice say—'how dare you'?"). Similarly, a therapist might ask the client to put words and meaning to their body posture, as in, "I notice your fists clenched as you speak. . . . Can you put words to that?" Secondary or reactive emotions that cover anger (e.g., guilt, fear, defeat, helplessness) are bypassed or implicitly discouraged by making selective reflections. Instead, the therapist validates and supports the client's authentic, spontaneous expression of anger at injustice, unfairness, or maltreatment.

A good example of gradual exposure to anger is in the client, John, presented in previous chapters, who, following the death of his mother, was sent to an orphanage where he was physically and sexually abused. Initially, he was completely resistant to acknowledging any anger about his life experiences. Intervention first needed to explore the client's resistance to anger ("It isn't 'Christian' to be angry . . . I just want to be good person"), then educate him about anger, and eventually used successive approximations to help him acknowledge his anger.

> T: When you think now about those things [i.e., beatings, sexual molestation] happening to other young boys, like maybe your nephew, how do you feel?

> C: Well, I don't like it. It bothers me.

> T: I'm sure it does. Can you stay with that, say more, what don't you like?

Eventually John was able to say that the abusive priests "shouldn't have done what they did, it wasn't right, they are to blame for all the emotional problems I've had." He was able to acknowledge his anger at "the system" for putting him in an orphanage and depriving him of his family and culture, and anger at individual priests for abusing him.

Explore Secondary Anger

Secondary anger typically needs to be changed. On one hand, changing anger generated by maladaptive thought processes is achieved by accessing, exploring, and restructuring these maladaptive cognitions. On the other hand, if possible, changing anger that masks more vulnerable feelings is best accomplished by simply bypassing it. This is because the goal ultimately is to access more core emotional experience and associated information as quickly and efficiently as possible. When defensive anger cannot be easily bypassed, it needs to be explicitly explored again to access core primary experiences. The client who routinely expresses anger at signs of interpersonal slight, for example, needs to gain access to underlying feelings of hurt, rejection, or sadness that likely give rise to the defensive anger.

Identify Instrumental Function of Anger

Appropriate intervention for instrumental anger involves confronting and interpreting the instrumental function of this anger and teaching more adaptive ways of getting one's needs met. Both secondary and instrumental anger can be problematic at the level of intensity, and, in this case, intervention needs to include teaching anger regulation strategies. All of the above types of anger can be problematic at the level of chronicity or frequency such that anger might be the dominant emotion some clients experience or express. These individuals typically have limited access to other feelings, and therapeutic intervention requires emotion awareness training. This consists of empathic responses that direct client attention to, and help them accurately label, their other feelings. It also can include the use of structured exercises that explicitly teach emotion awareness skills (see Linehan, 1997).

Symbolize Meaning

Through exploring anger experience, clients come to understand their anger, its associated values and needs, the effects maltreatment or injustice has had on them, perceptions of self and offending others, and so on. This new information is used to construct new personal meaning. In cases of maladaptive or secondary anger, the maladaptive meaning (e.g., misattributions of hostile intent) can be examined and modified.

INTERVENTIONS FOR CHANGING MALADAPTIVE ANGER

The following sections describe EFTT's approach to reducing maladaptive anger.

Regulating Anger

Before turning our attention to the process of resolving interpersonal trauma through the promotion of anger experience, it is important first to clarify what types of anger not to promote and how to work with them in alternative ways. As noted above, chronic and underregulated anger are frequently associated with exposure to trauma, particularly complex interpersonal trauma. Experts agree that problems with anger dysregulation and associated aggressive behavior can be difficult to change (Novaco, 2007). These responses might be reinforcing and be part of the individual's personality style. Just as in recovery from phobia, neural pathways never completely disappear, but motivated clients can carve out more preferred pathways and old responses can fade with time and disuse (Doidge, 2007; LeDoux, 1996). Maladaptive anger interferes with resolution of interpersonal trauma; the client is stuck in an earlier stage of emotional processing, characterized by hostile blaming and rejecting anger (refer to Figures 3.1 and 7.1, this volume).

Although EFTT has an affinity with CBT strategies with respect to this area, EFTT is not an anger management therapy. Rather, strategies for regulating or reducing this type of anger must be integrated into the resolution process. In many instances, it will be more important for clients with chronic anger problems to focus on grief and sadness expression (instead of anger) as a route to resolution. However, the dilemma is that when trauma involves injustice, violation, and maltreatment, anger is a legitimate response and should not be avoided as a means of control. Therapy must validate clients' experiences of adaptive anger and find ways to help them express it appropriately.

Moving Beyond Secondary Anger

The first step in working with chronic anger in EFTT is assessment of the client's capacity to attend to and identify the internal experiences associated with anger, and the factors (internal and external) that contribute to escalating and perpetuating anger. Limited awareness must be increased for clients to gain control of their anger experience (e.g., the therapist might say, "So, when you think your kids don't respect you and dwell on that, you feel yourself getting more and more angry"). The next step is to help clients distinguish between different types of anger experience so they know when to validate, express, modulate, or bypass their anger and attend to more core vulnerable experience. If necessary, intervention will include the use of emotion regulation or modulation strategies, such as breathing, relaxation, time-out, or distraction that have been well articulated in the CBT literature. Memory evocation strategies, such as those described in the preceding chapters, can be used to help clarify the triggers for problematic anger reactions. In instances of secondary anger, the underlying cognitive–affective processes need to be brought into awareness and maladaptive aspects changed. For example, Deffenbaker (1999) suggested, from a CBT perspective, the use of two-chair enactments similar to those used in EFTT to increase client awareness of the thought processes that contribute to problematic anger. Of course, EFTT characteristically focuses more on exploring meaning rather than directly challenging maladaptive cognitions (e.g., the therapist might ask the client, "What's that all about, this sense that disrespect from your teenage kids is so intolerable?"). Anger at perceived disrespect, in the above example, also could be understood as a defense against hurt or shame in which case the therapist directs client attention to the core experience (e.g., "So it triggers some sense that you're a bad father, incompetent . . . ? That must hurt a lot. Let's stay with that, it's important.").

In terms of confronting offenders in the IC procedure, anger intensification is avoided with clients who have problems with anger control. However, therapists model and sometimes directly teach appropriate assertive expression skills, using the guidelines for healthy anger expression presented above. For clients whose dominant emotion is anger, resolution of past trauma will include acknowledging appropriate anger at abuse, but such resolution may largely occur through accessing hurt and sadness, which initially is less available to the individual.

An example of this is Paul, again, who had a history of anger and aggression problems. He recognized that his violent father had been a bad role model and that he, himself, used anger as a way to feel powerful and to control others. He was motivated to change this behavior but still was quick to anger, and anger experience initially dominated therapy sessions.

Early in therapy, the therapist provided the observation that Paul's anger dominated and threatened to derail the therapy process. She collaborated with him on shifting this focus from anger to accessing more vulnerable feelings. Paul was able to attend to his internal experience and had learned strategies for deescalating anger arousal, so he was able to explore the thoughts and feelings that contributed to anger and its escalation. Different anger processes and underlying vulnerable experience were identified and explored as they emerged in sessions ("hot" processing). Over time, the client allowed himself to be vulnerable with the therapist. Resolution of past trauma finally involved the client acknowledging his contribution to his own pain through maladaptive anger and grieving the many losses he had endured. In particular, he was able to acknowledge and express, both in session and to his aging father in real life, the deep sadness he felt at having missed out on a healthy and supportive relationship with his father when he was growing up. This in turn strengthened his current relationship with his father.

INTERVENTION FOR PROMOTING PRIMARY ADAPTIVE ANGER

Unlike maladaptive anger that needs to be reduced, problems with anger also concern its constriction. These problems frequently are addressed in the context of resolving issues with perpetrators of abuse and neglect.

Model of Resolution Using IC in Phase 3

The model of resolution using IC (Greenberg & Foerster, 1996; Greenberg & Malcolm, 2002; Paivio, Hall, Holowaty, Jellis, & Tran, 2001) was presented in chapter 7 (see Figure 7.1). We review it here with a focus on later stages in the process and on the specific role of adaptive anger in the resolution process. Recall that IC is initially introduced during Session 4 at the end of Phase 1 and then is used in conjunction with other procedures throughout Phase 2 of therapy. The frequency of client participation in IC over the course of therapy will vary depending on individual client processes and their treatment needs.

Returning to the process, as fear and shame are worked through and desensitization to trauma feelings and memories occurs, client difficulties with confronting imagined perpetrators during the IC procedure gradually diminish. Clients become more freely able to express previously inhibited feelings directly to the other. Then, Phase 3 of EFTT begins with the clear and uninhibited expressions of adaptive emotion, in this case, anger at maltreatment.

The Degree of Resolution Scale (DRS; Greenberg & Hirscheimer, 1994) presented in chapter 7 and in Appendix C is used by therapists to track client progress and set session-by-session process goals. The following example of a client, "Julie," working through sexual abuse in EFTT illustrates these stages in the model. The process begins with blame and complaint toward the other, then moves through overcoming self-interruption, to assertive expression of anger and meaning exploration, entitlement to unmet needs, letting go of expectations regarding the other, and finally ends with a shift in perceptions of self and other.

C: He's [father] such a disgusting pig! Who treats their own daughter like that?

T: I hear how much you hate him, despise him. Tell him over there [*points to chair*], what you hate, make him understand.

C: Yes, I hate the way you manipulated and corrupted me for your own selfish needs. You perverted everything, I was innocent and you ruined my childhood, you made sex disgusting. I hope you rot in hell! [*sighs, withdraws*]

T: What happened just now, Julie, you sigh and kind of collapse?

C: I don't like it, I sound just like him.

T: But you're not him, you're nothing like him. You're justifiably angry and you want to see him punished for his despicable behavior, for his crimes. Tell him.

C: Yes, I do want to see you punished, you deserve to be punished for all the harm you've done. You fucked me up royally, my life has been such a mess, but I'm not going to let you ruin my life anymore.

T: How do you feel saying that?

C: It feels right, he was the adult, I was just a little kid, I deserved love and security not the twisted life he imposed on me.

T: How do you imagine your father over there would react if he knew how you felt—defensive, remorseful, blaming and angry . . . ?

C: It's funny. He used to seem so huge and powerful, now I see just a pathetic old man. I don't think he's capable of understanding, but it doesn't matter anymore. I know the truth.

In this example, therapist interventions supported the client's anger and entitlement to justice and helped her begin to articulate the effects of the abuse and hold the perpetrator accountable for harm.

One of the goals here is for clients to begin to have a more realistic perspective of the other. An important step toward this is to elicit the client's understanding of the imagined perpetrator's response to such a confrontation. Enacting or imagining the other can elicit client empathic resources. This can be particularly important in situations when healing attachment relationships is appropriate and important for the client. For example, a client may come to understand that one or both parents had themselves been victims and would have regretted their behavior vis-à-vis the client. In contrast, when healing the attachment relationship is not appropriate, as in the example of Julie above, accessing clients' empathic resources by imagining the other's response can help clients view the other as more human and less powerful.

Therapist Operations During IC: Anger Expression in Phase 3 of Therapy

The following discussion focuses on specific steps in the model of resolution that occur during Phase 3 of EFTT, as outlined in chapter 7, Exhibit 7.1.

This section describes therapist operations that facilitate processes in both self and other chairs and corresponding client DRS levels. Difficulties with resolution in general will be discussed in chapter 12 in the context of termination.

Before anger can be expressed assertively, it must be differentiated from other emotions (Step 4 in Exhibit 7.1). Of course, unpacking complex feeling states requires that therapists decide which, among the different specific emotional constituents that a client presents, should be focused on first. At this phase of therapy and stage in the model, the client has made considerable progress in working through self-related issues (fear and shame). The decision to focus on anger, therefore, is based on verbal and nonverbal indicators that anger is the most salient client experience in the moment. In the context of memory work or exploring self-critical process in two-chair enactments during Phase 2, for example, the client may spontaneously access anger at a parent for harsh criticism or other forms of abuse. This is a marker for switching to express that anger to the imagined parent in IC. Frequently, however, the decision concerns which adaptive emotion, anger or sadness, to focus on when both are present and mixed together (e.g., anger mixed with tears). This choice is based on previous in-session processes, the individual client's history, and treatment goals. Repeated client concerns with issues of autonomy, justice, fairness, and respect are indicators for promoting the expression of adaptive anger. Historical information about the client also informs one's clinical judgment as to whether empowerment or accessing vulnerability will be the most transformative for the individual. In general, therapists are attuned to and focus on the affect and meaning that has been least available or least salient (subdominant) in the client's repertoire.

Assuming that anger is the most appropriate emotion to activate, therapist interventions direct the client's attention to microsignals of anger (e.g., the therapist might say, "Lots of feelings there; for now let's just focus on your anger, stay in touch with that"). If the client shifts back to feelings of guilt, shame, hurt, or vulnerability, the therapist again selectively and explicitly redirects the client's attention to anger. In the above example of Julie, the therapist directly challenged the client's fear that she was like her father, and this was enough to help her push past her fear. In other instances, a therapist might say, "Let's not go there, stay away from your hurt feelings for now, stay with your anger" or "So her criticism really hurts your feelings, but I hear you also saying her criticism borders on abuse, is over the top, out of line—and that it makes you angry. (The client responds, "Yes, it does") Then tell her."

Throughout the process, interventions facilitate client enactment or vivid experiential memories of the imagined other (Step 5 in Exhibit 7.1) to evoke anger experience and track shifting perceptions of the other. As clients become more self-aware and assertive in their own expressions, they also begin to see the other in a different light. The following steps in the IC procedure, beginning at Step 6, are characteristic of Phase 3 in therapy (as outlined in Exhibit 7.1).

6. *Promote expression of adaptive anger toward the other.* Guidelines for promoting anger expression during IC are based on the criteria presented earlier in the chapter. First, anger is expressed concerning the specific damaging actions or behaviors of the other. Moreover, quickly and completely activating anger and associated meaning is possible only when verbal and nonverbal elements of expression are consistent with the presenting experience. Although therapists need to avoid being overly directive and concerned about "correct" expression, clients can be encouraged to look at the imagined other (or therapist) and to sit up straight, with their feet planted firmly on the floor, and speak firmly from the belly (not the throat).

In terms of appropriate levels of arousal, traumatic experiences vary in severity, and the intensity of associated anger experience similarly varies, from rage over rape to resentment over invalidation and neglect. Likewise, clients differ in terms of expressive style and their history of emotion regulation problems. For clients who tend to be overcontrolled, intensification strategies are useful and appropriate, but they are contraindicated for clients with anger control problems. Markers of clients' self-doubt about anger experience ideally can be bypassed, but if not, they need to be further processed by returning to treatment principles from Phase 2.

Dealing with revenge fantasies can be an issue both for clients who find them disturbing and avoid them and for clients who perseverate on them. Within limits, clients are encouraged to disclose their revenge fantasies (to therapist and/or imagined other). Clients can be directed to tell the other, "This is how hurt and angry I have been," but not to enact them or dwell on them. For most clients, these fantasies need to be validated as normal reactions to injury, reframed as unresolved hurt and anger, and reassurance needs to be provided that resolution will reduce such feelings of tension and the desire to hurt the other.

In terms of assertive expression, this includes the use of "I" language and specification of wants, needs, expectations regarding the other, as well as preferred alternative behaviors and the positive effects that these would have had. For example, the client might say, "I was your daughter. You should have believed me so I didn't have to spend my whole life second-guessing myself. This would have made such a difference." Assertive expression of anger also can involve setting limits and boundaries, particularly in current relationships. This is a central part of promoting a client's sense of entitlement to unmet needs, which is a necessary component of resolution and will be discussed in Step 7 below.

Again, the EFTT approach to assertiveness training usually involves gradually shaping client behavior through modeling and successive approximations rather than by explicit teaching. In the initial activation stage of IC, the client should not be concerned about "saying it right." Indeed, such a preoccupation can interfere with clients acknowledging their feelings. As clients are chastising or telling the other off (e.g., "You cared more about your bottle and your boyfriends than you did about me, your own daughter!"), the therapist should instead guide clients to expressing their anger verbally (e.g., "Yes, so furious about all the damage she caused, tell her more about what makes you so angry"). In this later phase of therapy, clients who do not spontaneously shift to more assertive expressions can be explicitly directed and coached to do so by the therapist (e.g., "Try saying 'I hated it when you . . .'"). In any case, it is essential that interventions help clients to use clear and specific anger words. Interventions that hint at or imply anger are not specific enough and may tacitly reinforce anger inhibition.

Finally, healthy anger expression requires interventions that promote experiencing (see guidelines in chap. 6, this volume). To that end, it is essential to help the client maintain a balance between outward expression and inward attention to inner referents. Verbal expression should emerge from authentic experience. Because of the expressive and interactional nature of IC, a common pitfall of novice therapists is to neglect the experiencing part of this process. Some therapists also get carried away and derailed by the drama of anger expression. An effective EFTT therapist looks for congruence between the client's internal experience and outward expression and frequently asks the client to "check inside" to ensure that verbal expressions fit with internal experience. Interventions that help promote anger exploration focus on the impact of the other's behavior on self. This is like formulating a victim impact statement that includes affective arousal. Some clients have asked whether they could formally prepare such a statement for homework or write a letter to the perpetrator (but not send it). These exercises can be effective as long as they are read aloud by the client, in session, and the client's experience of doing this is explored. These in-session experiences typically are quite evocative.

7. *Expression of unmet needs and expectations regarding the other.* An essential component of meaning exploration is clear expression of unfulfilled needs and expectations in relation to the other. In the case of anger, these include the need for autonomy or personal control, to defend oneself against threat or harm, and to correct injustices, as well as expectations concerning fair and respectful treatment from others. These needs are motivating and move the process forward. Clients, therefore, are explicitly directed to attend to and tell the other what they wanted or needed (or still want and need) and did not get. This can include what was damaging about the other's actions toward them, how clients feel they should have been treated, and why. For example, the therapist might say to a client, "Instead of the criticism and living in constant

fear, tell him what you needed as a child" or "Tell her how important it would have been if she had actually shown some interest in you."

8. *Track perceptions of self and other.* Therapist interventions highlight the quality of client expressions toward or regarding the imagined other (e.g., "You sound pretty clear" or "It's still not easy to stand up to him, is it?"). These client expressions also are markers for eliciting a response from the other (e.g., the therapist might ask, "How do you imagine he would respond to your demands?"). The quality of this relational process serves as a behavioral index of internalized object relations, which evolve as the client becomes increasingly able to express authentic feelings and needs. It is essential to track these evolving perceptions as indicators of the client's stage in the resolution process (see the DRS in Appendix C).

9. *Promote increased sense of entitlement to unmet needs and expectations regarding the other.* The goal in this step is to help a client not only identify unmet needs but also define self in terms of legitimate wants and needs. Ultimately, there is a shift, from client self-doubt (e.g., "Maybe I did something to bring it on") and the sense that their needs are unrealistic or unattainable to a sense of conviction. Clients come to believe that, like everyone, they deserve to be treated fairly and with respect, to be protected, and to have had a childhood of freedom and innocence, regardless of the opinions, behaviors, or limitations of the other (e.g., "I may not have been the easiest kid, but I was still just a kid. I needed guidance."). Such entitlement helps the client hold the other accountable (e.g., "You were the adult! You should have provided this regardless!") and motivates efforts to get interpersonal and existential needs met in current life and relationships.

Markers for promoting entitlement are clients' assertive expressions of need (e.g., "I needed encouragement, not those constant put-downs") or expectation from other (e.g., "I deserve to be treated with respect, just like anyone else"). Therapist interventions validate the client's assertions (e.g., "Yes of course, all people need and deserve this") and then direct clients to clearly express these to the imagined other. Working with anger in a way that promotes entitlement usually includes the use of verbs such as *insist, refuse, will,* and *will not.* Once again, it is essential to have clients check whether these expressions fit with their internal experience. If there is still some self-doubt, therapy needs to spend more time exploring and working this through. Fully experiencing entitlement to better treatment (as opposed to superficial self-affirmations) is what strengthens self-confidence and self-esteem.

10a. *Support client's emerging new view of self.* At this stage, interventions associated with anger experience promote and support gradual separation from the other, letting go of unmet needs and expectations concerning the other, and self-empowerment. Clients' enmeshment with perpetrators is evident in the ongoing attention they focus on the other, or their dwelling on past injustices and offenses. In situations in which there is ongoing inter-action with the other, the client may engage in extraordinary efforts to please these others, be unable to assert themselves for fear of offending them, or be preoccupied with forcing the imagined other to apologize, admit he or she was wrong, or change.

Therapist interventions should first heighten client awareness of enmesh-ment, victimization, and powerlessness (e.g., "It's like you can never be happy unless she changes, you are doomed!") or exaggerate a client's maladaptive efforts to force the other to change (e.g., "Try saying, 'I will force you to apol-ogize, I demand that you apologize'" or "Try saying, 'I cannot live until you respect me'"). Alternatively, the therapist might role-play the imagined other's response to promote a client's letting go of unmet needs (e.g., "And so, what if the response is like, 'It doesn't matter what you do, I will never give you what you want'?"). Through this kind of enactment or imagining, clients eventually come to see that they cannot force the other to change or acknowledge wrongdoing.

Letting go emerges partly from fully experiencing a sense of deserving or entitlement to one's unmet needs in an earlier step. Clients no longer feel like defenseless children and no longer seek the other's approval to feel good about themselves. For instance, a Canadian First Nations client who was taken from his family, stripped of his language and culture, and sexually and physically abused in an Indian residential school wanted official recognition and an apology from the church, government, and individual perpetrators. Partly through anger expression and validation, this client began to feel that an apology was owed and deserved, even though he may never get one. Many clients also become more aware of how important issues of justice and respect are to them and resolve to promote these values in their current life. For example, one client who had been abused as a child decided to become a lawyer, another volunteered to work for Victim Services, and yet another vowed to become a better parent.

10b. Support emerging new view of the other and relationship. In the early phase of therapy and IC, the other is perceived narrowly and negatively—one client viewed her physically abusive and rejecting mother as "the devil." However, at this step people are able to see the other more realistically partly because their own feelings and needs have been expressed and validated. Thus, as the client gets closer to resolution, the goal of intervention shifts when the client is enacting the other. Rather than using the imagined other strictly as a stimulus for evoking feelings in the client, the emphasis now is more on promoting experiencing while the client is in the "other" chair. This helps flesh out the imagined other's perspectives, feelings, and motives. Ulti-mately, this process draws on clients' empathic resources. Therapists can ask clients, for example, how they imagine the other would feel "on the inside" or "in their heart," even if they cannot imagine the other expressing remorse or directly apologize. Clients develop an increasingly rich understanding of the other and may develop an appreciation of the limitations and frailties of those who have mistreated them. Whether or not clients feel compassion toward the other, they begin to see them as more human and life-size and less powerful.

Compassion as well as forgiveness of the other comes through the acknowledgment and expression of legitimate anger and its associated meaning, not through denying anger. In the ideal situation, the client might imagine that the other is able to respond empathically to her or his feelings and needs. Some clients imagine that the offender regrets and takes responsibility for the harm done (or that they feel regret but could never admit it). In these cases, resolution is more likely to be accompanied by forgiveness. As we have discussed, this is particularly true when the other is or was a neglectful primary attachment figure, with whom the client wishes to restore relations. In other instances, clients begin to accept that the other will never be willing or able to respond to their feelings and needs, and they accept that the other does not have what is required to respond. Some clients come to perceive the other as mentally ill or pathetic. In any case, forgiveness, as we define it, is not excusing or condoning the other's behavior, rather the client clearly and appropriately holds the other accountable for harm.

11, 12. *Close contact with imagined other, then process meaning of IC experience.* These last two steps take place at the end of each IC and are particularly important aspects of the final IC and therapy termination. It is essential to identify and accept the degree of resolution achieved in each session whatever it is. If issues with the other remain unfinished, clients should be encouraged to say so and state their intention to return to the issue in the next session. Finally, resolution is a cyclical and reiterative process, so therapists should use the DRS to evaluate a client's progress and set process goals for the next session (e.g., facilitate clearer expression of anger, increase entitlement to need, elicit perceptions of the other).

In this chapter we reviewed the model of interpersonal trauma resolution that is the basis for EFTT. This model specifies experience and expression of adaptive emotion as the catalyst for change. We also reviewed the model with a particular focus on the role of anger in resolution. The following chapter focuses on the role of sadness and grief.

11

RESOLUTION THROUGH SADNESS AND GRIEF

Full experience and expression of sadness frequently follow the process of working through anger and resentment toward the other, and once the client has developed a stronger sense of self. While the focus on resolution through anger in emotion-focused therapy for trauma (EFTT) is controversial in some circles, researchers and practitioners alike tend to view resolution achieved through sadness and grief as healing and curative. Indeed, for many clinicians, trauma work is synonymous with grieving. However, despite a large literature on the complex process of grief, little has been written on working with the discrete emotion of sadness. Furthermore, although most approaches to therapy for complex trauma recognize the importance of grieving traumatic losses, only EFTT explicitly focuses on accessing adaptive sadness as a specific and essential step of that larger process.

In this chapter, we briefly review the literature on traumatic grief across theoretical perspectives, highlighting EFTT's distinct emphasis on sadness as a discrete component in the grieving and resolution process. We also describe different types of sadness observed in trauma therapy and principles of intervention with each of these types. The intervention sections provide guidelines for working with sadness and grief as a means to resolving interpersonal trauma during imaginal confrontation (IC), for resolving self-related losses, and for reducing depression.

TRAUMATIC GRIEF ACROSS THEORETICAL PERSPECTIVES

Fully experiencing the depths of one's sorrow and accepting losses can be the most difficult aspect of trauma recovery. Experiences include the loss of loved ones as well as cherished aspects of self. Sadness experiences related to trauma also frequently include intense feelings of loneliness, isolation, and an inability to communicate one's feelings. Profound losses are especially associated with childhood maltreatment, when children are deprived of innocence, self-respect, security, and love. In cases of neglect, the developing child is deprived not only of attention, recognition, contact, and comfort from attachment figures but also of basic stimulation and feedback from the environment. Neglect leads to profound loneliness and longing for attention and recognition. It often creates a sense of self as negligible or unworthy of attention from others. The absence of information and feedback from attachment figures results in uncertainty about self—one's feelings and values, for example—and anxiety about the expectations of others.

Grieving losses is a complex process that can take place over many years and involves many emotional processes, including denial, anger, despair, depression, and sadness. People seek therapy for traumatic separation and loss because they "can't get over it." In other words, they have not been able to complete the grieving process and move on with their lives. Several factors can interfere with normal grieving. People can be preoccupied with coping with the effects of the trauma or have limited support for coping, such that grieving is suspended and left incomplete for years. Grieving profound losses is possible only after traumatic fear becomes less intense and some sense of safety has been restored. When that time comes, a supportive therapeutic relationship, along with interventions that direct clients' attention to, affirm, and validate their losses, will provide the support that likely has been missing in the environment.

In other instances, the therapeutic process is more complex and involves actively changing certain maladaptive processes that have interfered with grieving and resolution. For example, other client emotions (anger, fear, guilt, shame) or injunctions against grieving (e.g., "I shouldn't be so upset about this, others have it so much worse") can either overshadow or interrupt sadness. Changing these maladaptive processes typically is the focus of the second phase of EFTT that was presented in Chapters 8 and 9. Resolution of past interpersonal trauma also can be complicated by ongoing interactions with the offender to whom the client is still attached—emotionally, financially, functionally, or socially. In these instances, healthy expression of sadness as part of grieving traumatic loss may need to be distinguished from a mal-adaptive sense of powerlessness and depression in current situations.

The client Monica, whose mother committed suicide, was a case of a client with complicated grief because she had not been able to get over the death of her mother. Her sorrow was more like anguish, and her tears were mixed with anger at betrayal and the chaos of her life. Being traumatized and saddled with the burden of memories, recurring trauma symptoms, and family responsibilities deprived her of a happy childhood and a normal family life. Monica blamed her mother for the premature death of her father and for her own and her siblings' subsequent struggles and suffering. She also felt shame, tainted by the "atrocity." These feelings had never been validated or fully expressed and interfered with her ability to come to terms with her mother's suicide. Over the years, the message she received from family and society was, "Let it go, don't think about it, what's done is done, your mom was sick, you should forgive and forget." These well-intended messages not only prevented Monica from being able to fully grieve but also prevented her from making sense of her mother's death. For example, she lamented, "I don't understand it. I don't accept those explanations; they just sound like excuses and what she did was inexcusable." Later, in an imagined confrontation with her mother, she eventually said, "I need to know why you did what you did." Over the years she had "cried buckets," but this global distress, without clearly articulated meaning, had not been therapeutic weeping. Before she could fully experience the depths of her sorrow, Monica first needed to achieve some desensitization to the pain and distress of the trauma, resolve her feelings of shame, and fully express her anger and resentment.

Coming to terms with traumatic loss involves the process of allowing emotional pain (Greenberg & Bolger, 2001; Greenberg & Paivio, 1997), which was introduced in chapter 8. Clients must make a conscious decision to allow the pain of separation or loss and to fully experience and express the associated sadness, sometimes for the first time. This process accesses the specific information and meaning associated with sadness and helps clients to identify what was missed—the needs that were not or are not being met. Needs that are brought clearly into awareness are motivational and act as behavioral goals. Although the client will never get back the lost person, part of self, or missed opportunities, he or she can still move on to build a new life, have personal needs met, and find new meaning.

Most contemporary models of mourning (e.g., Neimeyer, 2001) understand loss in terms of disruptions in meaning. For instance, a woman who lost her husband of 20 years in a plane crash lamented, "I can't seem to wrap my head around it. I am no longer Mrs. B. . . . Like, who am I?" Current cognitive–behavioral therapy (CBT) approaches for complicated grief (e.g., Boelen, Van den Hout, & van den Bout, 2006) use standard cognitive restructuring interventions to reduce depressive withdrawal and avoidance that interfere with recovery. These approaches also may use techniques such as IC used in EFTT, to foster "communication" with the deceased and thereby promote acceptance of the loss. Current narrative constructivist approaches (e.g., Neimeyer & Bridges, 2003) focus on disruptions in personal narratives (coherent meaning) that occur through traumatic loss. In these approaches, therapy is a process of constructing a new personal narrative that includes strength, survival, and growth. EFTT bears considerable affinity with these narrative-constructivist approaches except that we focus more explicitly on affect, particularly the central role of sadness, in the resolution of loss.

Through the experience and expression of sadness during Phase 3 of EFTT, clients develop a clearer view of self and are able to fully acknowledge and understand how experiences of loss functioned in their lives. Moreover, this process unfolds in the context of a therapeutic relationship and increases warmth, intimacy, and connection with the therapist, and clients come to appreciate the support of their therapist. This can be a new learning experience that increases the likelihood of clients seeking support in other relationships. Thus, the full experience of sadness at loss is, in particular, what seems to precipitate posttraumatic growth (Tadeschi, Park, & Calhoun, 1998). It is only in facing the emptiness of a loss, and in "saying goodbye," that one is able to build something new.

Although painful, full expression of adaptive sadness is a catalyst for resolving attachment injuries related to deprivation, separation, and loss. It is important to note that this is not a linear process. Often, in therapy, sadness can be fleeting, and the client may shift back into anger or fear. Clients need to anticipate and learn to cope with the recurrence of pain and sadness, for example, at the anniversaries of a loss. Resolution and growth do not preclude anniversary reactions or other periods of distress; rather these periods are associated with an increased capacity to cope with the distress and move on. Clients can learn to be kind to themselves and seek support from others but may need to accept that the pain of profound loss may never completely go away. They can learn to honor reoccurrences of pain as indications of the depth and extent of their loss—that the persons and lost aspects of self are worth the pain. For example, a client whose two grown daughters died of alcohol-related illnesses, with time, learned not to fear holidays like Christmas when memories often flooded her awareness and old wounds were revisited. Instead, she learned to accept that, at these times, she needed to honor her grief by withdrawing and allowing herself to grieve again for the loss of her daughters. Thus, fully experiencing sadness and awareness of the needs associated with this can help clients cope with anniversary reactions and learn what to do to better care for themselves.

PROCESS DIAGNOSIS: DISTINGUISHING
DIFFERENT TYPES OF SADNESS

The following sections describe sadness as a basic emotion and distinguish among different types of sadness observed in trauma therapy.

Characteristics of Sadness as a Basic Emotion

Whereas anger emerges from violation and its expression promotes separation and distance from others; sadness experience and expression promote closeness and connection to self and others. The latter occurs partly because sharing the vulnerability and distress of sadness elicits comfort and support. Sadness, unlike anger, is inwardly directed and involves loss of energy, feelings of heaviness and collapse, downcast eyes, and a weak quiet vocal quality. People may want to lie down or curl up into a ball. This has implications for therapeutic interventions that are intended to promote sadness experience and expression. There are two action tendencies associated with sadness. One is to withdraw in order to heal and recuperate from the loss; this frequently is observed in mourning the loss of a loved one. The other is to seek contact and comfort from supportive others in order to reduce distress (i.e., "a shoulder to cry on"). Community and family grieving, as well as rituals (e.g., funerals), strengthen bonds among group members. So these and other forms of shared sadness can strengthen interpersonal connection.

Emotional *pain* and *distress* are closely related to experiences of sadness. As we discussed in Chapter 8, emotional pain is a complex experience of feeling broken or shattered and involves complex and idiosyncratic meaning about a psychological injury. Emotional pain is associated with primary sadness only when the pain concerns deprivation, separation, or loss. In contrast, crying in distress is a general signal of suffering and a cry for help, and global distress, like emotional pain, is associated with a wide range of emotions such as fear, shame, anger, and sadness. At the beginning of therapy, clients frequently are highly distressed and might cry easily about the things that are bothering them. However, they usually are not expressing primary sadness at an articulated loss. Appropriate interventions, first, need to clarify the sources of distress and differentiate it into specific emotions (see Figure 7.1 in chap. 7, this volume). Subsequent interventions differ depending on the emotion.

Adaptive Sadness

The following sections describe primary adaptive sadness and specify criteria for its expression in therapy.

Primary Adaptive Sadness

Adaptive sadness can emerge as a fleeting moment embedded in the more complex process of therapy or can be deeply felt and involve intense sobbing. It is not uncommon for this type of sadness to be suppressed or not expressed in a manner that is clearly distinct from other emotions, which can make it difficult to address. Markers of sadness suppression include intellectualization, minimization of pain, covering with anger, tensing muscles, holding one's breath and holding back tears, and experiencing an explicitly stated unwillingness to let oneself cry or "go into the pain," along with concerns about being overwhelmed. Knowledge about the situation and the individual client helps a therapist distinguish adaptive from maladaptive sadness such as depression. Sadness involves accepting loss and the hopelessness of undoing the loss, which is distinct from the lingering hopelessness, resignation, and defeat of depression.

Knowledge of the situation also provides information about other emotions that are likely to be present, along with sadness, as part of an undifferentiated emotional experience. For example, in situations of betrayal, sadness typically is mixed with anger; in situations of trauma, sadness can be mixed with fear and anger; in situations of violation and abuse, sadness is usually mixed with anger, fear, and shame. All of these emotions can be primary and all need to be experienced and expressed separately and completely. To do this, interventions aim at helping clients articulate and experience each one at a time. Interventions for sadness focus on the aspects of loss in an experience (e.g., the therapist might say, "I understand how angry you are at her abandonment and, at the same time, it must be so difficult to be dealing with it all alone, so lonely . . .").

Criteria for Healthy Sadness Expression

Criteria for adaptive sadness experience and expression in therapy are similar to those described for anger. Healthy sadness needs to be differentiated from other emotions, for example, tears of loss rather than of powerlessness or fear. Arousal levels for sadness expression need to be suitable to the situation such as quiet weeping about missed opportunities or deep sobbing over the death of a loved one. Sadness also needs to be expressed assertively with an ownership of the experience (e.g., use of "I" language, inward focus, not blaming) and should include exploration of the meaning once arousal levels subside (e.g., after one has had a "good cry"). Unlike anger, however, adaptive sadness can be directed toward the self, as in acknowledgment of, and compassion for, one's own suffering.

Maladaptive Sadness

The following sections distinguish three main types of maladaptive sadness observed in trauma therapy.

Primary Maladaptive Sadness

It takes time to determine whether expressions of primary sadness associated with traumatic loss are in fact maladaptive. The situations that trigger feelings of sadness may be appropriate but, if after repeated expression, nothing shifts or there is a dysfunctional quality of fear, fragmentation, inability to cope with loss, or helplessness, it may suggest to the therapist problems with underregulation or a core sense of vulnerability or weakness. Fear, fragmentation, and regulation problems may be associated with the severity and magnitude of a loss. This is the case, for example, with some refugee trauma survivors who have witnessed the destruction of their community and the mutilation and/or murder of loved ones. In these instances, intervention focuses on containment and regulation of distress. Pathological or complicated grief concerning a loss is another example of primary maladaptive sadness in which the person is unable to cope with and move on from an important loss. Here, accessing and working through unexpressed anger and guilt (e.g., over failure to prevent the suicide of a loved one) may be an important part of intervention.

Another dramatic instance of primary maladaptive sadness is the paradoxical sadness that may be in response to expressions of kindness and tenderness from others. For the client, these expressions from others are like evocative reminders of a deeply felt sense of deprivation, unmet dependency needs, and an ocean of longing to have these needs met. In one case, for example, a client's eyes welled up in tears at expressions of compassion that came from the therapist. Intervention in these cases involves accessing and exploring the core maladaptive emotion structure or sense of self as alone and unloved, and then restructuring this sense of self. This process occurs partly through a corrective emotional experience with an empathically responsive therapist who reduces client isolation and distress, as well as by developing healthy internal resources such as the capacity for self-soothing and seeking comfort from others. Ironically, the person often needs to feel less deprived before he or she can tolerate and receive kindness.

Secondary Sadness

Once again, tears can accompany many experiences besides sadness. For example, clients who have been violated and abused can repeatedly collapse into hurt, helplessness, and victimization rather than experience any underlying anger. These secondary reactions are recognized by verbal or nonverbal cues indicating helplessness or resignation and, as in other secondary emotions, by their temporal sequence. In this case, tears are preceded by cognitive–affective processes, such as expressions of anger at a loved one and the anticipation of rejection because of one's anger, which then results in fear, distress, and sad feelings. Interventions explore the cognitive–affective sequences leading to this secondary emotion and promote understanding of the deeper meaning and arrive at the core underlying experience.

Depression

Depression is a complex maladaptive emotional state characterized by a chronically sad mood that can have unacknowledged primary adaptive sadness (and/or anger) at its core. Depression is most prominently associated with anhedonia, or the inability to experience pleasure and ruminative negative thoughts, typically about oneself. As noted in earlier chapters, emotion-focused therapy views depression as stemming from the activation of a maladaptive emotion scheme or structure characterized by a weak/bad sense of self (Greenberg & Watson, 2006). This consists of a network of meaning that includes clients' negative thoughts about self (e.g., "I'm such a freak—who could love me?") and feelings of worthlessness, hopelessness, power-lessness, and defeat. The depressive emotion scheme also includes somatic experiences, such as heaviness and low energy, and behaviors such as social withdrawal. A depressogenic sense of self like this frequently develops from complex trauma, that is, from repeated experiences of profound powerlessness and helplessness in the face of danger and betrayal.

People typically try to gain control over their depressed mood by suppressing or distracting themselves from negative thoughts. However, there is abundant evidence supporting the view that these strategies can be counterproductive—they can maintain or exacerbate the mood state (see chap. 8, this volume, on avoidance). Mindfulness-based cognitive therapy for depression is based on these observations (Segal, Williams, & Teasdale, 2002). In that approach, clients learn to nonjudgmentally observe and accept the inevitable flow of thoughts and feelings rather than ruminating or attempting to suppress them. EFTT intervention similarly involves helping clients allow bad feelings of hopelessness and defeat. Unlike mindfulness, however, this allowing is for the purpose of subsequently exploring and constructing new meaning. Client change is accomplished by finally arriving at some healthy resource, such as primary adaptive sadness, which accesses self-soothing responses and facilitates grieving, accepting the loss, and interpersonal connection.

CHANGE PROCESSES AND GOALS

The intensity of emotional pain and the duration of the grieving process vary depending on the nature of the loss, as well as the culture, personality, and a number of other demands faced by the griever. Traumatic grief takes longer to address because resolution first deals with the underlying trauma. Similarly, in EFTT, sadness associated with posttraumatic stress disorder (PTSD) often can only be adequately dealt with after fear and shame are addressed, and after the client's sense of self has been strengthened through the experience of anger. Grieving also is harder to bear and takes longer if traumatic loss involves horrible images and memories (e.g., suicide of mother through gunshot, refugees of war). The presence of PTSD also is indicative of recurring trauma memories and grief reactions. Trauma survivors are more reactive to recurring grief and need to accept that they have been wounded by the trauma and that wounds take time to heal. The point we want to emphasize here is that allowing the pain of loss, as part of the grieving process, is not a simple cathartic event but rather involves complex feelings and processes that usually take place over considerable time. The goal of therapy in the early stages of resolving traumatic loss was simply to help clients tolerate and stay with these complex processes. Sadness expression takes place in this larger context and usually is fully experienced and expressed during Phase 3 of therapy.

Steps in the process of allowing emotional pain and resolving interpersonal trauma using IC or empathic exploration (EE) were presented in earlier chapters. The following discussion summarizes and combines critical processes and goals with a focus on the specific role of sadness in grieving and resolution.

Allow the Pain, Accept the Loss, and Express Sorrow

The first goal is to help the client let go of the struggle to avoid pain or relinquish efforts to hold onto the lost object. Once a loss is accepted as irrevocable, at least for the moment (e.g., a client says, "I will never get back that innocence, it's gone forever"), a new and more realistic view of self can emerge. Thus, the client develops an increased sense of agency and is able to acknowledge the damage to self that has occurred. The goal of therapy in this phase is also to facilitate and support a process of deep grieving that includes the expression of sadness. This could take place in interaction with the therapist, an imagined supportive other, or an imagined part of self.

Promote Awareness of Specific Losses and Associated Needs

An important goal in working with sadness is to help the client specify what is and/or was missed, wished, or longed for, in terms of both interpersonal loss and personal losses (e.g., one's hopes, dreams, cherished beliefs, assumptions, identity). Awareness of specific losses provides motivation for replacing what is still missed and getting one's needs met.

Promote Self-Exploration

The goal here is to promote experiencing in the context of sadness, that is, exploration of feelings and meanings related to the loss. In narrative terms, this means shifting from chaos to coherence (Neimeyer, 2006), making new meaning, and coming to terms with the loss. Change processes of this kind begin when clients start to ask questions about themselves and their loss (e.g., "Why has God taken this away, what is my purpose?" or "All those years of degradation—what makes me think anyone would respect me?"), and the client engages in a deliberate effort to formulate answers and construct a more coherent understanding of self and traumatic events.

An important issue concerning meaning construction is illustrated in the case of Monica. A major focus of her therapy was Monica trying to make sense of her mother's suicide. Of course, it is impossible to know why the mother did what she did, and the challenge for therapists in situations like these is not to push for any particular content or ending to the story. Also, for clients like Monica, who cannot obtain more corroborating information about events or significant others, a new and more coherent understanding is one that makes sense to the clients themselves and that fits with their existing experiential memories and their existing stories. This understanding only emerges from the moment-by-moment process of exploring and clarifying aspects of experience and the story as they emerge in session.

INTERVENTION PRINCIPLES FOR PROMOTING ADAPTIVE SADNESS

This section presents intervention principles that are specific to promoting the experience and expression of healthy sadness about separation and loss.

Ensure an Appropriate Time and Therapeutic Environment Conducive to Sadness

First, the therapist and client may need to collaborate on an appropriate time to focus on grieving. Grief may have to be postponed to a time when clients are not overwhelmed by external demands and responding to problems imposed by the trauma. When grief is a focus of therapy sessions, therapists need to ensure that clients have a time and place to be with their feelings outside of therapy or can reasonably manage their feelings between sessions.

Establishing an appropriate therapeutic environment for working with sadness and loss begins with provision of safety. Clients must feel safe enough to allow themselves to collapse and be vulnerable with their therapist. Moreover, in IC work, clients must feel that the imagined other potentially will respond with compassion and comfort. They will not allow themselves to be vulnerable in the face of an imagined other who continues to be seen as cruel or abusive. Using or switching to the EE intervention in these circumstances effectively avoids this potential obstacle by having clients disclose without an imagined perpetrator. Thus, sadness expression takes place in interaction with an empathically responsive therapist, with another part of the self, or with an imagined other who is perceived as having the capacity for support. Typically, this last option will be an attachment figure (internalized or in real life) with whom the client wants to restore connection.

Vulnerability and expressed sadness increase the likelihood of intimacy because they invite the possibility of supportive reactions from imagined others. For example, the client Monica could fully express her sorrow toward her imagined mother only after she imagined that her mother would hear her anger and take full responsibility for the harm she had caused. However, the therapist should not assume that, because the client could not or would not express sadness toward an imagined other in the early phase of therapy, the situation will remain unaltered. As noted in earlier chapters, appropriate intervention requires ongoing tracking and assessment of a client's evolving perceptions and goals in terms of relations with the other.

Provide Validation, Encouragement, and Support

Above all, when working with sadness, therapists need to feel and communicate deep compassion for their clients' suffering and pain and validate the importance of the loss and how hard it is to approach these feelings (e.g., "It's terrible for a child to feel so alone and unloved, so hard to feel that again" or "How many tears you must have cried for your beloved daughters?"). These interventions normalize client grief and help them to allow the pain of sadness and loss because they are no longer suffering alone. Therapist compassion and nurturing are internalized by clients and contribute to their capacity for compassion toward self and self-soothing. Interventions that provide support include the therapist's soothing presence, vocal quality, and giving clients the space they need to focus inward and momentarily withdraw from personal contact in order to heal. In terms of eliciting self-soothing responses that do not spontaneously emerge, therapists can ask their clients how they would respond to a friend or loved one if those people were grieving such an important loss.

Strengthen Clients' Sense of Self

The conscious choice to allow the pain of loss comes about because clients feel safer in the environment but also because they feel less fragile.

One of the features of unresolved trauma is weeping in distress about feeling victimized and powerless rather than about accepting one's loss. We have noted throughout the book how accessing healthy anger at violation can help reduce a client's sense of victimization and powerlessness. Anger as a basic emotion is associated with strength and vitality, finding one's "backbone" and therefore contributing to strengthening the self while one is dealing with loss. For example, the client John, whose mother died of a drug overdose, resisted facing the pain of her death. After several sessions that focused on anger about his own subsequent abuse in an orphanage and brief expressions of sadness, John was able to focus more fully on grieving the loss of his mother and the many associated losses and suffering he had endured.

A number of basic emotion-focused therapy intervention principles, described in earlier chapters, also are particularly important in promoting sadness experience and expression. First, in terms of directing attention to internal experience, it is essential to create an environment that is peaceful and quiet so the client can withdraw and focus inward. Second, present-centeredness and responding to client moment-by-moment process are crucial because the emergence of primary sadness can be subtle and fleeting (e.g., eyes momentarily welling up in tears, downcast eyes, a wistful tone of voice). Therapists must be flexible in modulating the quality of their responses (e.g., vocal quality) to match the emerging experience of the client. Sadness also can quickly shift to other emotions such as fear or anger (and vice versa) or to self-protective withdrawal. For this reason, therapists need to recognize the difference between natural shifts to another primary emotion, such as anger, as opposed to shifts that indicate avoiding vulnerability or pain. These distinctions have obvious implications for appropriate intervention.

Promoting sadness at loss also can involve increasing arousal to the point at which suppressed sadness can no longer be ignored. Interventions include memory evocation (e.g., references to the client as a child); evocative empathic responses that are personal and poignant and that use imagery and metaphor (e.g., "a broken heart"; "a big gapping hole inside"); references to bodily experience (e.g., feelings of heaviness, aching, emptiness); and use of enactments. The client imagining self as a child and fully experiencing the pain of being unloved, for example, can elicit deep compassion or empathy for self and nurturing, soothing responses.

The final intervention principle is helping clients to symbolize the meaning of sadness and loss. Without the consistent effort of the client and the carefully refined reflections of the therapist, grief can quickly unravel into a much more global sense of distress. This is the essence of "therapeutic weeping" as opposed to clients who have "cried buckets" with no glimpse of resolution. The principles involved in promoting client experiencing presented in Chapter 6 also are relevant here. Targets of exploration include somatic experiences;

causes of the pain; specific losses and associated wants, needs, and desires; the effects of the loss on self and self-identity; and perceptions of self and others. Therapists encourage clients, for example, to put word to bodily experiences (e.g., "Put words to your tears" or " . . . that ache inside" or " . . . what weighs you down"). Symbolizing the pain of loss helps to create distance from it and make it comprehensible. Once again, identifying what is and/or was missed or missed out on is central to the meaning of sadness and the source of one's emptiness and pain. When clients feel sad, they need to know what they feel sad about (e.g., the therapist might ask, "What is that emptiness, what is missing?" or "What did you long for, or crave, more than anything?").

INTERVENTIONS FOR PROMOTING SADNESS AND GRIEVING LOSSES

Specific change processes ensue when pain and sadness are expressed concerning an attachment figure during IC; in particular, these processes promote empathy for and connection with the other. In the sections that follow, we identify steps in the process that parallel those related to anger, but here we highlight the role of sadness in the resolution process.

Promoting Primary Sadness Over Attachment Injuries

In response to client markers of unresolved deprivation, separation, or loss concerning an attachment figure (e.g., when a client says, "It tears me apart every time I think of her"), the therapist can initiate a focus on experiences of sadness (e.g., "Let's stay with this pain and sadness for a moment . . ."). Alternatively, the therapist and client may collaboratively decide that a focus on sadness and loss will be most productive for the client. In cases in which unproductive anger is a client's dominant experience, for example, the therapist can raise this issue for discussion and suggest the goal of expanding the client's emotion repertoire (e.g., "It seems as if you feel sad about this as well, never getting the attention you needed. I think it would be useful to explore that other side of the coin. I guess it would be hard to go there, but still . . ."). Once sadness has been activated, the client then can be directed to express his or her sadness to the imagined other in IC.

Therapist Operations During Steps in the IC Task

General steps in the IC task are outlined in Chapter 7, Exhibit 7.1, and steps specifically related to anger were outlined in the preceding chapter.

When the process relates to sadness, once the procedure has been set up (Steps 1 and 2), promoting psychological contact with the imagined other (Step 3) again requires that the other is seen as capable of responding with sympathy and support. If this is not the case, it is most beneficial for the client to express sadness to the therapist (e.g., in EE) or another part of self (e.g., in a two-chair dialogue). In terms of separating sadness from global distress and other emotions (Step 4), client weeping in the early phase of therapy typically is accompanied by hurt, blame, and complaint about the other. At the beginning of therapy with Monica, her tears were mixed with anger, and the process oscillated back and forth between anger and sadness. Despite an early focus on helping her work through her anger, the therapist was continuously attuned to the presence of sadness as Monica described new events concerning her mother (e.g., Monica said, "It's so sad seeing those old pictures of her, so young and beautiful") and empathically responded to the client's laments ("Yes, really tragic, you missed out on so much"). Later in therapy, the therapist explicitly encouraged Monica to stay with these feelings of pain and sadness ("Tell her how much you have missed her, all the things you have missed over the years"). Specifying the things she had missed out on elicited the softening typical of sorrow, that is, vulnerability, turning inward, and a longing for contact and comfort ("I missed you seeing me graduate, getting married, even just going shopping . . . I see other women with their mothers and it always hurts so much"). This marked the shift to steps in the resolution process typical of Phase 3 of therapy. These steps, as they apply to sadness, are outlined below, beginning with Step 6 in Exhibit 7.1.

6. *Promote sadness expression.* To promote full experience and expression of sadness, interventions first may need to address problems with emotion regulation. This includes providing empathic affirmation of vulnerability, reassurance, soothing, and comfort to reduce distress. In other cases, this would include the use of evocative language to increase arousal and activate core emotion structures. As noted, helping the client reexperience him- or herself as a child can be particularly evocative. It is critical that a therapist's nonverbal behavior (quiet soothing voice, leaning forward) is conducive to sadness experience and helps the client turn inward.

7. *Identify unmet needs.* As in the example of Monica, unmet attachment needs emerge from identifying specific losses in relation to the other. Clients can find it difficult to acknowledge the depths of their neediness and longing because of the emotional pain, unresolved anger, or difficulties admitting weakness or vulnerability. Effective intervention for client difficulties with vulnerability depends on whether the problem concerns avoiding the experience of vulnerability or the disclosure of vulnerability. The intervention also will depend on whether the client has concerns about vulnerability vis-

à-vis the imagined other or the therapist. When clients resist expressing need-iness to the imagined other, it can be helpful for therapist interventions to distinguish the present from the past (i.e., what was needed as a child) and direct clients to speak about their past needs, which frequently are more evocative than their adult situations.

For example, a client entered therapy saying she had been "sad for years." She perceived her mother as "mean," constantly criticizing, never telling the client she loved her or praising her. Although the client still maintained a relationship with her mother, she held her mother in contempt. In ses-sion, she was unable to acknowledge how much she wanted affection from her mother, such as a hug ("Not now, it's too late, it makes me sick even thinking of it"). This refusal to entertain her need for affection was con-flicted because of both her anger and the intensity of her longing ("It's yucky, embarrassing"). Intervention acknowledged both the client's resist-ance (e.g., the therapist said, "I hear how much you distrust her and would never expose your feelings to her right now") but then responded to her sadness. These responses validated the extent of the client's deprivation and pain and helped her acknowledge her hunger and longing for her mother's love. The therapist asked the client, "Feeling sad for years, what's that about? A big ache inside, can you put words to that ache? As a little girl, what did you long for more than anything? What was the worst part?" Client longing initially was expressed to the therapist, and later interven-tions returned to IC with the mother. Graded interventions like this help a client articulate and explore the effects of unmet needs on self and the significance of their absence in the client's life.

8. *Track perceptions of self and other.* Tracking client perceptions of self and other throughout the dialogue process is part of exploring and symboliz-ing meaning by promoting client experiencing. Clients also can be directed to tell the imagined other, or to tell the therapist in the case of EE, about her- or himself (e.g., the therapist might say, "Tell him what he [father] missed out on, what kind of a person you are"). Perceptions of the other are elicited by enacting or imagining the other's response to the client's expressed sorrow, disappointment, and longing. Aside from the other's perceived capac-ity for responsiveness, core issues regarding expressions of sadness concern whether the client wants to maintain or regain connection with the real or internalized attachment figure. This also is related to the importance a client places on forgiving an offending other. These issues will shape the process of interaction with the imagined other and determine the type of resolution that is possible.

9. *Increase sense of entitlement to needs.* It is important to increase clients' conviction that their unmet attachment needs are essential to their devel-opment and their happiness and that they are deserved, rather than seeing

one's personal needs as excessive, self-indulgent, or trivial. This is accomplished by directing clients' attention to and validating their needs, desires, and longings in relation to the other (e.g., the therapist might say, "Yes, of course, all children need attention and recognition, need to know that they are important"). Needs that are fully acknowledged and owned become the motivational aspects of meaning. Clients who can both experience and admit the extent of their loneliness and their need for connection and intimacy are more likely to seek out ways to get these needs met in their everyday life.

10a. *Support emerging new perceptions of self.* A clearer and more realistic view of self emerges, in part, from allowing emotional pain, letting go of needs and expectations regarding the other person, and accepting losses. Here we need to distinguish resolution and acceptance of loss from the untenable pseudo-resolution of resignation and powerlessness. Interventions in EFTT facilitate a gradual process of acceptance and letting go. Therapists need to avoid forcing or supporting premature or pseudo-acceptance. Difficulties in this area will be discussed in more detail in the following chapter on termination. Facilitating genuine acceptance requires helping the client to sink into the sense of hopelessness at the irrevocable nature of the loss (e.g., the therapist might say, "Stay with that, knowing you will never have the kind of family you wanted, it's so hard to let that go"). The therapist may direct clients to attend to their bodily experience, for example, "Go inside, speak from that heaviness. What does it say?" Along with interpersonal losses, clients also may need to accept the limitations imposed on them by the trauma (e.g., difficulties with intimacy and trust).

A particularly painful and difficult situation is when clients must accept and grieve the reality that they were not wanted or loved by an attachment figure. One of the clients described in an earlier chapter alternated between current issues of nonassertiveness with his employer and a focus on past issues with an alcoholic father who had been emotionally and physically abusive. In a pivotal session, the client recalled an incident in which his father showed up late and drunk for the client's birthday, then "proceeded to break my heart by breaking all my presents." Therapy with this client was a gradual process of approaching and accepting the painful reality that he had never been loved by his father and that all his efforts to secure that love were futile. The male therapist in this case provided a model of male compassion and warmth. Interventions to help the client with his sadness included affirmation of vulnerability, provision of comfort and support, and validation of the client's experience and perceptions. The therapist said to the client, "This is so painful, hard to accept that you were not loved by the one person you needed it from the most. You missed out on so much, you both did, what a shame." Therapy repeatedly returned to this theme until the client was able to fully acknowledge and accept the extent of his deprivation and loss.

One strategy used to promote letting go during IC or two-chair enact-ments involves saying goodbye to the imagined other, the relationship, or a lost part of self. There seems to be universal recognition that this can be powerful and valuable for clients, and many approaches to grief therapy incorporate some variation on this procedure. In some cases, symbolizing the process of letting go can be done by inviting the client to list all those things that are now gone. For example, in a formal and explicit fashion, a therapist could prompt a client to "Say goodbye to all the good things, what were they?"; then "Say good-bye to all the bad things, good riddance to what?"; and, finally, "Say good-bye to all the hopes and dreams, what were they? What is it that will never come to pass?"

In the process of allowing pain and accepting loss, clients also shift to acknowledging and accepting the self as having been shattered and devas-tated by the loss, and surviving despite this devastation. Moreover, there is an increased sense of self-control or agency in choosing to allow the pain of sadness and loss. One of the distinctive features of sadness expression, and especially in contrast to anger, is its association with the experience of vul-nerability. This feature contributes to particular healthy changes in object relations: Tears of sadness are accompanied by relief, softening, and compas-sion toward self and sometimes toward the other.

10b. *Support new perceptions of imagined other.* Primary adaptive sadness is free of blame, and, during IC, heartfelt expressions of sadness and longing can elicit (from the position of imagining the other) responses of comfort, soothing, and possibly regret for causing the client pain. However, sadness and acceptance of loss may mean accepting the limitations of the other in terms of relationship quality. The client above, for example, was able to accept that his father was incapable of love and felt sorry for him. In either case, when sadness is expressed to or about (as in EE) attachment figures, it almost always is associated with a softening toward the other (e.g., the client might say, "He did the best he could with what he had" or "She was a vic-tim herself"). Monica, for example, was able to see her mother's suicide as "a terrible mistake" stemming from desperation rather than self-centeredness and any lack of caring. Directing client attention to what they imagine the other would feel "in his or her heart" rather than focusing on the other's neg-ative behavior can help elicit client empathic resources. This is distinct from minimization and making excuses for the other as sometimes occurs in the early phases of therapy. Notice that, technically speaking, this involves a shift from using the imagined other as a stimulus to evoke a response in the self to promoting experiencing from the perspective of the other as a way of promot-ing empathic understanding.

A shift to more realistic perceptions of the other also is illustrated by John, the client who had been placed in orphanage after the death of his mother's overdose. Early in therapy he had idealized his mother, viewing her as an "angel." Deepening his experiencing resulted in a more authentic and less superficial experience, and a richer understanding of her:

T: Of course at age 5 she was your angel, your world. But she was a real woman. Now, as a grown man, how do you see her?

C: I know she must have had problems, my uncles always said she was an addict, but I always felt loved by her, we used to sit around the kitchen table and she would help me do my homework, stuff like that.

T: So, despite her problems she loved you. . . . How tragic to lose her, heartbreaking.

C: [His eyes well up with tears]

T: Stay with that, she is worth your tears. What is the worst part of it for you?

C: It makes me so sad to think of her suffering all alone, she was so young, sweet really.

T: Yes, she sounds like a gentle soul. And you, her beloved boy, thrown to the wolves, also suffering alone.

Through continued exploration, the client was able to acknowledge the reality of his mother's tragic life before her death and to experience deep compassion for her rather than superficially idealize her. At the same time, he also was able to feel compassion for himself, for his years in the orphanage feeling sad and alone, and the many other losses he had endured—his cultural identity (not only lost but demeaned) his family and childhood, his destroyed sexuality, his ruined health.

Many survivors of complex trauma are in ongoing relationships with perpetrators of abuse and neglect, and this can obviously make resolution more complicated. For example, a client, "Kim," felt angry and betrayed by her alcoholic mother who failed to protect her from sexual abuse at the hands of a babysitter. In their current relationship, the mother manipulated her daughter (the client) to get her own way. Her mother was unreliable and could not be supportive or play the role of a proper grandmother. All her life, Kim felt that she had been "mother to her own mother" and lamented her unmet dependency needs. She "walked on eggshells" with her mother and engaged in endless efforts to please her. The therapist commented, "It's as if, if you do just the right thing, your mother will finally wake up and see you and appreciate you." The client laughed and said that she had been unable to accept her mother for who she really was. Therapy involved many sessions of exploring the impact of the mother's current behavior on the client, the constant disappointments, what the client longed for, and the pain of never getting it.

In desperation, Kim also considered the possibility of ending the relationship entirely, and she explored both sides of this dilemma in a two-chair dialogue. This accessed deep sadness at all the disappointments, letting go of the hope that things would ever change, and accepting that her mother was incapable of meeting her needs. She was able to move on to explore alternative ways to get the nurturing and support she needed from others in her life. Finally, Kim was able to feel compassion for her mother ("She can't say it [referring to mother] but she would be devastated if I ended it. She is like a child, she needs me."). Moreover, Kim developed a clear sense that she, in fact, did not want to end the relationship. However, she became able to set limits in terms of the behavior she would not accept in that relationship. The latter was facilitated by expressing resentment (anger) at her mother's unacceptable behavior and having this validated by the therapist.

INTERVENTION FOR OTHER TYPES OF SADNESS

Not all sadness concerns interpersonal separation and loss. The following sections describe EFTT intervention with self-related losses and depression.

Accepting Self-Related Losses

Trauma can also result in numerous self-related losses, including alienation and isolation through inability to communicate one's feelings and experiences or trouble connecting interpersonally with others. In some sense, the horrors of trauma are locked up inside the individual. After fear is reduced, anger seems to be the adaptive experience that is most often associated with details of a trauma, whereas sadness is associated with experiences of loss that become so apparent in the wake of abuse and injury. These losses frequently are minimized or overshadowed by more powerful emotional experiences such as anger, shame, or fear, but eventually they need to be acknowledged and grieved in therapy.

Experiences of complex interpersonal trauma, particularly in development, can involve especially devastating losses to self: a ruined sexuality or capacity for intimacy, loss of innocence and self-respect, shattered hopes and dreams, as well as being deprived of basic attachment needs and the effects this has on adult functioning. When offenders, including attachment figures, continue to be seen as unrepentant, despicable, and cruel, resolution most often involves increased separation and empowerment through anger experience and grieving losses to self. Grieving loss is done in the context of the therapeutic relationship or in two-chair dialogues with the lost aspects of self. These enactments can be used alone or in conjunction with IC or EE. For example, an earlier chapter described how Clare, the client who had been sexually molested by her brother, shifted between angrily confronting the imagined brother and comforting herself as a little girl. The therapist's interventions helped Claire access compassion for herself and helped her develop self-soothing and comforting responses to herself by asking, "Imagine her, you, that little girl who feels bad about herself. What do you want to say to her? What do you want her to know?"

Other survivors of complex trauma have lost the capacity to connect interpersonally and are profoundly lonely. A client with a history of being emotionally terrorized and physical abused by her father and coldly rejected by her mother stated, "There was something odd about me as a kid" and "I have failed in my efforts to connect with people." Although she described herself as "climbing the walls" with loneliness, she found it difficult to experientially acknowledge her emotional pain. In an example of paradoxical sadness, her eyes welled up in tears at any sign of warmth or compassion from the therapist. Intervention helped her gradually acknowledge the extent of the deprivation she had experienced and the depths of her longing.

T: These demonstrations of kindness seem to touch a big emptiness inside you.

C: [in a little girl voice, suppressing her tears] I don't like it, it makes me feel foolish.

T: Foolish? There's nothing foolish about needing affection, it's like you're starved for it.

C: I hate admitting this.

During IC with her mother, the client could express anger but not admit her unmet need for mothering although her pain was very evident.

C: I don't *want* to want her.

T: Maybe not now, maybe it's too late . . . but as a child?

C: Oh yes, as a child. I remember standing close to her and thinking how nice it felt.

T: Wishing for what, maybe a hug?

C: Oh god, hugs were out of the question!

T: How sad, little children need lots of hugs and kisses, it's like food for the soul.

C: [sighs] Yes, well, I never got that food.

Interventions continued to focus on what it was like for this client as a child and helped her express sorrow about unmet attachment needs and the lifetime of loneliness she had suffered.

Still another client experienced regret about not realizing his career potential after growing up in an abusive environment. He was always fearful and nervous as a boy, did poorly in school, and, as a child, believed he was stupid. The client also regretted his ruined marriages, which he authentically attributed to his own limitations, not in self-blame but rather as part of his accepting responsibility for contributing to the marital breakdown. This client initially minimized these losses ("I shouldn't complain. I have a good job, right? I've even been promoted to supervisor, people respect me."). Intervention with this client validated his experience and helped him to fully acknowledge the significance of his loss. For example, the therapist said, "Yes you've accomplished a lot, despite your crappy childhood, but sounds like you never had a chance to really try other things, test your potential. I guess the truth is many opportunities are gone forever, you'll never know, and that's what makes you sad." This helped the client to grieve and accept the reality of his lost career potential, to let go, and to consider new possibilities rather than maintain his Pollyanna-like stance.

Working With Depression

Depression can be a normal part of grieving that occurs in an early stage of that process and then shifts. Resolving depression that does not shift typically is the focus of Phase 2 of EFTT because it involves changing maladaptive processes that interfere with resolving interpersonal trauma. Other volumes on emotion-focused therapy describe the approach for dealing specifically with depression (see, e.g., Greenberg & Watson, 2006). We briefly discuss therapeutic work with depression here to distinguish this process from promoting primary adaptive sadness at separation and loss, as was described above.

In terms of trauma, clients who were unable to protect themselves or loved ones can collapse into powerlessness, can feel numb, and are vulnerable to the reactivation of these feelings in their current life. Also, they may never have had an opportunity to express the sorrow they feel for their own and their loved one's suffering. We recently have been seeing a number of refugee trauma survivors in our clinic, and depression is quite prevalent among these individuals. After the initial "honeymoon" and adjustment period that is focused on meeting basic needs for housing, school, employment, and learning English, they begin to miss their family and home and may have difficulty connecting and adjusting to their new life. These clients also can have difficulty accepting that they probably will never see their family and home again. They may hang on to that fantasy but then regularly lose hope when the reality of their situation sinks in. This was the case with a client whose family arranged for her to leave her home country after she had been raped and held for ransom on two separate occasions. She had no hope that circumstances in her country would change and, therefore, no hope of returning safely and seeing her parents again. She also had found it difficult to find appropriate work and new friends in Canada; things were not working out as she had planned. Each new disappointment triggered a collapse into depression for her.

In instances like these, depression is secondary, a by-product that follows more primary sadness about loneliness, separation, and loss. This aftermath of continued depression represents the inability to accept that a given loss is permanent and the related collapse into defeat. Appropriate intervention is aimed at exploring and changing clients' sense of defeat, meaninglessness, and inability to cope. This is done, in part, by validating and promoting expressions of primary adaptive sadness at very real losses. Although providing hope is an important part of therapy for complex and cumulative trauma (Pearlman & Courtois, 2005), it must be realistic. Hopefulness cannot be clinging onto impossible dreams and unrealistic expectations. Thus, intervention with clients who feel destitute ultimately involves helping them face their hopelessness and accept the reality of unavoidable separations and losses that are indeed beyond their control.

Sadness is about endings and saying goodbye. The following final chapter describes Phase 4 of EFTT, which deals with ending therapy and the difficulties that may be encountered in that process.

PHASE FOUR OF EFTT

12

TERMINATION

Phase 4, the termination phase of therapy, is about completing the resolution process, consolidating client changes, saying goodbye, and bridging to the future. The length of the termination phase varies depending on a client's needs and the length of therapy, and it could range from one to several sessions. As in most therapies, discussions of therapy ending takes place long before the actual final session so that clients are well prepared. In our clinic, clients typically initially contract for 16 to 20 sessions. Before Session 16, we begin discussing client progress, their feelings about ending, and whether a few more sessions will be needed to wrap things up. For clients who are nervous about ending and losing the support of therapy, there is always the possibility of gradually tapering off sessions and returning for booster sessions.

In our experience, termination is not a major issue for most clients who are suitable for short-term therapy, and agreement about the number of sessions is easily determined collaboratively and adhered to. However, termination is more complex when therapy has continued for a longer term, trust was more difficult to cultivate, or the client is more vulnerable and has few external resources. Obviously, in these cases, provision for continuation of services (either emotion-focused therapy for trauma [EFTT] or referral to another service) is essential.

In this chapter we describe how to revisit core issues and use a final round of imaginal confrontation (IC) or empathic exploration (EE) interventions to help create closure and to consolidate client treatment gains. We highlight that one of the aims in these concluding interventions is to emphasize clients' new awareness of, and ability to monitor and control, their internal processes. We also provide guidelines for giving and eliciting mutual therapist–client feedback about the process and experience of therapy. Finally, we discuss difficulties that may emerge at the end of treatment in EFTT. On one hand, clients may have difficulties with reaching resolution, getting stuck on a final step of letting go. On the other hand, clients may have difficulties with termination itself and accepting the end of therapy. We end with some remarks on bridging the work clients have done in treatment with their future lives.

COMPLETION AND CONSOLIDATION OF CHANGES

Explicitly reviewing client changes at termination helps to consolidate those changes, assesses the degree to which goals have been accomplished, and identifies areas for further growth (either in or outside of therapy). The therapist discusses these positive changes with the client, introducing them as topics for exploration. This end-of-treatment discussion focuses on changes in self-related processes and in relation to those significant others who were the focus of therapy. Helping clients integrate therapy processes into their current daily lives also is part of this final goal.

Final IC or EE

A final IC or EE with the imagined other(s) who have been the target of therapy normally takes place one or two sessions before what has been agreed will be the final session.

Complete and Bring Closure to the Resolution Process

The purpose of the final IC (or EE) with the imagined other(s) is to help the client move forward toward resolution as much as possible, tie up any loose ends, and bring closure to the resolution process. The therapist might ask a client, for example, "How do you feel about ending, saying goodbye to her? Is there anything else you want to say to your mother before we end?" Before the session in which the final dialogue with the imagined other is initiated, it is important to review client goals. Therapists must be clear about their client's degree of resolution (see the Degree of Resolution Scale in Appendix C) and clear about what still needs to be, and feasibly could be, accomplished in one final dialogue with (or discussion about, in the case of

EE) the imagined other. For example, even though forgiveness previously may have been stated as a goal, the client may still be unable to forgive the other. In such a case, the focus of the final IC would be to explore what interferes with forgiveness, what is required to accomplish that initial goal, or whether the goal can be revised. One strategy in promoting forgiveness (or at least in increasing understanding) of the other could be to pay particular attention to client enactment and perceptions of the other and to promote experiencing from the other's perspective to elicit client empathic resources. An alternative strategy might be to help clients explore any lingering anger they may have that interferes with understanding the other's perspective, something we will discuss in more detail below.

Even though the final dialogue is an opportunity for promoting closure, the therapist also should be prepared for new information and new issues to emerge. Clients see this as their last opportunity to work through issues that have been the focus of therapy and may have given this considerable thought prior to the session. This reflection and preparation is helpful to the process, and therapists may want to encourage clients to consider their goals in light of the treatment process that has passed. For example, one client had been firmly entrenched in a completely malevolent view of his brutally violent and abusive grandfather who was his caregiver for a number of years. During the final IC, however, he imagined the grandfather in heaven, remorseful but also so prideful that it prevented him from apologizing. The client imagined that his grandfather was only able to say, "I wish I'd been a better husband to your grandmother—she was a good woman—and a better grandfather to you." This imagined response felt authentic to the client and he was able to let go of his own anger toward the grandfather and close the interaction satisfactorily. This same client was interviewed several months after therapy completion and reported continuing to feel fully resolved.

In other cases, new issues spontaneously (and unexpectedly) emerge in the course of completing the final interaction with the imagined other, and these issues need to be worked through. A good example of this was the final IC with Monica. Prior to this session, it appeared that issues with her mother were fully resolved but, when encouraged by the therapist to say goodbye to her mother in the final IC, she was unable to do so. This raised the issue of her attachment to her internalized mother that needed to be explored. In exploring this issue, the client expressed her deep need and longing to feel that she had been loved by her mother and her insecurity about this. The discussion that followed with her therapist elicited poignant and comforting memories for Monica of interacting with her mother when she was a girl. These experiential memories strengthened the attachment to her internalized mother and fulfilled these unmet needs in a healthy and realistic way, so that she could let go of the longing and move on with her life.

Consolidate Changes

Improvements in complex traumatic stress are more than simple symptom reduction. Furthermore, shifts in personal meaning and attachment to abusive or neglectful others are challenging to measure in a concrete way. To that end, the final IC or EE is intended and explicitly framed as an index of change, a performance-based measure in which therapist and client can witness how the client reacts differently. This is an opportunity for clients to experience their current status in relation to the core issues that brought them to therapy (e.g., the therapist might say to a client, "Let's see where you're at with your father. Tell him how you feel about him and those past issues, now. What's your current understanding?"). Therapists also can encourage clients also can compare their present state with that of the beginning of therapy (e.g., the therapist might say, "Pay attention to how you feel now compared with how you felt at the beginning. Maybe even tell your father how you have changed."). This increases clients' awareness of their current position and what has been accomplished over the course of therapy. It also orients clients by increasing their awareness of areas still requiring attention and for future growth.

Client Awareness of Changes in Internal Processes

Self-related goals in EFTT are to help clients to better tolerate emotional pain and self-soothe, stand up to critical self-statements, and be more confident in relation to others in real life. Basic EFTT intervention principles apply in consolidating these client changes. For example, when clients report that generally they no longer feel so anxious, the therapist typically asks them to recall a particular situation, attend to their internal experience, and describe how they now stop themselves from feeling anxious (e.g., "Can you think of a situation in which you felt anxious and then calmed yourself— what went on inside, what did you do or say to yourself?"). Therapists also empathically respond to clients positive feelings (e.g., pride, confidence) concerning their changes and accomplishments (e.g., "It must be such a relief to be free of that constant pressure" or "Your smile tells me something feels good about all this!").

First, a client's therapeutic gains are always genuinely framed in terms of accomplishments and mostly attributed to the client's own efforts. For example, during the last session, a therapist stated to the client, "You must feel pretty good about what you've accomplished. You've 'come a long way, baby!' [*They both laugh*]. Seriously, you've worked very hard." Second, of course, clients frequently will recall something meaningful that the therapist said or did. Therapists openly accept their clients' compliments and appreciation of their contributions but acknowledge the collaborative nature of the process, highlighting that "we did it together." In any case, the implicit message to be communicated by therapists to their clients is, "You are the sort of person who can forge a collaborative relationship and make use of what therapy has to offer." This not only enhances self-esteem but increases the likelihood that clients will seek out support in the future, should they need it.

AWARENESS AND ACCEPTANCE OF LIMITED CHANGE

In some instances, clients do not fully achieve their treatment goals and aspirations. The following sections describe strategies for addressing this during the termination phase of therapy.

Client Is Disappointed About Limited Gains or Degree of Resolution

Unfortunately, clients (and therapists) do not always achieve what they had hoped for in therapy. First, it is essential for both parties to have realistic expectations for change throughout the therapy process. Goals should be circumscribed (particularly in short-term therapy) and be realistically attainable. Clients can reasonably expect to make meaningful improvements in at least one or two important areas. If the client perceives that this has not occurred (and will not occur), his or her disappointment needs to be discussed and processed as therapy approaches the final session. Clients, for example, could be bothered by the fact that they still feel angry and unable to forgive a parent or other offender, that they still feel insecure in a current relationship, or that they still wrestle with depression. Creating meaning around this disappointment helps soothe it and sometimes can advance the resolution process a bit further still.

Assuming that the current course of therapy has come to an end and no more time will be devoted to working on these issues, the basic intervention strategy in these situations is to acknowledge and explore client disappointment, promote acceptance of "what is," and promote client self-acceptance in this particular area. Therapists can communicate that they sympathize with the client's disappointment (e.g., the therapist might say, "Yes, I wish you could feel completely at peace with this, but that's just not where you're at right now, is it? You can't force yourself to be someone you're not, feel something you don't feel."). Interventions also promote clients' experiencing to explore and help them understand their current position vis-à-vis their struggle for closure. However the case may be, interventions must instill confidence in the client's capacity for continued growth and hope for the future (e.g., the therapist might say, "The important thing is to continue to pay attention to and trust your experience. Be open to whatever comes your way, just as you've done in therapy. Trust that, if you do this, things inevitably will evolve."). Thus, the aim of interventions in this last phase is to provide clients with a sense direction for personal growth while acknowledging the status of changes to date and the current circumstances.

Client-Reported Changes Seem to Be Pseudo-Resolution/Forgiveness

Pseudo-resolution of issues with offenders typically is characterized by clients' assertions that they have resolved their issues and are "over it" while their therapists have concerns that this may not be entirely the case. For example, client wishful thinking can occur, especially when there is ongoing interaction and desired reconnection and reconciliation with an offender who is an attachment figure. Sometimes clients seem to have achieved a high degree of resolution during IC or EE, but when they interact with the other for the first time in real life this is completely undone and they are profoundly disappointed. Pseudo-resolution also can occur in cases when clients, for moral or religious reasons, want to bypass anger and quickly move into forgiveness. In other cases, client expressions of acceptance and letting go of expectations regarding the other are accompanied by a disappointed shrug and they are actually more like expressions of defeat and resignation. In still other cases, client separation from the other is characterized by cold, hostile distancing (e.g., as when a client says, "I don't give a shit about him any more. He is dead to me.") that is more characteristic of the earlier rejecting anger stage of the process. If not addressed, all of these situations can result in premature termination and relapse. Intervention to address pseudo-resolution involves challenging clients' perceptions of resolution without invalidating the underlying nature of their experience or a shift in goals.

When therapists suspect that a client's perceived resolution is not realistic or stable, the best approach is to be direct. For example, one client desperately wanted to reconnect with his alcoholic father who had abandoned him and his mother when he was an adolescent. Interactions with his imagined father during IC were poignant and genuine. He expressed forgiveness and enacted the father as regretful and wanting to make amends to his son. At one point in the course of his therapy, the client had arranged a live meeting with his father during which he intended to confront past issues and address them in real life. The therapist was concerned that the client might be setting himself up for disappointment because of his deep longing, combined with information suggesting the father might actually have a limited capacity for responsiveness. So, the therapist opened this up for discussion by noting, "I wonder if there is a bit of wishful thinking here, that you want very badly to reconnect with him but you might be setting yourself up for disappointment?" The client and therapist then discussed possible scenarios involving the father and how the client might handle them.

Similarly, in situations of client resignation or resentful distancing from the other, therapist interventions involve making tentative observations about these processes. For example, the therapist might say to a client, "I know you would like to just accept her for who she is and move on, but I hear a kind of resignation in your voice, like giving up rather than acceptance" or "I hear a lot of anger still in your voice—not that you can't be angry at times—but it seems like he still has the power to affect you in a negative way." After such an introduction, clients then are invited to explore the issue further. The therapist may also provide the client with information about the jagged process of resolution and validate common sources of difficulty. In the end, either more sessions can be offered to move the process forward or clients can be helped to be more realistic and accept that they are not as fully resolved or at peace with the other as they would like to be.

Of course, therapists also need to ensure that they do not push the client into pseudo resolution because of their own desire to help, hurry the process, or be successful at promoting change. Therapists also need to accept the reality of what is.

MUTUAL FEEDBACK

The following sections specify the types of feedback that are appropriate for both the therapist and client.

Therapist Gives Feedback to the Client

Therapists are experts on trauma and the processes of therapy. Their feedback, therefore, should concern their observations of therapy processes, not on the reported changes in clients' daily lives. Therapist feedback always is in relation to the target complaints and the client goals that were identified at the beginning of therapy and how these have evolved over the course of treatment. In general, feedback can be based on any number of factors or dimensions that are relevant to the core issues and processes in a particular case. It is essential that therapists review their case notes and think carefully about the client and the case prior to giving this feedback in the last session. Feedback should be specific and, if possible, should refer to particular phases of therapy or sessions and content. The most obvious areas for feedback and discussion are the client's process and degree of resolution with offenders, as well as any therapeutic relationship issues that arose during therapy. Therapists can refer to the Degree of Resolution Scale (see Appendix C) for guidance in terms of relevant dimensions of resolution for feedback. One might comment, for instance, on the degree to which a client's feelings were avoided or inhibited, or whether key adaptive emotions have been experienced and expressed. Other useful points for feedback include the core existential and interpersonal needs that may have been recognized and valued by the client, and any changes in his or her perceptions of self and other. These changed perceptions include new insights and understandings expressed during therapy as well as the accompanying affective qualities that a therapist observed a client express in sessions (e.g., reduced anger toward other; increased detachment/calm when confronted with trauma memories; feeling less needy for the other's approval; increased self-confidence and self-acceptance).

Other observed processes that might be the topic of therapist feedback include clients' emotional functioning and narrative quality features that reflect trauma resolution. Relevant aspects of emotional functioning include clients' attention to affective experience (or cognitive style, if this was an issue), their capacity to explore their internal experiences and use them to solve problems, or their capacity to make sense of and work through issues. In one instance, the therapist commented, "I noticed you became much calmer. Remember? You were quite agitated at first, and then you got really good at expressing your true feelings—your resentment toward your mother, for example—and really clear about your boundaries with her." In another case, the therapist reflected, "You were willing to wrestle with those difficult feelings and come to understand your father's limitations and, at the same time, not let him off the hook."

Other features of narrative quality that can be topics for feedback include clients' clarity and coherence in talking about trauma, as well as their confidence and conviction in expressing feelings and needs or in stating their opinions and perspectives. Observations about clients' narrative styles could further include the fact that the clients are focusing more on the present and future as opposed to the past, or their references to positive feelings. Of course, none of this should be news to the client. This type of feedback should have been already provided either directly, through process observations and reviewing goals, or indirectly throughout therapy. Thus, the last session is a summary, a take-home message, which captures the client's process developments. Even so, one must be careful not to paint an overly rosy picture. Therapists must also clearly acknowledge any observed areas of client disappointment in terms of achieving their goals and areas for further growth. In bridging to the future, therapists will help clients identify ways in which they can address their remaining challenges.

In terms of relationship issues, therapists need to highlight any observed struggles the client had in cultivating the therapeutic alliance, including difficulties with disclosure and trust (e.g., the therapist might say, "I saw how difficult it was for you to come in here and share those painful things with a perfect stranger"). Moreover, it is important to highlight client strengths in meeting those challenges (e.g., the therapist might tell the client, "I saw how dedicated you were—never missed a session—and how hard you were working to push through your fears"). Acknowledging client efforts and strengths in confronting his or her difficulties again will contribute to a client's self-esteem and self-confidence. This is another place where therapists can refer to the positive feelings associated with the attachment bond and collaborative process (e.g., "I was aware of what a relief it was for you when you finally were able to share that with me [identifies specific incident]" or " . . . how good it felt to connect on a deep level"). If appropriate, therapists may choose to disclose their own experience of the relationship (e.g., "I really appreciated your willingness to be vulnerable with me—I felt very close to you" or "It was a real privilege to be let into your life"). These personal exchanges can contribute to clients' appreciation of healthy attachment and their seeking it out outside of therapy.

Client Gives Feedback to the Therapist

Clients are the experts of their own experience. Therapists therefore will elicit clients' feedback concerning those facts of their lives and internal experiences that only they as clients have access to. This includes asking clients about areas of growth (positive outcomes from working through the trauma), current functioning and coping in their daily lives, and their changed views of self and others. Another important area is to elicit clients' feedback concerning helpful and hindering aspects of therapy, and the connection between therapy processes and improvements in their daily lives. The therapist should probe for specificity of examples and situations; not only is this useful information for the therapist in terms of improving one's practice, but it also contributes to consolidating client gains. In addition, for individuals who have felt ineffectual, helpless, and needy for much of their lives, it can be particularly meaningful to feel that their opinions are appreciated and valued and to have an opportunity to give back.

DIFFICULTIES WITH RESOLUTION

Clients can get stuck at any stage in the resolution process. The first step in addressing difficulties with resolution is for therapists to determine the stage their clients are at in the process and then the reasons clients are having trouble moving forward. In this last phase of therapy, the most frequent client difficulties concern accepting irrevocable loss, letting go of unmet needs and expectations regarding the other, insisting on an apology, hoping the other will change, and having difficulties imagining the other's perspective. Sometimes these difficulties are partly attributable to persistent self-related disturbances (e.g., difficulties with experiencing, fear and avoidance, entrenched feelings of worthlessness) that now, in turn, interfere with the resolution of relational difficulties. In these cases, it is necessary to return to processes that were the focus of therapy in Phase 2, and treatment likely will be prolonged. We now focus on difficulties that are typical of the last phase, Phase 4, of therapy and that can be addressed in a few sessions.

Client Has Difficulties Letting Go of Anger and Sadness

These refer to difficulties with Step 10 (see Exhibit 7.1) in the resolution process that takes place during Phase 3 (chaps. 10 and 11, this volume). In terms of sadness, although one may want one's clients to accept irrevocable loss and move on, it is important not to push for premature acceptance. This is consistent with a fundamental intervention principle of helping clients accept their own experiential reality. When clients have difficulty letting go, effective therapists help them attend to that experiential reality and accept that they "cannot say goodbye right now—maybe some day, but not now." In some instances, interventions of this kind involve supporting clients' need to hang on to hope, for example, that a relationship can be repaired or that they can return to their homeland, even if it seems like a fantasy. In instances of irrevocable loss, interventions should heighten clients' awareness of their own resistance and explore the block to letting go and saying goodbye (e.g., "So, it's almost like you are saying, 'I refuse to accept . . .' Can you try saying it like that, explicitly—just as a way of exploring this? [client says, "I refuse to accept . . ."] How does that sit with you?").

The client Monica did not want to say goodbye to her dead mother because to her mind it meant losing her mother completely; she wanted to maintain connection and keep the (internalized) relationship alive. A traditional Freudian view of recovery from loss would have interpreted Monica's wish as maladaptive, favoring a complete separation and detachment from the lost object. However, more contemporary thought focuses on constructing a new self-narrative, one that includes a new, changed, internalized relationship with the lost loved one (Neimeyer, 2001). So, in this spirit, Monica's therapist highlighted her desire to maintain connection and asked her to elaborate on the importance of this to her. Monica explained that she felt her mother was part of herself, and she had always wanted back the memories that had been destroyed by the trauma, memories she found comforting. In this case, intervention supported the client in her wishes: Her "internalized mother" would always be with her, she could always turn to memories of her mother for comfort, and this understanding became part of the resolution.

In other cases, a client might say goodbye to a malevolent other as a way of detaching from influence, control, and emotional pain. Of course, setting boundaries and severing ties in this way is more likely to emerge from the experience and expression of anger than from grief. In either case, saying goodbye means weeping for and accepting what is lost forever and being open to constructing a new internalized relationship with the other.

To let go of anger, it is important first to recognize that issues of dependence and struggles with separation may be partly a function of a client's developmental stage or underlying personality pathology. It follows then that any intervention strategy will need to take such factors into consideration. For example, a young client was hanging on until the very end of therapy, hoping for an apology from her mother that might never come, and hoping that her mother would change ("I wish she'd get into treatment"). The client's desperate wishfulness as well as persistent focus on the offending other was a function of both the nature of her injury and her youthful naiveté. One useful strategy in addressing this kind of obstacle is to validate the importance that those wished-for changes has for the client, while at the same time increasing the client's awareness of the futility of that effort. This can be done through exaggeration of neediness, by the therapist role-playing the other's refusal to change, or by directing the client's attention to implicit maladaptive cognitions. For example, the therapist might say, "It's like you can't live until she changes [or apologizes]. You can't be happy. You're doomed to live a painful and unfulfilled life." Even if the client cannot let go of these unrealistic hopes and move on, interventions like these highlight the direction for future growth.

Another client felt neglected by her parents and attempted to force them to pay more attention by "punishing them" in her daily life through various passive–aggressive behaviors (instrumental anger), to no avail. She was unable to accept that she would never get what she wanted from them and that they would never change. She also had difficulty enacting her parents in IC or imaging their point of view. Acceptance only began when the therapist enacted what seemed to be the implicit message from the parents, "We are never going to give you what you want, you can kick and scream and turn yourself into a pretzel all you like but we are never going to give you what you want." This brought the futility of her efforts into full awareness. She experienced the realistic hopelessness of her situation and broke into tears. This was the beginning of letting go.

Client Has Limited Capacity for Empathy With the Imagined Other

Sometimes clients are unable to let go of unmet attachment needs and resolve issues with offenders because they are unable to imagine the other's perspective or access personal empathy for them. The other remains the "bad object"—perceptions of him or her remain undifferentiated and globally negative. In these instances, intervention should be sure to explicitly promote experiencing when the client is enacting the other during IC.

However, empathy training in this way will not work and will seem invalidating if the client's limited capacity for empathy is a function of narcissism and a fragile sense of self. Therapy, under those circumstances, likely will need to focus on processes that are typical of an earlier phase of therapy. In particular, empathy in the therapeutic relationship should be used to strengthen the client's sense of self. Successful resolution with clients who have a narcissistic or fragile sense of self will also likely require longer term therapy.

DIFFICULTIES WITH THERAPY TERMINATION

In addition to difficulties resolving issues with attachment figures, clients also can have difficulty letting go of therapy itself. The following sections describe how to address these difficulties.

Client Is Afraid of Termination

Because the capacity for interpersonal connectedness frequently is disrupted by trauma—particularly complex relational trauma—clients should be encouraged early on to cultivate social support outside of the therapy session. Nonetheless, many clients still have impoverished social support networks and can find it difficult to let go of the intimacy and support provided by therapy. In most instances, fear about termination will be partly related to a client having limited external resources. Therapy can be gradually tapered off for vulnerable clients who fear they will be unable to cope without regular support. Of course, therapists need to ensure that clients have alternative coping resources and strategies for handling distress, and these issues need to be explicitly discussed prior to termination.

Client Is Angry or Sad About Termination

Clients' reactions to the therapist's role in terminating treatment will likely reflect the nature of the issues they struggled with in therapy. Although this is essentially transference, EFTT therapists do not usually confront clients with transference interpretations but rather address their real experience and subjective perceptions of the relationship ending by way of a genuine interpersonal encounter. One client struggled throughout therapy to overcome general issues of anger and distrust and wrestled, in particular, with being vulnerable with his therapist. Eventually, however, he was able to be vulnerable with her. He came to appreciate the intimacy, feeling attended to, and feeling deeply understood. He had never previously had this type of intimacy in his life and longed for it. As the last session drew closer and ending therapy was being discussed, he said angrily, "You don't really care about me. This is only a job." In situations such as this, immediacy and genuineness in the relationship are the first priority, along with other basic emotion-focused therapy intervention principles. The therapist bypassed the client's (secondary) anger and responded to his openness and disappointment (primary sadness) that therapy was ending, given that it took him so long to open up. This led to a discussion of the importance, to the client, of being himself and feeling accepted, and the therapist validated, "It must be hard to let this go." After getting angry, the client initially minimized his disappointment ("I know you're a professional, you can't keep seeing people forever"), but eventually he apologized for his anger ("I know you really are a kind person, you really want to help"), and in the end acknowledged his loneliness. Together they discussed ways in which the client could begin to get his intimacy needs met in his current life (e.g., allow himself to be appropriately vulnerable in other relationships rather than react with anger) and ways in which he could cope or endure in the absence of an intimate relationship.

For other clients, ending therapy will be perceived as a tremendous loss. For example, one refugee trauma survivor had found it difficult to connect interpersonally in her new life and, apart from her employment, she was extremely isolated. In session, she was open and vulnerable about her loneliness and longing for home, but therapy was sporadic and she frequently canceled sessions because of her changing work schedule and the demands of child care. When the therapist suggested termination, assuming that therapy was not that important to her, the client struggled to stifle her tears. When the therapist empathically affirmed her vulnerability and encouraged her to disclose, the client wept openly, saying that she would miss the therapist and that she had no one else she could talk to. The suggestion of termination was seen as yet another loss that the client could not bear. The therapist responded with compassion and apologized for underestimating the client's degree of vulnerability and need for support, and they collaborated to continue therapy despite unavoidable disruptions in the process.

Client Relapses in Reaction to Termination

A client relapse in reaction to termination must follow a relatively productive process of resolution, thereby differentiating it from complications related to premature termination. Normally, the possibility of relapse (following resolution) is discussed with the client, and further sessions are presented as an option should relapse occur. For some clients who have become dependent on therapy, however, symptoms can increase and crises emerge just as therapy is ending. One client with a history of aggressive and self-harm behavior in response to rejection became highly distressed as therapy was ending and expressed fear that he would hurt himself or his girlfriend (who had been one focus of therapy). Treatment goals shifted to managing this crisis, and termination was deferred. Intervention included giving the client comprising emotion regulation and distress tolerance exercises as homework and processing these in session using a more behaviorally-oriented style (for examples, see Linehan, 1993). This was combined with helping the client to explore feelings of insecurity and fear of abandonment at the prospect of therapy ending.

When termination is deferred in this way following a symptomatic reaction (despite there having been a productive course of treatment), it is useful to follow two guidelines. First, client and therapist should explicitly verbally contract to extend treatment for a specified number of sessions rather than making an open-ended deferral. To that end, it is likely not in the client's best interest to allow additional subsequent deferrals of termination. The reason for this is to avoid creating circumstances that reward clients (i.e., with additional sessions) for their expressions of distress (i.e., relapse). Second, the treatment goals should explicitly shift in these new sessions to symptom management and exploration of meaning with regard to termination in particular, rather than returning to earlier phases of treatment. The reason for this shift in focus is to ensure that clients are better prepared for the termination that is to follow and that it provides a successful therapeutic experience.

BRIDGE TO THE FUTURE

Bridging to the future includes discussing the connection between therapy processes and the client's current life. Discussions may include, for example, the impact of interventions to reduce avoidance or self-criticism on current self-confidence and self-esteem, or the impact of processes during IC on current relationships. This aspect of termination also includes discussion of clients' ongoing struggles and coping resources, and, most important, their hopes and plans for the future. It is useful to also provide clients with frank information on typical pattern of client recovery and the nature of relapse. For preventative measure, therapists should encourage clients to consider the possibility of relapse. For example, the therapist might say to clients:

> It's wonderful that you have really been able to make use of our work together. But you and I know that life has its ups and downs. So, one day something might happen and this stuff might raise its ugly head again. What do you think could go wrong or might be most distressing? . . . What sorts of things will be useful for you when that happens?

It also is useful to normalize the future possibility of issues surfacing or resurfacing and the client wanting to return to therapy. Therapists should express a willingness to "keep that door open" or refer to termination as "ending therapy with a semicolon, rather than a period." This assurance can serve as a preventative factor against relapse, whether or not clients make use of it.

In one example, a young man who had successfully worked through issues related to family sexual abuse terminated treatment without difficulty but then recontacted the therapist less than a year later. His personal growth had led him to go further and consider the abuse that his siblings had also suffered, and he reported feelings of guilt over not having protected them ("It's like, now that I'm clearer about all this in my head, I want to rekindle family relationships and fix my love life too"). The therapist agreed to resume brief treatment to focus on current relational issues. However, after only four sessions the client was again ready to terminate, saying, "I don't know, I guess I *am* doing okay. As long as I'm doing my part, I'm okay with them [siblings] not really reciprocating after all. . . . It just doesn't seem so much of a problem as it did a month ago."

Still another client, who had addressed issues of abandonment and neglect, found terminating therapy to be an especially daunting task. The client expressed a wish to "take the training wheels off really, really slowly." So, therapist and client agreed to taper sessions over a longer period of time posttermination, which included two booster sessions at 3-month intervals and then a final session that followed 1 year later. Moreover, it was important to the client (and feasible to the therapist) to firmly schedule the last appointment a full year in advance. In the final session, after a year without treatment contacts, the client explained:

> Ending seems like no big deal now because, really, I ended therapy a year ago. But still—there were times when I started to go to that negative place again and I felt really alone with it. And then I would think, well, at least therapy's not over yet. I could always go to my agenda and look up the actual appointment.

For this client, the assurance that the "door is still open," in the form of a concrete promise of an appointment, was enough to provide a sense of security and solidarity that fostered hope and continued personal recovery.

AFTERWORD

Anyone who works in the area of trauma is often appalled and saddened, and sometimes even distressed, by the cruelty, pain, and suffering people can inflict on one another, particularly on children. We are also often amazed and inspired by people's courage and resilience, and the human potential for healing and growth. Our hope is that this book will contribute to those processes. There is abundant clinical wisdom in the area of trauma recovery. This book is intended as an additional resource, giving clinicians new tools for helping their clients, and thereby giving clients new tools for problem solving, healing, and continued growth. Intervention strategies described in this book are intended to help clients value their own feelings, perceptions, values, and needs. The intention of this treatment approach is also for clients to come to feel compassion for their own suffering and respect for their strengths, to develop or renew trust in others, and to turn to others for the support they may need.

EMOTION-FOCUSED THERAPY FOR TRAUMA (EFTT): PAST, PRESENT, AND FUTURE

In light of the affect revolution that is occurring in both psychology and neuroscience, many have come to regard the old dichotomy of "feelings and arousal" versus "thoughts and meanings" as overly simplistic and untenable. For this reason, experiential, emotion-focused, and somatic-focused therapies are rapidly developing treatment approaches that, now, are regarded as perhaps the most promising in the field of trauma. However, many of these approaches are not particularly well researched, if at all. A historical reason for this lack of research on affectively oriented approaches is that clinicians with an experiential or humanistic penchant often have balked at the notion of being able to measure the nuances of clients' emotional experiences and scientifically determine optimal patterns of change.

Nonetheless, EFTT (as a development of emotion-focused therapy) comes from an experiential and humanistic tradition, and from its inception, it has been uniquely informed by professionals seeking to integrate science and therapeutic models. As a result, the theory and intervention principles of this specific treatment model have been directly informed by a larger body of emotion-focused therapy research; what is, collectively, perhaps the most comprehensive research program on emotional processes in the field of psychotherapy. Each intervention principle discussed in this book has been practiced and further developed hand-in-hand with detailed process and outcome research, while we were working with individuals who have suffered complex interpersonal trauma, among other related difficulties. This tradition of emotion-focused therapy research and practice, to which we have added, has allowed for EFTT to articulate key phases in a treatment model and to fine-tune specific aspects of interventions in a manner that accelerates treatment beyond what was possible using first-generation experiential treatments.

Research in affective neuroscience and on trauma, in particular, has played an important role in helping us understand how abuse and neglect harm individuals. This exciting line of emerging work provides new understanding of the problems being faced by both those individuals who are suffering and the therapists committed to providing treatment. However, although critically informative, affective neuroscience and brain imaging will only be able to help clinicians address complex relational trauma insomuch as there are sophisticated theories of emotion and of psychological functioning to interpret those findings. For this reason, we believe that emotion-focused theory and the process research that supports it will become increasingly important in mediating and interpreting relevant research on the neural substrates of trauma and recovery. To be effective, new directions in understanding trauma must inform what therapists do in session and in the context of a deeply empathic therapeutic alliance; we believe the conceptual framework presented in this book will help practitioners do this.

A BOOK WRITTEN FOR CLINICIANS

A frequent concern among practicing clinicians who are seeking to develop their skills is that although many evidence-based treatments are built on sound theory and enjoy strong research support, they all too often do not seem to be describing the complex patients or clients who are sitting in their waiting rooms everyday. So, for many practitioners, there seems to be a disjunction between published research and actual practice. Bearing this in mind, we have aimed to provide a lot of specificity in this book on "how to" and to include in-session details such that clinicians might, in some sense, recognize their own clients in these pages.

We have intended for this book to be accessible to those who seek to learn new sophisticated interventions in working with complex trauma. For those who are new to an emotion-focused approach, being familiar with the emotion markers and the relevant phases of therapy described in this book will help orient them to their client's moment-by-moment emotional processes. Simply by heightening one's perception of a client's shifts in emotion and by acquiring a basic knowledge of the patterns of productive process that we have described, this model can be used to inform intervention—the types of empathic reflections or skills training procedures that would be most fruitful at a given moment in therapy with trauma survivors.

As the field of psychotherapy enters into a second and third generation of integrative treatments, we believe this book will also lend itself to seasoned therapists who are already expert in another approach to trauma therapy and want to expand their repertoire. In short, we do not intend that EFTT be implemented in a formulaic way but rather that the ideas and principles presented here be integrated into therapists' own personal style and existing practice.

APPENDIX A: SHORT FORM OF THE CLIENT EXPERIENCING SCALE

Level	Content	Treatment
1	External events; refusal to participate	Impersonal, detached
2	External events; behavioral or intellectual descriptions of self	Interested, personal, participation in the process
3	Personal reactions to external events; limited descriptions of self; behavioral descriptions of feelings	Reactive, emotionally involved
4	Descriptions of feelings and personal experiences	Self-descriptive, associative
5	Problems or propositions about feelings and personal experiences	Exploratory, elaborative, hypothetical
6	A "felt sense" of an inner referent	Focused on there being more about "it" (the topic)
7	A series of "felt senses" connecting the content	Evolving, emergent

APPENDIX B: SHORT FORM OF THE WORKING ALLIANCE INVENTORY

Scale: 1 = never, 2 = rarely, 3 = occasionally, 4 = sometimes, 5 = often, 6 = very often, 7 = always.

Questions

1. My therapist and I agree about the things I need to do in therapy to help improve my situation.
2. What I am doing in therapy gives me new ways of looking at my problems.
3. I believe my therapist likes me.
4. My therapist does not understand what I am trying to accomplish in therapy.
5. I am confident in my therapist's ability to help me.
6. My therapist and I are working toward mutually agreed-upon goals.
7. I feel that my therapist appreciates me.
8. We agree on what is important for me to work on.
9. My therapist and I trust each other.
10. My therapist and I have different ideas on what my problems are.
11. We have established a good understanding of the kinds of changes that would be good for me.
12. I believe the way we are working with my problems is correct.

Note. Adapted from "Development and Validation of the Working Alliance Inventory," by A. O. Horvath & L. S. Greenberg, 1989, *Journal of Counseling Psychology, 36*, p. 226. Copyright 1989 by the American Psychological Association.

APPENDIX C: THE DEGREE OF RESOLUTION SCALE

The following scale describes hierarchically organized processes as clients move closer toward resolution of past issues with an identified other.

1. The client expresses a lingering bad feeling toward the significant other. The client may blame and complain about the other's treatment or express a longing about what was lacking. The client feels unresolved, may have a sense that nothing can be done, or suppresses associated feelings.
2. An emotional reaction is evoked by making psychological contact with the imagined other. The client expresses hurt, bitterness, fear, or hopelessness about ever resolving the bad feelings.
3. Bad feelings concerning the imagined other are differentiated into anger, disgust, or sadness, and these emotions are clearly and completely expressed. Expression occurs through reexperiencing an episodic memory concerning the other.
4. The client feels entitled to unmet needs; what had previously been judged as unacceptable is now experienced as valid and assertively expressed. The client clearly defines the self in terms of legitimate wants and needs and may begin to hold the other accountable for harm (rather than blame self).
5. The client is more separate from the other, no longer seeking retribution or to satisfy unmet needs from that specific other. There is a greater sense of autonomy and self-empowerment. The client views the other in a more differentiated fashion, may see the other's point of view, and may forgive the other. In any case, the client clearly holds the other accountable for harm.
6. The client feels more powerful in relation to the other and no longer blames self. The client lets go of expectations that the other will change or make amends and looks to her or his own resources to meet existential or interpersonal needs. The client either sees the other in a different light or experiences self as more powerful and legitimate and focuses more on personal strengths. The client feels finished and is able to complete the interaction with the other in a more satisfying way.

Note. From *Relating Degree of Resolution of Unfinished Business to Outcome*, by L. S. Greenberg & K. Hirscheimer, 1994. Paper presented at the meeting of the North American Society for Psychotherapy Research, Santa Fe, NM. Adapted with permission of author.

REFERENCES

American Psychiatric Association. (2000). *Diagnostic and statistical manual of mental disorders* (4th ed., Text Revision). Washington, DC: Author.

Angus, L., & Bouffard, B. (2004). The search for emotional meaning and self-coherence in the face of traumatic loss in childhood: A narrative process perspective. In J. Raskin & S. Bridges (Eds.), *Studies in meaning: 2. Bridging the personal and social in constructivist psychology* (pp. 137–156). New York: Pace.

Angus, L. E., & McLeod, J. (Eds.). (1999). *The handbook of narrative and psychotherapy: Practice, theory, and research.* Thousand Oaks, CA: Sage.

Barlow, D. H. (1988). *Anxiety and its disorders: The nature and treatment of anxiety and panic.* New York: Guilford Press.

Beck, A. T., Freeman, A., & Davis, D. D. (2004). *Cognitive therapy of personality disorders* (2nd ed.). New York: Guilford Press.

Beitchman, J. H., Zucker, K. J., Hood, J. E., DaCosta, G. A., Akman, D., & Cassavia, E. (1992). A review of the long-term effects of child sexual abuse. *Child Abuse and Neglect, 16*, 101–118.

Benjamin, L. S. (1996). *Interpersonal diagnosis and treatment of personality disorders* (2nd ed.). New York: Guilford Press.

Bernstein, D., & Fink, L. (1998). *Manual for the childhood trauma questionnaire.* San Antonio, TX: Psychological Corporation.

Beutler, L., Machado, P., & Neufeldt, S. (1994). Therapist variables. In A. Bergin & S. Garfield (Eds.), *Handbook of psychotherapy and behavior change* (4th ed., pp. 229–269). New York: Wiley.

Boelen, P. A., Van den Hout, M. A., & van den Bout, J. (2006). A cognitive–behavioral conceptualization of complicated grief. *Clinical Psychology: Science and Practice, 13*, 109–128.

Bohart, A. C. (1993). Experiencing: The basis of psychotherapy. *Journal of Psychotherapy Integration, 3*, 51–67.

Bohart, A., & Greenberg, L. S. (1997). *Empathy reconsidered: New directions in psychotherapy.* Washington, DC: American Psychological Association.

Bolger, E. A. (1999). Grounded theory analysis of emotional pain. *Psychotherapy Research, 9*, 342–362.

Borkovec, T. D., Alcaine, O. M., & Behar, E. (2004). Avoidance theory of worry and generalized anxiety disorder. In R. G. Heimberg, C. L. Turk, & D. S. Mennin (Eds.), *Generalized anxiety disorder: Advances in research and practice* (pp. 77–108). New York: Guilford Press.

Bourne, E. J. (2003). *Anxiety and phobias workbook.* Oakland, CA: New Harbinger

Bowlby, J. (1988). *A secure base.* New York: Basic Books.

Breslau, N., Davis, G., Andreski, P., Federman, B., & Anthony, J. C. (1998). Epidemiological findings on posttraumatic stress disorder and co-morbid disorders in the general population. In B. P. Dohrenwend (Eds.), *Adversity, stress, and psychopathology* (pp. 319–330). New York: Oxford University Press.

Breslau, N., Davis, G. C., Andreski, P., & Peterson, E. (1991). Traumatic events and posttraumatic stress disorder in an urban population of young adults. *Archives of General Psychiatry, 48*, 216–222.

Briere, J., & Scott, C. (2006). *Principles of trauma therapy.* London: Sage

Bushman, B. J. (2002). Does venting anger feed or extinguish the flame? Catharsis, rumination, distraction, anger, aggressive responding. *Personality and Social Psychology Bulletin, 28*, 724–731.

Castonguay, L. G., Goldfried, M. R., Wiser, S., Raue, P. J., & Hayes, A. M. (1996). Predicting the effect of cognitive therapy for depression: A study of unique and common factors. *Journal of Consulting and Clinical Psychology, 64*, 497–504.

Cavell, T. A., & Malcolm, K. T. (Eds.). (2007). *Anger, aggression, and interventions for interpersonal violence.* Mahwah, NJ: Erlbaum.

Chagigioris, H. (2009). *The contribution of emotional engagement with trauma material to outcome in two version of emotions focused therapy for trauma (EFTT).* Unpublished doctoral dissertation, University of Windsor, Windsor, Ontario, Canada.

Chagigiorgis, H., & Paivio, S. C. (2006). Forgiveness as an outcome in emotion focused therapy for adult survivors of childhood abuse (EFT-AS). In W. Malcolm, N. DeCourville, & K. Belicki (Eds.), *Women's perspectives on forgiveness and reconciliation: The complexities of restoring power and connection* (pp. 121–141). New York: Routledge, Taylor & Francis Group.

Chard, K. M. (2005). An evaluation of cognitive processing therapy for the treatment of posttraumatic stress disorder related to childhood sexual abuse. *Journal of Consulting and Clinical Psychology, 73*, 965–971.

Chilcoat, H. D., & Breslau, N. (1998). Investigations of causal pathways between PTSD and drug use disorders. *Addictive Behaviors, 23*, 827–840.

Cichetti, D., & Toth, S. L. (1995). A developmental psychopathology perspective on child abuse and neglect. *Journal of the American Academy of Child and Adolescent Psychiatry, 34*, 541–565.

Cloitre, M., Koenen, K., Dohen, L., & Han, H. (2002). Skills training in affect and interpersonal regulation followed by exposure: A phase-based treatment for PTSD related to childhood abuse. *Journal of Consulting and Clinical Psychology, 70*, 1067–1074.

Coleman, P. (2006). *Flashback: Posttraumatic stress disorder, suicide, and the lessons of war.* Boston: Beacon Press.

Courtois, C. A., & Ford, J. D. (Eds.). (2009). *Treatments for complex traumatic stress disorders.* New York: Guilford Press.

Damasio, A. R. (1999). *The feeling of what happens: Body and emotion in the making of consciousness.* New York: Harcourt.

Davanloo, H. (1995). *Unlocking the unconscious: Selected papers of Habib Davanloo*. Oxford, UK: Wiley.

De Girolamo, G., & McFarlane, A. C. (1996). The epidemiology of PTSD: A comprehensive review of the international literature. In A. J. Marsella, M. J. Friedman, E. T. Gerrity, & R. M. Scurfield (Eds.), *Ethnocultural aspects of posttraumatic stress disorder: Issues, research, and clinical applications* (pp. 33–85). Washington, DC: American Psychological Association.

Deffenbaker, J. L. (1999). Cognitive behavioral conceptualization and treatment of anger. *Journal of Clinical Psychology, 55*, 295–310.

Doidge, N. (2007). *The brain that changes itself: Stories of personal triumph from the frontiers of brain science*. Toronto, Ontario, Canada: Viking Penguin.

During, S. M., & McMahon, R. J. (1991). Recognition of emotional facial expressions by abusive mothers and their children. *Journal of Clinical Child Psychology, 20*, 132–139.

Ekman, P., & Friesen, W. V. (1975). *Unmasking the face: A guide to recognizing emotions from facial clues*. Englewood Cliffs, NJ: Prentice-Hall.

Elliott, R., Watson, J. C., Goldman, R. N., & Greenberg, L. S. (2004). *Learning emotion focused therapy: A process experiential approach to change*. Washington, DC: American Psychological Association.

Epstein, S. (1994). Integration of the cognitive and psychodynamic unconscious. *American Psychologist, 49*, 709–724.

Fairbairn, W. R. D. (1952). *Psychoanalytic studies of the personality*. London: Routledge.

Fiese, B. H., & Wamboldt, F. S. (2003). Coherent accounts of coping with a chronic illness: Convergences and divergences in family measurement using a narrative analysis. *Family Process, 42*, 3–15.

Finkelhor, D. (1994). The international epidemiology of child sexual abuse. *Child Abuse and Neglect, 18*, 409–417.

Foa, E. B., Hembree, E., Cahill, S., Rauch, S., Riggs, D., Feeny, N., & Yadin, E. (2005). Randomized controlled trial of prolonged exposure for posttraumatic stress disorder with and without cognitive restructuring: Outcome at academic and community clinics. *Journal of Consulting and Clinical Psychology, 73*, 953–964.

Foa, E. B., Huppert, J. D., & Cahill, S. P. (2006). *Emotional processing theory: An update*. In B. O. Rothbaum (Ed.), *Pathological anxiety: Emotional processing in etiology and treatment* (pp. 3–24). New York: Guilford Press.

Foa, E. B., Keane, T. M., Friedman, M. J., & Cohen, J. A. (Eds.). (2009). *Effective treatments for PTSD: Practice guidelines from the International Society for Traumatic Stress Studies* (2nd ed.). New York: Guilford Press.

Foa, E. B., & Kozak, M. J. (1986). Emotional processing of fear: Exposure to corrective information. *Psychological Bulletin, 99*, 20–35.

Foa, E. B., Riggs, D. S., & Gershuny, B. S. (1995). Arousal, numbing, and intrusion: Symptom structure of PTSD following assault. *American Journal of Psychiatry, 152*, 116–120.

Foa, E. B., Riggs, D. S., Massie, E. D., & Yarczower, M. (1995). The impact of fear activation and anger on the efficacy of exposure treatment for posttraumatic stress disorder. *Behavior Therapy, 26,* 487–499.

Foa, E. B., Rothbaum, B. O., & Furr, J. M. (2003). Augmenting exposure therapy with other CBT procedures. *Psychiatric Annals, 33,* 47–53.

Ford, J. D. (2005). Treatment implications of altered affect regulation and information processing following child maltreatment. *Psychiatric Annals, 35,* 410–419.

Ford, J. D., Racusin, R., Ellis, C. G., Daviss, W. B., Reiser, J., Fleischer, A., & Thomas, J. (2000). Child maltreatment, other trauma exposure and post-traumatic symptomatology among children with oppositional defiant and attention deficit hyperactivity disorders. *Child Maltreatment, 5,* 205–217.

Fosha, D. (2000). *The transforming power of affect: A model for accelerated change.* New York: Basic Books.

Fosha, D. (2003). Dyadic regulation and experiential work with emotion and relatedness in trauma and disordered attachment. In D. J. Siegel & M. F. Solomon (Eds.), *Healing trauma: Attachment, trauma, the brain and the mind* (pp. 221–281). New York: Norton.

Fosha, D., Paivio, S. C., Gleiser, K., & Ford, J. D. (2009). Experiential and emotion-focused therapy. In C. A. Courtois & J. D. Ford (Eds.), *Treating complex traumatic stress disorders: An evidence-based guide* (pp. 286–311). New York: Guilford Press.

Fredrickson, B. L. (2001). The role of positive emotions in positive psychology: The broaden-and-build theory of positive emotions. *American Psychologist, 56,* 218–226.

Frederickson, B. L., & Losada, M. (2005). Positive affect and the complex dynamics of human flourishing. *American Psychologist, 60,* 687–686.

Freud, S. (1961). New introductory lectures. In J. Strachey (Ed. & Trans.), *The standard edition of the complete psychological works of Sigmund Freud* (Vol. 22, pp. 3–182). London: Hogarth Press. (Original work published 1933)

Fridja, N. H. (1986). *The emotions.* Cambridge, UK: Cambridge University Press.

Friedman, M. J., Davidson, J. R. T., & Stein, D. J. (2009). Psychopharmacotherapy for adults. In E. B. Foa, T. M. Keane, M. J. Friedman, & J. A. Cohen (Eds.), *Effective treatment for PTSD: Practice guidelines for the International Society for Traumatic Stress Studies* (2nd ed.; pp. 269–278). New York: Guilford Press.

Gauthier, L., Stollak, G., Messe, L., & Arnoff, J. (1996). Recall of childhood neglect and physical abuse as differential predictors of current psychological functioning. *Child Abuse and Neglect, 20,* 549–559.

Gendlin, E. T. (1996). *Focusing-oriented psychotherapy: A manual of experiential method.* New York: Guilford Press.

Gilbert, P., & Irons, C. (2005). Focused therapies and compassionate mind training for shame and self-attacking. In P. Gilbert (Ed.) *Compassion: Conceptualizations, research and use in psychotherapy* (pp. 263–325). New York: Routledge.

Goldman, R. N., Greenberg, L. S., & Pos, A. E. (2005). Depth of emotional experience and outcome. *Psychotherapy Research, 15,* 248–260.

Gottman, J. M. (1997). *The heart of parenting: Raising an emotionally intelligent child.* New York: Simon & Schuster.

Greenberg, L. S. (2002). *Emotion-focused therapy: Coaching clients to work through their feelings.* Washington, DC: American Psychological Association.

Greenberg, L. S., & Bolger, E. (2001). An emotion-focused approach to the over-regulation of emotion and emotional pain. *Journal of Clinical Psychology, 57,* 197–211.

Greenberg, L. S., & Foerster, F. S. (1996). Task analysis exemplified: The process of resolving unfinished business. *Journal of Consulting and Clinical Psychology, 64,* 439–446.

Greenberg, L. S., & Hirscheimer, K. (1994, February). *Relating degree of resolution of unfinished business to outcome.* Paper presented at the meeting of the North American Society for Psychotherapy Research, Santa Fe, NM.

Greenberg, L. S., & Korman, L. M. (1993). Assimilating emotion into psychotherapy integration. *Journal of Psychotherapy Integration, 3,* 249–265.

Greenberg, L. S., & Malcolm, W. (2002). Resolving unfinished business: Relating process to outcome. *Journal of Consulting and Clinical Psychology, 70,* 406–416.

Greenberg, L. S., & Paivio, S. C. (1997). *Working with emotions in psychotherapy.* New York: Guilford Press.

Greenberg, L. S., & Paivio, S. C. (1998). Allowing and accepting painful emotional experiences. *International Journal of Action Methods: Psychodrama, Skill Training, and Role Playing, 51*(2), 47–61.

Greenberg, L. S. & Pascual-Leone, A. (2006). Emotion in psychotherapy: A practice-friendly research review. *Journal of clinical psychology, 62,* 611–630.

Greenberg, L. S., & Pascual-Leone, J. (1995). A dialectical constructivist approach to experiential change. In R. A. Neimeyer & M. J. Mahoney (Eds.), *Constructivism in psychotherapy* (pp. 169–191). Washington, DC: American Psychological Association.

Greenberg, L. S., Rice, L. N., & Elliott, R. K. (1993). *Facilitating emotional change: The moment-by-moment process.* New York: Basic Books.

Greenberg, L. S., & Safran, J. D. (1987). *Emotion in psychotherapy: Affect, cognition, and the process of change.* New York: Guilford Press.

Greenberg, L. S., & Watson, J. (2006). *Emotion-focused therapy for depression.* Washington, DC: American Psychological Association.

Gross, J. J. (1999). Emotion regulation: Past, present, future. *Cognition and Emotion, 13,* 551–573.

Hall, I. E. (2008). *Therapist relationship and technical skills in two versions of emotion focused trauma therapy.* Unpublished doctoral dissertation, University of Windsor, Windsor, Ontario, Canada.

Harvey, M. R., Liang, B., Harney, P. A., Koenen, K., Tummala-Narra, P., & Lebowitz, L. (2003). A multidimensional approach to the assessment of trauma impact, recovery and resiliency: Initial psychometric findings. *Journal of Aggression, Maltreatment and Trauma, 6*, 87–109

Hayes, S. C., Strosahl, K. D., & Wilson, K. G. (1999). *Acceptance and commitment therapy*. New York: Guilford Press.

Herman, J. L. (1992). *Trauma and recovery*. New York: Basic Books.

Hermans, H. J. M. (1996). Voicing the self: From information processing to dialogical interchange. *Psychological Bulletin, 119*, 31–50.

Holowaty, K. A. M. (2004). *Process characteristics of client-identified helpful events in emotion-focused therapy for adult survivors of childhood abuse (EFT-AS)*. Unpublished doctoral dissertation, University of Windsor, Windsor, Ontario, Canada.

Holtzworth-Munroe, A., & Clements, K. (2007). The association between anger and male perpetration of intimate partner violence. In T. A. Cavell & K. T. Malcolm (Eds.), *Anger, aggression and interventions for interpersonal violence*. (pp. 313–348). Mahwah, NJ: Erlbaum.

Horvath, A. O., & Greenberg, L. S. (1989). Development and validation of the Working Alliance Inventory. *Journal of Counseling Psychology, 36*, 223–233.

Horvath, A. O., & Symonds, B. D. (1991). Relations between working alliance and outcome in psychotherapy: A meta-analysis. *Journal of Counseling Psychology, 38*, 139–149.

Izard, C. E. (2002). Translating emotion theory and research into preventive interventions. *Psychological Bulletin, 128*, 796–824.

Janoff-Bulman, R. (1992). *Shattered assumptions: Towards a new psychology of trauma*. New York: Free Press.

Jaycox, L. H., Foa, E. B., & Morral, A. R. (1998). Influence of emotional engagement and habituation on exposure therapy for PTSD. *Journal of Consulting and Clinical Psychology, 66*, 185–192.

Jellen, L. K., McCarroll, J. E., & Thayer, L. E. (2001). Child emotional maltreatment: A 2-year study of U.S. army cases. *Child Abuse and Neglect, 25*, 623–639.

Johnson, S. (2002). *Emotionally focused couples therapy for trauma survivors*. New York: Guilford Press.

Kabat-Zinn, J. (1990). *Full catastrophe living*. New York: Delta Press.

Kessler, R. C., Sonnega, A., Bromet, E., Hughs, M., & Nelson, C. B. (1995). Posttraumatic stress disorder in the national comorbidity survey. *Archives of General Psychiatry, 52*, 1048–1060.

Kiesler, D. J. (1971). Patient experiencing level and successful outcome in individual psychotherapy of schizophrenics and psychoneurotics. *Journal of Consulting and Clinical Psychology, 37*, 370–385.

Kilpatrick, D. G., Edwards, C. N., & Seymour, A. E. (1992). *Rape in America: A report to the nation*. Arlington, VA: National Crime Victims Center.

Kirsch, I., Moore, T. J., Scoboria, A., & Nicholls, S. S. (2002). The emperor's new drugs: An analysis of antidepressant medication data submitted to the U.S. Food and Drug Administration. *Prevention and Treatment, 5,* Article 23. Retrieved from http://journals.apa.org/prevention/volume5/pre0050023a.html

Klein, M. H., Mathieu-Coughlan, P., & Kiesler, D. J. (1986). The Experiencing Scales. In L. S. Greenberg & W. M. Pinsof (Eds.), *The psychotherapeutic process: A research handbook* (pp. 21–71). New York: Guilford Press.

Kohut, H. (1984). *How does analysis cure?* Chicago: University of Chicago Press.

Kubany, E. S., Hill, E. E., Owens, J. A., Iannce-Spencer, C., McCaig, M. A., Tremayne, K. J., & Williams, P. L. (2004). Cognitive trauma therapy for battered women with PTSD (CTT-BW). *Journal of Consulting and Clinical Psychology, 72,* 3–18.

Kudler, H. S., Krupnick, J. L., Blank, A. S., Jr., Herman, J. L., & Horowitz, M. J. (2009). Psychodynamic therapy for adults. In E. B. Foa, T. M. Keane, M. J. Friedman, & J. A. Cohen (Eds.), *Effective treatments for PTSD: Practice guidelines from the International Society for Traumatic Stress Studies* (2nd ed.; pp. 346–369). New York: Guilford Press.

Kunzle, E., & Paivio, S. C. (2009). *Changes in narrative quality pro- and post-emotion focused therapy for childhood abuse trauma.* Manuscript submitted for publication.

Landy, S., & Menna, R. (2006). *Early intervention with multi-risk families: An integrative approach.* Baltimore: Paul H. Brookes.

Lanius, R. A., Williamson, P. C., Densmore, M., Boksman, K., Neufeld, R. W., Gati, J. S., & Menon, R. S. (2004). The nature of traumatic memories: A 4-T fMRI functional connectivity analysis. *American Journal of Psychiatry, 161,* 36–44.

Lazarus, R. S. (1991). Progress on a cognitive–motivational–relational theory of emotion. *American Psychologist, 46,* 819–834.

Le, T. (2006). *Use of emotion words and depth of experiencing as indices of alexithymia in trauma narratives.* Unpublished master's thesis, University of Windsor, Windsor, Ontario, Canada.

LeDoux, J. (1996). *The emotional brain: The mysterious underpinnings of emotional life.* New York: Simon & Schuster.

Linehan, M. M. (1993). *Cognitive–behavioral treatment of borderline personality disorder.* New York: Guilford Press.

Linehan, M. M. (1997). Validation and psychotherapy. In A. Bohart & L. Greenberg (Eds.), *Empathy reconsidered* (pp. 353–392). Washington, DC: American Psychological Association.

Luborsky, L., Popp, C., Luborsky, E., & Mark, D. (1994). The core conflictual relationship theme. *Psychotherapy Research, 4,* 172–183.

MacMillan, H. L., Fleming, J. E., Trocme, N., Boyle, M. H., Wong, M., Racine, Y. A., et al. (1997). Prevalence of child physical and sexual abuse in the community: Results from the Ontario Health Supplement. *JAMA, 278,* 131–135.

Main, M. (1991). Metacognitive knowledge, metacognitive monitoring, and singular (coherent) vs. multiple (incoherent) model of attachment: Findings and directions for future research. In C. M. Parkes, J. Stevenson-Hinde, & P. Marris (Eds.), *Attachment across the life cycle* (pp. 127–159). New York: Tavistock/Routledge.

Marotto, S. (2003). Unflinching empathy: Counselors and tortured refugees. *Journal of Counseling and Development, 81*, 111–114.

McCann, I. L., & Pearlman, L. A. (1990). *Psychological trauma and the adult survivor: Theory, therapy, and transformation*. Philadelphia: Brunner/Mazel.

McCullough, L., Kuhn, N., Andrews, S., Kaplan, A., Wolf, J., & Hurley, C. L. (2003). *Treating affect phobia: A manual for short term dynamic psychotherapy*. New York: Guilford Press.

McLean, L. M., & Gallop, R. (2003). Implications of childhood sexual abuse for adult borderline personality disorder and complex posttraumatic stress disorder. *American Journal of Psychiatry, 160*, 369–371.

Mitchell, S. A. (1993). *Hope and dread in psychoanalysis*. New York: Basic Books.

Morgan, T., & Cummings, A. L. (1999). Change experienced during group therapy by female survivors of childhood sexual abuse. *Journal of Consulting and Clinical Psychology, 67*, 28–36.

Mullen, P. E., Martin, J. L., Anderson, J. C., & Romans, S. E. (1996). The long-term impact of the physical, emotional, and sexual abuse of children: A community study. *Child Abuse and Neglect, 20*, 7–21.

Najavits, L. M. (2002). *Seeking safety: A treatment manual for PTSD and substance abuse*. New York: Guilford Press.

Neborsky, R. J. (2003). A clinical model for the comprehensive treatment of trauma using an affect experiencing–attachment theory approach. In M. Solomon & D. Siegel (Eds.), *Healing trauma* (pp. 282–321). New York: Norton.

Neimeyer, R. A. (2001). *Meaning reconstruction and the experience of loss*. Washington, DC: American Psychological Association.

Neimeyer, R. A. (2006). Chaos to coherence: Psychotherapeutic integration of traumatic loss. *Journal of Constructivist Psychology, 19*, 127–145.

Neimeyer, R. A., & Bridges, S. K. (2003). Postmodern approaches to psychotherapy. In A. S. Gurman & S. B. Messer (Eds.), *Essential psychotherapies: Theory and practice* (2nd ed., pp. 272–316). New York: Guilford Press.

Norris, F. H. (1992). Epidemiology of trauma: Frequency and impact of different potentially traumatic events on different demographic groups. *Journal of Consulting and Clinical Psychology, 60*, 409–418.

Novaco, R. W. (2007). Anger dysregulation. In T. A. Cavell & K. T. Malcolm (Eds.), *Anger, aggression and interventions for interpersonal violence* (pp. 3–54). Mahwah, NJ: Erlbaum.

O'Kearney, R., & Perrott, K. (2006). Trauma narratives in posttraumatic stress disorder: A review. *Journal of Traumatic Stress, 19*, 81–93.

O'Malley, S., Suh, C., & Strupp, H. (1983). The Vanderbilt Psychotherapy Process Scale: A report on the scale development and a process-outcome study. *Journal of Consulting and Clinical Psychology, 51*, 581–186.

Paivio, A. (2007). *Mind and its evolution: A dual coding theoretical approach*. Mahwah, NJ: Erlbaum.

Paivio, S. C., & Bahr, L. (1998). Interpersonal problems, working alliance, and outcome in short-term experiential therapy. *Psychotherapy Research, 8*, 392–407.

Paivio, S. C., & Carriere, M. (2007). Contributions of emotion-focused therapy to the understanding and treatment of anger and aggression. In T. A. Cavell & K. T. Malcolm (Eds.), *Anger, aggression and interventions for interpersonal violence* (pp. 143–164). Mahwah, NJ: Erlbaum.

Paivio, S. C., & Cramer, K. M. (2004). Factor structure and reliability of the Childhood Trauma Questionnaire in a Canadian undergraduate student sample. *Child Abuse & Neglect, 28*, 889–904.

Paivio, S. C., & Greenberg, L. S. (1995). Resolving "unfinished business": Efficacy of experiential therapy using empty-chair dialogue. *Journal of Consulting and Clinical Psychology, 63*, 419–425.

Paivio, S. C., Hall, I. E., Holowaty, K. A. M., Jellis, J. B., & Tran, N. (2001). Imaginal confrontation for resolving child abuse issues. *Psychotherapy Research, 11*, 433–453.

Paivio, S. C., Holowaty, K. A. M., & Hall, I. E. (2004). The influence of therapist adherence and competence on client reprocessing of child abuse memories. *Psychotherapy: Theory, Research, Practice, Training, 41*, 56–68.

Paivio, S. C., Jarry, J. L., Chagigiorgis, H., Hall, I. E., & Ralston, M. (in press). Efficacy of two versions of emotion focused therapy for child abuse trauma: A dismantling study. *Psychotherapy Research*.

Paivio, S. C., & Laurent, C. (2001). Empathy and emotion regulation: Reprocessing memories of childhood abuse. *Journal of Clinical Psychology, 57*, 213–226.

Paivio, S. C., & McCulloch, C. R. (2004). Alexithymia as a mediator between childhood trauma and self-injurious behaviors. *Child Abuse and Neglect, 28*, 339–354.

Paivio, S. C., & Nieuwenhuis, J. A. (2001). Efficacy of emotion focused therapy for adult survivors of child abuse: A preliminary study. *Journal of Traumatic Stress, 14*, 115–133.

Paivio, S. C., & Patterson, L. A. (1999). Alliance development in therapy for resolving child abuse issues. *Psychotherapy: Theory, Research, Practice, Training, 36*, 343–354.

Pascual-Leone, A. (2005). *Emotional processing in the therapeutic hour: Why "the only way out is through."* Unpublished doctoral dissertation, York University, Toronto, Ontario, Canada.

Pascual-Leone, A. (2009). Emotional processing cycles in experiential therapy: Two steps forward, one step backward. *Journal of Consulting and Clinical Psychology, 77*, 113–126.

Pascual-Leone, A., & Greenberg, L. S. (2006). Insight and awareness in experiential therapy. In L. G. Castonguay & C. E. Hill (Eds.), *Insight in psychotherapy* (pp. 31–56). Washington, DC: American Psychological Association.

Pascual-Leone, A., & Greenberg, L. S. (2007). Emotional processing in experiential therapy: Why "the only way out is through." *Journal of Consulting and Clinical Psychology, 75*, 875–887.

Pascual-Leone, J. (1990). An essay on wisdom: Toward organismic processes that make it possible. In R. J. Sternberg (Ed.), *Wisdom: Its nature, origins, and development* (pp. 244–278). New York: Cambridge University Press.

Pascual-Leone, J. (1991). Emotions, development, and psychotherapy: A dialectical-constructivist perspective. In J. D. Safran & L. S. Greenberg (Eds.), *Emotion, psychotherapy, and change* (pp. 302–335). New York: Guilford Press.

Pearlman, L. A., & Courtois, C. A. (2005). Clinical applications of the attachment framework: Relational treatment of complex trauma. *Journal of Traumatic Stress, 18*, 449–459.

Pelcovitz, D., Kaplan, S. J., DeRosa, R. R., Mandel, F. S., & Salzinger, S. (2000). Psychiatric disorders in adolescents exposed to violence and physical abuse. *American Journal of Orthopsychiatry, 70*, 360–369.

Pennebaker, J. W. (1997). Writing about emotional experiences as a therapeutic process. *Psychological Science, 8*, 162–166.

Pennebaker, J. W., & Campbell, R. S. (2000). The effects of writing about traumatic experience. *NC-PTSD Clinical Quarterly, 9*, 18–21.

Pennebaker, J. W., & Seagal, J. D. (1999). Forming a story: The health benefits of narrative. *Journal of Clinical Psychology, 55*, 1243–1254.

Perls, F. S., Hefferline, R. F., & Goodman, P. (1951). *Gestalt therapy*. New York: Julian Press.

Pilkington, B., & Kremer, J. (1995). A review of the epidemiological research on child sexual abuse: Clinical samples. *Child Abuse Review, 4*, 191–205.

Pollak, S. D., Klorman, R., Thatcher, J. E., & Cicchetti, D. (2001). P3b reflects maltreated children. *Psychophysiology, 38*, 267–274.

Polusney, M. S., & Follette, V. A. (1995). Long-term correlates of child sexual abuse: Theory and review of the empirical literature. *Applied and Preventive Psychology, 4*, 143–166.

Pos, A. E., Greenberg, L. S., Goldman, R. N., & Korman, L. M. (2003). Emotional processing during experiential treatment of depression. *Journal of Consulting and Clinical Psychology, 71*, 1007–1016.

Ralston, M. (2006). *Emotional arousal and depth of experiencing in imaginal confrontation versus evocative empathy.* Unpublished doctoral dissertation, University of Windsor, Windsor, Ontario, Canada.

Resick, P. A., Nishith, P., & Griffin, M. G. (2003). How well does cognitive–behavioral therapy treat symptoms of complex PTSD? An examination of child abuse survivors within a clinical trial. *CNS Spectrums, 8*, 351–355.

Resnick, H. S., Kilpatrick, D. G., Dansky, B. S., Saunders, B. E., & Best, C. L. (1993). Prevalence of civilian trauma and posttraumatic stress disorder in a representative national sample of women. *Journal of Consulting and Clinical Psychology, 61*, 984–991.

Rice, L. N. (1974). The evocative function of the therapist. In L. N. Rice & D. A. Wexler (Eds.), *Psychotherapy and patient relationships* (pp. 36–60). Homewood, IL: Dow-Jones Irwin.

Rice, L. N., & Kerr, G. P. (1986). Measures of client and therapist vocal quality. In L. S. Greenberg & W. M. Pinsof (Eds.), *The psychotherapeutic process: A research handbook* (pp. 73–105). New York: Guilford Press.

Rind, B., Tromovitch, P., & Bauserman, R. (1998). A meta-analytic examination of assumed properties of child sexual abuse using college samples. *Psychological Bulletin, 124*, 22–53.

Robichaud, L. (2005). *Early client experiencing and outcome in emotion focused trauma therapy*. Unpublished master's thesis, University of Windsor, Windsor, Ontario, Canada.

Rogers, C. R. (1951). *Client-centered therapy: Its current practice, implications, and theory*. Boston: Houghton Mifflin.

Rogers, C. R. (1957). The necessary and sufficient conditions of therapeutic personality change. *Journal of Consulting and Clinical Psychology, 60*, 827–832.

Rogers, C. R. (1959). The essence of psychotherapy: A client-centered view. *Annals of Psychotherapy, 1*, 51–57.

Romans, S., Martin, J., & Mullen, P. (1996). Women's self-esteem: A community study of women who report and do not report childhood sexual abuse. *British Journal of Psychiatry, 169*, 696–704.

Roth, S., Newman, E., Pelcovitz, D., van der Kolk, B., & Mandel, F. S. (1997). Complex PTSD in victims exposed to sexual and physical abuse: Results from the DSM–IV field trial for posttraumatic stress disorder. *Journal of Traumatic Stress, 10*, 539–555.

Safran, J. D., & Greenberg, L. S. (1987). *Emotion in psychotherapy: Affect, cognition, and the process of change*. New York: Guilford Press.

Safran, J. D., & Muran, J. C. (2000). *Negotiating the therapeutic alliance: A relational guide to treatment*. New York: Guilford Press.

Samoilov, A., & Goldfried, M. (2000). Role of emotion in cognitive behavior therapy. *Clinical Psychology: Science and Practice, 7*, 373–385.

Saxe, B. J., & Johnson, S. M. (1999). An empirical investigation of group treatment for a clinical population of adult female incest survivors. *Journal of Child Sexual Abuse, 8*, 67–88.

Schore, A. N. (2003). *Affect dysregulation and disorders of the self*. New York: Norton.

Scoboria, A., Ford, J., Hsio-ju, L., & Frisman, L. (2006, May). *Exploratory and confirmatory factor analysis of the Structured Interview for Disorders of Extreme Stress*. Paper presented at the meeting of the Society for the Exploration of Psychotherapy Integration, Los Angeles, CA.

Sedgwick, E. K., & Frank, A. (Eds.). (1995). *Shame and its sisters: A Silvan Tomkins reader*. Durham, NC: Duke University Press.

Segal, Z. V., Williams, J. M. G., & Teasdale, J. D. (2002). *Mindfulness-based cognitive therapy for depression: A new approach to preventing relapse*. New York: Guilford Press.

Siegel, D. J. (2003). An interpersonal neurobiology of psychotherapy: The developing mind and the resolution of trauma. In M. F. Solomon & D. J. Siegel (Eds.), *Healing trauma: Attachment, trauma, the brain and the mind* (pp. 1–54). New York: Norton.

Silberschatz, G., Fretter, P. B., & Curtis, J. T. (1986). How do interpretations influence the process of psychotherapy? *Journal of Consulting and Clinical Psychology, 54*, 646–652.

Singh, T., Pascual-Leone, A., & Greenberg, L. (2008, June). *The influence of therapist intervention on client emotional processing and emotional variability*. Paper presented at the meeting of the Society for Psychotherapy Research, Barcelona, Spain.

Shapiro, F., & Maxfield, L. (2002). Eye movement desensitization and reprocessing (EMDR): Information processing in the treatment of trauma. *Journal of Clinical Psychology, 58*, 933–946.

Solomon, M., & Siegel, D. (2003). *Healing trauma: Attachment, trauma, the brain and the mind*. New York: Norton.

Spates, C. R., Koch, E., Cusack, K., Pagoto, S., & Waller, S. (2009). Eye movement desensitization and reprocessing. In E. B. Foa, T. M. Keane, M. J. Friedman, & J. A. Cohen (Eds.), *Effective treatments for PTSD: Practice guidelines from the International Society for Traumatic Stress Studies* (2nd ed.; pp. 279–305). New York: Guilford Press.

Sroufe, L. A. (1996). *Emotional development: The organization of emotional life in the early years*. New York: Cambridge University Press.

Stein, M. B., Koverola, C., Hanna, C., Torchia, M. G., & McClarty, B. (1997). Hippocampal volume in women victimized by childhood sexual abuse. *Psychological Medicine, 27*, 951–959.

Stern, D. B. (1997). *Unformulated experience: From dissociation to imagination in psychoanalysis*. Hillsdale, NJ: Analytic Press.

Tadeschi, R. G., Park, C. L., & Calhoun, L. G. (1998). *Posttraumatic growth: Positive changes in the aftermath of crisis*. Mahwah, NJ: Erlbaum.

Talbot, N. L., & Gamble, S. A. (2008). IPT for women with trauma histories in community mental health care. *Journal of Contemporary Psychotherapy, 38*, 35–44.

Taylor, G. J., Bagby, R. M., & Parker, J. D. A. (1997). *Disorders of affect regulation: Alexithymia in medical and psychiatric illness*. Cambridge, UK: Cambridge University Press.

Teicher, M. H., Ito, Y., Glod, C. A., Andersen, S. L., Dumont, N., & Ackerman E. (1997). Preliminary evidence for abnormal cortical development in physically and sexually abused children using EEG coherence and MRI. In R. Yehuda &

A. C. McFarlane (Eds.), *Annals of the New York Academy of Sciences: Vol. 821. Psychobiology of posttraumatic stress disorder* (pp. 160–175). New York: New York Academy of Sciences.

Tracey, N. L., & Kokotovic, A. M. (1989). Factor structure of the Working Alliance Inventory. *Psychological Assessment: A Journal of Consulting and Clinical Psychology, 1*, 207–210.

Turner, A., & Paivio, S. C. (2002, August). *Alexithymia as a transmission mechanism between childhood trauma, social anxiety, and limited social support*. Poster presented at the 100th Annual Convention of the American Psychological Association, Chicago, IL.

Vaillant, G. E. (1994). Ego mechanisms of defense and personality psychopathology. *Journal of Abnormal Psychology, 103*, 44–50.

van der Kolk, B. A. (1993). Biological considerations about emotions, trauma, memory, and the brain. In S. L. Ablon, D. Brown, E. J. Khantzian, & J. E. Mack (Eds.), *Human feelings: Explorations in affect development and meaning* (pp. 221–240). Hillsdale, NJ: Analytic Press.

van der Kolk, B. A. (2003). Posttraumatic stress disorder and the nature of trauma. In M. Solomon & D. Siegel (Eds.), *Healing trauma: Attachment, mind, body, and brain* (pp. 168–195). New York: Norton.

van der Kolk, B. A., & McFarlane, A. C. (1996). The black hole of trauma. In B. A. van der Kolk, A. C. McFarlane, & L. Weisaeth (Eds.), *Traumatic stress: The effects of overwhelming experience on mind, body, and society* (pp. 3–23). New York: Guilford Press.

van der Kolk, B. A., Pelcovitz, D., Roth, S., Mandel, F., McFarlane, A., & Herman, J. (1996). Dissociation, somatization, and affect dysregulation: Complexity of adaptation to trauma. *American Journal of Psychiatry, 153* (Festschrift Suppl.), 83–93.

Vrana, S., & Lauterbach, D. (1994). Prevalence of traumatic events and post-traumatic psychological symptoms in a nonclinical sample of college students. *Journal of Traumatic Stress, 7*, 289–302.

Walker, E. A., Katon, W., Russo, J., Ciechanowski, P., Newman, E., & Wagner, A. W. (2003). Health care costs associated with posttraumatic stress disorder symptoms in women. *Archives of General Psychiatry, 60*, 369–374.

Watson, J. C., Gordon, L. B., Stermac, L., Kalogerakos, F., & Steckley, P. (2003). Comparing the effectiveness of process–experiential with cognitive–behavioral psychotherapy in the treatment of depression. *Journal of Consulting and Clinical Psychology, 71*, 773–781.

Wild, N. D., & Paivio, S. C. (2003). Psychological adjustment, coping, and emotion regulation as predictors of posttraumatic growth. *Journal of Aggression, Maltreatment and Trauma, 8*, 97–122.

Winnicott, D. W. (1965). *The maturational processes and the facilitating environment*. New York: International University Press.

Woldarsky, C., & Greenberg, L. S. (2009, May). *The transformational power of shame in forgiveness*. Paper presented at the annual conference of the Society for the Exploration of Psychotherapy Integration, Seattle, WA.

Wolfe, D. A. (2007). Understanding anger: Key concepts from the field of domestic violence and child abuse. In T. Cavell & K. Malcolm (Eds.), *Anger, aggression and interpersonal violence* (pp. 393–402). Mahwah, NJ: Erlbaum.

Wolfe, D. A., Welkerle, C., Scott, K., Strautman, A. L., & Grasley, C. (2004). Predicting abuse in adolescent dating relationships over 1 year: The role of child maltreatment and trauma. *Journal of Abnormal Psychology, 113*, 406–415.

Yamamoto, M., Iwata, N., Tomoda, A., Tanaka, S., Fujimaki, K., & Kitamura, T. (1999). Child emotional and physical maltreatment and adolescent psychopathology: A community study in Japan. *Journal of Community Psychology, 27*, 377–391.

Zlotnick, C., Shea, T. M., Rosen, K., Simpson, E., Mulrenin, K., Begin, A., & Pearlstein, T. (1997). An affect-management group for women with post-traumatic stress disorder and histories of childhood sexual abuse. *Journal of Traumatic Stress, 10*, 425–436.

INDEX

and experiential differentiation,
128–130
historical roots of, 84–86
intervention guidelines for
promoting, 134–142
in major tasks of EFTT, 93–97
measurement of, 90–91
as process, 81–83
promoting with focusing, 142–146
rationale for, 128
therapeutic environments for,
131–133
in therapy, 91–93
value of, 130–131
Experiential approaches, 8, 86, 142,
294
Experiential avoidance, 16
Experiential differentiation, 128–130
Experiential focusing, 54
Experiential knowledge system, 78–79
Experiential system, in trauma
interventions, 31–32
Experiential therapy, 7, 35
Exploration, cultivating, 132, 135–136
Exploration phase (emotional pain
work), 191–192
Exposure-based procedures
dropout rates of, 173
emotional processing in, 64
experiencing in, 78, 88
IC procedure vs., 153–154
for trauma, 152
Exposure therapy, 132
Expression analysis, 210
Expression and exploration stage, of IC,
163, 169
External details, in memory evocation,
200
External focus of attention, 148–149
Externalizing disorders, 22
Eye movement desensitization and
reprocessing (EMDR), 67, 88,
153, 180, 189

Failure, 221
False self, 205
Family environment, effects of abuse
on, 29
Family violence, 29
Fantasies, revenge, 248

Fear
about termination, 288
accessing and restructuring, 198–202
action tendency of, 137
adaptive, 181–182
anxiety, avoidance, and, 179–202
change processes for, 184–187
in EFTT vs. other approaches,
180–181
and emotional processing, 64
emotional transformation of, 71–72
interventions for managing, 187–189
maladaptive, 72, 179
and overcontrol of emotion, 114
and posttraumatic stress reactions, 60
regulation of, 113–114
and shame, 45–46, 220
types of, 181–184
Fear structures, for trauma, 19
Federman, B., 18
Feedback
from clients, 285
and constructing new meaning, 80
during IC, 167
from therapists, 283–285
Feelings
admitting vs. allowing, 180
"bad." See ìBad feelings"
differentiation of, in IC, 167–168
in IC, 166–168
labeling of, 5, 50–51, 128, 136, 149.
See also Symbolization
in LES, 161
maintaining focus on, 131–132
unresolved, 121, 236
Female abuse survivors, 4–5, 42, 119
Foa, E. B., 132
Focusing, 54, 138, 142–146
Foerster, F. S., 159
Forgiveness
and adaptive anger, 252
as client goal, 172
and pseudo-resolution, 282–283
and termination, 279
Fredrickson, B. L., 71
Freud, S., 79
Functional validation, 106
Functioning, general theory of, 35–36
Furr, J. M., 132
Future, bridging to, 290–291

Malcolm, W., 159
Maltreatment, childhood, 4, 15, 17–18
Marital distress, 25
Marker-based approach, to intervention, 40, 107
Maternal depression, 25
Meaning
  cocreation of, 129, 133
  constructing, 80, 132, 262
  exploring, 48, 51, 77, 89
  and IC, 153
  and implicit messages, 140
  maladaptive, 15, 78
  and needs, 268
  personal, 36, 88, 242
Measurement, of experiencing, 90–91
Medical morbidity, 22
Medications, 120
Memory(-ies)
  from adult perspective, 201, 202
  autobiographical, 23–24, 49
  and change, 37–38
  distal, 47
  dual coding theory of, 79
  and emotion, 56–57
  episodic, 47–49, 53, 165–166, 215
  and experiencing, 95–96
  exploration of, 85
  and IC, 156
  maladaptive meaning of, 78
  narrative, 5
  neuroimaging studies of, 19–20
  reexperiencing, 226–227
  self-related, 49
  and shame, 211
  trauma, 19–20
Memory evocation (memory work)
  anger in, 247
  and episodic memories, 48–49
  maladaptive emotions in, 200–202
  for motivations of clients, 214
  sadness in, 264
  shame in, 216–220
Memory gaps, 23–24
Men, applicability of EFFT for, 42–43
Mindfulness practice, 89–90, 186, 260
Modulation
  of anger, 241
  emotion, 104–105
  of emotional experience, 51–52
  of emotional intensity, 47–48

Mothers, nonprotective, 234
Motivations, of clients, 120, 214, 235
Mourning, 255

Narcissistic rage, 204, 215
Narrative approaches, 89, 256
Narrative memory, 5
Narratives, 23–24, 36, 69, 81, 284
Neborsky, R. J., 14
Necessary and sufficient conditions of change (term), 205
Needs
  assertive expressions of, 250
  awareness of, 268
  existential and interpersonal, 138
  unmet, 138, 226, 249–250, 266–267
Neglect, 30, 216, 234, 254
Negotiation, between aspects of self, 223
Neuroimaging studies, of trauma memories, 19–20
Neuroplasticity, 83
Neuroscience, affective, 294
Neutrality, and EFTT, 111, 125
Nonprotective mothers, 234
Nonspecific emotional distress, 68, 73–74
Nonverbal behavior, 161, 266
Normalization, 51
Nurturing, by therapists, 263

Object relations, 58, 87, 153
Observations, 108, 157, 211
Observer stance, of therapists, 124–125
Offenders, relationships with, 233, 246, 251, 270–271
Off-theme experiencing, 92
Ongoing process diagnoses, for EFTT, 40
Outcome of treatment, experiencing and, 91–92
Overcontrol
  of anger, 238, 248
  of emotions, 26–28, 113, 114, 123
Ownership of experience, 47, 48, 156, 190, 238

Pain, emotional. See Emotional pain
Painful emotions, 63, 225
Painful experiences, allowing, 186
Paivio, S. C., 23, 49, 173
Panic, 48
Paradoxical sadness, 259

Unconditional acceptance, 107
Unconditional positive regard, 212, 214
Unconditional positive self-regard, 35
Underregulation of emotion, 27, 113,
    123
Undifferentiated hurt, 136
Unfinished business, 175
Unmet needs, 138, 226, 249–250,
    266–267
Unproductive styles, of therapists,
    147–148
Unresolved feelings, 121, 236

Validation
    and alliance, 105–106, 111
    and exploration, 135–136
    functional, 106
    and maintaining focus on feelings,
        131
    of sadness, 262–263
    to soothe clients, 114
    of trauma story, 123–124
Venting, 66
Victim impact statements, 249
Victimization, 204, 264

Vietnam war, 15, 18
Violence, 15, 27, 29
Vrana, S., 17
Vulnerability
    affirming, 51, 135, 209
    and anger, 244
    in core sense of self, 182–183, 198–200
    and sadness, 266–267
    and secondary shame, 224

WAI. *See* Working Alliance Inventory
War, trauma from, 15
Warmth, in therapeutic relationship, 124
Weeping, therapeutic, 264
Winnicott, D. W., 205
Wishful thinking, 282
Withdrawal, 149, 257
Wolfe, D. A., 29
Women, as abuse survivors, 4–5, 42, 119
Working Alliance Inventory (WAI),
    104, 299
Worry, 132
Worthlessness, 138, 183, 215

Zlotnick, C., 30

ABOUT THE AUTHORS

Sandra C. Paivio, PhD, C.Psych, received her PhD in psychology from York University in 1993. Her program of research and clinical interests in complex trauma began at that time when she conducted and participated in published clinical trials of emotion-focused therapy. This approach proved to be particularly well-suited to clients dealing with complex trauma.

Since that time, Dr. Paivio has published, with colleagues and graduate students, numerous chapters and articles on emotion-focused therapy and emotion-focused therapy for trauma (EFTT) and is the coauthor, with Les Greenberg, of *Working With Emotions in Psychotherapy*. Her research has continued to focus on clinical trials evaluating emotion-focused therapy and the emotional processes contributing to disturbance and recovery from complex trauma. Recent studies have evaluated the efficacy and processes of change in EFTT, and the benefits of different re-experiencing procedures.

Dr. Paivio is a professor in and head of the psychology department at the University of Windsor, Canada, and director of the Psychotherapy Research Centre. Most recently her clinical work and supervision has focused on EFTT with refugee trauma survivors. She also maintains a part-time private practice.

Antonio Pascual-Leone, PhD, C.Psyc, is a clinical psychologist and a professor of psychology at the University of Windsor, Canada. Originally from Toronto, he completed his early graduate training in France and then returned to Toronto to complete his PhD with Les Greenberg at York University. Since that time, he has published a number of articles on the process and outcome of psychotherapy, with a special focus on the role of emotion. More recently, he coauthored an outcome study on an emotion-focused treatment for domestically violent men as well as several articles on psychotherapy skills training. In 2009, Dr. Pascual-Leone received the New Researcher Award from the Society for the Exploration of Psychotherapy Integration for his contribution to the field.

He currently runs a research group studying emotion and intervention at the University of Windsor, where he is also a graduate faculty member teaching emotion-focused therapy and integrative approaches to psychotherapy. In addition, Dr. Pascual-Leone has been a returning faculty member at the Emotion-Focused Therapy Summer Institute (Toronto) for many years, where he helps instruct intensive seminars on emotion-focused therapy skills for professionals. As well as being involved as a therapist in several of the published clinical trials of emotion-focused therapy—for both individual and couples therapy—he has also been trained in dialectical behavior therapy and cognitive–behavioral therapy. He runs a private practice in Windsor, seeing individuals and couples.